❖   Theorizing Feminist Policy

Gender and Politics represents the most recent scholarship in the areas of women, gender, and politics, and is explicitly cross-national in its organization and orientation. Recognizing the contribution of women's studies to gendered political analysis, the goal of *Gender and Politics* is to develop, and to publish, frontier analysis, the empirical research exemplary of the intersection between political studies and women's studies.

The series is edited by Professor Karen Beckwith at the Department of Political Science, College of Wooster and Professor Joni Lovenduski, Department of Politics and Sociology, Birkbeck College.

Theorizing Feminist Policy

Amy G. Mazur

OXFORD

UNIVERSITY PRESS

OXFORD
UNIVERSITY PRESS

Great Clarendon Street, Oxford OX2 6DP

Oxford University Press is a department of the University of Oxford.
It furthers the University's objective of excellence in research, scholarship,
and education by publishing worldwide in

Oxford New York

Auckland Bangkok Bogotá Buenos Aires Cape Town Chennai
Dar es Salaam Delhi Hong Kong Istanbul Karachi Kolkata
Kuala Lumpur Madrid Melbourne Mexico City Mumbai Nairobi
São Paulo Shanghai Singapore Taipei Tokyo Toronto

with an associated company in Berlin

Oxford is a registered trade mark of Oxford University Press
in the UK and in certain other countries

Published in the United States
by Oxford University Press Inc., New York

British Library Cataloguing in Publication Data

Data available

Library of Congress Cataloging in Publication Data

Mazur, Amy.
Theorizing feminist policy/Amy G. Mazur.
p. cm.
Includes bibliographical references.
1. Women—Government policy.   2. Feminism.
3. Women—Employment—Govenment policy.   I.Title
HQ1236.M3672002   305.42—dc21   2001054562
ISBN 0–19–829393–3
ISBN 0–19–924672–6 (Pbk.)

10 9 8 7 6 5 4 3 2 1

Typeset by Hope Services (Abingdon) Ltd.
Printed in Great Britain
on acid-free paper by
T. J. International Ltd.,
Padstow, Cornwall

❖ Preface and Acknowledgements

This book grows out of my own interest and involvement in feminist politics. My feminism is scientific rather than political. Throughout my life I have taken great pride in being a feminist and have supported a variety of feminist political causes. It has been pursuing a feminist agenda through social science research that has sparked my interest the most. I identify with empirical feminism more than with any single current of feminist political thought. To be sure, traditional male-dominated political science has blatantly ignored feminist policy issues and the scholarship that studies them; however, the baby should not be thrown out with the bathwater. One should confront directly and show a highly androcentric political science community that it is doing woefully incomplete social science when feminist considerations of gender issues are excluded. Thus, the incorporation of the feminist study of feminist policy and politics can strengthen political science as an academic discipline.

Given my analytical feminist interests, I was very pleased to be approached to write the book in 1995. With conflicting feelings of trepidation and accomplishment, I agreed to draft a book prospectus. Three years and numerous prospectus drafts later, I signed a contract with Oxford. Even then, I did not fully grasp the scope of the project.

It was not until I began to search the literature, with the help of several research assistants, that I finally understood the sheer magnitude of the project. Over 450 different pieces of literature were consulted for this book. It took another five years to carry out this huge and what seemed at times overwhelming project. In reading the work of so many different scholars on such a wide range of feminist policy issues, I gained a profound understanding of what was clearly a new field of study: Feminist Comparative Policy. While I take full responsibility for the analytical choices, arguments, and flaws of the book, it should stand as a tribute to the accomplishments of over 30 years of research by more than 80 feminist scholars.

Throughout my career, dedicated feminist scholars inspired me, taught me, and provided me with their analyses of feminist policy development. Beginning in 1987, a network of European feminist policy researchers first took me under their collective wings and then taught me the tools of their trade. Since then, they have welcomed me into research networks and have joined me in research projects as co-organizers and as participants. It was my training and background that led me into this vital feminist policy network. I completed a joint Ph.D. in French Studies and Political Science at New York University. I spent two years of my graduate work in Paris, including a year of field work for my dissertation on French equal employment policy. Since then I have continued to develop comparative theory from research on French feminist policy formation. I have taken positions at universities in the USA but have returned regularly to France for research stays.

I work with scholars of feminist policy issues in Western Europe on a regular basis and have participated in several European Consortium Political Research (ECPR) workshops on gender and politics. It was at an ECPR workshop in Leiden in 1993 that I presented my first paper on feminist public policy in post-industrial democracies. Earlier, in 1987, I met Dorothy McBride Stetson, who became a mentor, collaborator, and friend. We were both fascinated by the Ministry of Women's Rights in France and embarked together on a scholarly journey with European, North American, and Australian colleagues to study these fascinating state feminist institutions more generally in Western post-industrial democracies. Both of us believed that for such a study to be useful it needed to operationalize feminist concepts and use non-feminist methods of qualitative, comparative analysis. With an initial edited book and the creation of a new 45-member research group in 1995—the Research Network on Gender, Politics, and the State (RNGS)—under our co-direction, a ten-year-long study of women's policy offices in seventeen countries across five different policy areas was then launched and is now well under way.

Through my training, experiences, and exchanges, I have developed a keen interest in studying overtly feminist government action through an empirical, comparative, and feminist lens. My mentors taught me that it is not anathema to the feminist project to conduct studies based on the principles of social science inquiry. In my involvement in the field of political science, outside of feminist networks, I have noticed that little attention is paid to what is an exciting and cutting-edge area of research. I have often been puzzled by what appears to be at best scholarly carelessness, at worst intellectually or politically motivated exclusion. My aim, therefore, is to contribute to feminist scholarship and to convince scholars, practitioners, and citizens outside of feminist circles that feminist policy and its study is more than just a fad; it is a permanent reality of the modern state and therefore worthy of policy studies.

This book is about the growing community of feminist academics and their work. They are tied together not only by their scholarly interest but also by their rejection of feminist dismissals of social science as being too patriarchal to use tools of 'male' social science in advancing a feminist agenda. I hope to do justice to the work of this community in the pages that follow without diluting the collective wisdom that underpins this body of work. In this context, readers should consider this book as a part of ongoing collective conversations about feminist policy issues rather than any definitive statement. Ultimately, I hope that the study generates new and different ways to strengthen and enrich the traditions of this new feminist research community.

There are many people to recognize and to thank. First, I must acknowledge the three feminist scholars who guided my apprenticeship in feminist policy studies: Joni Lovenduski, Dorothy McBride Stetson, and Joyce Outshoorn. In addition to their mentoring, their published work has made major contributions to the field of Feminist Comparative Policy. Joni Lovenduski helped me produce a strong prospectus and provided me with crucial feedback and support throughout the project. Her copious and tireless editing hopefully saved this book from the traps of unclear social science writing. Karen Beckwith provided me with priceless suggestions on the prospectus and on the final version of the manuscript. Specific thanks go to the anonymous reviewer who did an extraordinary job of reviewing the final manuscript. I hope my revisions have done justice to the highly thoughtful and thorough comments.

My work on projects with Elizabeth Meehan, Jet Bussemaker, Terrell Carver, and Selma Sevenhuisjen has been very important. I would particularly like to thank Ulrike Liebert for inviting me to present an earlier version of this manuscript to her research seminar on gender policy at the University of Bremen. The critiques and insightful comments from the seminar participants—Birgit Locher, Henrike Müller, Konstanze Platt, Silke Reuter, Verena Schmidt, Holger Schneider, and Stefanie Sifft—were important in producing a stronger final manuscript. Mary Hawkesworth, Alice Brown, Phil Cerny, and Steven Stehr made useful comments on the prospectus.

Cynthia Cendagorta, Jocelyn Silva, Sarah Quigley, Jaana Manns-Brooks, and Dorigen Caldwell put in many hours in compiling the bibliography, searching journals, and tracking down books and articles. Cyndy, Jocelyn, and Sarah put in the most time on the project. I could not have completed this project without their assistance. Many individuals gave me bibliographical advice and sent me their publications. Specific thanks go to: Celia Valiente, Evelyn Mahon, Yvonne Galligan, Jocelyn Praud, Annette Borchorst, Leslie Eliason, Karen Anderson, John Keeler, James Caporaso, Tom Preston, Eric Einhorn, Anne Good, Constanza Tobió, Kimberly Morgan, Laurel Weldon, Jacqui True, Michael Mintrom, Marila Guadagnini, and Jacques Gerstlé. Andrew Appleton provided me with essential intellectual and moral support and advice throughout the project. My collaborations with Janine Parry and Claudie Baudino have also been of great help. I must also recognize my colleagues in RNGS for their collective contributions to my thinking about feminist policy formation. I extend my thanks to Dominic Byatt and Amanda Watkins at Oxford for their hard work, good humour, and understanding throughout the long process of producing this book.

I would like to thank the Department of Political Science at Washington State University for providing me with institutional support, and my colleagues for tolerating my more stress-filled moments while working on this project. Lisa Janowski, Diane Berger, and Cynthia Avery were particularly helpful. Thanks also go to Lance T. LeLoup and Cornell Clayton, both chairs during the project, for providing me with much needed financial support and with the conviction that my time was being well spent focusing on the book. I could not have done such an in-depth literature search without this financial support. Robert Mazur, with the help of Mary Mazur, came through with crucial copy editing of the entire manuscript at the eleventh hour. His scientific eye made me rethink many different passages of the book. I must heartily thank all my friends and family for supporting and tolerating me throughout the many years of this project. As always, special thanks go to Geno and Minerva. I could not have completed this project without their companionship and support.

Amy G. Mazur

Pullman, July 2001

❖ Contents

❖ List of Figures

❖ List of Tables

1 ❖ Introduction

This book is a response to three realities. First, since the 1980s, a new area of feminist study has been taking shape within the field of political science. Building from and contributing to feminist and non-feminist scholarship, Feminist Comparative Policy (FCP) seeks to answer the highly complex questions of if, how, and why contemporary Western post-industrial democracies are feminist.[1] An ever-growing community of over 80 researchers in Europe, North America, Australia, and New Zealand shares a common comparative approach to the study of gender, policy, and the state. By 2001, FCP scholars had produced a significant body of literature to be reckoned with and created permanent research and teaching infrastructures on three continents.

Second, it has been over 30 years since second-wave women's movements took to the streets to change society in Western democracies. In part, as a response to women's demands, governments across the ideological spectrum have developed a complex and varied set of machineries and policies. These policies and agencies were specifically charged with promoting women's rights and status and, in some cases, with addressing the deep-rooted causes of gender-based inequalities between men and women. Like the women's movements that inspired them, they have had varying levels of success in achieving ambitious goals.

Such an international imperative of feminist policy development provides a unique laboratory in which to examine the emergence and consolidation of a new arena of government action inextricably linked to social movements over an extended period. Moreover, studying state responses to women's movements in Western post-industrial democracies can provide profound insights into the perennial question of the capacity of democracies to respond to social change and demands for expanded rights; in other words, whether stable democracies can become more democratic. Yet it has been for the most part feminist social scientists who have explored feminist policy and the related issues of gender, policy, and the state. Indeed, the third reality faced by this book is that traditional political science has paid little attention to gender and policy issues or the wealth of new research that studies them.

In response to the first reality of Feminist Comparative Policy, this book systematically maps out the new field for the first time.[2] It strengthens FCP by addressing the theoretical and methodological gaps in one area of scholarship in this new area, namely, research on feminist policy formation. The FCP approach to empirical inquiry is also used as a guide to take stock of the large but fragmented literature on feminist policy issues in Western post-industrial democracies and to conduct a comparative study of feminist policy formation.[3] This book, therefore, responds to the second reality of feminist policy in three ways. First, it identifies feminist policy as a separate sector of policy with eight sub-sectors. Second, it develops a comparative framework that focuses on policy processes and outputs rather than the social outcomes of policy, to tackle the question of whether, how, and why governments pursue purposefully feminist action. Third, it generates testable propositions about the processes of feminist policy formation from the cross-national analysis of policy dynamics and determinants in 13 Western post-industrial democracies.

The final academic reality is addressed through the intersection of feminist and non-feminist scholarship in the design of this study's analytical framework and the comparative analysis of feminist policy formation. In pursuing these intersections, the book ultimately shows how FCP should be an integral part of theory building and the cumulation of knowledge in traditional political science as well as in newer areas of feminist political analysis.

This first chapter previews the book's aims, arguments, approach, and outline. It then turns to the task of mapping out the new field of Feminist Comparative Policy by examining the overall approach, scientific community, and research infrastructure.[4]

❖ AIMS, ARGUMENTS, APPROACH, AND OUTLINE

A central assumption of this book is that feminism is a concept that generates a great deal of debate and is used to describe a wide variety of ideas, actions, and strategies; in other words, it is a classic case of a 'contested concept'.[5] As Beasley (1999: ix) states in the first sentence of her book, *What is Feminism?*, 'Feminism is a troublesome term'. Feminism is used often to describe a wide variety of actions: 'the practical politics of women's movements', the 'history of ideas' (Delmar 1986, cited in Beasley 1999: xiii), political positions of actors outside of the women's movement, and various epistemological stances. This book uses the term 'feminism' to refer to an approach to conducting policy analysis in Feminist Comparative Policy, to an arena of public action in feminist policy, and to different feminist political ideologies used by or identified with specific social movements, organizations, and individuals.

Some theorists and activists avoid using the term 'feminist' altogether; others assert that the divisions between the different currents of political and academic feminism make it difficult to identify a single meaning.[6] This book explicitly uses the word 'feminist' because of the full range of core ideas it has come to represent at the beginning of the twenty-first century in Western post-industrial democracies. Instead of identifying a single fixed definition of feminism, this book takes the approach of recent FCP work that recognizes the core ideas of Western feminism from which academics, activists, and policy practitioners choose.[7] The following are the core ideas typically recognized:

- a certain understanding of women as a group within the context of the social, economic, and cultural diversity of women;

- the advancement of women's rights, status or condition as a group in both public and private spheres; and

- the reduction or elimination of gender-based hierarchy or patriarchy that underpins basic inequalities between men and women in the public and the private spheres.

A major argument of this book is that governments in Western post-industrial democracies have formulated, and in many cases implemented, an enormous array of feminist policies. The pervasiveness of these policies and their shared feminist intent suggest that the state in post-industrial democracies may be taking on a new feminist function, equivalent to other functional areas of public policy, such as agriculture, business, and employment. The degree to which the new policy sector has a single set of instruments, actors, and interactions, like other policy sub-sectors, is a central concern for this study. This book shows that feminist policy, due to its highly transversal nature which cuts across a wide range of policy sectors, does not display a uniform set of political patterns like other more established policy sectors in contemporary democracies. While the feminist intent of these policies is clearly stated by government officials or flagged in the content of the policy itself, not all feminist policies, reflecting the multiform nature of feminism itself, share the same goals or define women's rights and status in the same way. The degree to which feminist policies are implemented to effectively achieve their goals also varies across the range of feminist policies.

This book identifies eight sub-sectors of feminist government action: blueprint, political representation, equal employment, reconciliation, family law, reproductive rights, sexuality and violence, and public service delivery. A separate chapter covers each sub-area, except for public service delivery policy.[8] In Chapter 2, the broad operational definition of feminist policy for this study is presented and feminist policy as a separate sector with eight sub-areas is described. The first sections of Chapters 3 to 9 examine the range and general feminist aims of policies in each area and show the boundaries between feminist and non-feminist government action.

4

The analytical framework for this study, presented in Chapter 2, provides one way of beginning to determine systematically whether nominally feminist policies are actually feminist. In-depth qualitative analysis of specific cases of policy formation based on published studies of feminist policy development provide the data. The effectiveness of feminist policy is assessed by whether it makes the policy process more open to feminist actors and issues; the question of the feminist impact of policy on society at large is not an object of this study. At issue is whether women are represented, descriptively—through the presence of women—and substantively—through the expression of women's interests—in the pre-formulation, formulation, implementation, and evaluation of a specific policy and whether the policy generates institutional feedback in the state and society. The relationship between women's representation in the policy process, the policy profile, and the way state and society actors mobilize around a given policy in the different stages of the policy process, the policy style, as well as other external factors such as institutional design, culture, and extra-national influences, are scrutinized in each case analysis.

The politics of feminist policy formation is observed in 13 post-industrial democracies. As Chapter 2 shows, these 13 countries are exemplars of the four 'feminist families of nations' identified by gender and welfare state scholars in the post-industrial world. The 13 countries are: Ireland, Italy, and Spain for the 'Late Female Mobilizing' family; Denmark, Sweden, and Norway for the 'Protestant Social Democrat' family; France, Germany, and the Netherlands for the 'Advanced Christian Democrat' family; and the United States, Great Britain, Canada, and Australia for the 'Protestant Liberal' family. A total of 27 cases is analysed: one case in the seven policy sub-sectors for each country from each of the four feminist families of nations.[9] The second part of the sub-sectoral chapters presents the individual national cases of feminist policy formation in terms of this study's analytic framework.

As the book's conclusion asserts, all cases of feminist policy attained certain levels of women's substantive and descriptive representation. There was significant variation in the levels of feminist policy process outcomes. In other words, feminist policies may be feminist in action, but to varying degrees. Policies that achieved the highest level of feminist activity did not correspond to a particular country, a particular feminist policy sub-area, a particular feminist family of nations, or even a particular time period. Instead, a complex line-up of factors came together at different moments, in different policy sub-sectors, and in different countries to produce the most successful feminist policies. One of the most important conditions for feminist success was the presence of a 'strategic partnership' (Halsaa 1998) or 'triangle of empowerment' (Vargas and Wieringa 1998) between women in elected office, feminist/women's movements and organizations, and women's policy offices in the development of a specific policy. Given that only 27 cases were investigated and 16 of those were either incomplete or had comparability problems, it is important to point out, as Chapter 10 does in more detail, that any conclusions from this study about the determinants of feminist policy are tentative and should be seen as propositions to be tested in future studies.

❖ APPROACH AND CORE CONCEPTS OF FEMINIST COMPARATIVE POLICY AS A FIELD OF STUDY

Feminist policy scholars in Western Europe first acknowledged the empirical gaps and gender biases in theory and methodology related to the state, gender, and public policy in the early 1980s. By the early 1990s, researchers in North America and Australia had joined their Western European counterparts in this new feminist academic enterprise. In the mid-1990s, a loose consensus in this international community around conventions for conducting research, developing theory, and reporting findings, moved the field into a new stage of vitality and institutionalization. The six following features constitute the different features of the new consensus.

❖ *Feature 1: An Applied Feminist Empirical Approach*

Labels commonly used to identify different strands of Western feminist thought are not useful in identifying the feminist approach of FCP,[10] given that individuals who contribute to this new field mostly carry out a feminist agenda through designing, conducting, and disseminating their research and teaching about the topics they study. Some FCP scholars participate in women's movements and organizations and serve periodically as experts on government women's commissions. Most researchers, however, pursue their political action in academia. In addition, unlike many feminist scholars who seek to 'transform' (Staudt and Weaver 1997) or 'revolutionise' (Silverberg 1990) the study of politics, FCP practitioners have a more moderate agenda aimed at working within the rules of the scientific game and contributing to non-feminist and feminist bodies of knowledge. They tend not to take a separatist approach to research; most would say that men are just as capable as women to conducting feminist research.

This moderate empirical feminist agenda can be identified with 'feminist empiricism'.[11] Whereas FCP scholars agree that past social science research was androcentric, and dominated by men—hence the research problems and methodology excluded considerations of gender and women—they do not seek to dismiss the entire social scientific process. At the same time, FCP scholars recognize that social science inquiry is not entirely value-free. In their view, social scientists who claimed to be conducting 'objective science' in the past essentially ignored empirical gender policy issues in the formulation of research problems and research designs. Lovenduski and Randall (1993: 9) articulate the FCP approach to research in the beginning of their study of feminist politics in Great Britain:

> Although we have denied ourselves the freedoms of the post-modernist rejection of the entire epistemological basis for social science, we fully recognize the problems of attempting to conduct 'unbiased', 'scientific' social research.

Most FCP practitioners seek to use empirical observation to test and explore hypotheses in order to contribute to theories about gender, politics, and the state. When FCP scholars talk about constructing theory, they mean empirically based theory and not normative or critical theory. Theory-building is not the only goal of their work. FCP studies are often designed so that findings can be used to help public policy practitioners and feminist activists in women's policy agencies, political parties, movements, and organizations learn more about the causes of gender-based inequities and their solutions, including different ways of designing 'good practices'.

The applied feminist empiricist approach of FCP scholars underpins their attitudes to identifying with specific feminist currents of thought and to adhering to a single fixed definition of what constitutes feminist policy, feminist states, and feminist political action more generally. FCP scholars tend not to articulate a specific political stance on feminism in their research and teaching. They do not deny adhering to a certain type of feminist politics; they just do not apply their specific political views of feminism to their research.

Similarly, the definitions of feminism FCP researchers use in their analyses come from comparative studies of feminist politics rather than their own feminist politics. FCP scholars tend to be dubious of pinning down a single narrow definition of feminism connected to a specific current of Western political thought. They often argue that definitions of feminism should come from observation and study, reflecting the specific patterns of politics across many different countries. Feminist policy analysts from continental Europe often criticize earlier FCP work for making Anglo-American assumptions about feminist policy and politics in their studies. Many argue also that there is a growing consensus around broad analytic definitions of feminism that can be used in a variety of national contexts in the West.

Increasingly, FCP scholars acknowledge the debates over defining feminism and the diversity of feminist ideas and action in the context of putting forward a simple and base-line definition. In the context of comparative research on feminist movements, for instance, Beckwith distinguishes feminist movements from women's movements in their 'challenge to patriarchy' (2000: 437) and the way they are 'women-based' and 'mobilized around issues of gender equality' (2000: 436). Lovenduski (1997b) bases her working definition of feminism in the Western European context on Dahlerup's definitions of feminism, 'those ideologies, activities, and polices whose goals it is to remove discrimination against women and to breakdown male domination in society' (1986a: 6). Stetson and Mazur (1995: 16) advance a similar definition of feminism in their study of women's policy offices: 'An ideology, policy organisation, or activity is feminist to the extent that it has the purpose of improving the status of women as a group and undermining patterns of gender hierarchy.' In her analysis of the institutionalization of gender equality in Nordic countries, Borchorst (1999b: 164) refers to work of other Nordic FCP scholars—Halsaa, Van der Ros, and Dahlerup—in establishing the 'minimum requirement of the structural background of gender differences.'

❖ Feature 2: Operationalizing Normative Feminist Theory on Democracy

Normative political theory has been an integral part of the development of feminist studies. Feminist theorists such as Carol Pateman, Catharine MacKinnon, Anne Phillips, Luce Irigary, and Rosemary Pringle, to name a few, have made fundamental contributions to rethinking core ideas about politics and democracy that represent the different currents of Western feminist thought. The enormous canon of feminist political theory is clearly oriented toward activism and social criticism. When feminist theorists use empirical analysis, it is usually as a means to advance normative arguments about politics rather than providing solutions to empirical puzzles.

A major question asked by feminist theorists who write on the West is whether our stable democracies are as democratic as observers think, particularly given the degree to which women and women's issues have been excluded from politics, in the context of the formal articulation of universal, and gender-blind, values of equality, freedom, and representation. Feminist theorists who write on democracy argue for the greater inclusion of women and ideas that favour women's rights in the political process through substantive and descriptive representation (for example, Phillips 1991;1995; Squires 1999b; Pateman 1988). These themes of representation and democracy are at the centre of Feminist Comparative Policy studies when they ask the empirical questions of whether, how, and why democratic states can be feminist. The issue is less about the specific form and design of democracy than about its capacity to incorporate women's interests and issues and in doing so to promote gender equality.

FCP scholars take concepts, arguments, and theoretical constructs from feminist theory in designing their empirical studies; in other words, they operationalize feminist theory. Most FCP studies refer to feminist theory in the definition of analytical frameworks and concepts. Some studies are constructed to test the propositions coming out of normative feminist theory. Increasingly, there is a canon of feminist theory to which most FCP work refers.[12] The links with feminist theory are also reflected in many FCP books that are divided into theoretical and empirical sections (for example, Meehan and Sevenhuijsen 1991a) or have theoretical chapters intermingled with more empirical chapters (for example, Savage and Witz 1992; Sassoon 1992; and Duerst-Lahti and Kelly 1995). Although not considered 'feminist theorists', many FCP scholars write theoretical pieces from their own research to improve empirically based feminist theory on the state.

❖ Feature 3: Bringing the Patriarchal State Back In as a Question for Research

One of the core concepts of feminist and non-feminist political theory is the state, used here to indicate government structures rather than country or nation. The state is a not a simple idea. As Elman (1996a: 2 n. 2) articulates, 'States are more than mere governments; they consist of numerous systems and elusive methods of legal coercion that structure the relations between civil society and public authority'. Many see the state as a contested concept, with significant debate over where the state ends and society begins (for example, Skocpol 1985; Cerny 1990). Often at issue is the extent of the state's coercive power.

For many feminist theorists, the state is highly problematic given that they see it as a product of systems of power based on male domination or 'patriarchy'. From the assumption of the patriarchal nature of the state, whereby state actions, structures, and actors seek to perpetuate systems of gender domination that keep women in their inferior positions in the public and private spheres, many feminist analysts dismiss or are highly critical of the state as an arena for positive social change (for example, MacKinnon 1989). Other feminist theorists provide a more malleable view of state patriarchy and argue that certain state arenas may be appropriate sites for feminist action.

Whether for or against the state, feminist analysts have looked to the state as an important framing element of politics. As traditional political science moved from its behavioural orientations in the 1980s, non-feminist political analysts also became concerned with the state as an object of analysis. By the late 1980s, much of comparative political analysis had followed the calls of Skocpol (1985) and others to 'bring the state back in'. The emphasis on state institutions in the 'new institutionalism' (March and Olsen 1984) has also drawn unprecedented attention to the state in comparative research.

Reflecting the importance of the state for feminist theory and comparative politics, FCP places the state and its institutions at its analytical core. The four major areas of FCP research—feminist policy formation, feminist movements and policy, state feminism, and gender and the welfare state—examined in the next section all focus on some aspect of the state or state action. National conceptions of the state and political culture are often included as important explanatory variables in many FCP studies. Research in all four areas takes seriously the difficulties of defining the state, paying close attention, as theorists like Nettl (1968) do, to the ways the state is defined in different national contexts.

FCP scholars do not assume that the state is a single monolithic entity that acts 'uniformly . . . to maintain patriarchal relations'; rather, they see the state as a 'series of arenas' (Pringle and Watson 1992: 53) that can be seized upon by different groups, in different ways and at different moments. In this view, the state in its shifting form can be used by feminist groups and actors to pursue feminist ends. FCP analysts, however, do not entirely dismiss the possibility of a patriarchal state; they see the issue of state patriarchy as a question for empirical research. Indeed, some parts of the state may be patriarchal while other parts may have the potential to be quite woman-friendly.

❖ Feature 4: Using 'Gender as a Category of Analysis'

Since the mid-1980s, feminist research across different disciplines has been shifting its focus from sex, a dichotomous variable based on biological differences between men and women, to gender, the social construction of sexual difference between men and women (Lovenduski 1998; Acker 1992; Nelson 1989; Sapiro 1991; Silverberg 1992). As Scott (1986) articulated early in the genesis of the feminist studies, the relational concept of gender should be the prime 'category of analysis' in theoretical frameworks and research designs.

Whereas some theorists question the sex-gender dichotomy, arguing that sex differences should be also considered as social constructions (for example, Gatens 1991), most feminist theorists assert that gender is a useful analytic concept that is complex, relational, and should go beyond being a synonym for 'sex', 'female', or 'women' (for example, Carver 1995; Di Stefano 1997; Squires 1999a). This holistic approach to the use of gender is intended to push analyses beyond 'the add women and stir' phase where 'sex' or 'women' is added as an analytical afterthought (Sapiro 1991). Eleven years after Scott's plea, Lovenduski (1998: 350) asserted that a critical mass of feminist studies on 'political representation, public policy, and welfare states' has used the complex notion of gender to structure studies. Beckwith (2000) points out as well that gender has been woven into the design of comparative research on women's movements.

Since the mid-1990s, FCP scholars have incorporated the complex relational notion of gender into their research designs in a variety of ways. Many FCP studies are concerned about the connection between dominant notions of men's and women's roles in public policy—often referred to pejoratively as the 'gendered' nature of the state or public policy—and the impact of those policies on gender roles in society. As an author of one recent study on gender and welfare state regimes states,

The major purpose of this book is to enlarge our understanding of how gender is constructed in welfare state policies and how these policies are a force in ordering gender relations through an examination of a wide range of contexts. (Sainsbury 1999a: 4)

Other studies see the introduction of gender ideas into public debate and public policies in a more positive light: as the basic first step to adopting policies that can effectively strike at the causes of inequalities between men and women (for example, Stetson 2001a; Mazur 2001a; Rees 1998). From this perspective, policy actors and the policies themselves must formally acknowledge the dominant gendered division of labour between men and women, whereby women are seen as full-time family carers and part-time workers and men are seen as full-time workers and part-time family caretakers, in order to achieve feminist and/or woman-friendly outcomes. FCP analysts also use gender in the study of public administration. They determine how the gendered organization of state bureaucracies excludes the women and benefits the men who work in them through the promulgation of masculine approaches to the affairs of government (for example, Cockburn 1991; Savage and Witz 1992; Kelly and Newman 2001).

❖ Feature 5: Comparative and Qualitative Theory-building in Western Post-industrial Democracies

FCP scholars seek to develop theory through comparative, cross-national analysis, often employing comparative and qualitative principles of research design and methods developed outside of a feminist perspective.[13] Beckwith first identified the 'methodological problems' of the 'cross-cultural study of women and politics' in 1980. More recently, calls have been made to improve theory-building potentials (for example, Orloff 1993; Sainsbury 1999a) by more systematically situating case studies and multi-country analyses of patterns and variations 'in the context of the range of cross-national variations' (Orloff 1993: 73). Up until 2000, with a few exceptions (for example, Norris 1987), FCP work utilized small 'n' analysis, case studies and the comparative method.[14] Geertz's (1973) 'thick description' is also used as an essential tool. Archives, content analysis, historical analysis, elite interviewing, and participant observation are used to 'unearth' the complex causal connections between cultural context, gender, policy, and the state in order to 'inductively build up generalisations' (Heclo 1974: 12). With the recent move toward cross-national studies that include more observations, many FCP studies now use the statistical tools of large 'n' analysis (for example, Meyers, Gornick, and Ross 1999; Young 2000; O'Regan 2000; Weldon 2001).

FCP work focuses on Western post-industrial democracies. The label 'post-industrial democracy' is used instead of 'advanced industrialized democracy' or 'stable democracy' to avoid the value-laden and ethnocentric implications of comparing the 'First World' with the 'Third World'. This terminology also reflects the stage of economic and political development of the 23 or so countries that fall into this category. Post-industrial countries tend to have relatively similar levels of national wealth, similarly large service or 'post-Fordist' economies, relatively stable democratic political systems since the Second World War, and mass-based political behaviour characterized by 'postmaterial values' (Esping-Andersen 1999; Wiarda 2001; Inglehart 1990; Hayes, McAllister, and Studlar 2000).

FCP studies take a most similar systems approach (Lijphart 1971; 1975) where economic and political development are the control variables and variations in national political culture are examined as they influence the gender, state, and policy issues. Most FCP work assumes that post-industrial countries in the West, unlike other countries of the world, share certain politico-economic environments and institutions, with notable cross-national variations in cultural contexts. A part of the common heritage is that women's movements have emerged with strategies aimed at least in part to influence the democratic policy process and the development of large welfare states. Theory building, therefore, is a 'middle range' enterprise, in the tradition of Merton (1949) and LaPalombara (1968). Few FCP scholars claim that their theory is directly applicable to countries outside of the West, including Japan or Israel. Instead, they leave it to area specialists of non-Western countries to operationalize and test FCP propositions.

Like non-feminist qualitative comparative political analysts, FCP scholars develop and use concepts that are able to 'travel' across national boundaries. As Sartori (1970), Collier (1993), and Collier and Mahon (1993) caution, general concepts should not be automatically used in cross-national analysis without acknowledging different cultural contexts. If the cultural context is ignored in the articulation and application of concepts, they argue, the core meaning of the concept may be lost or ethnocentric notions derived from one cultural context may be imposed on another context. When concepts are 'stretched' too far they risk losing their analytic usefulness. Whereas some of the first FCP studies were less sensitive to the cross-national compatibility of concepts, many of the cross-national research projects that follow the FCP approach are careful to use concepts that take into consideration the different cultural and social contexts of the countries included in a given study.

❖ *Feature 6: One-way Intersections with Non-feminist Political Science*

Many FCP scholars since the mid-1990s have actively sought to intersect their work with non-feminist literature. Intersection here means cross-fertilization.

Rather than seeking to unite or to integrate non-feminist and feminist work, FCP scholars find arenas of overlap that can be used as a foundation for closer collaboration with non-feminist scholars. Instead of completely rejecting traditional political studies or uncritically using feminist studies, FCP work purposefully develops the strengths and shores up the weaknesses of each to advance knowledge in both areas. As Sainsbury (1996: 2) argues, intersecting is a two-way process whereby 'the shortcomings of each', non-feminist and feminist, are identified 'to combine their insights in order to transcend their limitations'.

Welfare state research has sought to gender non-feminist welfare state theory by adding gendered dimensions to conventional typologies of 'gender regimes' (for example, Sainsbury 1994; 1996; 1999a). Work on feminist movements and public policy has applied and modified theories on new social movements and political opportunity structures (for example, Gelb 1989; Lovenduski and Randall 1993; Banaszak, Beckwith, and Rucht 1996; Ferree and Martin 1995). One study of women's organizations in Sweden is explicitly defined as 'a feminist project' related to 'the traditional political science approach as well as to the advances made by feminist researchers' (Gustafsson, Eduards, and Rönnblom 1997: 7). Non-feminist concepts have been used frequently in feminist policy analyses, including Lowi's policy typology (1964; 1972), Schattschneider's (1975) notion of 'mobilisation of bias' in policy formation; Kingdon's (1995) and others' (for example, Cobb and Elder 1983) work on problem definition and agenda setting, Edelman's (1985) work on symbolic reform; and Jenkins-Smith and Sabatier's (1993) advocacy coalition framework.

In general, efforts to intersect feminist work with non-feminist political science tend to be one-way. FCP scholars seek to contribute to non-feminist work and non-feminist work ignores adjacent FCP theory-building. For example, in debates about the application of Lowi's policy typology in mainstream policy journals (Kellow 1988; Lowi 1988; 1997; Anderson 1997a, b), no mention was made of any of the feminist modifications (for example, Outshoorn 1986a; Newman 1995; Boneparth and Stoper 1982b; Lovenduski 1986a). Even within the context of political science's new 'era of eclecticism' (Lane 1990: 927, cited in McCool 1995: 7) guided by 'methodological pluralism' (Roth 1987, cited in McCool 1995: 7), few political studies outside of the purview of feminist analysis use the findings or concepts of FCP research.[15]

Although the gender and welfare state literature has received some acknowledgement in non-feminist circles (for example, Liebfried and Pierson 1995; Esping-Andersen 1999; Pierson 2000; Castles 1999) and a few comparative policy studies have brought in feminist policy issues and literature (for example, Caporaso and Jupille 2000), the norm in non-feminist political science is to ignore the new burgeoning area of scholarship, even when non-feminist areas share common methodological and theoretical ground with FCP. For example, policy analysts involved with the new 'policy science of democracy' (Kelly 1992) in the USA, virtually ignore FCP scholarship. Like FCP scholars, they see the systematic, but not purely value-free, study of policy as a way of making democracies more democratic. They are also committed to doing research for use in designing better policies (for example, Kamienicki 1991; Mead 1995; Ingram and Smith 1998; De Leon 1998; Ashford 1992).

Despite the move in comparative politics to 'bridge the divide' between qualitative and quantitative approaches (for example, Ragin 1987; King, Keohane, and Verba 1994; Collier 1993; Putnam 1993; Bunce 1981; Esping-Andersen 1990; Caporaso 1995; Laitin 1995; Collier 1995) and hence to value qualitative comparative policy analysis, work in this major sub-field seldom mentions FCP scholarship. Feminist scholarship was mentioned in only one of the contributions (Pierson 2000) to a recent collection of essays on the state of the field of comparative politics in the journal *Comparative Political Studies*. This particular journal is arguably the major outlet for articles that take a qualitative or bridging approach. Comparative public policy work that divides public policy into specific sectors (for example, Adolino and Blake 2001; Feick 1992; Heidenheimer, Heclo, and Adams 1990; Wilensky *et al.* 1985; Jones 1985; Desario 1989; Andersen and Kjell 1993) and even recognizes newer sectors like 'ethnic minorities policy' (Harrop 1992) does not identify feminist/gender/women's policy as a separate sector of public policy.

❖ FCP LITERATURE

Published work in FCP can be understood in two ways: first, through the different ways research examines the state's role, and second, through the 'research cycle' that drives the cumulation of knowledge on gender, the state, and policy in Western post-industrial democracies.

❖ Four Approaches to the State

The FCP literature takes four analytical approaches to the state and its institutions. Rather than being discrete, each area emphasizes a different part of the larger empirical puzzle of gender, policy, and the state and, hence, partly overlaps with other areas. The first approach, feminist policy formation, scrutinizes the ways in which public policy promotes women's status and strikes down gender hierarchies through studying the obstacles, actors, content, and processes of feminist policy (see Appendix B). The major object of analysis is the policy process itself, or the 'politics of policy formation', and not the impact of policy on society. It is not that feminist policy formation studies ignore whether public policy improves women's status or changes gender relations in society; indeed, many of them include some discussion of women's and men's status.

Rather, many researchers who work on feminist policy formation recognize the problem of uniquely attributing changes in gender relations in women's status to a specific set of policies rather than to other explanatory factors unrelated to public policy.

Feminist movements and policy work—the second approach— is concerned with the interplay between women's movements, the state, and public policy.[16] One issue treated by much of this literature is whether, how, and why women's/feminist movements ideas and action get translated into state policies. Whereas some research focuses on the first wave of feminism in the nineteenth and early twentieth centuries, it is usually the activities and repercussions of second-wave feminism that interest FCP scholars who work on social movement topics.[17] It is also important to note that this literature goes beyond examining the activities of women's movements to scrutinizing how social movements interact with the state through policy formation and other state activities such as women's policy offices.

A major issue of interest here is to evaluate the success of women's movements in influencing the content of public policy and the structures of the state. Many analysts are interested in how movements change the 'frame' of policy discussions on relevant issues (for example, Gamson 1988; Snow and Benford 1992; Beckwith 2001). Women's movement research does overlap with feminist policy formation and state feminism, but it tends to remain distinct in the way much of the work refers to social movement theory to aid understanding of the role of women's movements in policy development.

An area of some debate in the feminist movement literature is over the difference between women's movements and feminist movements. Beckwith (2000) provides an excellent discussion of this debate in her review of comparative women's movement research. She calls for a differentiation between 'women's movements', 'women in movement', and 'feminist movements'. While women's movements are ' . . . characterised by the primacy of women's gendered experiences, women's issues, and women's leadership and decision-making', feminist movements 'are distinguished by their challenge of patriarchy' (2000: 437).

State feminism—the third approach in FCP—considers whether state structures and actors can promote feminism through focusing on women's actors in the state as policy-makers, the gendered nature of state agencies that influence women's—and men's—roles, and the activities of women's policy machineries in a wide variety of government agencies and branches.[18] FCP analysts studying women's policy offices are also interested in studying the women and sometimes men—'femocrats'—who staff these new action agencies and who make careers in women's policy (for example, Borchorst 1999b: 165; Van der Ros 1995; Outshoorn 1998a).

Following the lead of feminist scholars such as Pringle and Watson (1992) and Molyneux (1985), but still assuming that 'women's interests are interesting' (Sapiro 1981), more recent literature on state feminism tends to conceptualize women's interests in their full complexity, taking into account that any consideration of women as a group must also recognize the class, ethnic, and racial differences that can undercut the collective identity of women. State feminism work assesses the links between the 'substantive' representation of women's interests in policy and the state and the presence of women in elected office: their 'descriptive' representation (Pitkin 1967). A major issue of inquiry is whether an increased presence of women in elected and appointed office leads to more woman-friendly or feminist policies: in other words, whether descriptive representation leads to substantive representation (for example, Young 2000; Oldusma 2002; Tremblay and Pelletier 2000; Burrell 1997). This analytical cut is also inspired by an adjacent literature that focuses on the political recruitment of women in public office, usually via political parties.[19]

The final approach to the state, the gender and welfare state literature, scrutinizes the welfare state as a prime obstacle and/or promoter of gender discrimination and equality.[20] Much of this scholarship looks at the link between women's and men's roles in the public and private domains in relation to the policies of the welfare state. Work on this topic is not concerned with the development of purposefully feminist policy but rather with the impact of non-feminist policies on the status of women, often compared with men's, and gender relations. A recent major shift in gender and welfare state literature is to study policy issues related to women's and men's roles in caring.

Two other areas of research that tend to be conducted by FCP scholars cut across all four areas of research. Comparative European Union (EU) scholarship that focuses on relations between the EU and member states provides important insights into the interface between supra-national and national policies.[21] National governments, the EU, and the Council of Europe often contract reports on feminist policy issues.[22] Quite often FCP scholars organize these studies or are employed to carry out country-based research. The EU uses these reports to evaluate the implementation of its sex equality policy in member states.[23]

There are several other areas of work that overlap with FCP literature but do not fully embrace the FCP approach. Identifying work that is adjacent to FCP literature highlights FCP's separate identity. Most feminist public policy literature on the USA studies some of the same objects of analyses as FCP work in the US context with virtually no reference to comparative theory-building or FCP literature.[24] Work on policy in the USA can be used as case study data for comparative studies that include the USA, but does not contribute to FCP theory.

Global feminist policy literature looks at the same analytical approaches to gender, policy, and the state, refers to some FCP work, has a comparative frame, and since the mid-1990s has focused on gender.[25] It tends to take an interpretive cross-systemic approach without concern for theory development, usually including, quite randomly, countries from different parts of the world for reasons that are more linked to global coverage than to theory-building. FCP scholars are invited to write chapters in some of these books.

Scholarship on non-Western countries is more systematically concerned with theory-building, but it develops theoretical and conceptual tools adapted to quite different political, cultural, economic, and social environments of the country or regions in the study.[26] Authors like Kammerman and Kahn (1978), Yohalem (1980), Field (1983), Hallett (1996), and Cossman *et al.* (1997) take a comparative empirical approach by examining public policy areas that are related to women's issues and gender without seeking to analyse explicitly feminist action, to operationalize feminist theory, or to orient research findings toward applied feminist outlets.

❖ The FCP Research Cycle

Although some FCP authors are less explicit than others about comparative aims, most work takes part in a comparative, feminist theory-building 'research cycle'. Based on Skocpol and Somers' (1980) analysis of the theory construction process in comparative politics, the FCP research cycles consist of four separate streams. As they observe about non-feminist comparative analysis, all four streams work together, each from different approaches to comparison, to develop middle-range theory.

The first stream consists of theoretically driven, single-country case studies that often increase the number of observations by conducting 'within country case studies' (Collier 1993) or examine a wide variety of policies within one country.[27] These case studies generate hypotheses that are examined by research in the second stream. The next stream, explicitly or implicitly employing the comparative method, selects two or three countries as a means of sorting through hypotheses about the determinants of the state and gender, usually derived from single-nation case studies.[28] The third stream consists of mostly edited books that bring together scholars with expertise on the countries in the volume to examine loosely, in a broad selection of countries, a specific issue, like abortion policy, equality principles, or gendering welfare states. The extent to which this work discusses specific contributions to theory-building is varied. Nonetheless, whether through filling significant empirical and conceptual gaps or by sharing common analytical goals, these books are important building blocks in the broader FCP research cycle.[29]

The fourth stream is more recent and is indicative of the consolidation of FCP as a field of study. Following recent calls for systematic cross-national analysis and building from the findings of scholarship in the other three parts of the research cycle, these studies use the comparative method and quantitative analysis to test hypotheses about a well-defined set of relationships through a systematic cross-national research design. The latest generation of FCP studies includes three or more countries. The studies are quite often a product of research groups that meet on a regular basis to discuss methodology and data collection issues (for example, Sainsbury 1999*a*; Mazur 2001*a*; Lewis 1997; Stetson 2001*a*).

❖ FCP SCIENTIFIC COMMUNITY AND INFRASTRUCTURE

Roughly 80 scholars work regularly on FCP research topics.[30] With a few exceptions, members of the FCP scientific community are women. More than a result of any collective decision to exclude men, their absence is a result of the realities of self-selection in academic training; women tend to be more interested in the study of feminist politics than men. One half of FCP scholars is based in English-speaking countries: Ireland, the United Kingdom, Canada, Australia, and the USA. Less than one-quarter of these are from the USA. The other half is based in continental Europe: the Netherlands, Germany, Austria, Italy, Spain, Denmark, Norway, Sweden, Finland, and Belgium. If we control for national population and size of university infrastructure, this community is quite evenly spread among the different countries. Furthermore, many FCP researchers are trained in one country and then work and live in others, sometimes moving between several countries during their careers. Even when scholars are trained and work in a given country, they frequently spend significant parts of their careers in other countries.

Because of the different national languages spoken by the members of the community, the lingua franca is necessarily English. For the most part, members can speak English fluently; many publish in English. Many of the native English speakers also speak at least one other language. A major hallmark of the FCP community, therefore, is its cosmopolitan nature. The FCP community actually contradicts the larger trends in political science identified by Norris (1997*a*: 19) toward localism, 'with a primary concern to delineate political processes within the context of a particular nation-state'.

FCP community members work primarily in universities. Many are also frequently hired as government consultants. Approximately two-thirds are trained political scientists. The next largest group are sociologists; and the rest specialize in social policy, history, women's studies, or law. Most FCP scholars are active teachers and seek to further the FCP agenda in the classroom at both graduate and undergraduate levels. FCP scholars, for example, participated in a workshop at the University of Washington in 1997 on how to introduce gender into Western European Studies courses (Mazur and Appleton 1997; Stetson 1997*a*; Eliason 1997; Lovenduski 1997*c*; Elison 1997). For many, the relationship between research and teaching is two-way, where researchers can gain valuable feedback from their students to develop their research designs and agendas.[31] Most FCP research projects include doctoral students. A new generation of FCP scholars coming out of doctoral programmes in North America and Western Europe provides strong evidence of the importance of mentoring and graduate teaching in FCP.[32]

FCP practitioners began to develop research networks in the early 1980s. The networks often meet at the conferences of the European Consortium of Political Research, the American Political Science Association, the International Political Science Association, or the International Studies Association. At least ten FCP books have come out of ECPR workshops.[33] In the 1990s, FCP scholars increasingly developed multinational research projects. Once in place, the network convenors secure funds from a combination of supra-national, national, university, and private funding agencies, and other institutionalized sources that are not overtly feminist. Whereas some feminists might consider this strategy as a sign of mainstream cooption, FCP practitioners see it as a necessary 'political adjustment' to institutional imperatives.[34] These projects implement a complex, gendered research programme, produce a series of publications, and often create more permanent infrastructure like newsletters, journals, and graduate funding and permanent programmes.

FCP networks have been active in three of the four areas of scholarship on the state. Networks on gender and the welfare state include 'Crossing Borders' with a research core named 'Gender, Citizenship and Welfare States'. First convened in Sweden in 1994, the network produced one book (Hobson and Berggren 1997) and a regular newsletter. The organizers received 4m kronor ($US421,000) from the Bank of Sweden for their research programme in comparative gender studies. A new graduate programme affiliated with the network received funding from Stockholm University. A feminist collective of researchers first brought together in 1993 to study lone mothers and the welfare state published an edited book (Lewis 1997) with the help of a Human Capital and Mobility Grant from the European Union. A USA-based network used seed money from a Council for European Studies workshop grant to hold several meetings in Europe and the United States. Bock and Thane's (1991) edited collection originated in a research programme housed at the European University Institute in Florence.

At least three research networks have been active in the women's movements and policy area. Ferree and Martin's edited collection (1995) was a product of a conference funded by the National Science Foundation in the USA. An in-progress project on social movements and the state, directed by two Americans and a German and funded by the Council for European Studies in the USA, has had several meetings over the past three years and plans to produce a final edited book in 2001 (Banaszak, Beckwith, and Rucht 1996). Gustafsson, Eduards, and Rönnblom (1997) carried out a study of women's organizations in Sweden in conjunction with a larger state-funded project on government change, named 'Democracy in Transition'.

Several research networks have been active since the mid-1990s in the area of state feminism. A three-person British research effort on Gender and the New Urban Governance received funding from the UK Economic and Social Research Council and was based at the London School of Economics (Abrar, Lovenduski, and Margetts 1998). Andrew and Rodgers' (1997) edited collection originated in a conference sponsored by the Social Sciences and Humanities Research Council (SSHRC), the Department of Justice, the Department of the Secretary of State, and the University of Ottawa. It assesses the impact of 20 years of state feminism in Canada. A partnership between nationally based feminist researchers and the European Union through the Community Action Programs on Equal Opportunities for Women and Men has been an important catalyst in the development of a consolidated FCP community.

The Research Network on Gender, Politics, and the State (RNGS) is a 45-member group working on women's policy offices. It produced an initial edited volume (Stetson and Mazur 1995) and then developed a comparative research design to undertake a long-term study of women's policy offices in 17 countries (Stetson and Mazur 2001). Two books were published on its research findings and three more will be produced by the end of the project in 2004 (Mazur 2001a; Stetson 2001a; Lovenduski in-progress). The group received funding from the National Science Foundation (USA), the University of Leiden, the University of Southampton, the European Science Foundation, and the University of Washington. The French, Italian, and Canadian governments provided funding for RNGS research as well.

An update of the ground-breaking study of gender, policy, and state in Nordic countries (Haavio-Mannila et al. 1985) was published in English as well as in all of the Scandinavian languages in 1999 (Bergqvist et al. 1999). This study cuts across all four areas of FCP research. The Gender, Empowerment and Politics project in Denmark is also conducting research that addresses the analytical issues from the FCP paradigm. A new Centre for the Advancement of Women in Politics at Queen's University of Belfast promotes research and teaching on FCP related topics as well.

The Women and Restructuring Network in Canada, funded by an SSHRC grant and a grant from the Canadian International Development Agency, examines how state restructuring has affected women and women's movements in the context of the global economy. At least three publications have been inspired by this network (Bakker 1996; Brodie 1995; 1996). The project, Public Policy Discourses, Mass Attitudes and the Governance of Gender Equality in Europe at the University of Bremen, funded by the German government, is a current seven-nation study on 'the institutionalization of gender equality norms' in EU member states in 1975–2000.

The feminist journal *Social Politics* is an important part of active FCP networking on welfare states; not all articles published in the journal follow the FCP approach. It is edited by three welfare state scholars, two in the USA and one in Sweden, and was created in 1994 during the take-off period of FCP. A second journal created in 1999, the *International Feminist Journal of Politics*, identifies explicitly with the goals of FCP. Given that 'a vital professional field must possess the means to regenerate itself, publicly and intellectually' (Lawlor 1996: 117), these two journals are both indicators of as well as vehicles for FCPs institutionalization and growth.

❖ CONCLUSION

At the beginning of the twenty-first century, the field of Feminist Comparative Policy has a consolidated and distinct approach connected to a well-networked and cosmopolitan scientific community. Driven by feminist empiricism and institutional pragmatism, FCP scholars have successfully developed an infrastructure on three continents. Whereas the accomplishments of FCP are clear, its impact on non-feminist political science and adjacent disciplines is less obvious. Given that the field has moved into a more institutionalized phase only within the last several years, it may be too early to assess FCP's long-term impact. There is only anecdotal evidence that the pattern of past resistance to FCP work may be in the process of being replaced. Only a handful of non-feminist political scientists appear interested in turning the one-way intersection between FCP and traditional political studies into a two-way exchange.

To be sure, there are still gaps in FCP scholarship itself. Lacking systematic cross-national analysis through FCP research networks, the literature on feminist policy formation is arguably less methodologically and theoretically advanced than the other three areas of FCP. Chapter 2 identifies the weaknesses of this area of research and proposes a framework, inspired by the FCP approach, for making use of the large literature to analyse more systematically feminist policy formation. In shoring up the gaps in one area of FCP, this book seeks to strengthen this young, vital, and ever-expanding field of study.

❖ NOTES

1 For more on the different ways this study uses the term 'feminist' see the next section, Chapter 2, and Appendix A.

2 The plethora of state-of-the-field assessments of feminist political studies has made passing references to Feminist Comparative Policy work without identifying FCP as a separate area of feminist studies. On gender and politics studies, see Lovenduski (1981), Boals (1975), Carroll (1980), Ferguson (1984), Nelson (1989), Sapiro (1991), Carroll and Zerilli (1993), Randall (1991), Silverberg (1992), Githens (1983), Meehan (1986), Staudt and Weaver (1997), and Kelly and Fisher (1993); on feminist policy

studies, see Hawkesworth (1994), Ackelsberg (1992), Lief Palley (1976), and Cichowski (2000); on feminist welfare studies, see Orloff (1993), Kornbluh (1996), and O'Connor (1996); on feminist scholarship in specific countries, see Outshoorn (1992) on the Netherlands and Valiente (1998*a*) on Spain; and on work that uses gender as an analytical lens, see Lovenduski (1998), Acker (1992), and Nelson (1992). I conducted an initial review of FCP as a new field of study in 1998 (Mazur 1999).

3 Over 420 published English-language pieces on feminist policy formation were identified for this study. See Appendix B for a guide to the literature consulted for the comparative analysis of feminist policy formation.

4 This assessment is partially based on an article I wrote on FCP in 1998 (Mazur 1999).

5 Both non-feminist comparative politics (for example, Sartori 1970; Collier and Mahon 1993) and feminist analysis (for example, Bacchi 1996) are concerned with the problem of developing analytically useful definitions of thorny concepts: 'contested concepts'.

6 See Beasley (1999: Ch. 1) for an excellent discussion of whether there is a single feminist ideal or not. She also discusses how feminist activists and scholars deal with the tension between the multiplicity of feminist positions and practice and the need to identify a core set of ideas. Beasley avoids presenting a single set definition of feminist political thought, instead opting to identify the seven major strands of 'current feminist viewpoints' (1999: 48).

7 Like the working definitions of feminism used by other FCP scholars, this definition attempts to incorporate the diversity of Western feminism. Providing a general definition of feminism based on core ideas does not mean, however, that this study eschews conventional labels for different types of feminist action and ideas. For the operational definition of feminist policy see Chapter 2. For the categorization system this books uses to label feminist ideas in political action in Western post-industrial democracies, see Appendix A.

8 Public service delivery policies were not included due to their highly cross-cutting nature and the lack of published studies on them.

9 Three, instead of four, cases of family law policies are analysed due to the absence of published studies of this policy area in the three Protestant Social Democrat countries. See Table 2.1 for the distribution of analysed policy cases across the eight subsectors and 13 countries.

10 Beasley (1999), for example, identifies the following currents in Western feminist thought: liberal, radical, Marxist, socialist, psychoanalytic, postmodern, and 'feminist concerns with race and ethnicity'.

11 First identified by Harding (1987*b*), the notion of feminist empiricism has been used by Randall (1991), Hawkesworth (1994), and others to describe one of several feminist stances on empirical inquiry.

12 Some feminist theory mentioned in FCP work includes Conway, Bourque, and Scott (1987); Ferguson (1984); Jones and Jonnasdottir (1988); Pateman (1988); MacKinnon (1989); Bock and James (1992); Phillips (1991; 1995); Sassoon (1992); Duerst-Lahti and Kelly (1995); DiStefano (1991); Carver (1995); Hernes (1987); Pringle and Watson (1992); Squires (1999*a*).

13 Qualitative studies focus on a limited number (n) of cases to observe the dynamics and determinants of a given political phenomena. Quantitative studies use large sample sizes to statistically analyse correlations between continuous independent and dependent variables. Qualitative studies in comparative politics are often referred to as 'small n analysis' and quantitative studies as 'large n analysis'. Many political scientists across different sub-fields in recent years have attempted to overcome the quantitative-qualitative divide in analysis. Whereas quantitative analysts use more in-depth study of specific cases, qualitative researchers apply analytical principles from quantitative analysis in designing research (for example, King, Keohane, and Verba 1994).

14 In comparative politics theory-building, case studies are used to investigate theories and generate hypotheses but not to test hypotheses (Lijphart 1971; 1975). The comparative method uses two or more cases to sort through rival explanations and to test hypotheses (Collier 1993; Ragin 1987).

15 The poor reception of FCP scholarship echoes similar trends identified by assessments of the impact of feminist scholarship across all of the major sub-fields of political science (see n. 3 for the list of review essays).

16 To name some examples: Jenson (1985); Dahlerup (1986a); Duchen (1986); Katzenstein and Mueller (1987); Beckwith (1987); Black (1989); Gelb (1989); Kaplan (1992); Ferree and Martin (1995); Threlfall (1996a); Brodie (1995); Banaszak (1996); Gustafsson, Eduards, and Rönnblom (1997); Andrew and Rodgers (1997); Bashevkin (1998); Andreasen *et al.* (1991).

17 Although there is some disagreement as to whether the 'new women's movements' of the 1960s and 1970s constitute the third or the second consecutive wave of feminist activity in Western democracies (Rossi 1973), most agree that a new feminist wave developed during this period. This second wave brought together mass women's movements, women's rights pressure groups, and women's groups in political parties and trade unions to pursue a variety of feminist aims (Dahlerup 1986a).

18 See, for instance, Epstein and Laub (1981); Baldcock and Cass (1983); Haavio-Mannila et al. (1985); Hernes (1987); Sassoon (1992); Franzway, Court, and Connell (1989); Watson (1990); Sawer (1990); Pringle and Watson (1992); Cockburn (1991); Savage and Witz (1992); Stetson and Mazur (1995); Eisenstein (1996); Davis (1997); Burrell (1997); Abrar, Lovenduski, and Margetts. (1998); Tremblay and Andrew (1998); Mazur (2001a); Stetson (2001a); O'Regan (2000).

19 See for example, Lovenduski and Hills (1981); Siltanen and Stanworth (1984); Cook, Lorwin, and Daniels (1984); Bashevkin (1985a); Lovenduski and Norris (1993); Karvonen and Selle (1995); Norris and Lovenduski (1995); Tremblay (2000); Bayes (1991); Young (2000); Tremblay and Pelletier (2000).

20 For more on gender and welfare state research see, for example, Daly (2000); Lewis (1983a; 1992; 1993a; 1997; 1998); Gordon (1990); Bock and Thane (1991); Orloff (1993; 1996); Sainsbury (1994; 1996; 1999a); Ostner and Lewis (1995); Bussemaker and Voet (1998); Hobson and Berggren (1997); Carlsen and Larsen (1993); Hirschmann and Liebert (2001); Hobson (2000b); Harrington (2000); Evans and Wekerle (1997); Boje and Leira (2000); O'Connor (1996); Adams and Padamsee (2001); Mahon (2001); Mutari and Figart (2001).

21 For some examples, see Buckley and Anderson (1988b); Vallance and Davies (1986); Meehan (1994); Hoskyns (1996); Elman (1996b); Rees (1995; 1998); Van Doorne-Huiskes

and Roelofs (1995); Pillinger (1992); Egan (1998); Meehan and Collins (1996). In addition see Meehan (1992) for a review of the literature on equality policy and the EU.

22 See, for instance, Corcoran and Donnelly (1988); Vogel-Polsky (1994); Braithwaite and Byrne (1995); Cockburn *et al.* (1994; 1995).

23 The study, 'Women in Decision-making', is an example of an FCP-networked report for the EU (Lovenduski and Stephenson 1998). Joni Lovenduski coordinated over 18 country-based researchers to review research on women in economic, social, and political decision making, women's policy machineries, and assessments of sex equality policy in all member states.

24 See, for example, Diamond (1983); Boneparth and Stoper (1982*a*; 1988); Gelb and Palley (1982; 1987); Stetson (1997*b*); Tolleson (1992); Costain (1992); Thomas (1994); Borrelli and Martin (1997).

25 Examples of global feminist literature include Lipman-Bluman and Bernard (1979); Black and Cottrell (1981); Dominelli (1991); Bystydzienski (1992*a*); Chow and Berheide (1996); Nelson and Chowdhury (1994); Lycklama à Nijeholt, Vargas, and Wieringa (1998); Randall and Weylen (1998); Abels and Sifft (1999); Basu (1995); Weldon (2001).

26 See, for example, Beckman and D'Amico (1994); Scott, Kaplan, and Keates (1997); Staudt (1998); Wieringa (1995); Bystydzienski and Sekhon (1999).

27 Examples of research in the first research cycle include Lovenduski and Randall (1993); Stetson (1987) ; Mazur (1995*a*); Elman (1996*a*); Gregory (1987); Gelb and Palley (1987); Gustaffson, Eduards, and Rönnblom (1997); Bashevkin (1998); Cockburn (1991); Watson (1990); Eisenstein (1996); Sawer (1990); Abrar, Lovenduski, and Margetts (1998); Boneparth and Stoper (1982*a*; 1988); Bussemaker and Voet (1998); Franzway, Court, and Connell (1989).

28 Examples of the second research cycle are, Ruggie (1984); Meehan (1985); Randall (1982; 1987); Kahn and Meehan (1992); Leira (1992); Heatlinger (1993); Hart (1994); Black (1989); Gelb (1989); Hernes (1987); Burrell (1997); Davis (1997); Bashevkin (1985*a*); Gardiner (1997*a*); Haavio-Mannila *et al.* (1985); Savage and Witz (1992); Lewis (1983*a*); Daly (2000); Jenson and Siheun (2001).

29 The following are examples from the third research cycle: Lovenduski (1986*a*); Norris (1987); Kaplan (1992); Ratner (1980); Lovenduski and Outshoorn (1986*a*); Jenson, Hagen and Reddy (1988); Meehan and Sevenhuijsen (1991*a*); Githens and Stetson (1996); Drew, Emerek, and Mahon (1998); Dahlerup (1986*a*); Katzenstein and Mueller (1987); Ferree and Martin (1995); Epstein and Laub (1981); Bock and Thane (1991); Lewis (1993*a*; 1997, 1998); Sainsbury (1994; 1999*a*); Threlfall (1996*a*); Hobson and Berggren (1997).

30 See Mazur (1999) for a more detailed breakdown of FCP community members. Scholars with two or more publications on an FCP topic were counted as a part of the FCP community. The list of active FCP scholars used for this analysis is available on request.

31 Lewis, for instance, attributes the idea for her 1983 book to her students. 'Indeed, it was the desire of a group of students at the London School of Economics to discuss the subject of gender roles in relation to social policy which gave rise to the seminars on which this book is based' (1983*a*: i).

32 I know four current doctoral candidates in FCP and seven recent Ph.D.s working on FCP who were placed in permanent academic jobs in the past three years. All seven have FCP books in press.

33 See, for example, Haavio-Manila *et al.* (1985); Lovenduski and Outshoorn (1986*a*), Dahlerup (1986*a*); Meehan and Sevenhuijsen (1991*a*); Jones and Jonassdottir (1988); Sainsbury (1994, 1999*a*); Stetson and Mazur (1995); Gardiner (1997*a*); Carver and Mottier (1998).

34 Rönnblom uses this concept in her analysis of women's projects in Sweden. She argues that local Swedish women's projects are feminist because they assess the imperatives of their institutional environment and use state funds to further 'gradually' women's interests in a 'step by step' manner. She neither criticizes this strategy nor indicates that women's interests have been coopted. Instead she argues that these women's projects uncover the patriarchal nature of the state through demanding 'their share of the public pie on their own terms . . . and a political order which is based on women's daily lives . . .' (1997: 119).

2 ❖ Towards Solving the Feminist Policy Formation Puzzle

To what degree do Western post-industrial democracies purposefully pursue feminist ends? Once governments make nominally feminist policies, are the policies actually feminist? If so, what are the ingredients for successful feminist policy development? These questions constitute the analytical puzzle for the rest of this book. Whereas some scholars of Feminist Comparative Policy (FCP) have been turning their attention to solving the puzzle, most of the vast literature on feminist policy issues lacks a single, overarching theoretical framework or methodological approach. *Sex Equality Policy in Western Europe* provides useful insights into defining and studying sex equality policy as a separate arena of government action. As the editor of the volume states,

> What is increasingly clear . . . is the need for a comprehensive assessment of equal-
> ity policy as a substantive area of policy, subject to evaluation in its own right, like
> other areas of governmental policy. Analysis is needed both within and between
> sectors (to which equality policies apply) within and between nations and an
> overall schema to chart the progress of equality policy within a comparative
> European framework. (Gardiner 1997*b*: 7)

It is to the task of proposing an 'overall schema' to comprehensively assess this new sector of policy 'in its own right' that this chapter now turns. The chapter first discusses how this study follows the FCP approach. Given the need to spell out the parameters of feminist policy as a sector, the next section explains why the term 'feminist' is preferred to other commonly used labels. The operational definition for feminist policy is then supplied. The succeeding section presents the notion of feminist policy as a sector and furnishes a brief overview of the eight sub-areas of feminist policy to be scrutinized in the rest of the book. The last section turns to an analysis of the framework and methods of the study. The chapter concludes with a summary of the road map for the rest of the book.

❖ Putting into Action the Feminist Comparative Policy Approach

This study develops propositions about feminist policy formation in Western post-industrial democracies through empirical analysis that follows the basic conventions of social science research, such as replication, falsifiability, sampling, and hypothesis-testing. Feminist policy is the object of analysis, not only because activists believe that it should be a major factor in promoting a woman-friendly polity, but also because of the empirical reality of public policies that formally announce some type of feminist aims in all Western post-industrial democracies: a reality documented by a critical mass of research conducted by analysts from all over the world.

This study also seeks to help activists and policy practitioners; the concluding chapter specifically addresses this project's practical implications. The general definition of feminism in Chapter 1 and the operational definition of feminist policy presented below reflect the ecumenical and analytical approach of FCP to defining feminism. Rather than associating feminist policy with one type of Western feminist political thought, this study opts for a broad definition that incorporates the full range of feminist ideas and actions found in Western post-industrial democracies.

The puzzle of feminist policy formation is related to one of the central issues of normative feminist theory: how to gender democracy? In identifying and mapping out feminist policy as a sector and analysing if, how, and why nominally feminist policies are feminist, this study suggests that democracies may very well be capable of being gendered in meaningful ways: meaningful for at least some feminists. Feminist theories of democracy are used more specifically to examine whether policy processes represent women both substantively and descriptively. This study also follows the cues of feminist theorists that have presented the state as a malleable and multi-sited entity, capable of being influenced by feminist movements and feminist actors. It does not ignore, however, the possibility that other state arenas outside of feminist spheres of influence remain patriarchal. The relational concept of gender is an integral part of the working definition of feminist policy and is used to evaluate whether women's interests are represented substantively in policy content and discussions.

This study takes a qualitative cross-national approach by analysing policy processes within a relatively small sample of countries and policy cases. It uses the comparative method to identify different explanations for variations in feminist policy formation in Western post-industrial democracies. In this light, neither the taxonomy for feminist policy as a sector nor this study's tentative conclusions claim to shed light on democracies outside of the West, even those that many comparativists argue are at the same level of political and economic development as Western post-industrial democracies, like Japan and Israel. Within this context of similarity, the sample of countries selected for comparative analysis also represents the full range of cultures, political systems, and gender relations found across Western democracies.

Also reflecting the FCP approach to comparative research, core concepts are designed to travel across national boundaries without stretching their analytical meanings. Feminist policy as a sector and each sub-area of feminist policy are defined to include the gamut of nominally feminist policies in all Western post-industrial democracies. Similarly, feminist policy effectiveness is measured in terms of the policy process and not in terms of a given policy's impact on women's and men's status or on dominant attitudes about gender. An emphasis on process over impacts avoids what many have identified as the value-laden and ethnocentric biases inherent in cross-national studies that measure the social effects of public policy. It also reflects the approach of FCP researchers interested in state feminism and women's movements. They argue that evaluating the influence of women's policy agencies and women's movements on the democratic process itself is just as important as, if not more important than, determining whether agencies and movements affect women's status and gender relations in society.

Finally, this study is a textbook case of intersecting feminist and non-feminist scholarship. It follows the lead of non-feminist comparative public policy analysis that uses existing qualitative studies of policy to develop theory. It uses some of the major concepts of traditional comparative policy analysis in a study with feminist aims. The hypotheses about the national and regional determinants of effective feminist policy formation are derived from both conventional and feminist family-of-nations comparative classification systems as well.

❖ Why Call Feminist Policy 'Feminist'?

The term 'feminist' is used to label this new arena of government action to avoid the semantic problems and analytical ambiguities of other terms. One of the most frequently used labels in FCP research is the catch-all notion of 'woman-friendly'. Hernes (1987) first coined the term to examine whether states can create 'gender just' societies through 'state feminism'. For Hernes and other Scandinavian analysts, state feminism consist of 'feminism from above in the form of gender equality and social policies' (1987: 162). Others see state feminism in terms of the presence of women in state decision-making positions as administrators, elected politicians, appointed officials, and femocrats (Siim 1991; Stetson and Mazur 1995). Thus, from the beginning woman-friendly states linked the presence of women in government with policies.

Gardiner and Leijenaar (1997: 61) define 'woman-friendly policies' as the 'broad range of options available to European governments to improve the status of women, the adoption of and implementation of which reflect the existence of a culture of equality'. For Borchorst (1994a), woman-friendliness is about the degree to which welfare states put into question 'patriarchal patterns of power' in society. Although Dahlerup (1987: 123) does emphasise the unintended consequences of 'sex-neutral' policies as well as 'sex- specific' policies in her conceptualization of woman-friendly policy, most studies that employ this concept do not separate 'sex-specific' from 'sex-neutral' policies. They also tend to focus on the impact of policy on women rather than the intricacies of the policy formation process. Given the scope of the concept woman-friendly policy, this study opts for the term 'feminist' to pinpoint policies that have the specific intent of promoting women's rights and equality between the sexes.

Comparative work on feminist policy in Western Europe uses interchangeably the terms 'sex equality', 'gender equality', and 'equality' (for example, Gardiner 1997a; Lovenduski 1997c; Meehan 1992; Hobson and Berggren 1997; Borchorst 1999b, c). Studies of European Union (EU) policy on sex-based inequities in paid employment often label this policy area 'equality policy' (for example, Buckley and Anderson 1988b).[1] Scandinavian authors also tend to use the term 'equality policy', given that gender-oriented policies are often formally expressed in sex-neutral ways (for example, Holli 1992; Borchorst 1999b). These terms are also too general for this study. As Borchorst (1999b: 164) points out, gender equality policies, at least in the Nordic context, are not necessarily feminist: ' . . . gender equality initiatives can be pro-feminist or non-feminist, and we will not exclude the possibility that they can also be anti-feminist.'

An array of terms is used to describe equal employment policies: 'equal opportunities', 'equal treatment', 'equal pay', 'positive action', to name a few. Some of these terms are used to describe specific types of equal employment policies. In other instances, analysts use them to describe different policies that target equality between the sexes beyond paid employment. Thus, there has been some degree of confusion between general equality policies that cut across a variety of areas and more specific equality policies that target only equality in the labour force. Part of this confusion stems from the fact that most Western governments first tackled sex equality through the lens of wage labour (Lovenduski 1986a: 250).

Another problem with the label 'equality' is that it potentially excludes affirmative or positive action policies that favour women over men.[2] Taking a wide variety of forms in both employment and political arenas, these policies target women in order to bring them into previously male-dominated positions and, ultimately, to achieve some level of equality or balance between men and women in positions (Baachi 1996: 15).[3] As Gardiner (1997a: 3) points out, 'to favour one sex over the other for employment opportunities or to compensate one sex more so when market/state failure threatens their employment opportunities is regarded as sex discrimination'. Yet, as feminist policy scholars and practitioners assert, it is necessary to pursue a host of positive actions to specifically target women in order to redress deep-seated sex and gender-based inequities. 'In short, [equality] policy must accommodate preferential treatment for its target groups' (Lovenduski 1997b: 94).

Focusing on pure equality between men and women, rather than 'equity' or 'parity' (Lovenduski 1997b), may also preclude taking into consideration the real and socially constructed differences between men and women:[4] that is, the sex- and gender-based differences in life situations and societal expectations that keep women inferior to men. Whereas many scholars argue that notions of equality can bring in sex and gender differences, it still remains a politically and theoretically troublesome concept in the way that it has been used, particularly by some liberal feminists, to imply the sameness between men and women and to erase the fundamental differences between their life courses and choices.[5] This study, therefore, uses the general term 'feminist policy' rather than 'equality policy' to avoid the potentially politically divisive meanings and ambiguities associated with the contested concept. It does not, however, completely eschew the core principles contained in equality, so essential in bringing women's status, rights' and conditions in line with men's. Instead, the notion of equality is gendered so as to allow for differences between men and women that translate into politically, socially, and economically empowering men and disempowering women.

In many Western European countries, when notions of equality are articulated in public debates and in formal policy statements, whether the policies are employment-oriented or more broadly based, equality is often assumed to be sex-based rather than based on equality between different racial or ethnic groups. Alternatively, in the USA, affirmative action policies are often associated only with the promotion of minority rights, even though they officially target sex discrimination as well. Outside of the USA, racial or ethnic discrimination and sex discrimination are often treated in separate legislation and by different enforcement agencies. For example, in France the notion of égalité professionnelle refers to sex-based but not race-based equality, in both public discussions of equality and in the array of policy agencies and instruments that have been designed to promote égalité professionnelle. The degree to which racial and ethnicity issues become intertwined with gender issues in public policy formation depends on the ethnic composition and the way racial differences are transposed into the politics of a given country. Race-based and ethnicity-based equality issues, therefore, are addressed in this book as they are raised in the politics and processes of specific instances of feminist policy development.[6]

Hosykns (1996: 6) in her study of EU sex equality policies uses the term 'women's policy' to describe 'the area of political action and activity which particularly concerns (or targets) women or groups of women, or where issues are forced onto the agenda by women'. For her, the usual terms 'equal treatment', 'equal opportunities', or 'women's rights' do not 'convey the ramifications and unintended outcomes' of policies in the area of women's policy. Conway, Ahern, and Steuernagel (1999) also employ the label 'women's policy' in their study in the USA. Whereas they do not define clearly what is meant by policy for women, their cross-sectoral analysis does imply that they are interested in looking at how different policy areas affect women's lives. Hallett (1996) uses a similar rubric of women and social policy when looking at gender-specific policy in the United Kingdom, without attaching notions of feminism, equality, or equity.

In her sectoral analysis of policy for women in the USA (1997*b*) and France (1987), Stetson calls this category of policies 'women's rights policies'. While an important Anglo-American concept in terms of individual autonomy and law, the label does not travel well to Western countries like Sweden, France, or Italy, without rights-based cultures. Stetson's conceptualisation is still useful as it suggests the inclusion of a broad range of activity. 'More than statutes, rules, and court cases, women's rights encompasses all conflicts—the ongoing public debates—over what it means and should mean to be a female citizen . . .' (1997*b*: xi).

❖ THE OPERATIONAL DEFINITION OF FEMINIST POLICY

After this elaboration of why 'feminist' is the most accurate label for this new area of policy, it is now necessary to define what 'feminist policy' means. Analysts have taken three tacks in developing analytical definitions of feminism. The first is to provide a definition based on different currents of feminist political thought (for example, Beasley 1999; Tong 1989; Jaggar 1977). Many comparative analysts criticize this approach for being ethnocentric and for ignoring newer areas of feminist thought. A second approach is to inductively base operational definitions on the activities of groups that call themselves 'feminist' (for example, Offen 1988, 2000; Black 1989; Lovenduski 1997*c*). The problem with this approach is that it begs the question of what a feminist group is in the first place, particularly if groups and individuals do not identify with the term 'feminist'. The third tack is to use the term 'feminist' without defining it at all. Here, scholars and activists often use the label 'women', as in 'women's movements', as a synonym for 'feminist'.

The first two approaches to defining feminism are used in developing this study's operational definition of feminist policy. In order for a policy to be considered feminist, the formal intent, in public presentations or written policy statements, must include at least three of the following five components: three out of the five because of the scope and complexity of feminism. The policy statement does not actually need to mention the term 'feminist', just put forward clearly three of the following five ideas:

(1) the improvement of women's rights, status, or situation to be in line with men's, however rights, status, and situation are culturally defined within a given context;

(2) the reduction or elimination of gender-based hierarchies or patriarchy;

(3) a focus on both the public and the private spheres or an approach that avoids distinctions between the public and the private;

(4) a focus on both men and women;

(5) ideas that can be readily associated with a recognized feminist group, movement, or individual actor in a particular national context.

This definition is used in identifying the aims and the limits of each of the subareas of feminist policy and in determining whether the 27 cases of feminist policy formation have feminist results. It includes both the improvement of women's autonomy, contained in Black's (1989) definition of feminist action, and the recognition of the patriarchal system that must be struck down, a central tenet of Offen's (1988) view of feminism. It also allows for different cultural conceptions of what is the appropriate object of change: women's rights, situation, or status. The idea that women's situations need to be targeted in comparison with men's without making them the same, an idea advanced by feminists focused on difference, is an important element as well.

Both gender hierarchies and patriarchy are included to account for anti-system feminism and reform-oriented feminist action.[7] Moderate feminists may shy away from what they see as more radical terms 'patriarchy' and 'male oppression'. Here, gender hierarchies consist of socially defined asymmetric relations between men and women that have been a part of the development of contemporary Western societies and that underpin women's inferior status in comparison with men's.

Related to gender hierarchies and the improvement of women's status is the radical feminist assumption that analyses of the causes of and the remedies for women's inferior social position must be grounded in both the public and the private spheres. As Kate Millett (1971) articulated over 30 years ago, 'the personal is political'. Thus, the content of feminist policies should state how the traditional divide between public and private spheres is overcome and formally recognize that gender-based inequities are a result of dynamics in the home and in people's private lives as much as in the public arena of formal politics and paid work. This definition does not preclude, however, government action that targets the private or the public arenas alone. Feminist policy should also be aimed at both men and women, given that for many feminists real social change can occur only if both sides of gender relations are addressed. The fifth component of the definition emphasizes how nominally feminist policies should reflect the demands of groups, movements, and individuals that identify with real-life feminist struggles within a given country.

❖ FEMINIST POLICY AS A SECTOR

Studying public policy in a sectoral perspective is an important tradition in Comparative Public Policy research.[8] It allows the analyst to divide policy formation into sub-areas of government action based on the functions the ever-growing modern state has assumed in the twentieth century (Harrop 1992: 14). A sectoral approach assumes that policy actors operate within sub-systems or policy communities, based on the functional areas of government, composed of a given set of state and society actors, and with a certain pattern of interactions or styles. Research on policy sub-systems shows that there is variation in the way policy actors interact, the degree of 'sectorization' (Hayward 1992: 382), across different sectors within a given country.

This study conceptualizes feminist policy as a separate sector of government action as well. Given the vastness of the highly transversal new sector, eight major sub-sectors, or sub-areas, of domestic feminist action can be identified: (1) blueprint, (2) political representation, (3) equal employment, (4) reconciliation, (5) family, (6) body politics I: reproduction, (7) body politics II: sexuality, and (8) public service delivery.[9] *Blueprint policy* (BP) consists of the range of policies and agencies that establish general principles for feminist government action. *Political representation policy* (PRP) covers state action that promotes women's representation in the political arena as appointed and elected officials. *Equal employment policy* (EEP) includes any policy that seeks to promote feminist aims in paid labour. Policies that target how women and men deal with the double burden of work and family are in included in *reconciliation policy* (RP). This policy sector is considered separately because it often involves different actors and processes from those of equal employment policy, which targets uniquely paid labour issues. *Family law policy* (FLP) addresses gender hierarchies and men's and women's rights in the family through legal instruments. The fifth and sixth sub-sectors cover feminist government action that focuses on women's bodies or *body politics policy*. There are two different types of body politics policies: policies that promote women's *reproductive rights* (RRP) and policies that promote feminist approaches to *sexuality and violence* (SVP).

Public service delivery policy includes government efforts to deliver public services, like health, housing, education, and transportation It is often made and implemented at the local and/or sub-national levels of government. These polices tend to be raised in the context of other sub-sectors of feminist policy. For example, childcare delivery is dealt with in reconciliation policies and many issues related to women's health are taken up in body politics policies. Public education issues can also be covered in equal employment policies through job training. Public service delivery policy is not analysed in a separate chapter because of its highly transversal nature and because it has only recently become an object of systematic empirical scrutiny.

❖ THE FEMINIST POLICY FORMATION PUZZLE

❖ FRAMEWORK AND METHOD

❖ Questions and Unit of Analysis

The analytical framework in this study addresses the following questions:

1. Are nominally feminist policies actually feminist in the way they represent women descriptively and substantively in the long-term process of policy development?
2. If nominally feminist policies actually have feminist results in the policy process, what are the determinants of that feminist success? Does success correspond with a specific sub-area of feminist policy, with a specific country, or with a specific regional cluster of countries? Are there other important factors that can be identified at the level of the policy sub-system, the nation-state, or outside of the nation-state that produce feminist policy success?
3. Is there a single policy style or pattern of sectorization within specific sub-areas of feminist policy or across the entire sector of policies with formal feminist intentions?

The framework is designed to use the large but eclectic literature on feminist policy formation to analyse the unfolding of the complex process of feminist policy development over an extended period of time in the seven sub-areas of feminist policy in Western post-industrial democracies. As both feminist and non-feminist policy analysts argue, studying policies over an extended period of time provides a more accurate picture of policy dynamics and determinants. For instance, Abrar, Lovenduski, and Margetts (1998: 169) find in their study of policy in municipal government in Britain that 'feminist success in highlighting the gender dimensions of a policy resulted from activity sustained over a long period of time'. Likewise, Sabatier (1993: 16) asserts that 'understanding the process of policy change . . . requires a decade or more'.

This study uses the policy 'stage heuristic' (Sabatier 1993) to capture the unfolding of policy over the long haul. The unit of analysis is the development of policy through the different stages of the policy process from the time an issue becomes identified as a public problem to when policy actors evaluate formally the outcome of the policy years later. The stages of feminist policy development are observed in discrete policy decisions, usually at the national level, through 'process-tracing' (George and McKeown 1985) and 'thick description' (Geertz 1973). Process-tracing is the technique used by many policy analysts to follow the unfolding of a particular set of policy decisions over time. It allows the analyst to identify events and actors in order to explain the causes of a given series of policy decisions and/or outcomes. Tracing the evolution of a given issue over time typically involves archival research and elite interviews. This study replaces these primary data sources with published analyses of feminist policy formation.

With the unit of analysis being individual policy development over a significant time period, the universe of feminist policies within a given country is quite large. Indeed, it would be impossible to analyse the development of all feminist policies within a single sub-area of feminist policy within one country, much less across all eight sub-areas or across all Western post-industrial democracies in a single study. It is necessary, therefore, to select a limited number of cases to study. This study uses theoretical criteria, presented later in this chapter, to select the sample of 27 policy cases analysed in the rest of this book. The published studies of feminist policy formation are used to identify patterns in feminist policy success and failure over time in order to avoid becoming mired in the minutiae of thickly describing the quite messy processes of policy formation in democracies. The analytical template and scoring system designed for this study, also presented below, helps to keep the case analyses focused on the essentials of feminist policy formation.

❖ Using the Literature on Feminist Policy Formation

Out of the four major areas of FCP work, the literature on feminist policy formation is one of the largest and, arguably, has the least theoretical and methodological coherence. Over 420 pieces on empirical feminist policy issues were located and consulted for this study. Taken together, the published scholarship on feminist policy in Western post-industrial democracies lacks a uniform framework in the way information on feminist policy formation is collected and reported. Many of the studies are path-breaking in that they scrutinize for the first time a new area of government action in a single country or collection of countries. Yet much of the literature is more concerned with describing the unfolding of specific policies within national contexts than addressing any larger theoretical puzzles about feminist government action.

Feick (1992: 26) identifies a similar problem with the battery of national policy studies in non-feminist Comparative Policy Analysis.

> The problem with these studies is well-known: empirical data and their coding can hardly be controlled by the reader, the sample of cases is small, and attempts at generalisation seem to be highly eclectic and difficult to accumulate across studies.

He uses the qualitative policy analyses as a source for his study, placing the issue of whether 'the studies selected for secondary analysis . . . lend themselves to integrative comparisons' (1992: 257) at the centre of his inquiry. Baumgartner (1996) also uses existing policy studies to generate propositions about variation in policy-making styles in France.

This book uses the plethora of country-based studies of feminist policy formation in a similar fashion. Given the methodological unevenness of these studies, it is not certain whether they can be used as a reliable source of data for the case analyses of feminist policy formation in this book. This methodological issue is revisited in the concluding chapter once the individual case analyses have been carried out. A major part of this project is to sort through the vast literature on feminist policy formation in order to identify for analysis specific policy cases that have the best coverage. In sorting through the literature, this study also provides a survey of the field, classifying over 420 pieces by the seven sub-sectors of feminist policy, by the four feminist families of nations, and by the countries in those four groups.[10] For the most part English-language literature was consulted; some studies in French were examined and used as well. Whereas this limits the number of available analyses to a certain degree, given that most FCP scholars publish in English, the language barrier does not pose an insurmountable problem. There was insufficient literature for only one policy case, on Family Law policies in the Nordic countries.

❖ Operationalizing Styles, Profiles, and the Policy Process

The analytical model presented in Fig. 2.1 shows the various potential ways the policy styles of policy sub-systems and other factors outside of the sub-system may interact to influence the processes and outcomes, or policy profiles, of individual policies. The model structures the individual analyses of the 27 cases of feminist policy in this book and generates the study's hypotheses, presented at the end of this chapter. Information from the feminist policy literature for each component of the model is recorded in each case in a template adapted from the cross-national study of women's policy offices by the Research Network on Gender, Politics and the State (RNGS). This template assures that, even though the source data for the cases is uneven, the information recorded for each case is placed in uniform categories to make the case analyses as comparable as possible.[11]

As Fig. 2.1 illustrates, exogenous factors at the level of the policy sub-system, the nation-state, or the region can potentially influence the policy style in policy development. These factors may include a broad range of cultural, economic, and political phenomena. The start-to-finish process of each individual policy is called a 'policy profile' (Feick 1992). While the policy styles of sub-systems have the potential to remain the same across a range of policies through sectorization, policy profiles tend to vary on each individual policy. Figure 2.1 indicates the hypothesized complex relationships between styles, profiles, and exogenous factors. In particular, the model suggests that the policy style of a given sub-system may actually be an important intervening influence between contextual factors and the specific profile of individual policies.

First introduced in the 1980s by Richardson (1982), Freeman (1985), and others, the notion of policy styles is used to analyse the general dynamics of how state and society actors interrelate and eventually influence policy-making processes within the policy sub-system. This study does not seek to participate in

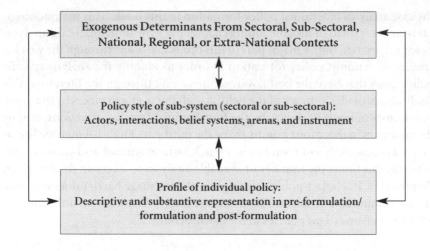

Figure 2.1 Model for hypothesized relationships
in feminist policy formation

recent debates about the properties of policy sub-systems, called also 'networks', 'communities', and so forth. As Dowding (2001) argues, the 'intellectual fatigue' that surrounds what many see as an unending debate may have clouded over the usefulness of the notion. Instead, the policy sub-system is used here as a heuristic device to explore how the constellation of society and state actors that swirl around policy issues affects the flow and outcome of policies. The concept is not intended to indicate any particular pattern of interaction or structure.

The particular dynamics of a given sub-system or policy style is a part of solving the analytical puzzle of feminist policy formation in this study. As Fig. 2.1 illustrates, it is important to determine the following components of a given sub-system in order to determine the style: principal actors, the interactions between the actors, belief systems shared by the actors, the major instruments used to make policies, and the principal arenas where policy discussion and decisions take place.

An important aspect of the policy sub-system identified by many policy analysts is the overall approach taken to policy problems by the policy actors or their shared 'belief system' (Sabatier 1993). Sabatier and Jenkins-Smith (1993) call the various state and societal actors that group around a given policy area 'advocacy coalitions'. The argument here is that the constellation of society and state actors that mobilize around a given issue area shares a certain set of ideas about the direction of policies: 'a set of basic values, causal assumptions, and probable perceptions' (Sabatier 1993: 25). Other analysts also point to the importance of values and of ideas espoused by policy actors in determining policy outcomes.[12]

Students of policy sub-systems and policy styles have disagreed about whether policy formation is characterized by a single national policy style or by sectoral-level style and potentially by sub-sectoral policy styles (for example, Feick 1992; Atkinson and Coleman 1989; Van Waarden 1992). Policy analysts who take this approach in designing their studies examine whether 'there is differentiation within individual countries across sectors and convergence across nations in similar sectors' (Freeman 1985: 486). Today, many comparativists agree that 'a great number of policy styles naturally co-exist' (Baumgartner 1996: 88) in a given country. There is no consensus, however, on whether policy styles vary by sub-sectors or by individual policies.

The issue of whether policy styles or other factors matter in explaining policy development is examined in each case of feminist policy formation through the RNGS template and the feminist policy-formation model and discussed generally in the concluding chapter. The hypothesis of sectoral variation of policy styles versus a single national policy style is also scrutinized in the policy cases. The relationship between policy styles, policy profiles, and exogenous factors is addressed in the comparative summary of the 27 case analyses in the concluding chapter.

Whether an individual policy has a feminist policy profile is determined by tracing a single policy through the different stages of the policy process.[13] In pre-formulation, social conditions are defined into public problems, for which proposals are generated, by a variety of state and non-state actors. The government then chooses some of these issues to place on its agenda for eventual formulation. Formulation ends when the state makes an authoritative decision reflected in an official policy statement that is supposed to be implemented. The policy statement does not necessarily have to be a piece of legislation; it can be a court decision, an executive order, or any other instrument that reflects the authoritative decision made by the state.

Once a decision is made, the policy may or may not be implemented and evaluated. Evaluation of the impact of the policy can be undertaken officially by government agencies or unofficially by watchdog groups. In some cases, policy evaluation leads to re-formulation. Implemented policies have the potential to generate government outputs—for example, programmes, structures, policy orders—and feedback in society. Societal feedback includes the emergence of new groups and group action around the implementation and evaluation of a policy.[14] For example, in many countries equal employment policies generated an equal employment network grounded in both society and the state, consisting of a panoply of government offices and groups that oversaw policy enforcement (Mazur 1995a).

❖ Measuring Feminist Policy Success

Pitkin's (1967) notion of descriptive and substantive representation is used to evaluate feminist policy success. As feminist theorists argue, post-industrial democracies are deficient because they fail to represent women's interests and needs adequately, whether through descriptive representation—the direct placement of women in positions of power—or through substantive representation—the incorporation of woman-friendly issues into the policy process (for example, Phillips 1991). Empirical studies in Europe and North America also show that the absence of women in positions of power is a central explanatory factor of the extent to which public policies in many Western democracies are gender-biased.[15]

A feminist policy is considered a feminist success here if women's interests are represented in both substantive and descriptive ways in pre-formulation, formulation, and post-formulation. Feminist descriptive representation in policy formation consists of the active participation of women in forwarding overtly feminist ideas at any stage of the policy process, including women as individuals or as representatives of organizations or movements. Substantive representation of women's interests throughout the policy process is measured in two ways. First, the analysis determines whether the formal content of the policy is actually feminist: that is, whether it contains at least three out of five parts of this study's operational definition for feminist policy.

An essential part of ascertaining the feminist content of the policy is to observe whether policy content formally acknowledges the gendered nature of the social problems and designs solutions that attempt to redress gender-based inequities; in other words, whether a specific policy was gendered in a feminist way. This formal expression may be written in the policy statement or elaborated orally at the time of policy adoption. It is also important to determine to what degree the policy was formulated with an overtly feminist frame, regardless of the type of feminism: that is, whether policy discussions adopted a feminist approach in a meaningful manner. Second, the policy cases study whether there is evidence of institutional feedback in state and society in the implementation and evaluation stages. If this is the case the policy is considered a feminist success.

The RNGS template in Appendix C provides a way of structuring and reporting the data for each case. Each of the seven sub-area chapters includes a presentation of the four policy cases in terms of the different components of the model. It is not enough, however, to present an analysis of the cases; it is also important to have some way to systematically compare them. A numerical measurement for feminist success is therefore developed. Assigning numerical values is not intended to be a feminist scorecard that indicates the most feminist country or groupings of countries. An ordinal scale is used to measure descriptive and substantive representation in pre-formulation/formulation and post-formulation, in order to allow for more systematic comparison between the cases and to identify more effectively patterns in dynamics and determinants of feminist policy formation.

Three points are given for each dimension of representation for the two major stages of the policy process—pre-formulation/formulation and post-formulation—for a total of twelve points for each policy case.[16] The highest feminist scores—three points—for descriptive representation are given when there is a critical mass of women advancing feminist demands. High scores on substantive representation in pre-formulation/formulation are given when the content and/or frame of the policy take on at least three of the five components of feminist policy. High scores on substantive representation on post-formulation are given when there are high levels of state and society feedback around implementation, evaluation, and, in some cases, re-formulation. Scores of the policy cases are presented in the titles of each policy case analysis, in the conclusion of each sub-sector chapter for the cases covered in that sub-area, and in the conclusion chapter for all 27 cases.

❖ Determining the Determinants of Feminist Policy Formation: Case Selection and the Feminist Family of Nations

Once the analysis presents the 27 cases of feminist policy formation, it is possible to begin to consider the impact of the determinants of feminist public policy, or what the analytical model refers to as 'exogenous factors'. The literature on feminist policy identifies a dizzying number of determinants of effective woman-friendly policies: to name a few, women in the policy process, women's movements, women's policy offices, type of governing majority, parliamentary or presidential system, unitary or federal territorial distribution of power, structure of the bureaucracy, type of legal system, level of woman-friendliness in social polices, type of welfare state regime, level of women in the workforce, presence of strong social democratic parties, political culture, religion, gender consciousness in society, and type of state-society relations. Much of the literature emphasizes the interplay between institutional factors, left-wing governments, and the role of women and women's movements and organizations in creating feminist policies.[17] No matter what the combination, analysts agree that there is 'no single factor that can explain women's policy' (Dahlerup 1987: 121).

The particular categorization system this study uses to classify post-industrial countries helps to sort through the myriad of determinants. One explanatory tack is to identify patterns in policy development with general regional groups of countries in the West or 'families of nations'. This approach emphasizes the common geographic, historic, ethnic, linguistic, and religious backgrounds of countries. It classifies Western democracies into four families: English-speaking, southern European, Nordic, and Germanic (for example, Castles 1993). There is some debate as to the extent of each group's cohesiveness and commonalties. Many feminist (for example, Siaroff 1994; Sainsbury 1999a; Langan and Ostner 1991; Lewis 1992) and non-feminist (for example,

Esping-Andersen 1990) welfare state researchers base their cross-national classification systems on a regional families-of-nations scheme.

Gornick (1995) and Duncan (1995) examine the interface between feminist and non-feminist welfare state classification systems and the array of new gendered cross-national categorization systems. In addition to the gendered welfare-state comparative classification systems, Duncan (1995: 264) distinguishes two other 'strands in theorising European gender systems' in Western Europe: 'differential patriarchy' and 'gender contracts'. All three strands contain a certain level of regional compatibility in terms of classifying specific countries on different measurements of gender-equal societies and polities. Kaplan's (1992) analysis of 'European feminism' also takes this regional approach. Liebert (1999) also refers to the importance of regional 'gender orders' in explaining cross-national variations in men's and women's voting in European elections.

This study uses Siaroff's (1994) feminist categorization system of welfare states to identify patterns of causal factors in feminist policy formation because it includes relevant dimensions of gendered welfare states and cultural factors that correspond roughly to the non-feminist 'family of nation' classification systems. Siaroff's typology categorizes welfare states along three gendered dimensions: 'family welfare orientation, which parent is the recipient of benefits, and female work desirability' (1994: 93). Together, these three components comprise the ingredients for a woman-friendly society. Siaroff develops composite measurements for each dimension from the non-feminist and feminist literature on welfare states. He classifies post-industrial democracies into four different regional categories by their scores on each of the three dimensions of woman-friendly welfare states and the political saliency of religion: 'Protestant Liberal', 'Late Female Mobilizing', 'Protestant Social Democratic', and 'Advanced Christian Democratic'. The Protestant Social-Democratic countries have the most favourable welfare states for women and the Late Female Mobilizing the least. The following 13 countries are analysed within the four feminist nations:

Late Female Mobilizing: Ireland, Italy, Spain
Protestant Social Democrat: Denmark, Sweden, Norway
Advanced Christian Democrat: France, Germany, the Netherlands
Protestant Liberal: USA, Great Britain,[18] Canada, Australia.

This particular selection includes countries from all three continents of the Western post-industrial world. These countries also represent a broad range of variations on other potentially important exogenous determinants, including territorial division of power, type of legislative-executive relations, role of the bureaucracy, type of electoral system, level of women's representation in elected office, structure of the feminist movements, and political party system. In addition, they have some of the highest levels of coverage in the feminist policy-formation literature.

Using this feminist family-of-nations categorization enables assessment of whether countries with more woman-friendly welfare states produce feminist policy successes. As Bussemaker (1997:180) asserts, 'Equality policies in Western European democracies [as well as other post-industrial countries] are being implemented in the context of welfare states'. On the one hand, more woman-friendly welfare states might produce fewer policies that are feminist because they provide more gender-just social benefits in general and so have fewer gaps to address in society. This is the argument made by Jenson (1987) about national-level policies and Caporaso and Jupille (2000) with regard to the activities of EU member states in bringing their own policies in line with EU policy. They argue that feminist policies have been more prevalent in Great Britain than in France because British policies have not been as woman-friendly as in France. On the other hand, countries with more woman-friendly welfare states may produce more actively feminist policies in the context of the culture of equality embedded in the policy formation system. Given the emphasis in Siaroff's taxonomy on religion, analysing cases from these countries allows the exploration of the influence of national patterns of religion in feminist policy formation as well.

Table 2.1 on the next page shows the distribution of analysed cases across the sub-sectors, the family of nations, and the countries. Policy cases for analysis are selected for even coverage across all feminist families of nations, seven from all categories except for the Protestant Social Democratic countries, due to missing information for family law policies, and across all policy sub-sectors, and four for each sub-area, except for family law. This even distribution assures that the sample of cases will have optimal variation across all of the analytical dimensions, sub-sector, family of nations, and country. The selection of the 27 cases also depended on coverage in the published policy literature.[19] The policy cases selected for analysis, therefore, should not be seen as exemplars of policies from each sub-area, each country, or each feminist family of nations. Additional criteria for selecting cases for each sub-sector are presented in each sub-area chapter. For most sub-sectors, specific cases are selected for analysis to reflect a range of policies in each sub-sector.

❖ SUMMARIZING THE ROAD MAP: ROUTES TO FEMINIST POLICY FORMATION

Each sub-sector chapter uses the same analytical road map to study cross-regional, cross-national, and cross-sub-sectoral trends in feminist policy formation. The chapters are divided into three sections: overview, case analysis, and comparative discussion. In the overview section, the analysis first defines

Table 2.1 Coverage of 27 cases by feminist family of nation, country, and sub-sector

	BP (4)	PRP (4)	EEP (4)	RP (4)	FLP (3)	RRP (4)	SVP (4)
LATE FEMALE MOBILIZING							
Ireland (3)		x	x	x			
Italy (2)		x				x	
Spain (2)	x						x
PROTESTANT SOCIAL DEMOCRAT							
Denmark (1)				x			
Sweden (2)			x				x
Norway (3)	x	x				x	
ADVANCED CHRISTIAN DEMOCRAT							
France (3)		x	x				x
Germany (2)				x	x		
The Netherlands (2)	x					x	
PROTESTANT LIBERAL							
USA (2)				x		x	
Great Britain (2)			x				x
Canada (2)	x	x					
Australia (1)					x		

BP: Blueprint policy.   PRP: Political representation policy.   EEP: Equal employment policy.
RP: Reconciliation policy.   FLP: Family law policy.   RRP: Reproductive rights policy.
SVP: Sexuality and violence policy.

the general feminist aims and parameters of the sub-sector. Next, it discusses the range and timing of policies found in the 13 countries; a systematic inventory of all policies in all countries is not a part of this discussion. This first section closes with a discussion of the criteria for selecting the policy cases.

In the second section, the results of the analysis of the case literature reported in the RNGS template is presented for each country, including the feminist policy-profile scores.[20] The progress of the policy is first examined in terms of whether the policy has been implemented and evaluated; in some cases, policies do not make it through the entire process. Next, each case analysis summarizes the policy profile in pre-formulation/formulation and in post-formulation. In both stages, women's descriptive representation is covered, with a focus on outputs and feedback in the post-formulation stages. Each case also scrutinizes the dynamics of the policy sub-system that surrounds policy development, focusing on the line-up of actors and the interactions between them, evidence of shared belief systems of advocacy coalitions, the primary policy instruments used in the community, and the arenas for policy discussions. Additional factors important in the unfolding of the policy process in each case are also presented. Each chapter concludes by presenting the scores on feminist policy success for all four policy cases, discussing cross-national similarities and differences in policy profiles and policy styles across the four cases, and forwarding tentative explanations for these trends suggested by the case discussions.

The final chapter returns to the original theoretical and methodological questions related to solving the puzzle of feminist policy formation. On a methodological level, it assesses whether the literature on feminist policy formation proved to be useful in conducting complete and empirically reliable case analyses of feminist policy formation. On a theoretical level, the chapter evaluates how much light the 27 cases shed on the dynamics and determinants of feminist policy formation as they were expressed in this study's analytical model. The hypotheses raised in this chapter are summarized in the following list. The conclusion analyses each hypothesis in light of a comparison of all 27 case studies. Propositions about other important causal factors that came out in the case analyses are also scrutinized.

❖ On the dynamics of feminist policy formation

Hypothesis 1. Nominally feminist policies are feminist in action.
Hypothesis 2. Feminist policy dynamics in formulation coincide with feminist implementation and evaluation.
Hypothesis 3. When women are represented descriptively in policy formation they are substantively represented as well.
Hypothesis 4. Feminist policies are not guided by a uniform feminist approach; feminist success in policy formation does not correspond with a specific type of feminism.

❖ On feminist policy as a sector

Hypothesis 5. Feminist policy as a sector does not have a single policy profile or style; feminist policy is not sectorized.

❖ On the determinants of feminist policy formation

Hypothesis 6. The determinants of feminist policy formation are highly complex.
Hypothesis 7. Variations in policy profiles and styles correspond with variations in sub-sectors.
Hypothesis 8. Variations in policy profiles and styles correspond with variations in feminist families of nations; a specific pattern of policy profile is found in each feminist family of nation.

Hypothesis 9. Woman-friendly polities produce more feminist policy.

Hypothesis 10. National/regional patterns in religion correspond with patterns in the profiles of feminist policies.

Hypothesis 11. Success in feminist policy formation tends to occur under left-wing governments.

Hypothesis 12. Variations in policy profiles occur in function of variations in policy styles.

Hypothesis 13. Feminist policy success is a result of the emergence of feminist advocacy coalitions. The coalitions are sometimes characterized by 'a triangle of empowerment' (Vargas and Weiringa 1998) or 'strategic partnership' (Halsaa 1998) among women's policy offices, feminist-oriented women in elected office, and women's movements/organizations that share a feminist approach to the policy problem in question.

The concluding chapter suggests several avenues of research to take this study a step further in developing a sound theory of feminist policy formation in post-industrial democracies. It concludes by showing how this study contributes to FCP, to non-feminist political science, and to the pursuit of practical feminist politics by policy practitioners and movement activists.

❖ Notes

1 The term 'European Union' (EU) is used throughout the book to refer to the policies, activities, and structures associated with the supra-national organization that binds together, after 1995, 15 Western European member states. The name 'European Union' was not formally adopted until 1991 by the Treaty of the European Union and came into effect in 1993. Prior to that, the geo-political entity and its policies were referred to as 'European Community' (EC). In the same manner as Hoskyns (1996: 4 n.1), this study uses the term 'European Union' to apply to the supra-national entity and it policies in general, if policies prior to 1991 are the object of discussion the term 'European Community' is used.

2 In the US, Canadian, and Australian contexts, the term 'affirmative action' is used to describe this policy; in Western Europe, 'positive action'. Many use the term interchangeably (for example, Baachi 1996). This book uses the label 'positive action' when referring to the general category of policies and 'affirmative action' when specific policies in the Australian, Canadian, and US contexts are being treated.

3 Bacchi (1996) shows the highly contested political nature of the notion of affirmative action for feminists and non-feminists alike.

4 The label 'parity' is not used in this book because *parité* in the French context is used to describe the new constitutional principle of the equal representation of men and women in parliament.

5 For a discussion of the equality/difference debate and the efforts to develop a middle way between the two often opposing approaches within feminist theory, see Squires (1999*a*: Ch. 4).

6 For more on the intersection of race, class, and gender issues in social policy see, for example, Hoskyns (1996), Williams (1989), Raissiguier (2001) and Hobson (2000a).

7 See Appendix A for an explanation of the different labels this study uses for feminist political action.

8 For more on sectoral approaches to comparing public policy see Hancock (1983); Adolino and Blake (2001); Feick (1992); Heidenhemer, Heclo, and Adams Teich (1990); Wilensky *et al.* (1985); Jones (1985); DeSario (1989); Andersen and Kjell (1993); Jordan and Schubert (1992); Sabatier (1993); Anderson (1994); Ashford (1978).

9 Not all purposefully feminist policies are covered in these eight areas. Other sectoral taxonomies of women's policy include additional policy areas. For instance, Stetson (1997b) includes economic status policy; Conway, Ahern, and Steuernagel (1999) adds gender and insurance and women in the criminal justice system, and Hallett (1996) brings in women and poverty policy. Also, foreign policies are not covered in this taxonomy because of the different dynamics they follow and the sheer magnitude of undertaking a systematic analysis of domestic feminist government action by itself. Excluding feminist foreign policies also reflects the conventional division made between foreign and domestic spheres in non-feminist public policy analysis.

10 Appendix B provides a guide to the feminist policy literature. The various steps taken to conduct searches for this literature are also discussed in the Appendix.

11 See Appendix C for the RNGS template. Individual templates completed for the 27 policy cases in this book are available on request.

12 For applications of the advocacy coalition framework in the analysis of feminist policy see Abrar, Lovenduski, and Margetts (2000) and Oldasama (2002).

13 For a review of the literature that uses the policy 'stages heuristic' see Jenkins-Smith and Sabatier (1993) or Hancock (1983).

14 Outputs and feedback are analysed here instead of impacts to avoid the thorny problems of impact evaluation research. Not only is the evaluation of how policies impact society laden with subjective judgements that are difficult to verify, but it also is very difficult to identify whether a particular change in society can actually be attributed to a specific policy. For instance, to what degree can the shrinking gap between men's and women's salaries be a direct result of pay equity policies rather than of other factors, like better childcare facilities for women or a change in attitudes about gender roles? A focus on institutional feedback also follows the lead of social movement research that uses procedural change in the state as an indicator of social movement success over the long term (for example, Rochon and Mazmanian 1993).

15 See for example, Hernes (1987); Lewis (1993a), Sainsbury (1994); Lovenduski and Norris (1993); Meehan and Sevenhuijsen (1991a); Gelb (1989); Haavio-Mannila *et al.* (1985); Lovenduski (1986a); Weldon (2001); Lycklama à Nijeholt, Vargas, and Wieringa (1998a); Bergqvist *et al.* (1999).

16 Pre-formulation and formulation are combined, given the continuous way problem definition, agenda setting, and formulation flow together. Post-formulation includes both implementation and evaluation, and the potential re-formulation, of policies.

17 For example, Gelb (1989); Bashevkin (1998); Mazur (1995*a*); Lovenduski (1997*c*); Stetson and Mazur (1995); Dahlerup (1986*a*); Elman (1996*a*); Watson (1990); Galligan (1998); Bussemaker and Voet (1998); Vargas and Wieringa (1998); Halsaa (1998).

18 The term 'Great Britain' is used instead of 'United Kingdom' because feminist policies in Northern Ireland are quite different from policies in Great Britain: that is, Scotland, England, and Wales. With the recent changes in Scottish politics, feminist policy formation there may become even more distinct from policy development in Great Britain. For more on feminist policy in Scotland see, for example, Brown (1996).

19 The policy cases selected were covered by at least two or more published sources in order to cross-check different analyses of the same set of events. Triangulating several different sources in this manner is one way of assuring validity in qualitative policy analyses. Case selection was a lengthy process. I first conducted systematic searches for potential published sources with the help of research assistants. I then skimmed the English-language literature on all of the countries in each sub-sector to identify which cases had the best coverage. Appendix B is a record of the initial search and survey of the feminist policy literature. Given that the final selection of cases was limited and based on ensuring even coverage of all feminist families of nations across all sub-sectors, not all cases with adequate literature coverage were analysed. There are published studies available for approximately 50 additional policy cases of feminist policy formation.

20 The titles of each policy case include the name of the specific policy, the particular feminist dynamics of feminist policy formation found in the case analysis, and the summary policy-profile scores for each phase of the policy process: pre-formulation/formulation is abbreviated as pre/form and post-formulation as post.

3 ❖ Blueprint Policy

❖ OVERVIEW

Blueprint policies—often referred to as equality policies—consist of the range of constitutional provisions, legislation, equality plans, reports, and policy machineries governments use to establish general principles, or a blueprint, for feminist state action at the national and sub-national levels. In unitary systems—Ireland, Italy, Denmark, Sweden, Norway, France, Great Britain, and the Netherlands for this study—national policies may set up a procedural or structural frame for sub-national governments. In federal—Germany, US, Canada, and Australia—and quasi-federal systems—Spain—sub-national levels of government may establish their own blueprint policies separately from federal policies. The term 'blueprint' is used here to indicate the overarching nature of the formal framework contained in a given policy statement. It also has a more subtle connotation than other terms, like 'framework' or 'general principles', that are often used to describe this area of policy. The notion of blueprint, or design, is intended to reflect how policies in this sub-sector are not always adopted to authoritatively promote sex equality and women's rights. In many countries, governments adopt blueprint policies far from the public view and do little, if anything, to implement them.᾿

Blueprint policy focuses on two or more domains. Policies that uniquely target paid labour are not considered a part of this sub-area. In some countries, blueprint statements and structures focus primarily on the workplace, with only brief mention of other target areas. For example, the 1978 Equal Status Act in Norway, 'designed primarily as a regulation covering working life' (Skjeie 1991a: 8), is still considered a blueprint policy here because it also aimed at 'equal status problems in general' (Halsaa 1995: 5). Great Britain's 1975 Sex Discrimination Act had initially a similar employment-oriented frame, but was 'extended to housing and provision of goods' (Lovenduski and Randall 1993: 185). The Italian Equal Status and Equal Opportunity National Commission, established in 1984 and given 'the task of dealing with all women's issues, except for employment' (Guadagnini 1995: 155) is also a blueprint office. Its counterpart, the Equal Status Committee, is not a blueprint instrument because its formal remit is limited to gender equity issues in paid employment.

Policies in this sub-area can institute principles of anti-discrimination that prohibit discriminatory behaviour and of procedural equality between the sexes. They can also formalize more structural principles of sex equality that proactively target the causes of women's inferior status in the public and private spheres. There are six major instruments of blueprint policies: symbolic constitutional statements, material constitutional provisions, legislation, executive orders, equality plans and reports, and governmental agencies.

Table 3.1 shows the range of policy instruments found in each core country at the national level. It lists the year the first policy or structure appeared for each type of policy instrument that has been used in a given country. The table is by no means an exhaustive list of all different modes of policy in each country. *Länder-* and State-level blueprint efforts in Germany and the USA are not counted here. In both countries, women's status and women's equality offices at the State and local levels can be more active than federal-level agencies (Ferree 1995; Stetson 1995*a*). It is important to note that Table 3.1 is not intended to indicate whether blueprint policies are actually feminist in action, particularly since blueprint policies do not necessarily lead to effective feminist policies in all sub-areas.

The table provides the year of establishment of women's policy machineries for the first formal agency at the national level, but not necessarily for a full-fledged ministerial office. For instance, in Ireland, whereas the Commission on the Status of Women was created in 1972, a more developed ministerial office (Connolly 1999: 83), the Ministry of State of Women's Affairs, with its own staff did not appear until 1982 (Mahon 1995; Mahon and Morgan 1999). Likewise, the

Table 3.1 Range of blueprint policy instruments in core countries

	Symbolic	Material	Legislation	Equality plans/reports	Machineries
Italy				1986	1984
Ireland	1937			1972	1972
Spain	1977		1988	1991	1983
Denmark					
Sweden	1970		1979		
Norway		1978	1978	1990	1972
France	1948/58			1975	1975
Germany	1949	1957		1972	
Netherlands		1983	1985	1976	1974
United States		failed in 1982		1963	1960
Great Britain		1975		1998	1997
Canada		1982		1970	1968
Australia		1984			1973

Sources: See literature in Appendix B under Blueprint Policy.

US President's Commission on the Status of Women was created in 1960, but the Women's Bureau, with a remit uniquely to cover paid labour issues, had been in existence since 1920 (Stetson 1995a).

There are two types of constitutional provisions for blueprint policies: symbolic and material.[1] *Symbolic statements* in the constitution recognize formal equality between men and women without establishing any real authority over new feminist policies or establishing constitutional rights to sex equality. Found in the constitutions of Spain, Sweden, and the Netherlands, principles of equality between men and women and anti-discrimination are often included in the original constitution without any active feminist sponsorship. In many cases, constitutional principles do not inform feminist policy until activists, groups, movements, or policy machineries mobilize around them. Feminist mobilization quite often occurs well after the initial blueprint law is adopted. Whether these symbolic statements are actually implemented depends on the national legal culture and the role the constitution plays in policy formation as well.

Procedural equality is not a part of Sweden's formal constitution, but the principle of equality between the sexes is in the 'instrument of government' that accompanies the constitution (Vogel-Polsky 1995: 172). There is no codified constitution in Great Britain; thus constitutional provisions take a different form. In Ireland, Vogel-Polsky (1995) identifies a sex-specific clause in the current constitution in Art. 9: 'no person may be excluded from Irish nationality and citizenship by reason of the sex of that person.' As feminist students of the Irish constitution point out, however, any sex specific aspects of the constiution are underpinned by Arts 41 and 42, which have created a 'gendered distribution of power and status which greatly favours men' (Connelly 1993: 92, cited in Galligan 1998: 92).

Material constitutional statements establish constitutional rights for equality between men and women that are actually implemented. The wording of the Equal Rights Amendment to the US constitution, which failed to be ratified in 1982 after many long years of mobilization, cited below, captures the all-encompassing nature of material constitutional provisions, including implementation.

> Section 1. Equality of rights under the law shall not be denied or abridged by the United States or by any States on account of sex.
> Section 2. The Congress shall have the powers to enforce, by appropriate legislation, the provisions of this article.

In France, the symbolic equality clause of the 1958 constitution, originally from the preamble of the 1948 constitution, that states 'the law guarantees to women in all domains the same rights as men', was made more material by a 1971 Constitutional Court decision. The Court decided that new legislation violated the 'political, economic, and social principles particularly necessary for our times' (Stone 1992: 66–9). The principles in question, however, were related to freedom of association and not sex equality. The preamble has not been used as a tool in making feminist policies (Mazur 1995a). Constitutional blueprint policies are not the norm in Nordic countries either (Bergqvist *et al.* 1999). In Canada, material feminist provisions are contained in the Charter of Rights and Freedoms of 1982. A material provision was inserted into the first article of the Dutch constitution through revisions in 1983. It puts forward the equality of all citizens under the law, regardless of sex and other characteristics. Several laws were put into place to further elaborate the new sex-based provisions.

In Germany , the Basic Law contains two provisions on sex equality. The Parliamentary Council of 1949 intentionally 'recognized the need to revise the German civil code' from the Weimar Republic's 'because the Weimar code, had defined formally women's rights only in terms of their role as wife and mother'. The revision of the civil code began in 1957 and it took another 20 years 'before the intentions of the Basic Law had reshaped the legislation on the place of women in society' (Kolinsky 1989: 43). Unlike the French case, the campaign for the inclusion of the sex-based equality clause was led by a feminist activist from the Social Democrats and 'joined by women politicians and newly formed women's organizations' (Ferree 1995: 97). Still, the implications of this federal provision were limited by Constitutional Court decisions justifying 'different treatment of women and men' as well as different rates of pay and other interpretations of the constitution that protect the life of the fetus. As Ferree (1995: 99) argues, 'the concern for women's rights is held hostage to the constitutional mandate to protect the family'.

Blueprint policies, outside of the constitutional arena, are adopted through legislation, equality plans, and the establishment of women's policy machineries. The creation of women's policy offices, however, does not necessarily lead to blueprint policies. At the same time, these agencies typically produce a general report or White Paper at least once—in some countries on a regular basis. As Table 3.1 indicates, there are no blueprint women's policy agencies in Denmark, given that the mandate of the women's policy office, the Equal Status Council, is formally limited to the 'political niche' of equal opportunity in employment (Borchorst 1995). Its members and staff have attempted unsuccessfully to move its mandate incrementally into other areas. Prior to the election of the Labour Party in 1997, there was no blueprint machinery in Great Britain (Lovenduski 1995). Under the government of Tony Blair, the shadow Ministry of Women, previously maintained in the Labour Party, became a part of the new government.

Many executive-initiated and parliament-approved equality plans were elaborated in response to the recommendation coming from the 1975 United Nations International Women's Year Conference. It called for countries to establish their 'own national plan of action and specify individual objectives and priorities in conjunction with the international plan of actions' (cited in

Eduards, Halsaa, and Skjeie 1985: 149). In some countries, women's policy machineries were created in response to the first conference; in other countries policy offices were established following ensuing UN Conferences on Women, held every five years.[2] The European Union Five Year Equality Programmes have also been important frames for blueprint policies, alongside the more authoritative equality directives at the national level. Both programmes and directives tend to focus on sex equality in paid employment. The UN conference on women does not have the same formal authority over member states as European Union equality policy directives. Australia, Norway, and Great Britain are the only countries to adopt blueprint legislation. The 1978 Equal Status Act in Norway, the 1984 Sex Discrimination Law in Australia, and the 1975 Sex Discrimination Act in Great Britain were the first blueprint laws.

This chapter examines the development of blueprint policies in Canada, Norway, the Netherlands, and Spain. The four cases cover a range of policy instruments. The Spanish case is an example of symbolic blueprint policy initiated by a women's policy office. Norway provides two examples of blueprint legislation. The equality plans scrutinized in the Dutch and Spanish cases represent instances of equality plans initiated by women's policy offices in quite different cultural settings. The policy for Canada is a case of material constitutional policy.

❖ THE POLICY CASES

❖ *1. The 1982 Charter of Rights and Freedoms in Canada: Liberal Feminist Constitutional Policy Formation (Pre/Form.: 3/2 Postform.: 3/2 =10)*[3]

The adoption and implementation of the sex equality sections of the Charter of Rights and Freedom in the federal constitution of Canada represents the clearest feminist success, particularly in descriptive representation and policy feedback, out of the four cases of blueprint policy. Three different parts of the Charter, approved in 1982 and fully implemented in 1985, include sex-specific principles. Article 15 covers 'equal protection' and 'equal benefit under the law without discrimination based' on 'sex', among other attributes. The second part of Art. 15 essentially allows for programmes that 'target disadvantaged groups', again based on sex, and Art. 28, a stand-alone provision, simply states that 'rights and freedoms referred to in it [the Charter] are guaranteed equally to male and female persons' (cited in Bashevkin 1985a: 152).

The process by which these clauses were inserted was a product of an active feminist lobby at the federal and provincial levels, grounded in autonomous women's groups like the umbrella organization, the National Action Committee on the Status of Women, and associations set up for the campaign, like the Ad Hoc Committee of Canadian Women on the Constitution—the 'Ad Hockers'—and the federal-level women's policy office, the Canadian Advisory Council on the Status of Women (Hausmann 1992; Burt 1988; Geller-Schwartz 1995). Women parliamentarians as well as women members of the cabinet outside of women's policy offices also played important roles in the inclusion of the sex equality provisions in the Charter (Haussman 1992).

It was not, however, entirely a feminist or women's effort. Indeed, as Haussman (1992), Bashevkin (1994), Geller-Schwartz (1995), and Burt (1988) agree, the opportunity to insert these clauses was given by the Liberal government's decision in 1980, under Pierre Trudeau, to repatriate the Canadian constitution and to include a Charter of Rights and Freedom that would be 'entrenched' in the constitution. Hausmann (1992: 110) in particular argues that the version of the Charter originally proposed by Trudeau to Parliament mentioned equality for women. From this perspective, the women's campaign that developed around the adoption of the Charter was a reaction to Trudeau's first proposal. Whatever the chain of events, it was certainly an important factor that the Liberal government majority and the Prime Minister were publicly in favour of the Charter, had placed the reform high on the agenda, and had not come out against the inclusion of sex equality clauses.

The campaign to include the sex provision of the charter was a highly public one that mobilized a significant number of women at elite and grass-roots levels. Once the Charter was placed on the government's decision agenda, women mobilized by the thousands behind the incorporation of feminist provisions. For example, 1,300 women attended a conference on 'Women and the Constitution', an important rallying point for this feminist campaign. The Liberal government was not entirely pro-feminist as it resisted the demands of the federal-level women's policy agencies. In fact, the Canadian Advisory Council on the Status of Women was supposed to have hosted the original feminist conference and was asked not to by the government. All members of the women's policy office acquiesced except the director, who resigned (Geller-Schwartz 1995: 53). With the organizational support of the women's lobby—the National Action Committee on the Status of Women—and the Ad Hockers, women pursued letter-writing campaigns and distributed flyers to gain support, particularly for Art. 28 of the Charter.

The women's lobby that developed around the Charter was an equal partnership between autonomous women's groups, the women's policy offices, and women in the Cabinet and Parliament. The different segments of this coalition were from a wide spectrum of parties as well. Women's groups, including the National Action Committee on the Status of Women, received funding from the women's policy offices, but they were not dependent on the money for survival. The state feminist offices that distributed the money did not attach political strings to these subsidies either (Geller-Schwartz 1995). Furthermore, unlike the Equal Rights Amendment in the USA, there was no strong counter-movement against the sex provisions of the Charter. Haussman (1992) asserts also that a pro-government collectivist political culture in Canada under-pinned the success of the Charter movement and the absence of a counter-movement.

In this context, the clauses generated a relatively high level of feedback in state and society, although no specifics about implementation were included in the original provisions. The National Action Committee on the Status of Women was committed to focusing on feminist issues through legal rights since the 1970s (Bashevkin 1994: 152). The umbrella organization continued the emphasis on equal rights into the 1990s (Burt 1995). Across the women's movement in general there was 'a growing preoccupation . . . with the language of the Charter' (Burt 1995: 92). Burt's survey of 22 women's groups in 1993 found that 16 of them saw the Charter 'as a positive force in Canadian women's lives' (Burt 1995: 92). There have been some important court cases that used the principles of the Charter as well (Bashevkin 1994: 152). The government provided a significant amount of money for its Court Challenges Program: 9m Canadian dollars in 1985. Program funds help legal defence organizations take equality cases to court. The decisions of many of these cases contribute to the growing sex equality case law and jurisprudence (Burt 1995: 95). The program was cancelled in early 1993 and rein-stated a few months later in the run-up to parliamentary elections.

The liberal feminist approach of the Charter and ensuing court decisions was reconfirmed in 1993. Recommendations that legal interpretations of the Charter should be based on more radical feminist assumptions that take into consideration women's equality in the context of difference, which came out of a symposium on women and the law organized by the Conservative Minister of Justice, were rejected by the government. Thus, a policy shift toward equality principles that account for sex difference is not a part of the feminist successes of the Charter. Some analysts have provided more mixed reviews about the extent to which the Charter has generated feedback in society. For instance, a 1989 report conducted by Brodsky and Day (1989) for the federal women's pol-icy office found that women were pursuing a small number of cases under the Charter and men were using the Charter to 'strike back at women's hard won protections and benefits' (cited in Bashevkin 1994: 152). In the words of Brodsky and Day (1989: 2), the 'news is not good'. Still, the very existence of the report indicates that there have been official government efforts to evaluate the Charter and hence there is clear evidence of government outputs beyond court cases. Whether these evaluations or the court cases have created a permanent institutionalized culture that defends women's rights under the Charter is not entirely clear.

❖ *2. The 1978 Equal Status Act in Norway: Qualified Feminist Policy Formation (Pre/Form.: 2/2 Post-form.: 3/3 = 10)*

The idea for an Equal Status Act was originally included in the Labour Party's 'election program' in 1973 (Skjeie 1991a: 87). It became the object of a 'party committee' within the Labour Party in 1978 and was later approved by the minority government under the Labour Party dependent on the support of the Socialist Left Party (Skjeie 1991a: 88). After being returned to the cabinet by Parliament one time, the bill was adopted in 1978 (Halsaa 1998: 177–9). The act created a new enforcement agency called the Ombuds and a process for fielding complaints which aimed ultimately for voluntary settlements. The head of the Ombuds was unpaid; it did have a Board of Appeals. There is some disagreement over whether the law was uniquely oriented toward employment (Skjeie 1991a) or was a true blueprint law covering more than two areas (Halsaa 1991; 1998; Bytsydzienski 1995a; Vogel-Polsky 1995). Halsaa (1991: 17) states clearly that the act 'ensures substantial equality of treatment in all areas of life; and to influence attitudes and sex roles, committing the authorities to work actively for equal status'. Whereas the act has not addressed overtly women's status in the private sphere, it did open the door for the use of positive discrimination in employment, education, and politics.

Eduards, Halsaa, and Skjeie (1985) show that the limited content of the act was a compromise between the Labour, Socialist Left, and Conservative parties. The powerful Confederation of Trade Unions (CTU) also played an important role in the final compromise bill. The Socialist Left Party invited socialist and radical feminists to participate in drafting one of the original versions of the bill (Halsaa 1998: 177). There were two major focuses of the bill: the prohibition of sex-based discrimination in salaries based on comparable worth and the provision of positive action programmes to strike down sex discrimination. Feminists involved with the process generally sought a gendered approach that would address the causes of women's inferior status in both public and private domains.

The feminist-inspired draft proposal on the salary issue was rejected by the CTU before the bill was presented to Parliament. Like trade union confederations in other countries (Cook, Lorwin, and Daniels 1984), the Norwegian confederation was hostile to a feminist definition of work of equal value, in particular rejecting the notions that different jobs could be compared (Skjeie 1991a: 88). It also refused to support a bill that allowed the new enforcement agency to supersede trade union-controlled labour courts and the salary negotiation process. The final bill reflected the power accorded to the CTU in this process by the Labour Party, including a toned-down version of the principles of equal value and positive discrimination. Article 3 states that women's special rights can be covered without violating the principle of equality between the sexes; thus the law was not entirely gender-neutral. While the political parties and the CTU ultimately limited the authority and scope of the 1978 act, the content of the law did take into consideration women's difference within the context of equality. Women, as representatives of feminist groups, also participated in policy formulation to a limited degree within the confines of the Socialist Left Party. As Halsaa (1998: 178) states, 'women's liberationists did not have much impact on the legislative process'.

In contrast, feminist groups significantly influenced the act's implementation and enforcement. To be sure, there were limitations on the enforcement power of the new Ombuds. As with equal pay legislation in France and other countries (Mazur 1995a), the new Ombuds was not allowed to promote pay equity for women in salary negotiations and, as a 1982 analysis showed, the established approach to the presentation of evidence limited the areas where the Ombuds could adjudicate sex discrimination. (Eduards, Halsaa, and Skjeie 1985: 148.) These two limitations, however, did not prevent the development of significant societal feedback and administrative outputs. The state feminist bureaucracy and women's organizations used the Ombuds to implement more effective feminist policies on a 'wide range of measures' (Halsaa 1998: 179). Thus, women's interests were better represented in both descriptive and substantive ways in post-formulation than in formulation.

The style of the policy community differed from one stage to the next. Skjeie's (1991a: 89) analysis of the policy formation dynamics of the act up to the late 1980s shows 'the power of different actors at different stages of the decision making process'. Clearly, in formulation it was the parliamentary process with its arenas in party, Cabinet and Parliament, influenced by the dominance of the CTU in the area of wage negotiations, that dictated the dynamics of the policy community. Ultimately, as Skjeie contends, the dominant political parties— Labour and the Socialist Left—decided who would be invited to the negotiation table, including the CTU. The party composition of Parliament dictated the final terms of the act. The political parties allowed feminist ideas and actors to enter the process only because their platforms included certain feminist issues.

For implementation, the dynamic was quite different, dictated less by party politics and more by the growing state feminist bureaucracy, female elected officials, and society-based women's groups. Buttressed by the activities of the Equal Status Council and in close partnership with the autonomous women's movements, the Ombuds was able to effectively enforce the act in mandated areas, moving into new areas not specifically indicated by the original act. This act, therefore, generated important feedback around its enforcement and contributed to strengthening the women's movement. Although the dynamics of party politics were less present in post-formulation, the context for enforcement was enhanced by the presence of a Labour Party majority in Parliament in1985–6 and 1989–91. In the final analysis, the law's enforcement both contributed to and benefited from a 'strategic partnership' (Halsaa 1998: 183) where women in organizations, public administration, and political parties and elected office worked together to push forward new feminist policies.

❖ *3. The 1985 Emancipation Program in the Netherlands: Feminist Formulation, Symbolic Outcomes, Uncertain Future (Pre/Form.: 2/3 Post-form.: 1/1 = 7)*

The Emancipation Plan (Beleidsplan) has been the principal government instrument in the Netherlands for feminist policy since the mid-1970s.[4] There have been three plans, in 1976, 1985, and 1995. Each proposes action over five years. The 1985 Emancipation Plan is examined here. It was adopted at the height of Dutch state feminism in the mid-1980s and has since been implemented—or not implemented—in a political context quite hostile to government-run programmes (Outshoorn 1995; Outshoorn and Swiebel 1998). The first plan was elaborated by the national-level Emancipation Committee—composed of representatives from the reform-oriented branch of the women's movement, 'Man-Woman-Society'. In 1982, the state secretary of the Department of Coordination of Emancipation (DCE), Hedy d'Ancona, one of the founding members of Man-Woman-Society, produced a draft for a new five-year plan with the help of her staff and a committee, composed of women from the feminist movements and civil servants from several ministries (Leijenaar and Niemöller 1994: 509).

Formulated under a Socialist-Christian Democrat government and inspired by the feminist ideas of the reform wing of the women's movement, the first draft of the plan defined women's issues in terms of gender-based power imbalances. Parliamentary elections took place nine months later and a new Liberal-Christian Democrat coalition controlled the Cabinet. The new Liberal state secretary of the DCE changed the focus of the plan to 'women's choice between work and family and made the constitutional principle of bodily integrity the cornerstone of her policy against sexual violence' (Outshoorn 1995: 175). As the final Emancipation Policy Program stated, its main goal was

> a pluriform society in which everyone has the opportunity to lead an independent existence irrespective of their sexual or marital status and in which women and men have equal rights, opportunities, freedoms and responsibilities.[5]

In 1985, the Second Chamber of Parliament adopted the plan with the support of women Members of Parliament from different parties. Women MPs began to actively support women's policy efforts in the mid-1980s and contributed to forming a women's policy network composed of women parliamentarians, women's movement activists, and femocrats. The DCE intended to act as a 'spider in the web' between these three actors By the early 1990s it became clear that the DCE was not a very 'powerful spider' (Outshoorn 1997: 123).

❖ BLUEPRINT POLICY

Nonetheless, the increased activity of women MPs on women's policy during the mid-1980s occurred through the 1985 Emancipation Policy Program. Therefore, the 1985 Program had a feminist policy profile with regards to both descriptive and substantive representation of women in the formulation process. At the same time, women's movement activities did not appear to be generally focused on the formulation of the plan, concentrating instead on creating a coalition of women's groups and political parties through the Broad Platform of Economic Independence (Outshoorn 1995: 180).

As with the first plan, the 1985 plan provided the foundation for policy initiatives in all ministries. It was monitored by the DCE through regular visits to ministries implicated in the plan. Although Outshoorn (1995: 175) asserts the Beleidsplan 'strengthened the position of the DCE, made for more effective policy in a number of areas, and laid the groundwork for the integration of women's policy into all ministries', it did not appear to generate any significant policy feedback outside of the DCE's monitoring role. Outshoorn and Swiebel (1998: 159–61) argue that women's policies with a clear feminist content in general have had more symbolic outcomes in implementation and evaluation, particularly beginning in the early 1990s when political elites from across the ideological spectrum began to embrace government downsizing and the free market as major governing principles.

The symbolic nature of post-formulation on the 1985 Emancipation Program was threefold (Outshoorn and Swiebel 1998: 159–61). First, on the state side, the fragmented structure and integrative approach of emancipation policy meant that the women's policy offices had little authority in different ministries to assure that provisions of the plan were being actually implemented. Combined with the absence of any specific positions responsible for these policies in each target ministry and the reduction of women's policy office budget in the 1990s, the feminist provisions of the original plan tended to be ignored. Second, the way in which the DCE subsidized women's groups created a supportive constituency dependent on the agency for funding. The feedback around the Beleidsplan, therefore, did not include an autonomous movement, capable of mobilizing around blueprint policies, as in the case of Norway. Furthermore, feminist groups were diluted by the same policy of integration as the women's policy office, leaving the women's groups 'robbed of their major ally and point of access into the government bureaucracy' (Outshoorn 1997: 124). Third, the new political consensus around less government undermined implementation through weakening the power of the women's policy offices. Thus, the fate of blueprint policy in the Netherlands has been inextricably linked to the fate of the women's policy machineries.

❖ 4. The 1988 Equality Plan in Spain: Feminist in Content, Not in Practice (Pre/Form.: 1/3 Post-form.: 1/2 = 7)

Two equality plans with feminist intent were adopted in 1988 and 1993. The national level women's policy office, the Instituto de la Mujer (IM), initiated and shepherded both through a cabinet-based policy process (Valiente 1995; 1997b; Threlfall 1996b; Mendez 1994). The 1988 plan included 120 measures in six areas: procedural sex-based legal reforms, non-sexist education, women's health, international cooperation through women's associations, and support to Spanish feminist groups (Valiente 1995: 131). The Equality Plan was presented to the Cabinet in 1988 and was an object of a written evaluation published by the IM in 1990. It was neither presented to the Parliament nor an object of any formal executive orders.

The Plan was a success in the substantive representation of feminist ideas in formulation; it was less successful in descriptive representation and in generating policy feedback in post-formulation. On one hand, the IM successfully negotiated with all of the relevant ministries a plan underpinned by a complex understanding of the causes of women's inferior status in both the public and the private spheres. Indeed, the 120 measures corresponded with the different ideas of the fragmented feminist movements, perhaps most of all to the Spanish social democrat party (PSOE) feminists who founded the IM. The content of the Equality Plan as well as the discussions surrounding it, therefore, were gendered in a feminist way, with the complex causes of gender discrimination taken into consideration. On the other hand, the power of the IM was limited to 'persuasion' rather than sanction (Valiente 1995).

The outcome was that the IM was able to convince ministries only to agree to abstract measures that were difficult to translate into effective feminist policies (Valiente 1997b: 132–3). Valiente shows two examples of how this 'high level of abstraction' made it difficult to make feminist policies. Moreover, the process of formulating the Equality Plan was quite closed. The femocrats from the IM used its advisory council, composed of ministry representatives, without inviting any other women. Any enhancement of women's descriptive representation in the policy process was, thus, held to a minimum.

Valiente (1995; 1997b) shows that there was no authoritative process to assure that the 120 measures would be actually carried out. Although a commission, initially composed of feminists from women's organizations, was established to monitor implementation and to recommend future directions in policy, its work was fraught with 'numerous disagreements' between the members, objections made by the feminist members to having been excluded from the formulation of the original plan, and general suspicion as to whether the IM would follow their recommendations. Most of the feminist group representatives left the committee; none were invited back to elaborate the 1993 Equality Plan.

❖ BLUEPRINT POLICY

The absence of any real enforcement mechanisms, the chaotic oversight process, and the abstract nature of the original plan undermined the effectiveness of the Equality Plan. Whereas the IM's evaluation of the plan states that 116 out of the original 120 measures were followed, Valiente (1997b) points out that this assessment should be examined with 'extreme caution.' At the same time, there have been reforms in some of the areas identified by the Equality Plan. Threlfall (1996b: 127), for instance, asserts that the changes in equal employment law in 1990 'can be traced back to the first Plan'.

There was some feminist success in creating concrete administrative outputs, but limited society-based feedback. Women's Institutes at the regional and local levels instituted their own equality plan processes (Threlfall 1996b: 126). Whether the plans become substantial feminist policies, however, remains to be seen. Also, the tense relationship between the national-level Institute and feminist groups in society, partially due to feminist suspicions about the motivations behind women's policy agency subsidies to women's associations (Valiente 1995), limits the degree to which women, other than female femocrats, are represented in the policy formation process of the equality plans at both the national and sub-national levels.

The policy community style on the Equality Plan was a top-down process, driven by the Instituto de la Mujer and its relationship with the PSOE-controlled cabinet. Feminists other than the PSOE femocrats were not important players in this process. Valiente (1997b: 135) characterized the relations between women activists and the IM as 'scarce and conflictual'. Two trade union representatives were invited to participate in the process on the 1993 Equality Plan only after the government asked the two feminist representatives to step down from their positions on the commission. The driving force behind the limitations of the feminist effectiveness of the 1988 Equality Plan, therefore, appears to be the position and power of the Institute in the politics of the PSOE-controlled Cabinet.

Another important factor at work was the indirect influence of European Union sex equality policy. Both Threlfall (1996b) and Mendez (1994) assert that one of the 'inspirations' for the first Equality Plan was EU equality policy. The Spanish government may have been particularly interested in looking as if it was supportive of EU policy given that Spain became a member of the EU in 1986. This supra-national pressure, rather than pressure from organized feminists outside of the PSOE within the country, may explain why the government was willing to support the Institute's demands for feminist blueprint policies in content, but not in practice.

❖ Comparative Discussion: Strategic Partnerships and Non-Feminist Allies

As the scores in Table 3.2 show, even the most successful case of the four instances of blueprint policy, the Canadian Charter, was limited to ten out of the possible twelve feminist policy profile points.[6] While women's descriptive and substantive representation was favourable in formulation, the feedback was limited to a certain degree, particularly in establishing a permanent and authoritative mechanism for implementation. The continuing resistance to parity equality—a much more gendered and arguably feminist approach to equal rights—also placed limits on the Charter. Still, women's representation was clearly enhanced in formulation and implementation. The Norwegian Equal Status Act was also a feminist success, less in formulation than in post-formulation. Clear compromises were made in the final act; they did not seem to circumscribe the development of an active feminist policy community that mobilized around the implementation of the act and its expansion into other policy areas.

The two instances of equality plans were in some ways similar despite the quite different social, political, and cultural contexts. In both Spain and the Netherlands, governments allowed feminist plans to be designed, but were reluctant to allow for any active implementation. In the case of Spain, there was virtually no authority given to the Instituto de la Mujer, or any other agency, to implement the plans. For the Netherlands, the turn towards integrating and downsizing women's policy machineries contributed indirectly to what some policy analysts saw as implementation failure. Unlike Canada and Norway, Dutch women's groups' approach to the policy process was far more ambivalent. It was the elite-oriented women's policy offices and their policies of selective subsidization that drove policy community interactions, not the women's groups or movements.

Whereas in the Netherlands women's groups took a more active role in policy formation than in Spain, there was still the same tendency for the women's policy offices to determine the line-up of participants. Unlike Spain, the feminist

Table 3.2 Policy profile scores for cases of blueprint policy

	Pre/Form.		Post-form.		Total
	D	S	D	S	
Canada: 1982 Charter of Rights and Freedoms	3	2	3	2	10
Norway: 1978 Equal Status Act	2	2	3	3	10
Netherlands: 1985 Emancipation Policy Program	2	3	1	1	7
Spain: 1988 Equality Plan	1	3	1	2	7

policy profile in the Netherlands was stronger in pre-formulation and formulation because of the alliance that had developed between women MPs, women's policy offices, and certain women's groups. Contrary to some studies of feminist policy formation, the Dutch and Spanish cases show that policy content does not necessarily lead to feminist success; the feminist-oriented policy plans were not actively implemented.

In terms of the dynamics of the policy sub-system, the more successful cases of feminist policy displayed an equal partnership between the various feminist actors. Although the cases of the Netherlands and Spain show that feminist formulation can occur in policy content without such a partnership, it did not continue into post-formulation. The 'triangle of empowerment' (Vargas and Wieringa 1998) between femocrats, feminist activists, and women elected officials was formed through interactions of collaboration rather than control. When state feminist offices attempted to control the feminist organizations it seemed this weakened any unified feminist front, particularly around implementation. The policy sub-systems based either around parliament or grassroots women's organizations also seemed to produce more feminist policy formation.

Another factor important in all four cases was the support of the non-feminist decision-making elite. Whether they were party leaders, prime ministers, or trade union representatives, when these elites opposed feminist actions the process failed to move ahead. This was certainly the case of the CTU and the equal value provision of the Equal Status Act in Norway. In the Netherlands, once the government elite decided to embrace neo-liberalism, the work of the blueprint policy and offices was severely undermined. The cases of Norway and Canada both show the importance of the support of the governing party or parties in advancing a feminist policy agenda. The Dutch and Canadian cases suggest that it is not necessarily parties of the left that favour feminist policy. The feminist Beleidsplan was passed under a centrist—Liberal-Christian Democrat—coalition government in the Netherlands and the proposal to develop equal rights based on sexual differences between men and women in Canada was produced through a symposium organized by the Conservative Minister of Justice. The Conservative government did eventually reject the proposal.

There are other salient factors that may have been important in these four instances of feminist policy formation. For example, Haussman (1992) emphasizes the role of the collectivist pro-government political culture in the success of the Charter in Canada. The Dutch and Spanish cases suggest that Equality Plans in general may produce symbolic policy outcomes in post-formulation, particularly given the highly contrasting cultural settings of the two countries. The successes of Norway and Canada are more difficult to compare, since they represents two quite different policy instruments. Still, the success of the

Canadian case may be due to the constitutionally oriented legal culture found in the English-speaking countries, where constitutional law and the precedent-setting court cases that implement it are politically meaningful policy-making arenas.

❖ NOTES

1 This discussion of constitutional treatments of sex equality is based on Vogel-Polsky (1995: 169–72) . She does not use the terms 'symbolic constitutional statements' or 'material statements', but does differentiate between 'the mere recognition of formal equality' in constitutions and a given country's 'formal' and 'autonomous' inclusion in 'its constitution of equal rights of women and men'. The concepts of symbolic and material policies come in part from Edelman's (1985) work on symbolic politics. 'Material' or 'concrete' policies go beyond a paper existence and are actually implemented and enforced. Anderson (1994) first advanced the idea of a continuum from symbolic to material policies to evaluate policy outcomes in the USA. Symbolic policies make formal statements with little or no government outputs. For more on symbolic and material reform in comparative perspective, see Mazur (1995a).

2 For an analysis of the UN women's conferences since 1975 see Lycklama à Nijeholt, Sinehel, and Wieringa (1998), Pietila and Vickers (1996), or Winslow (1995) .

3 Feminist policy scores are presented for both policy phases—pre-formulation and formulation (pre/form.) and post-formulation (post-form.)—and for each policy case in the case sub-headings. They are also presented for all four policy cases in summary tables at the end of each sub-sector chapter—Table 3.2 in this chapter—and in Chapter 10. See Chapter 2 for the criteria used to assign the scores.

4 Feminist policy in the Netherlands was originally called 'emancipation policy'. It has its historical roots in the nineteenth century when religious freedom—'emancipation'—was granted to Roman Catholics and Protestants. Later, the Dutch word for 'women's policy' was also used to cover feminist/emancipation policy (Outshoorn and Swiebel 1998: 159–60, n. 9).

5 Cited from Kuzenkamp (1985:2) in Leijenaar and Niemöller (1994: 509 n. 27).

6 See Chapter 2 for the values of the feminist policy profile scores.

4 ❖ Political Representation Policy

❖ OVERVIEW

Beginning in the early 1970s and gathering momentum by the mid-1980s, governments and major political parties adopted symbolic and material policies to enable women to achieve positions in elected and appointed office, semi-public and public advisory boards, political parties, trade unions, and, more recently, organizations in the private sector.[1] Political representation policies, however, have only recently been identified as a discrete area of government action (for example, Lovenduski and Norris 1993; Nelson and Chowdhury 1994). Gardiner and Leijenaar (1997), for example, discuss 'partner policies' in their analysis of women-friendly state action, and political representation is one of the five policy areas in a cross-national women's policy office project (Lovenduski in-progress).[2] In their role as gatekeepers, political parties play a pivotal role in the pursuit of women's political representation in elected office, as both supporters of and detractors to such a policy (Lovenduski and Norris 1993). Political representation policies elaborated within political parties, therefore, are also a part of what would otherwise be considered government-only action.

A recent Inter-Parliamentary Union Action Plan for addressing gender power imbalances divides political representation policies into two broad categories: general legal sanctions regarding men's and women's equality and 'political involvement at the national level' (cited in Vogel-Polsky 1995: 164).[3] The first category covers blueprint policies. Many political representation policies are made within the larger framework of sex equality and are often linked to policies that aim to improve women's inferior status in the work place, particularly when women in top jobs in business are involved. For example, policies on the 'glass ceiling' for women in political offices in the USA use the logic of equal opportunity laws.

Bacchi shows the direct link between employment and political representation in affirmative action policies that target women as a group in order to bring them into previously male-dominated positions and to redress sex-based inequities. She identifies two forms: 'policies to alter the composition of the labour force, and/or policies to increase the representativeness of public committees, political parties, and educational institutions' (1996: 15). Although equal employment and political representation policies may overlap, a policy must specifically target sex equality in decision-making positions, within government or private organizations, in order to be situated in this second sub-sector.

Three types of political representation policy can be identified: symbolic, positive action, and positive discrimination.[4] *Symbolic* political representation policies state general principles of women's and men's equality without providing specific target numbers for women or the means to actively pursue sex balance in top positions. Like all symbolic policies, rhetorical political representation policies have the potential to become material policies and often are followed up with more meaningful and effective action. A Royal Decree in Norway, for instance, established the principle of nominating at least one man and one woman for each position in public commissions. It took nine years for this principle to be implemented, in a 1981 amendment to the Equal Status Act. The amendment imposed a minimum quota of 40 per cent of members from each sex (Halsaa 1991: 34–5).

Positive action policies actively promote women in decision-making positions through recruitment activities, public information campaigns, the extension of basic political rights to women—voting and the right to stand for public office—women's commissions, and reports on the presence of men and women in public office. Reports on women's representation, often an integral part of positive action policies, do not necessarily lead to concrete action. Positive action policies are often carried out by government actors at different territorial levels of the state. For example in France, certain regional and departmental women's policy offices use their small budgets to develop public awareness campaigns on the advantages of electing women to public office.

Many political parties have internal women's commissions often intended to bring women and women's issues into the affairs of the party. Some parties have been known to create separate sister organizations for women, that are not formally part of the party, with the intent of excluding women from the party. The French Communist Party's sister organization, for example, is the Union des Femmes Françaises. The party also has an internal women's commission that has supported a variety of feminist causes in France (Jenson 1980; Jenson and Sineau 1995). There is not necessarily a feminist division of labour between internal women's commissions and sister organizations, with commissions being designed to empower women and sister organizations to disempower women.

In France, both women's commissions and sister organizations have been instrumental in marginalizing women in political parties (Appleton and Mazur 1993). The women's wing of the Liberal Party in the Netherlands has been active in promoting women within the party since 1948 (Leijenaar and Niemöller 1994: 507). In some cases, women's commissions are important advocates of women's rights within the party. In the 1960s and 1970s, women party members, inspired by second-wave feminism, created new women's commissions clearly oriented toward feminist action. The Women's Action Committee created in the British Labour Party in 1981 is one example of a feminist-networked internal women's committee (Lovenduski 1994: 304).

Positive discrimination policies officially state the specific balance between men and women, sex or gender balance, in decision-making hierarchies of organizations, public commissions, or on candidate lists.[5] Achieving the particular balance between men and women, sometimes set at 50:50, means that positions must be reserved for women rather than men. The desired goal is usually articulated in the form of a quota that establishes the minimum number or percentage of women or the minimum number or percentage of individuals from a given sex. Quotas are most commonly enacted by political parties.

All countries in this study have pursued political representation policy, with a major trend toward positive action and discrimination policies beginning in the 1980s. Prior to this period, policies in this sub-sector consisted mostly of the extension of women's voting rights, their right to hold office, and isolated symbolic statements about sex balance in positions in party constitutions. For example, in the USA, following campaigns by the League of Women Voters in the 1930s, certain State legislatures adopted requirements for political parties to have equal representation of men and women, or 50:50 representation, in State-level political parties (Stetson 1997b: 72). In most Western countries, women were granted the right to vote in the first half of the twentieth century. National-level positive discrimination policies are found in Sweden— the national action programme to promote sex balance in public commissions of 1987; in Norway—the 1982 law on a 40 per cent quota for women in public commissions; in Denmark—the 1985 law on sex balance in public commissions; in France—the 1999 parity amendment to the constitution; and in Italy—the 1993 and 1995 laws creating quotas for female candidates in regional and municipal elections (Vogel-Polsky 1995: 178–82).

Most political parties adopt political representation policy. Often, numerical targets for women in decision-making positions within the party or on election lists are formally articulated in party rules. Feminist groups and individuals outside of the party tend to lobby political parties to take a stand on political representation issues. In many cases, feminists from outside the party work with feminist party members. In some countries and in some historical periods, political parties have been the only actors to make any formal political representation policies. For instance, in Germany, while there are no formal quota laws on the books, most of the political parties have instituted quotas. The Green Party, in 1986, was the first party to formally establish a 50 per cent quota for women. The other parties adopted lower quotas in the late 1980s (Lemke 1994: 278).

In Great Britain, all three major parties set quotas for women on parliamentary short-lists in the mid-1980s (Lovenduski 1994: 304). In Canada, the New Democratic Party of Ontario adopted an affirmative action policy in 1982 (Bashevkin 1985a: 81). Australia's Labor Party formulated a formal positive discrimination policy in 1981 (Sawer 1994: 82). In Ireland, in 1985, Fine Gael, a centre-right party, adopted a positive action strategy, but rejected the use of quotas. A 25 per cent quota for female candidates for local elections considered by the Progressive Democrat party in Ireland failed (Galligan 1993: 162–3). In the Netherlands, the Labour Party set a quota of 25 per cent women for party delegates in 1977 (Leijenaar and Niemöller 1994: 507). The Democratic Party in the USA adopted an internal party quota in 1972 (Stetson 1997b: 72) as well.

International pressure for effective political representation policy has been growing since the early 1990s. Since its first Women's Policy Conference in 1975, the United Nation's was a lone international voice in this area up to the 1990s. The UN included calls for these policies in a long list of feminist policy recommendations (Fouque 1995). The Inter-Parliamentary Union's reports and action plans, first issued in early 1990s, have been important touchstones for national policy development. The Council of Europe's Committee for Equality between Men and Women organized conferences in 1989 and 1995 to discuss strategies for promoting women's and men's equal rights 'to participate in the functioning of democratic institutions' (cited in Vogel-Polsky 1995: 166).

Since the early 1990s, the European Union has taken some significant steps. The Third Action Plan for Women (1991–1995) included a section on increasing the number of women in decision-making positions. The European Commission sponsored a research network on 'Women in Decision-making' in 1997 (Lovenduski and Stephenson 1998). EU member states signed a declaration in 1992 and, in 1996, the Council of Ministers signed a recommendation. Both were on 'gender balance in decision-making'. It is difficult to determine the effect of international initiatives, particularly in the context of the limited authority of the UN and the absence of any real authority of the Council of Europe and the Inter-Parliamentary Union. EU policy in this area has the most potential for influencing national policies; however, for only nine out of the 13 countries covered in this book.

In the activist world of women in politics and feminist studies, notions of 50:50 representation of men and women are often based on the assumption that the presence of more women in decision-making positions greatly enhances the possibility of feminist policy outcomes: in other words, that the descriptive representation of women leads to their substantive representation, regardless of the political stances of the women being elected to public offices.[6] Studies of the question of whether women make a difference as political leaders increasingly suggest that, when there is a critical mass of women in public office, policies are more likely to be woman-friendly (for example, Bergqvist 1995b; Thomas 1994;

Skjeie 1991*b*; Dahlerup 1988; Davis 1997; Sainsbury 1999*b*). Experts agree, however, that there is still work to be done in designing replicable studies and working definitions of key concepts, like women's interests and woman-friendly policies, before any definitive conclusions can be drawn. This study does not assume that women in public office automatically make a difference.

Italy, Norway, France, and Canada are covered in this chapter. The policy cases were selected for the range of different policy instruments they represent. The adoption of the 1982 affirmative action measures in the Ontario New Democratic Party provides a well-documented example of party-level policies of the 1980s. A positive action policy is examined in Norway: the pre-election public awareness campaigns that were first initiated by feminist groups as early as 1967 and were institutionalized through the national-level Equal Status Council and Equal Status Committees in the mid-1980s. Given that Norway is seen as a 'role model for woman-friendly policy' (Gardiner and Leijenaar 1997: 87 n. 2) and has some of the highest levels of women's descriptive representation—in 1997 36.4 per cent in its national legislature (Bergqvist *et al.* 1999: 298)—it is interesting to see whether political representation policies display a high level of feminist activity in their policy styles and policy profiles. The French policy case is included because it is the only example of a constitutional amendment on positive discrimination policies among the 13 core countries. The two Italian laws are clear examples of positive discrimination policies at the national level. Given that the cases of Italy and France take place in the 1990s and both countries are EU member states, they also provide an opportunity to scrutinize more closely the interplay between EU and national policy-making.

❖ THE POLICY CASES

❖ 1. The 1982 Affirmative Action Resolution of the ONDP in Canada: Feminist Policy Formation in a Provincial Party Environment (Pre/Form.: 3/3 Post-form.: 3/3 = 12)

The formulation and implementation of the 1982 Affirmative Action Resolution in the Ontario New Democratic Party (ONDP) is a near text-book case of feminist policy formation. It is important to note, however, that any theory-building potential from this example is limited because policy-making took place at the provincial level of a political party and not the national level of government. The resolution and the politics that swirled around it were more progressive than at the federal level of the party (Bashevkin 1985*a*: 89). The ONDP also was an opposition party at the time the resolution was approved. It became a governing party in the early 1990s.

The origins of the resolution are linked to the rise of the Women's Committee in the ONDP, created in 1973 in the wake of the Royal Commission's Report on the Status of Women in 1973 and of the emergence of an active and strong liberal feminist lobby through the National Action Committee (NAC). With its 'positive orientation toward established parties and the electoral process' during these early years, the NAC directed a good portion of its action at political parties and developed 'significant interpersonal ties' with three major parties, including the National Democratic Party (Young 1998: 199–200). What Bashevkin (1985a: 112) identifies as a 'waffle' group composed of radical feminists, that had participated in creating a feminist women's committee in the NDP, helped to organize the Women's Committee in the ONDP. As a result, radical feminist ideas about women's difference and the importance of sexual subordination of women by gender power relations were brought into party discussions. The ONDP Women's Committee was an overtly feminist committee, actively pursuing the promotion of women in leadership positions within the party and as potential candidates and lobbying the party to place feminist issues on the party's platform (Bashevkin 1985a: 85).

A central part of the Women's Committee's strategy was the development of an affirmative action resolution, including both affirmative action and positive discrimination policies, for consideration at the provincial party convention. Seven years of Women's Committee work produced a 'Policies for Equality Resolution'. The resolution was presented and adopted at the group's 1980 convention with little opposition. In addition to other pro-women resolutions passed in the same year, the party approved the hiring of a 'women's organiser' in provincial party offices and a 'women's co-ordinator' in the ONDP legislative caucus. What was seen by many feminists as surprising support from the party leadership was put into question in the campaign for the 1981 provincial elections when the ONDP attempted to unseat incumbents. The Women's Equality Policies Resolution was not discussed and the two new women's positions were given secondary responsibilities (Bashevkin 1985a: 85). The Women's Committee leadership responded to this reversal by calling for the formulation of a more formal feminist policy statement.

The Affirmative Action Resolution approved by the Women's Committee in 1981 embodied the very essence of political representation policy. 'Taken together, this program represented a very significant, and probably the most systematic and formalised attempt thus far to increase female involvement in a Canadian political party' (Bashevkin 1985a: 87). There were four components to the resolution:

(1) to broaden the female electoral base of the ONDP by emphasizing policies of particular relevance to women both between and during election campaigns;
(2) to encourage equal ('at least 50%') representation of women in reading executives, and to require this in provincial council delegations, the provincial executives and party committees;

(3) to develop a leadership training programmes for women; and
(4) to recruit female candidates in strong ridings—that is, districts—and to assist with childcare and household management expenses of all candidates (cited in Bashevkin 1985*a*: 86–7).

The resolution called also for action against societal obstacles that prevented women from entering politics, like family obligations, and sought to place women in strong winnable districts: both policy positions rarely embraced by mainstream party leaders in most countries. The resolution was presented at the party leadership conference in 1982 where three male candidates were competing. All three candidates supported the proposal. Although there were vocal opponents to the resolution, including three women, the party adopted it with a majority of voting delegates (Bashevkin 1985*a*). The only feminist wording that was changed was that constituencies were 'urged' rather than 'required' to place women in 50 per cent of district executives positions.

According to members of the Women's Committee interviewed by Praud, the implementation and enforcement of the affirmative action parts of the resolution were pursued with great enthusiasm by the party. However, the positive discrimination provisions where women would need to be favoured over men in leadership appointments were more controversial (1997: 181–2). One feminist activist of the Women's Committee was concerned about the potential negative impact of the provisions on women (Praud 1997: 181–2). Still, there were positive results, at least in terms of the increase of women in provincial party decision-making, with executives reaching 51.4 per cent women and councils 39.5 per cent in 1990 (Praud 1997: 179). Also, over half of ONDP cabinet members were women. In 1992, the ONDP government promised to set aside half of the seats for women for the newly elected Senate (Praud 1997: 182). As two members of the Women's Committee stated, 'there has been a commitment to real power' for women that 'grew out of what the party had been talking about for a long time' (cited in Praud 1997: 182).

There has been a steady flow of institutional feedback around the 1982 Resolution. In 1989, the party passed a second affirmative action resolution reinforcing the feminist aspects of the 1982 version and extending the provision to ethnic minorities and gays (Praud 1997: 183). Throughout the 1980s, the party supported the Women's Committee in its active implementation of the ONDP's affirmative action policy. Thus, the Women's Committee became the functional equivalent of a feminist women's policy agency within the political party. It is not clear to what degree the interconnections between the feminist lobby, the NAC, and the work of the ONDP has continued. Nonetheless, the NAC, with the help of the national level women's policy machinery, remained very active in promoting women in campaigns throughout the 1980s (Geller-Schwartz 1995; Young 1998). In the final analysis, a well-received feminist unit, partially founded on radical feminist ideas, successfully introduced feminist policy in a slightly diluted form. Women's descriptive representation was also clearly increased in the affirmative action decision-making process within the ONDP and through the implementation of the 1982 and 1989 resolutions.

❖ *2. Institutionalizing Pre-Election Campaigns in Norway:*
 A Strategic Partnership Produces Feminist Policy Formation
 (Pre/Form.: 3/3 Post-form.: 2/3 = 11)

The pre-election campaigns in Norway were a series of systematic efforts, first initiated by feminist groups in 1967 and supported by the Equal Status Council in the 1980s, to promote women candidates. The campaigns were aimed at decision-makers in the political parties and the electorate in parliamentary, regional, and municipal elections. In 1967, the Norwegian Association for the Rights of Woman organized the first campaign to persuade political parties to nominate more women for the municipal elections. The government and all of the political parties backed the initiatives (Halsaa 1991: 27). The National Council of Women was also involved. Women at the local level mobilized, in particular to take advantage of the right to 'cumulate' candidates.[7] Women candidates written-in through this campaign successfully won seats in the 1967 elections. In one municipal council, 14 out of 43 seats were won by women who were written-in (Halsaa 1991: 27). The achievements of the first campaign led to the same partnership between grass-roots women and national level women's groups to organize a larger pre-election campaign for the next municipal elections in 1971. The outcome was even more successful. In 1971, the press declared a 'women's coup' with women gaining the majority of seats in the Oslo city council and several other key municipalities.

The election of women nominated outside of the political parties generated public controversy. Political party leadership criticized the movement for undermining the electoral process. Yet, as Halsaa (1991: 27) points out, men had long used cumulation without criticism. The ensuing public debate brought more women into the electoral arena and developed a widespread movement around the promotion of women candidates in local elections through 'effect-ive co-operation between independent women's organizations, women in political parties, and women in public administration' (Halsaa 1998: 174).

With the adoption of the Equal Status Act in 1978 and its increasing focus on positive action in political representation in the 1980s, the Equal Status Council and the Ombuds helped to institutionalize the campaigns through funding and providing office space for women candidates running for parliament. Beginning in 1985, the two national level women's policy offices organized strat-egy sessions for parliamentary elections that brought together women candi-dates, women's groups, and political parties to develop election campaigns for women (Halsaa 1991: 24–5; Bystydzienski 1995*b*: 48–9). The collaborative model for women's campaigns was further developed at the regional and local levels with the help of the Equal Status Committees, the field offices of the national-level women's policy machineries. The model has continued to be used in elections through the 1990s (Bystydzienski 1995*b*: 49).

At the national level, campaigns were aimed at party leaders to nominate women; at the local level, the campaigns promoted write-in women candidates. In the 1990s, women's campaigns became a permanent fixture of the election process (Halsaa 1991: 24). Up until 1991 at the municipal level, the pre-election campaigns were pursued randomly in municipalities, depending on local feminist interest and the orientation of the local Equal Status Committees. After 1991, the campaigns were organized in municipalities where councils were composed of less than 20 per cent women (Halsaa 1998: 174). In 1988, strategy meetings were organized in every region (Bystydzienski 1995*a*, *b*).

The Equal Status Committees were given the mandate and funds to help organize these campaigns. Studies of the local level women's policy agencies (Halsaa 1995; Van der Ros 1995) indicate that their effectiveness varies greatly. Without any formal enforcement authority their work depends largely on the femocrats who staff them. While on the one hand a vital and permanent movement at all levels of Norwegian society has developed, on the other the number of women elected to public office has increased since the first campaign in 1967. From 1981 to 1990 the share of women members of parliament went from 26 per cent to 39 per cent (Bergvist *et al.* 1999: 298). There was a drop in women municipal and county council members from 1989 to 1993, but this downward trend appeared to have been reversed by 1995 (Halsaa 1998: 174).

More recent analyses of the campaigns indicate that they may have lost the broad-based support as women's policy offices have institutionalized them. As Bystydzienski (1995b: 49) states, 'the number of workers involved in the campaigns has dwindled and the Council has provided pay for only one person each time who acts as a co-ordinator'. It is difficult to determine the degree to which government support has actually declined and campaigns themselves are actually losing support.

Nonetheless, women's descriptive representation was enhanced throughout policy development with significant institutional feedback in state and society around the campaigns. Societal feedback was both the cause and the effect of the strategic partnership between women in public office, state feminist agencies, political parties, women's groups, and individual women. Although the movement to bring women's representation to the levels of men's was initiated by non-governmental groups and movements, it was arguably strengthened by the principle of positive action contained in more general Equal Status policy.

❖ *3. The 1999 Constitutional Parity Amendment in France: Symbolic*
Constitutional Politics Without Feminists (Pre/Form.: 3/2 Post-form.:
2/3 = 10)[8]

In early 1999, the French National Assembly adopted a law that inserted the following provision into Art. 3 of the Fifth Republic Constitution: '*the law must favour the equal access of men and women to elected office.*' The inclusion of this clause was a culmination of nearly ten years of feminist mobilization, mostly among Paris-based feminists, intellectuals, and women members of the political elite, around the demand for *parité*: the notion of equal numbers of men and women in all public offices.[9] Up until the early 1990s, parity was not a central demand of the French women's movements. In 1982, Gisèle Halimi, president of the fading reproductive rights group Choisir, sponsored successfully a private member's bill to introduce a 25 per cent quota for women on municipal electoral lists. The adoption of the bill was significant given the rarity with which private members' bills actually get approved. However, the same year, the Constitutional Council nullified the law by declaring it in violation of the equality provision in the Constitution.

In the context of persistently low levels of women's representation,[10] feminist activists and intellectuals from the left began to develop the demand for an authoritative policy. A book published in 1992 by the founders of the Parity movement outlined the major problems and solutions, both within the parties and government (Gaspard, Servan-Schreiber, and LeGall 1992). The book did not identify a constitutional amendment as a major solution. Many feminists felt that the high politics of amending the Constitution would, at best, produce a weak policy and, at worst, stall indefinitely the entire process.

In the next several years, the parity issue mobilized a new group of women through mostly Paris-based groups. In 1994, the elite-dominated movement expanded its scope by creating an umbrella organization named Demain la Parité. Gaspard (1997:6) puts the number of members at two million. Among other things, the network circulated a petition to political parties on parity. In 1994, the Manifesto of 577 was published in *Le Monde*. Signed by 233 female and 344 male politicians, the manifesto called for the adoption of a framework law on parity. During the next two years, two of the most active feminist groups, the Association for Feminist Studies (ANEF) and the Association Against Violence Toward Women at Work (AVFT) held symposia on the issue in Paris. Both conferences produced special issues of the group's journals (ANEF 1994; AVFT 1996). In 1996, a prominent Paris-based political science journal, *Pouvoirs*, also published a special issue on women and politics with a focus on parity. In 1994, under a left-wing president, a right-wing parliament and, a right-wing government, two private members' bills on parity were presented; neither was adopted. One was sponsored by Gisèle Halimi and the other by Jean-Pierre Chevènement, a Socialist Party leader in the left wing of the party.

In 1995, the right-wing government of Alain Juppé created a new type of women's policy office, the Observatoire de la Parité, to examine the causes of and solutions to women's under-representation. Many saw l'Observatoire to be highly symbolic, involved more with stalling concrete government action than with actually pursuing effective policies to address what was seen by feminist activists as a major embarrassment for French democracy. Not only was the Observatoire created outside of the highly developed women's policy machinery, a legacy of the Socialist government (Mazur 1995b), but the previous right-wing government had downgraded the Socialist Women's Rights Ministry to an administrative agency without portfolio in 1993. The complex subcommittee structure of what essentially was a study group, the absence of any clear chain of command, and limited resources undermined the Observatoire's ability to take effective action. Headed by Halimi, a sub-commission on parity published its report in October of 1995. In June 1996, yet another manifesto was published, this time in the weekly magazine *L'Express*, calling for, among other policy initiatives, a constitutional amendment 'if necessary'. It was signed by ten former ministers, all women.

In March 1997, the Gaullist Prime Minister, Alain Juppé, participated in a debate in the National Assembly on parity. Immediately following the debate, the Prime Minister pledged that his government would begin drafting an amendment. The symbolic nature of these statements was pointed out by many feminist observers in the context of Juppé's remarks that the problem would be resolved once women had been through the initial period of political apprenticeship. After all, asserted Juppé in front of a half-empty assembly, women had obtained the vote only in 1945 (Gaspard 1997).

Following the victory of the Socialists in the 1997 elections, the new left-wing government under Lionel Jospin proposed a draft amendment to Parliament without any mention of parity. Furthermore, as one parity feminist observed, the government failed to consult any feminist supporters of parity in drafting the bill.[11] Indeed, the parity movement was still divided over whether a constitutional amendment would even be the best option. The final law was supported by left-wing and right-wing deputies, and a newly appointed Deputy Minister of Women's Rights and Job Training, Nicole Perry, presented the feminist arguments for the bill. Although the preface of the law treated the notion of parity, the final wording of the amendment itself did not specifically mention the term.

The amendment to the constitution was ratified in 1999 and implementation measures were adopted one year later. The new principles were clearly implemented in the 2001 municipal elections. Political parties presented an equal number of women and men candidates. The Ministry of the Interior was also exploring the implementation of the parity principle in administration in 2000. At the same time, the women's policy offices were not given any formal authority over the implementation of the new policies. The new policy gave no formal role to watchdog groups outside of the political parties and government either. None of the parity groups mobilized in the 1990s have come forward to oversee implementation.

Thus, while the descriptive representation of women's interests was significant in the pre-formulation of the parity amendment, there has been little significant feminist involvement by women in the post-formulation stages. In contrast to the Norwegian case, there was little evidence of a strategic partnership in the formulation or the implementation of this policy. There was more of a partnership in pre-formulation, through the leaders of the new parity movement and the Observatoire.

Another part of the partnership that has been lacking in France is the political parties. Feminists inside political parties have tried to compel party leaders to take action to address the low level of women in politics. Only the Communist Party has brought more women into leadership positions and on to electoral lists. The Socialist Party has pursued a highly rhetorical stance on quotas since the 1970s, paying lip service to them without actually following through (Appleton and Mazur 1993). The new constitutional amendment on parity may be forcing parties to re-evaluate their strategies of putting forward female candidates. It is still too early, however, to assess the degree to which the parties have actually adhered to the new parity rules in the 2001 elections.

A major factor in the French government's decision to formulate a parity amendment may have been pressure from the EU more than any internal feminist pressure. The treaty signed at Athens in 1992 and the Council of Ministers' recommendation in 1996 made it increasingly difficult to avoid taking an official stand on parity. Finally, an authoritative feminist policy has not been the usual French response to the EU sex-equality directives in employment (Mazur 1995a). In this light, the future direction of parity policy in France may very well continue to be symbolic.

❖ 4. 1993 and 1995 Quota Legislation in Italy: Divided Substantive Representation and Feminist Feedback (Pre/Form.: 3/2 Post-form.: 3/2 =10)

Two laws on the new Italian electoral system included positive discrimination provisions for women on electoral lists, in essence quotas, in the context of the institutional overhaul and political upheaval of 1993. The first law was adopted by Parliament on 25 March. It included wording that prohibited men or women from occupying more than two-thirds of an electoral list for municipal and provincial elections. This principle was extended, without any change, to regional council elections in a 1995 law. The second law on the new electoral system for the Chamber of Deputies was voted in on 23 August 1993. It required that, for the 25 per cent of the lower house elected by proportional representation, candidates be alternated by sex on the electoral list.[12]

The laws were implemented without any challenge in elections at the national and local levels in 1994. A 1995 Constitutional Court decision annulled both provisions. The 25 July ruling stated that the laws violated the 'fundamental right to equal access' based on sex guaranteed by Arts 3 and 51 of the Constitution. The Court also maintained that the laws failed to correspond to other constitutional provisions on positive action (Art. 3); neither law specified a plan to remove obstacles blocking women from elected office (Guadagnini 1998*b*: 3). Italian observers asserted that the quotas helped women in the elections in modest proportions. In the legislative elections, the quotas compensated women's losses in seats covered by the single district system. When the quotas were annulled, women's positive showing in municipal elections disappeared: for Guadagnini (1998*b*: 3) and others, a clear sign that quotas were necessary.

The published analyses do not make clear the precise channel through which the sex quotas were introduced into the two major pieces of legislation. The studies do show that the Equal Status and Equal Opportunity National Commission (ESONC) played a key role in the process. 'In the course of the debates on the electoral law, the ESONC urged parliament to introduce rules to guarantee women's representation' (Guadagnini 1995: 160). Also, the Commission had been actively pushing for women's representation, working with women politicians in public awareness and media campaigns since 1987. Femocrats worked with party leaders to promote women in internal party councils in 1989 and 1990 as well (Guadagnini 1995: 160). Thus, through the work of the ESONC, women entered into the pre-formulation process and may have been involved with formulating the quota provisions.

Substantive representation was less obvious in the formulation of the laws. Guadagnini's and Becalli's analyses of the debates over the quota systems show that feminists were divided into two camps. Both camps were involved in 'a fierce debate', along with non-feminist policy actors (Guadagnini 1998*b*: 2). Right-wing and liberal parties were against quotas, asserting that they overly protected women. Feminists in the Socialist Party (PSI) were divided, as were members of the newly reformed Communist Party (PDS). Feminist activists who supported 'difference feminism' opposed the quotas on the basis that it accentuated 'the weaknesses rather than the authoritativeness of women' (Guadagnini 1998*b*: 2)' Women in favour of the quota were associated with ESONC and the centre-left. Despite the disagreement, the debate brought women into a major policy-making arena on a high-priority reform issue for the country on a debate that involved a wide range of feminist and non-feminist actors. The President, for example, took a vocal position against the quotas, describing the system as 'disgusting, almost offensive' (Guadagnini 1998b: 2 n. 7).

The quota provisions of both laws incorporated at least one of the feminist positions and were implemented in a timely manner up to the annulment by the Constitutional Court. Although it stopped implementation, the decision did not end the movement around positive discrimination in Italy; if anything it unified the two feminist camps. The increase of women in the 1994 elections with the new quotas and the decrease in the municipal elections in 1996 without quotas for many observers illustrated the importance of quotas for getting women into public office. More recently, feminist jurists developed a bill proposal with wording that would not discriminate against one sex over the other (Guadagnini 1998b: 4). Other women associated with the 'difference' wing of the feminist movement called for the introduction of a gendered provision in the constitution that would allow for different treatment of women. Guadagnini (1998b: 4) identifies a series of measures that were being actively pursued in 1999 by a variety of feminist and non-feminist actors.

As Italian observers like Guadagnini point out, the mobilization in the 1990s came partly from Italy's poor record of women's representation (1998b: 1). Also, the emerging political landscape of the Italian system was not necessarily woman-friendly. For example, the increasingly popular northern regional party, the Lega, publicly supported the return of women to the home (Becalli 1996: 180). Here vocal anti-feminist movements may be causing women's groups to mobilize. The Bicameral Commission that was drafting constitutional reforms in 1998 had only six women members out of 70 (Guadagnini 1998b: 4 n. 24). Nonetheless, there has clearly been significant feminist feedback to counter the negative impact of the Constitutional Court decision. This feedback is even more striking given that it took over ten years for feminists to mobilize against a similar Constitutional Council decision in France that struck down a 1982 law on quotas.

❖ Comparative Discussion: Strategic Partnerships in Formulation, Constitutional Culture, and Non-Feminist Allies

As Table 4.1 illustrates, the four instances of policy formation suggest that political representation policies reach high levels of feminist success. In all four cases, affirmative action or positive discrimination policies were the site of significant levels of women's descriptive representation. Feminist groups and movements mobilized around their pre-formulation and formulation. In Italy and Canada the same line-up of feminist groups pursued implementation of the new policies. Even in the context of the Italy's Constitutional Court's nullification of the quota laws, feminists developed alternative strategies. In Norway, women's activists and groups may have become less involved in campaigns to promote women in public office in the 1990s. In France, the parity movement has not mobilized around policy implementation. The government has apparently failed to invite feminists to participate in implementation either. Nevertheless, persistently low levels of women in public office, the emergence of a new consensus around parity policy, and continuing pressure from EU policy may break the potential for symbolic politics in policy implementation.

The French amendment is arguably the least feminist. The content of the political representation policies in Italy, Norway, and the Canadian ONDP were much more feminist, with the ONDP's affirmative action resolution containing a highly feminist approach. Although the Italian legislation did not include any treatment of how obstacles to women's representation would be removed—indeed, this was one of the reasons the Constitutional Court annulled the law—it was implemented quickly, without any apparent opposition.

The styles of the policy communities varied across the four cases. Italy and Norway displayed quite similar policy styles. In Norway, feminist policies were a product of a coalition of women's groups, women's policy agencies, and women in public office. In Italy, incomplete analyses of the process make any definitive conclusion difficult. Nonetheless, it does appear that there was a certain degree of collaboration between women in political parties and public office, the women's movement, and the women's policy offices, although this collaboration has occurred more at elite levels than in Norway. The policy community style in Norway was the most grass-roots oriented. The actions of individual women outside of parties, organized feminist groups, and government played quite important parts in all stages of feminist policy formation. In France, the policy sub-system was highly divided between two camps. On the one hand a Paris-based, elite-dominated parity movement called for government action; on the other, governments of the right and the left resisted feminist calls for parity until 1997. Even then, they were reluctant to work with the society-based parity movement.

The closed nature of the arena for elaborating the ONDP's affirmative action resolution necessarily precluded links with groups outside of the political party.

Table 4.1 Policy profile scores for cases of political representation policy

	Pre/Form.		Post-form.		Total
	D	S	D	S	
Ontario: 1982 affirmative action in ONDP	3	3	3	3	12
Norway: election campaigns in the mid-1980s	3	3	2	3	11
France: 1999 Constitutional Parity Amendment	3	2	2	3	10
Italy: 1993 and 1995 quota legislation	3	2	3	2	10

In the analyses of the resolution, there was little mention of any contacts between outside feminists or women's policy agencies and the feminists within the ONDP. Still, there was a great deal of consensus within the party between the feminists in the Women's Committee and the non-feminist party leaders over the importance of taking a feminist stance on affirmative action. Furthermore, the party did not just reluctantly follow the feminist directives. It actually empowered party feminists to implement the new resolution.

While low levels of women's representation certainly served as important mobilizing points in all countries, and particularly in Italy and France in the 1990s, the same low levels in Italy and France did not produce the same policy styles and profiles. While in Italy the government embedded a policy response to women's low numbers in elected office into important institution-building legislation, the French government adopted what to many was a rhetorical constitutional amendment, with little feminist input. As constitutional scholars argue, the French constitution has only recently been used as an important policy-making device, through the decisions of the Constitutional Council (Stone 1992). The absence of an active constitutional culture, therefore, may generally limit the impact of the amendment. Still, the importance of the inclusion of this principle in the Constitution for future policy should not be underestimated.

The fact that women quickly mobilized to address the reversal made by the Italian Constitutional Court in 1995 but did not in France in the wake of the Constitutional Council's 1982 decision suggests that constitutional feminist politics in the two countries diverge. The difference between the French and Italian cases may be a function of institution-building in the Italian political system. Another explanation for the difference is that the political environment for parity in the early 1980s in France was quite different from Italy in the 1990s.

In both the French and Italian cases, the timing of the policies corresponds with the development of policy at the EU and other international levels. Whether the policy incentives have any concrete impact on getting member states to develop authoritative feminist policy is still not clear. It is certain, however, the European-wide pressure, particularly in the context of the move to a unified currency, compelled non-feminist decision-makers to pay more attention to this policy area than in the past . Policies in both Norway and the ONDP in Canada were quite feminist outside of the arena of the EU.

Finally, as in the case of blueprint policies, successful feminist political representation policy appears to be a result of the extent to which non-feminist decision-makers in government and political parties agree to pursue feminist demands for public policy. In other words, it seems that feminists must persuade non-feminists to take feminist action.

❖ NOTES

1 A recent European Commission report, for example, examined women in decision-making positions in state and society, including corporations, religious institutions, and business (Lovenduski and Stephenson 1998).

2 The term 'political representation' is used rather than 'partner' to avoid any confusion with partner policies in the USA that target the rights of unmarried couples.

3 The Inter-Parliamentary Union is a non-governmental organization that speaks for 125 national parliaments. It has been an important watchdog of women's representation throughout the world and has taken an active feminist stance on women's descriptive representation issues. Its reports are important sources of information for political representation issues (for example, IU 1995).

4 This categorization is based on Lovenduski's (1993: 8) taxonomy for political party strategies to promote women. She uses the term 'rhetorical' for the first category of strategies: a synonym for what is called here symbolic policy.

5 Opponents to quotas tend to use the label 'positive discrimination' in a derogatory manner. It is purposely used here to distinguish these policies from indirect positive action and to indicate that ultimately in order to promote equal or balanced representation of men and women in public office women must be selected over men in a preferential manner.

6 Not all feminist activists make this assumption. For example, in the Netherlands two separate feminist coalitions emerged in the 1980s around the issue of increased women's political representation: one group pushed for more women in politics (MWIP) and the other mobilized around the demand for more feminists in politics (MFIP) (Oldusma 2002:4).

7 In Norway, candidates are allowed to be nominated outside of political parties in a process called 'cumulation'.

8 For more on the parity politics in France see the special issue of *Contemporary French Civilization* (Praud 2001). This analysis is partially based on my article on the parity movement in that issue (Mazur 2001*b*).

9 The demand for 50:50 representation of men and women did not become known as parity until the early 1990s with the publication of the book *Au Pouvoir les Citoyennes! Liberté, Égalité, Parité* (Gaspard, Servan-Schreiber, and Anne LeGall 1992).

10 In 1997, 10.2% of deputies in the National Assembly were women compared with 5.7% in 1946 and 6% in 1993. In 1995, 5.1% of departmental councillors were women and 21.2% of municipal councillors, with 7.5% of all mayors being women (Mossuz-Lavau 1998: 21).

11 Interview with Françoise Gaspard (June 1998).

12 The other 75% was to be elected under a first-past-the-post system.

5 ❖ Equal Employment Policy

❖ OVERVIEW

Feminist policy studies show that achieving equality between men and women in paid labour is a much larger enterprise than merely focusing on work place decisions and programmes.[1] Feminist employment policies also need to take into consideration the causes of employment inequities that stem from the way gender roles are perceived and played out throughout society. Mahon (1998a: 158) argues, for example, that 'a broader view of equal opportunities must include structural factors which facilitate mothers' participation in the labour market: child care policies, tax and maternity benefits'. Steinberg-Ratner (1980b: 41–2) identifies direct and indirect barriers to 'the full integration of women into the paid labour market'. She places primary emphasis on the direct barriers that 'operate in the job market' and secondary emphasis on indirect obstacles related to 'women's home and family responsibilities, and with more intangible, yet crucial effects of prior socialisation of men and women in appropriate expectations and patterns of behaviour'. A feminist approach to employment policy, therefore, includes policies directed at the labour market and at other spheres outside of the labour market, or 'equal employment opportunity policy'.

Combining labour market and non-labour market policies, however, is analytically problematic. Government action that addresses barriers outside of wage labour inevitably overflows into other sub-sectors of feminist policy. In contrast, policies that focus on employment-related barriers are more distinct and usually involve the same array of actors: equal employment and/or labour administration agencies and officers, trade unions, feminist groups, management, consulting firms, and courts. This book groups together policies that seek to affect wage-labour mechanisms under the rubric 'equal employment policies'. Most policies that address the causes of wage-labour inequities located outside the labour market are covered in the reconciliation policy sub-sector in Chapter 6.

Separating out non-labour market policies, however, does not mean that the complex sources of employment inequities should be ignored in policy formation. The design of equal employment policies still needs to recognize that inequities in wage labour are actually a product of forces outside of the labour market. They also need to address both direct and indirect forms of employment discrimination against women.[2]

At the same time, policies that do not take into account gender-based social inequities outside employment are still considered feminist as long as they cover three out of the five components of this study's operational definition of feminist policy (see Chapter 2). In this light, equal employment policies consist of government action that addresses some, if not all, of the full range of barriers in the paid labour market that prevent women from participating in employment in the same manner as men. The major focal points of equal employment policies are employment decisions and the processes surrounding them on hiring, training, wages, promoting, and firing.

The term 'equal employment', rather than other terms, like 'equal opportunity', is used here for two reasons. First, although a major operating assumption of much equal employment policy is that women should be given the same opportunities as men to compete in the paid labour force, not all policies that fall into this category have formally focused on job opportunities. On the one hand, much legislation has been elaborated to eliminate discriminatory employment practices without making any reference to opportunities; on the other, policies in some countries seek to affect actual employment outcomes. Also, the term 'equal opportunity' often implies labour market and non-labour market policies. The general rubric 'equal employment', therefore, incorporates the different levels of commitment to equality in the actual labour market—treatment, opportunity, and outcomes—and avoids the conflation of workforce policies with policies that target other arenas.

Second, the notion of equality is retained because equal employment policies tend to be elaborated on the backdrop of showing the inequities between men's and women's employment profiles. The intent of policies in this third subsector of feminist policy is also based on the argument that the major goal of government action should be to reduce sex-based gaps as much as possible; in other words, to achieve some level of equality or equity between men and women.[3] Not all equality advocates, however, call for pure equality in outcomes between men and women: that men and women should have identical employment profiles in lifetime work patterns, occupational distribution, job status, training opportunities, salary, training, and promotions. Nonetheless, equal employment policy tends to be designed in the context of comparing women's and men's position in paid labour.

It is also important to note that neither the operational definition of equal employment policy nor the comparative propositions made here apply to policies that target employment inequalities experienced by other groups than women. This does not mean that the analysis ignores policy issues that treat discrimination against other groups, particularly given that sex-based equal employment policy is often intertwined with policies targeting other forms of discrimination. Rather, examining sex- and gender-based employment equality policy separately suggests the differences between policy formation dynamics in this area and equal employment policies that target other generalized forms of discrimination.[4]

There is a large literature on equal employment policy, particularly on the English-speaking countries where equal employment has been an important arena for feminist movement activities.[5] Given that employment was the first area of feminist state action and arguably the most acceptable to a wide variety of policy actors, feminist scholars were particularly interested in this area of policy in the 1970s. Many worked in this area because of the promise of the European Community equality policy as well. Not all of the literature, however, provides a start-to-finish analysis of policy formation. While many fields are interested in equal employment for women—law, labour studies, political science, sociology, and feminist studies—many analyses do not examine government action. Both feminist and government-funded evaluations favour assessing impact over political process or administrative outputs. There is a great deal of work on the equal employment acts of the 1970s, the cornerstone of policy in many countries. Scholarly interest in equal employment policy decreased in the late 1980s. This shift was partially due to the search for other solutions to the persistence in sex-based wage differential and occupational segregation and partially due to the elimination of the most overt forms of sex-based discrimination. In other words, equal employment policies were regarded simultaneously as a success and a failure.

Policies in this sub-sector are divided into two categories: anti-discrimination and positive action.[6] Anti-discrimination policies punish both intended and unintended employment discrimination. They include equal-pay and equal-treatment laws that essentially set up legal norms and procedures for trying cases in courts of law, civil or labour. In countries with litigation-oriented legal systems and a recourse to high-priced collective action settlements, discrimination policy can be an important deterrent to businesses treating women unfairly either directly or indirectly. The elimination of discriminatory protective policies targeted at women is also considered an anti-discrimination policy, as long as it is pursued in a feminist optic.[7]

Positive action policies promote employment equality between men and women, through the design and funding of firm-based programmes, subsidies with strings attached—in the USA government contracts to firms that meet certain target numbers—and the preferential treatment of women in training and jobs, or positive discrimination. Job training has been an important focus of positive action policies. Training policies include a wide range of programmes administered in the context of the paid labour market and public education through on-the-job training, training to re-enter the labour market, vocational training, and other employment-oriented education and placement pro-grammes. Job market-based training involves employment actors like manage-ment, private job-training providers, trade unions, and women's groups.[8]

Comparable-worth or equal-value policies assure that women are paid the same as men in jobs that are not identical but are equivalent in skills and work-place responsibilities. Originally an elaboration of limited equal-pay laws, equal-value policies can be classified as anti-discrimination and positive action policies. Court decisions, for instance, can force employers to pay equivalent salaries to women for work of equal value, essentially an anti-discrimination policy, and to actively develop the complex evaluation schemes and wage equiv-alencies necessary to achieve equal value.[9] Anti-sexual harassment policies adopted in the 1990s also fall into both categories. These policies often simultaneously define sexual harassment as a punishable offence and promote programmes that heighten sexual harassment awareness and reporting. Sexual harassment policy is examined in Chapter 9 in the Sexuality and Violence sub-sector given that in many countries anti-sexual harassment laws are linked to feminist demands for policy to address sexual violence toward women.

Table 5.1 shows the range of and timing for major national-level equal employment policy decisions. Like all feminist policy, the elaboration of equal-ity principles in an official policy statement does not necessarily lead to imple-mentation. The overview, therefore, is not intended to make a systematic inventory or evaluation of policy effectiveness. Equal employment policies include legislative acts, court decisions (Decision), equality plans, constitution-al provisions, and collective agreements (CA). Anti-discrimination policies are covered in the first two columns of the table; positive action and equal value policies are treated separately. The overall frame or approach, discussed further below, for equal employment policy is also listed for each country. A given piece of legislation may cover more than one of the four areas of equal employment policy. The first national-level, official treatment of a given principle in domes-tic policy is also listed. Ratification of international agreements, such as the International Labour Organisation's convention on equal pay, does not count as a national-level policy response in the table. Where policies cover several dif-ferent issues, either the dates are listed across the areas or dotted lines extend across the pertinent policies.

As Table 5.1 shows, equal employment policy began with equal pay in the early 1970s, usually in the form of national acts. Restricted equal pay laws were on the books in some countries as early as the late nineteenth century. Equal pay was usually followed by equal treatment laws that made direct discrimination against women in hiring, promotion, training, and firing a punishable offence. In European Union member states, equal pay and equal treatment laws were adopt-ed in conjunction with European Community equality directives of the 1970s.[10] The failure of anti-discrimination laws to address occupational segregation and

Table 5.1 Equal employment policies in core countries: type, timing, and approach

	Equal pay	Equal treatment	Positive action	Equal value	Approach
Italy	Early 1960s	1977 Act	1991 Act		PA
Ireland	1974 Act	1977 Act	1996 Bill	1977 Act	D/PA
Spain	1980	1979 Act	1979 Act/1986 Equality Plan		PA
Denmark	1976 Act	1978 Act	1988	1986 Amend.	EO/PA
Sweden	1970s CA	1979 Equal Opportunity Act			EO/PA
Norway	1959 Committee	1978 Equal Status Act			EO/PA
France	1972 Act	1975 Act	1983 Act		PA/EO?
Germany	1949 Const.	1980 Act/1994 Act			Weak PA/EO?
Netherlands	1975 Act	1980 Act	1994 Act		Weak PA/EO?
United States	1963 Act	1964 Act	1965/68 Exec. Orders		AD/PA
Great Britain	1970 Act	1975 Act	1986 Act	1983 Amend.	AD/PA?
Canada	1971 Code	1977 Charter	1986 Act	1977 Act	AD/PA
Australia	1969 Decision	1984 Act	1986 Act	1972 Decision	PA/EO/AD

Sources: See literature listed in Appendix B under equal employment policy.
Key: AD = anti-discrimination; PA = Positive Action; EO = expanding opportunities

persistently large pay gaps between men and women increased feminist mobilization for equal employment policy; and equality policy compelled most EU member-states in the late 1970s and 1980s to examine 'more complex anti-discrimination measures' (Lovenduski 1986a: 291). In many of the EU member states, EC/EU directives and the European Court of Justice decisions that came out of them served as powerful policy incentives to compel countries to take active positions on equal employment policy.

In the 1980s, there was a return to considering persistent sex-based wage differentials, this time through the lens of comparable worth/equal value. Bellace (1991: 27) calls this turn in public policy the 'third wave' in 'legislative responses to the equality movement'. The formal principle of equal pay for work of equal value is on the books in all of the countries except Australia and Italy. In Italy a broader non-gendered approach through collective bargaining has alleviated some sex-based wage differentials (Del Boca 1998). Significant sustained comparable worth efforts have been pursued in Canada, Australia, the USA, and Great Britain (O'Connor 1999; Bellace 1991) with important cross-national divergences. In the USA, for example, there is no federal-level comparable worth policy and in Australia the language of comparable worth has not been officially adopted.

Steinberg-Ratner's (1980b: 40–5) three-way categorization is used to understand cross-national variations in how governments generally approach equal employment policy; covered by the fourth column in Table 5.1. The scheme was first designed to discuss patterns in equal employment opportunity policies in the USA, Germany, the UK, and Sweden in the 1970s. It was further developed and applied in O'Connor (1999) and Steinberg-Ratner and Cook (1988). The framework provides a useful way of comparing different culturally-based approaches to this highly complex policy area.

There are three approaches to achieving employment equality: anti-discrimination (AD), positive action (PA) and expanding opportunities (EO). The first two approaches correspond with the two major types of equal employment policy listed above. The expanding-opportunities approach consists of systematic government efforts to link women's inferior status in wage labour to barriers operating outside the labour market and to design policies to help women surmount non-labour market obstacles in areas such as day care, education, family leave, and so on. Non-labour market policies must be intentionally designed within a feminist optic in order to be considered an indicator of an expanding opportunities approach. For instance, pre-school provisions for children beginning at age three in Spain and France undoubtedly help men and women lighten the double burden of work and family. The original logic behind these policies, however, had little to do with the pursuit of sex-based employment equality (Threlfall 1996b). As Table 5.1 shows, neither country takes an expanding opportunities approach.

Countries tend to follow one general approach. In some countries, a dominant approach to employment equality coexists with a second, less pronounced, policy stance. Only Australia follows all three approaches. For the Late Female Mobilizing countries, Spain and Italy both take a positive action approach. Goals and programmes are enunciated in national-level legislation and plans and family policies tend to have unintended feminist consequences without an explicit expanding-opportunities intent. The major approach to employment equality in Ireland is anti-discrimination, partially due to the rights-based legal culture in Ireland and the central role of EU equality directives (Gardiner 1999). In Ireland, unlike the other English speaking countries, there has been little policy activity on equal value (Callender and Meenan 1995: 52). Irish policy also incorporates positive action; and family policy is not overtly feminist.

The Protestant Social Democrat countries all share a primary emphasis on the expanding-opportunities model and a secondary recourse to a positive action approach. While mechanisms for the anti-discrimination model, such as courts and employment agencies, have been established, discrimination cases are not as important an avenue to achieving equality as policies formulated through the collective negotiations process. Equal pay in Sweden, for example, was mediated through the collective negotiation process before anti-discrimination laws were placed on the books (Ruggie 1984; Victorin 1991). The expansion of childcare and the establishment of family leave in the context of promoting sex equality tended to precede equal employment laws as well (Haavio Mannila *et al.* 1985; Dahlerup 1987; Ruggie 1984; Borchorst 1999c). To be sure, there are differences between the countries. For example, Leira (1993) points out that childcare provisions in Norway are not overtly linked to the promotion of women's equality in paid labour; and Eduards, Halsaa, and Skjeie (1985) argue that equality institutions are more developed in Sweden and Norway than in Denmark. Still, Parvikko (1991), Siim (1991), Borchorst (1999c) and others assert that more than in other countries general attitudes in Nordic countries tend to support the feminist notion that men and women should share the double burden of work and family.

The Advanced Christian Democrat countries take far less pronounced approaches to employment equality than the first two groups of countries. Given that equal employment agencies have not been assigned real enforcement powers, none of the countries followed the anti-discrimination model. France more than Germany and the Netherlands has a positive action approach, defined by the 1983 *égalité professionnelle* law. Positive action in Germany and the Netherlands has been piecemeal with no clearly defined national-level policy. Certain cities and *Länder* in Germany have developed positive action and anti-discrimination schemes in public sector employment (Ferree 1995). Whereas France and Germany pursue active childcare and family support policies, the policies are usually instituted outside of any specific equal employment logic.

❖ EQUAL EMPLOMENT POLICY

In Germany, analysts show that the constitution, predominant social attitudes, and certain non-feminist policies combine to make the male breadwinner-female caretaker model still dominant (Ostner 1993). This model is also still prevalent in France, though with the norm of women working in paid labour and taking on the family caretaker role. France has more of an expanding-opportunities approach than Germany; however, different segments of the French state simultaneously adopt a family-oriented and feminist-oriented discourse, often at odds with each other (Jenson 1988; Hantrais 1993a; Jenson and Sineau 1998b; Lanquetin, Laufer, and LeTablier 2000). In the Netherlands, there was no overt expanding opportunities strategy until the 1990s, when the government began to support childcare (Outshoorn and Swiebel 1998: 158).

The four Protestant Liberal countries share a strong emphasis on the anti-discrimination approach. Comparable worth has been a relatively important focus since the 1980s; some argue more systematically followed in Australia and Great Britain than in Canada and the USA (O'Connor 1999 and Wilborn 1991). In Great Britain, the struggle for equal employment for women has primarily taken place in the courts and industrial tribunals and through the application of European Court of Justice rulings (Lovenduski and Randall 1993). Voluntary affirmative action schemes are publicly funded to a certain degree in Great Britain, but are less focused on national policy than in the other three countries, where significant national-level positive action legislation or executive orders are actively implemented. Since the 1990s, only the Australian national government has taken an expanding-opportunities approach, committing officially to the full provision of 'work-related child care needs by the year 2000–2001' and instituting a childcare rebate to lighten specifically women's and men's double burden (O'Connor 1999: 16).

The four cases of equal employment policy in action are examined in this chapter in Ireland, Sweden, France, and Great Britain. They were selected to represent the full range of equal employment policies. Given that legislation has been a major tool for defining the general lines of policy in the sub-sector, legislative acts are examined in three out of the four cases: the 1977 Employment Equality Act in Ireland, the 1983 Égalité Professionnelle Act in France, and the 1979 Act on Equality Between Men and Women in Working Life in Sweden. The 1977 act in Ireland represents anti-discrimination legislation on equal treatment. The 1979 Swedish act represents the Nordic answer to employment equality: a single catch-all piece of legislation that targets all of the different areas of equal employment—pay, treatment, and positive action. The 1983 French legislation primarily focuses on positive action programmes. The British 1983 Amendment to the Equal Pay Act represents equal value policies. It is one of the few countries where equal value was the object of a national law.

❖ The Policy Cases

❖ 1. Discrimination Policy in the 1977 Act in Ireland: Feminist Policy Formation in a 'Political Niche' Within the Context of the Irish Rules of the Feminist Game (Pre/Form.: 3/2 Post-form.: 3/1 = 9)

Any analysis of feminist policy formation in Ireland must be situated within the strength of the male breadwinner-female caretaker model, the institutionalization of Catholic doctrine in the Constitution, the comparatively poor integration of women into the economy and politics, and the extent to which Ireland is rural. Irish analyses of feminist issues state clearly the particular cultural and structural impediments to women's status in Ireland. The situation has been improving in the context of changing social attitudes, women's mobilization and the ensuing feminist reforms, and Ireland's entry into the European Union in 1973 (for example, Mahon 1995; 1996; Galligan 1998). Thus, in a cross-national comparison of woman-friendliness, Ireland is rated often at the low end. If individual policy reforms are taken as the unit of analysis, however, Ireland presents a more positive picture of women's action and of the translation of feminist ideas into concerted feminist action. In this perspective, the profile and style of policy formation is feminist within the parameters of Ireland's 'rules of the feminist game'.[11] At the same time, the feminist success of the 1977 act was limited to the 'political niche'[12] of equal treatment, with feminist policy efforts in equal pay and expanding opportunities meeting insurmountable obstacles.

The 1977 act was the second piece of major equal employment legislation in Ireland, following the 1976 Equal Pay Act. It was modelled after legislation in Britain, Northern Ireland, and the USA to bring Ireland in line with the 1976 EC Equal Treatment Directive (Galligan 1998: 80) The law established legal definitions and the litigation process for all forms of direct and indirect discrimination in hiring, firing, and training and inserted equality clauses in collective agreements (Callender and Meenan 1995: 155). It also established an Equal Employment Agency (EEA) to monitor equal treatment and equal pay through overseeing discrimination cases and making annual reports on the progress of the laws (Callender and Meenan 1995: 167–75). Not only did the government allow the EEA to implement the law, but reform proposals were developed through the evaluation of the effectiveness of the original legislation: in other words, long-term and short-term government outputs and societal feedback

Unlike the 1976 Equal Pay Law, the content of the 1977 act corresponded to the demands of the liberal feminist movement. The Irish rules of the feminist game prevent radical forms of feminism from emerging (Galligan 1998). The Women's Advisory Committee (WAC), 'a women's ancillary group' of the Irish Congress of Trade Unions (ICTU), elaborated the list of demands for equal treatment at a meeting of the ICTU in 1973. The demands were eventually addressed in the final act. The Fine Gael-Labour government minister, Michael O'Leary, agreed to sponsor the legislation at a Women's Advisory Committee seminar on equal pay in April 1975. Some critics argued that O'Leary supported the law only to win women's support in the context of the International Year of the Woman (Galligan 1998). The law was adopted by the Irish parliament in 1977 without controversy. There was all-party support and backing from feminist groups, including more militant groups like the Trade Union Women's Forum. Among other feminist demands the law stipulated that women's groups would be fully represented on the new Equal Employment Agency, even in the context of opposition to an overtly feminist enforcement agency in the state bureaucracy (Galligan 1998: 81). Thus, in pre-formulation and formulation the policy profile was clearly feminist.[13]

The feminist trend was continued in implementation within the Act's niche. The first head of the Equal Employment Agency, Sylvia Meehan, used the full powers of the agency to turn it into 'the voice of working women, lobbying for the removal of discrimination and the promotion of positive action programmes within individual employment's, while monitoring and enforcing the legislation' (Galligan 1998: 84). In 1995, in the context of a reform-oriented government, the newly created Minister for Equality and Law Reform, and a woman President, the Agency issued a report in which it called for the government to take an active expanding opportunities approach through a strong commitment to childcare facilities for working parents (Mahon and Morgan 1999). The government resisted these calls since the Agency did not have the authority to pursue any policy formally outside of paid labour equality.

The absence of concrete reform since the original two acts also demonstrates the act's limits. The government responded finally to calls for reform in 1996. The Supreme Court overturned the 1996 reform one year later. Galligan argues that the 1980s was a very low period for political support for sex equality as well. It was not until the newly restructured Labour Party decided to take up the liberal women's rights agenda in the 1980s that new reforms were considered. Indeed, it was only the particular combination of factors that came together from 1974 to 1977 that led to the successes of the 1977 act.

> For a short period of time, political forces combined to open the tightly controlled corporatist economic interest structure, dominated by patriarchal values, to meet women's demands, satisfy EU rules and legitimise the concept of equality at work. The slight move in policy agenda was assisted by the mildly reformist ideology of the government in power between 1973 and 1977 (Galligan 1998: 84).

As long as trade unions and management are not asked to directly pay for equal employment—through salary equity, for instance—they are willing to support it. In the context of increased male unemployment in the 1980s, trade unions moved away from women's employment equality. Still, the policy profile and policy style continued to remain feminist within the political niche throughout the process.

❖ *2. Nordic Catch-all Policy in the 1979 Swedish Act: Growing Feminist Success From Within the State (Pre/Form.: 1/2 Post-form.: 3/2 = 8)*

The 1979 act represented a significant shift in the Swedish government's approach to women's employment equality. Prior to the act, the major approach was based on a gender-neutral universal model whereby women's equality was assured by creating economic independence and alleviating the double burden of work and home for both men and women, closing sex-based pay differentials, and developing some targeted measures for women in job training, all within the confines of a closed process of collective bargaining. After the adoption of the law, government policy became more woman-specific whereby national level feminist offices monitored and proposed new sex equality measures. It took 20 years for the universal model to be gendered, and, as analysts show, there is still progress to be made.

It is important to note that the original model was not inherently anti-feminist, because of its focus on expanding opportunities. Nonetheless, the major advocates of the gender-neutral model—the Social Democratic Party and the LO, the major trade union confederation—rejected any articulation of women's specific needs. 'Indeed, it became nearly immoral to talk about the need and demands of women when the push was for equal opportunities for everyone' (Westrand 1981: 13, cited in Elman 1995: 243). This suspicion was expressed in the 1975 state feminist report that led to the adoption of the act. 'There is always a danger that taking special measures on behalf of one sex will entrench traditional modes of segregated treatment and work against equality between men and women in the longer run' (cited in Ruggie 1984: 172).

Unlike the usual equal pay-equal treatment sequence of many other post-industrial countries, the 1979 act treated simultaneously equal treatment, equal pay, and positive action. For the first time, it provided legal definitions of discrimination in treatment and wages and charged an Equal Opportunities Commission and a newly created office, the Equality Ombuds, to oversee discrimination cases and complaints under the law. Equal pay was not a new area for public policy in the context of earlier collective agreements providing for the relatively effective treatment of equal pay issues (Ruggie 1984). Victorin (1991) argues, however, that labour-management negotiations had not satisfactorily dealt with sex-based occupational segregation through a meaningful comparable worth policy.

The act gave the Commission and the Ombuds together the authority to help individuals plead cases, to fine employers for infractions, and, in certain cases, to compel employers to develop positive action measures. The scope of the act was highly circumscribed by the provision that only workers treated in collective agreements were covered by the law. Given that only 10 per cent of women workers were in jobs that were covered by collective agreements, the new policy effectively applied to very few women workers (Elman 1995: 245). Neither employers nor trade unions nor collective agreements were the targets of the final act. The law imposed an equal burden of proof on plaintiff and defendant, a legal development that did not occur in most other countries until the 1980s and 1990s. While some trade unions introduced the new specific measures into collective agreements, the new equality machineries were not allowed to police this voluntary process. The demand for a broader remit for the act was definitely forwarded; organized labour and management successfully excluded this demand from the text of the final act (Eduards, Halsaa, and Skjeie 1985: 149).

It was not until the Social Democratic Party lost the elections to the Liberal Party in 1976 that a Liberal-Conservative coalition agreed to sponsor the new type of equality legislation. Although the Social Democratic government rejected an equal employment bill proposed by the liberals in 1970 (Elman 1995: 242), Prime Minister Olaf Palme appointed the first committee to examine equality between men and women in 1972. Sainsbury (1993) asserts that the late 1960s and 1970s were a period of increased women's activity within all of the political parties that resulted in putting women's equality on party agendas for the Social Democrats in 1969. Thus, a gender- specific approach to women's employment equality was at least articulated within the social democratic left.

Any pressure from internal efforts by party feminists, however, was significantly circumscribed by the context of the relatively marginal and new nature of women's demands, the long-established patterns of politics that underpinned the universal model to equality, and the absence of any strong autonomous feminist movement demands.[14] The Liberal Party's success in the 1976 elections was therefore an important turning point. The party did not have the institutional ties to organized labour and, as Ruggie (1984: 175) posits, more than other parties at the time, it 'wanted to make a symbolic gesture on behalf of women' to court their vote. Another factor that placed the act on the government's legislative agenda was the degree to which Sweden was out of line with other post-industrial countries in terms of the absence of a national-level discrimination policy. The pressure was quite indirect because Sweden was not a member of the EU at the time.

The Social Democrat government appointed the first advisory commission on sex equality that became the major state actor in favour of the new approach to women's employment equality. Under the Liberal government, the commission was transposed into a parliamentary committee, establishing a feminist presence in the legislative process. As an executive-based commission, the feminist advisory council had also recommended the act; as a parliamentary committee it contributed undoubtedly to shepherding the bill through Parliament. Analyses indicate that there were more men on the committee than women. Cook (1989: 77 n. 30) mentions the 'women' of the committee and explicitly states that the members were from all parties. There is no conclusive evidence, however, that women participated in pre-formulation and formulation.

In the immediate years following 1979, the narrow scope of the law limited the enforcement activities of the Equality Commission and Ombuds. In the late 1980s, in the context of efforts to bring policy in line with the EU equality directives for Sweden's impending entry into the EU, the new agencies spearheaded reform of the act in 1992 that included provisions on protection from sexual harassment, addressed some weaknesses in equal value, and provided a broader definition of indirect discrimination (Borchorst 1999*b*). There is no conclusive evidence on how far the new reforms have gone in changing the entrenched patterns of the process and policy inherent in the universal model. One commentator (Elman 1995: 247) did state that 'cautious restraint continues to best characterise the state's approach to sexual equality'.

There is a strong possibility that mainstream approaches to women's equality may very well be gendered in a feminist way. What is certain is that this shift has been inextricably linked to the development of a women-centred policy community created and nurtured within the arena of the women's equality agencies, outside the regular channels of employment decision-making. The outsider status of the women's policy offices, therefore, may be both a bane and a boon.

❖ 3. The 1983 Equal Value Amendment in Great Britain: Limited Feminist Success in 'Conservative Times' (Pre/Form.: 2/1 Post-form.: 3/2 = 8)

Despite the chilly climate for feminist reform during the Thatcher years, an emerging strategic partnership between the feminist Equal Opportunities Commission (EOC), certain feminist groups, and trade unions was instrumental in making the best of what was seen by many critics as a highly limited equal-value amendment to the 1970 Equal Pay Act. This feminist success in 'conservative times' reflects the relative successes of feminist reform in Thatcher's Britain compared with similar reforms during the Reagan years (Bashevkin 1998). Indeed, in the context of a neo-liberal government philosophically opposed to developing policy solutions that challenged individualism and market forces, the 1983 amendment generated a great deal of government outputs and societal feedback. It was used to advance comparable-worth policy beyond a restricted 'bureaucratic-managerial model', with an emphasis on expert evaluation and individual adjudication, to a more feminist 'labour mobilization model' aimed at improving women's pay status as a group through the mobilization of women workers and trade unions.[15] Although the UK does not entirely embrace the more feminist 'comparable worth from below', it has a hybrid of the two (Kahn 1992).

Analysts agree that the 1983 amendment was a direct result of infringement proceedings against the UK that were brought before the European Court of Justice by EU Commissioners in 1982 (Kahn 1992; Gregory 1992; Forbes 1989; Lovenduski 1995; Lovenduski and Randall 1993). Britain had not brought its policy in line with the 1975 Pay Equality Directive; in particular, there was no system of compulsory job evaluation, a central mechanism in assessing and redressing pay differentials in equivalent jobs. The Thatcher government had no choice but to adopt the amendment. As more detailed accounts of the European Court of Justice document shows (for example, Gregory 1992; and McCrudden 1991), the EOC brought several critical cases through the courts that put pressure on the government as well; some of them were aimed for appeal to the ECJ.

In the first years of the EOC, the commission was a reluctant actor, not taking full advantage of its powers and avoiding any direct contact with feminist groups. Throughout the 1980s, the EOC developed a much more activist strategy. The Commission capitalized on its existing resources and authority and secured additional funds from the Thatcher government. It also reached out to supportive feminist groups and trade unions to use existing laws to improve women's employment status (Lovenduski and Randall 1993; Lovenduski 1995). At the centre of the emerging partnership was the EOC strategy of using judicial review, through the European Court of Justice, to effect important policy shifts in limited legislation. From this perspective, women were present through the equality network in the pre-formulation stages of the 1983 amendment; hence, the policy profile of the amendment was at least in part feminist.

In contrast, the policy profile in terms of substantive representation on formulation appears to be a feminist failure; however, even this evaluation is nuanced. The content of the 1983 amendment was highly constrained and, as some analysts maintain, actually counterproductive, particularly in the context of the complex procedures for filing claims and the absence of any mandated collective action for job evaluation schemes. Forbes (1989: 31), for example, stated after the amendment's adoption, 'it is now even harder for women to claim equal pay'. In the same vein, Gregory (1992: 58) asserts, 'These procedural difficulties have had a stultifying effect on the development of pay equity campaigns in Britain'.

The analyses do not make clear the degree to which the Thatcher government heeded EOC recommendations. For instance, Gregory (1992: 49) implies that EOC proposals were ignored, calling the amendment 'an exercise in damage limitation, designed to concede as little as possible'. In the same article, she describes how the EOC was able to persuade the government to widen the scope of the final regulations (1992: 55). It appears that the EOC may have introduced last-minute changes despite the appearance of powerful government opposition. The House of Lords' adoption of what was essentially a protest amendment clearly indicates the laws inherent shortcomings (Gregory 1992: 50–1).

The implementation of the 1983 amendment displayed a feminist policy profile in both substantive and descriptive representation. Through the active participation of the feminist equal employment policy community led by the feminist EOC, the amendment generated outputs and significant feedback, including nearly 4,000 equal value cases for 1984–9, which actually involved 374 employers (Kahn 1992: 7), and a second reform in the 1986 Sex Discrimination Act designed to reduce the remaining gaps in equal value. Kahn (1992: 7) states that the activities of the equal employment policy community contributed to a shift in attitudes about equal pay.

> The significance of the British law is not only that it provides possible remedy in individual cases of pay discrimination, but also that it has contributed to a broad social consensus that not paying women equally for work of equal value is a form of discrimination.

Moreover, in contrast to the Swedish case, the Trade Unions Congress (TUC), major trade union confederation, played an important role in pursuing equal value cases and working with the EOC in individual cases as well as through collective bargaining. If successful, the strategy could overcome the absence of recourse to formal collective action on equal value. This action was pursued in conjunction with the creation of a Women's Rights Department in the union that also established an Equal Value Working Group (Kahn 1992; Gregory 1992). The TUC response is an indication that societal feedback on the 1983 amendment included organized labour.

The relatively feminist policy profile in implementation must be tempered, however, by the absence of any successful connections between equal employment and expanding opportunities policies. While the TUC put maternity and parental leave and childcare on its 'bargaining agenda' (Kahn 1992: 10), and the EOC's 1988 policy document, *From Policy Practice: An Equal Opportunities Strategy for the 1990s*, listed indirect barriers to women's equal employment as an important target, the equality policy community appeared to focus most of its energies on job-market specific solutions. The outcome was that 'the relationship between work and family has been little affected by EOC action' (Lovenduski 1995: 127).

❖ 4. Positive Action in the 1983 Égalité Professionnelle Act in France: The Promise of State Feminist Policy Fails to Translate into Feminist Success (Pre/Form.: 2/2 Post-form.: 1/1 = 6)

The[16] 1983 *égalité professionnelle* law was primarily focused on getting social partners—the state, organized labour, and management—to develop firm-level positive action programmes. The programmes required management and organized labour to present annual reports comparing men's and women's status and then to design training and promotion programmes to close the gaps. The law provided that government funds would be available to subsidize up to 50 per cent of each equality contract. Other provisions in the law addressed some important legal loopholes in the 1972 and 1975 discrimination laws. The central concern of the law, however, was establishing the firm-level positive action measures: what was henceforth referred to as *égalité professionnelle*. A culmination of nearly 20 years of feminist discussions, the pre-formulation and formulation of the 1983 law was the site of a certain level of women's descriptive representation. The content of the law, however, did not transform the demands of the small state-based feminist policy community for effective *égalité professionnelle* into government policy.

The notion of a firm-based positive action approach was first forwarded in the arena of low-level government agencies on women's labour in the Labour Ministry in the mid-1960s and the early 1970s. The femocrats who staffed the Women's Labour Committee invited representatives from trade unions and women's groups and feminist policy experts to regular meetings to assess and discuss the causes of and the solutions for women's inferior status in paid labour. A feminist policy network centred on equal employment emerged around the meetings of the committee from 1965 to 1983.

It was in the state feminist forum that the notion of *égalité professionnelle* was brought to the public agenda in the mid-1970s. Feminists in the Socialist Party advanced similar firm-level positive action strategies in internal party discussions at the same time. At the end of the 1970s, the Socialist Party, two major trade union confederations of the left, the Women's Labour Committee, and the Deputy Ministry of Women's Employment coalesced around the demand for *égalité professionnelle* legislation. The agreement took place in the context of a government report on sex-based discrimination and individual conferences on women's employment held simultaneously by the Socialist Party and each left-wing trade union. In the context of the electoral threat from the left in 1980, the centre-right Deputy Ministry of Women's Employment was allowed to draft a bill in 1980. The victory of the Socialists and the Communists in the 1981 elections stopped the bill from being considered by Parliament.

A very similar bill was elaborated by Socialist Minister of Woman's Rights, Yvette Roudy, as the major piece of legislation for her ministry. Roudy was one of the major feminist advocates of *égalité professionnelle* within the Socialist Party. Backed by the Socialist President, François Mitterrand, who had supported her rise in the party and made women's equality an important part of his election platform, Roudy presented a draft bill to the Cabinet in 1982. The promise of the feminist consensus and the support of the President were stymied by the realities of mainstream employment policy-making, in some ways quite similar to the politics of the universal model in Sweden. That is, organized labour, business, and non-feminist elements of the bureaucracy and the Socialist government together blocked the feminist demands for a law with real teeth. The feminist provisions that were removed included quotas for women in job training programmes, legal requirements for employer participation in new equality programmes, the creation of an autonomous equality authority with enforcement power, and the extension of prosecution rights to women's groups.

The final law created a national-level council, Conseil Supérieur d'Égalité Professionnelle (CSEP), composed of representatives from the state—the Ministries of Labour, Justice and Employment—labour—all five major confederations—management—the two major employer associations—agriculture, women's groups, and individual experts. The CSEP was charged with evaluating equal employment policy, but not to enforcing it. Only the Ministry in which the Council was housed, up until 1993 a ministerial-level office of women's affairs, was given the authority to convene the Council. A small administrative office, also under the authority of a ministry, was set up to coordinate the work of the CSEP and to oversee new *égalité professionnelle* programmes. In 1985, at the height of government support for *égalité professionnelle*, the Mission Pour l'Égalité Professionnelle (MEP) was staffed by eight full-time employees.

As of 2000, the implementation of the 1983 *égalité professionnelle* law failed to leave a significant institutional trail in state and society. State feminist offices have been the most active promoters of implementation with one of the left-wing trade unions—the CFDT—taking an active role in several of the 30 completed equality plans. Four thousand women were affected by these plans. One women's group, Retravailler, participated in the programmes. Half of the government funds originally set aside for these plans have been used. In 1985, the MEP announced that 3,000 firms had presented annual reports. Studies of the reports showed them to be incomplete and poorly updated. The evaluations concluded that, without broad-based support, incentives or penalties, management and union representatives had not been devoting the necessary time to analyse the position of women in the firm.

After 1993, the right-wing government abandoned promoting the employment of women. As femocrats in the women's policy agency in 1999 reiterate, without a gendered policy on women's equality, gender-neutral measures will be diluted by the sex-based biases inherent to the employment policy-making arena. These biases define women's work as marginal in light of their family duties (*sic*). Thus, the relatively high level of women's descriptive representation in the formulation of the 1983 law did not translate into a feminist profile in the post-formulation phases. The collaborative and cross-feminist style of the coalition around the formulation of the 1983 law was replaced by a bureaucratic state-feminist style. Only the femocrats formally in charge of *égalité professionnelle* take any significant interest in a policy in which, one democrat plainly stated, 'no one really believes'. For most French feminist activists, *égalité professionnelle* became a synonym for the limits of French state feminism.

❖ COMPARATIVE DISCUSSION: A STRATEGIC PARTNERSHIP WITH LABOUR, AUTHORITATIVE EQUALITY AGENCIES AND EUROPEAN UNION EQUALITY POLICY

The experiences with four different types of national equal employment legislation suggest some interesting tentative lessons about making feminist policies in this sub-sector. In both Sweden and Great Britain, questionably feminist policies in formulation—in women's substantive, but not necessarily in descriptive, representation—became feminist in post-formulation. In France, what seemed to be an emerging feminist policy profile in pre-formulation was stymied in formulation. The feminist forces interested in effective positive action were not able to reverse the trend in post-formulation. In Ireland, the 1977 act had a feminist profile in both substantive and descriptive representation throughout the unfolding of the policy process in the narrow context of equal treatment. Resistance to reform and to addressing the weakness in later reform indicated the limits of the feminist consensus around anti-discrimination laws in the late 1970s. In all four instances, a long-term view on the policy process from pre-formulation to evaluation revealed important changes in the policy profiles.

Equality agencies were key players in all countries. In France, Ireland, and Sweden the legislation established agencies that oversaw the implementation and enforcement of the policies. The ability of the agencies to make policies work depended in part on their formal legal remit. In Great Britain, Ireland, and Sweden the laws afforded the agencies relatively far-reaching powers; in France the CSEP was limited to an advisory council. In the three countries where the agencies had some formal influence they were able to expand their powers to new areas, generate new feminist policy initiatives, and, perhaps most important, work together with trade unions and women's groups to move equal

Table 5.2 Policy profile scores for cases of equal employment policy

	Pre/Form.		Post-form.	Total
	D	S	D	S
Ireland: 1977 Equal Employment Act	3	2	3	1	9
Sweden: 1979 Equality Act	1	2	3	2	8
Great Britain: 1983 Equal Value Amendment	2	1	3	2	8
France: 1983 *Égalité Professionnelle* Act	2	2	1	1	6

employment policy forward and to develop cultural norms about employment equality.

The ability to expand powers was achieved through partnerships between women's autonomous organizations, women's employment equality agencies, and organized labour. Indeed, the absence of a strong feminist policy profile in the formulation stages of Swedish policy was a result of labour's opposition. Later, with the weakening of corporatism and declining unionization, organized labour was more supportive of equal employment policy in Sweden. Although the TUC in Great Britain was originally more supportive of equal value than the LO in Sweden, this came at a time when British trade unionism was in decline; an appeal to women was seen as a way of reversing the downward trend. In France, the fragmented labour unions in general do not have the same power over policy as in Sweden or Great Britain. Feminist influence within the French unions played an important role in softening the unions to symbolic equal employment policy, particularly at the end of the 1970s when the feminist infiltration of the trade unions was at a high point. However, the trade unions did not embrace equality policy as a means to strengthen their position as the TUC had done in the UK. The absence of trade union opposition in Ireland most likely came from the narrowness of the 1977 act.

The later successes of Swedish policy suggest that feminist success in this sub-sector of policy can be achieved without the participation of autonomous feminist groups. In the other three cases, women's groups appeared to be important. In France, the absence of feminist group action made this a less compelling area for reluctant decision-makers in the government and organized labour. In Great Britain, equal value became a successful policy because of the support of the autonomous women's groups once they overcame their earlier suspicions of the EOC in the early 1980s. In Ireland, liberal feminist organizations provided some of the proposals for the 1977 act.

Other factors appeared to play a role in making equal employment policies more feminist in tandem with the presence of a labour-influenced 'triangle of empowerment'. To be sure, in Ireland and Great Britain the EC directives compelled otherwise reluctant governments to make a formal response. There was nothing in the directives, however, to force governments to go beyond paper policies. In France, there was far less interplay between the formulation and the implementation of the 1983 law and EC directives than in the other three countries. In Ireland, where national policy matched the directives the most closely, the rise of women's issues and feminist influence from within the parties were also a significant influence in the Liberal government's decision to back feminist proposals on the 1977 act. Moreover, the feminist legislation did not go beyond what the powerful non-feminist players were willing to allow.

EU equality policy itself also has its limits. A host of feminist critiques have shown from a variety of analytical perspectives that sex equality policy—

directives, infringement proceedings, recommendations, and European Court of Justice jurisprudence—tends to emphasize a liberal, anti-discrimination approach over an expanding-opportunities approach to equality through collective bargaining (for example, Elman 1996*b*; Nielsen 1995; Hervey and Shaw 1998; Luckhaus and Ward 1997; Borchorst 1994*b*; Ostner and Lewis 1995; Egan 1998). Hervey and Shaw (1998: 62), for example, conclude in their analysis of ECJ decisions, 'as long as the Court of Justice remains unwilling to make use of the interpretive space which it has carved out for itself, EC sex equality law will remain strictly limited in its utility'. Not only does the emerging EU equality policy model clash with the national institutions and modes of policy formation on sex equality, but it also limits the areas of national-level equality policy in which the EU equality process can be pursued as a strategy to make government policies more feminist.

Contrary to the conclusions of much comparative work on feminist policy formation, feminist polices were not necessarily the result of left-wing governments. In fact, three out of the four pieces of legislation were adopted by liberal or conservative governments. Interestingly, the legislation with arguably the least feminist success in France was formulated in the most left-wing environment. Like the analyses in the two preceding chapters, these four cases point to the importance of the presence of the feminist strategic partnership. The comparative question raised here is why these partnerships emerged in Great Britain, Ireland, and Sweden, but not in France. Success may have been a result of broader cultural factors that underpinned decisions to grant authority to the equality agencies, the development of an active feminist stance on equal employment policy from organized labour, and the emergence of equality-friendly women's groups. Still, the comparative puzzle here is that an equal-employment coalition emerged in three countries with quite different cultural contexts. In the case of the third area of feminist policy, culture may not be that important in making effective policy.

❖ NOTES

1 For the most part, feminist analyses of equal employment issues since the 1980s make the argument that effective policy must go beyond individual equal treatment (for example, Lewis 1983*a*; Buckley and Anderson 1988*a*; Chamberlayne 1993; Forbes 1989; 1991; 1996; 1997; Gardiner 1997*a*; Heatlinger 1993; Lovenduski 1986*a*; Jenson 1988; E. Mahon 1998*a*; Meehan and Sevenhijsen 1991*a*; Ruggie 1987; Siim 1993; Steinberg-Ratner 1980*a*; Borchorst and Siim 1987).

2 Direct discrimination consists of employment decisions that intentionally treat women unfairly because of their sex. Indirect discrimination entails employment decisions that are not intended to discriminate but have 'a disparate impact' on women as a group, often because of their maternal and family duties; for example, holding job-training programmes at times when working mothers need to take care of children.

3 For discussions of different feminist approaches to notions of equality see Meehan and Sevenhuijsen (1991a) and Squires (1999a: Ch. 4).

4 For discussions of how gender politics differs from other areas of identity politics and of policies that intersect race/ethnicity, class, and gender, see, for instance, Hoskyns (1996), Williams (1989), Raissiguier (2001), and Hobson (2000a). The word 'sex' is not used to modify equal employment policy because it is a sub-sector of feminist policy, which, by definition, treats sex-based issues. Outside of the context of feminist policy, however, this area of policy should be referred to as 'sex-based equal employment policy'.

5 There are 116 separate studies on equal employment policy listed in Appendix B. The next largest number of studies listed for a single policy sub-sector is 80 for reconciliation policy.

6 There is no uniform language to classify equal-employment policies. Several authors differentiate between 'two models of law on equal opportunity' in Europe, negative and positive (Lovenduski 1986a: 251 and Randall 1987: 313). These European-based categories coincide with the first two groupings in Steinberg-Ratner's (1980b: 42–2) three-way classification scheme for equal employment opportunity policy in post industrial democracies: 'discrimination', 'affirmative action', and 'expanding opportunities'.

7 In most countries, protectionist policies have generated a great deal of feminist debate. The original assumption of protectionist policies when they were first put on the books in the nineteenth century was that women workers were mothers and the weaker 'second sex'. For some feminists, restricting women's work conditions to protect them can be a good thing. Other feminists are virulently opposed to any restrictions on women's work hours and conditions. Governments that remove policies that protect women workers as a category do not always do so for feminist reasons. In France, for example, the right-wing government in 1987 under Jacques Chirac lifted the ban on women working at night for some categories of workers for mostly market reasons. For a discussion of protectionist policy in France, see Mazur and Reuter (forthcoming); Lanquetin, Laufer, and Letablier (2000); for protection policy issues in Great Britain, see Jarman (1991).

8 Comparative feminist researchers have only recently turned to analysing training policies. For more on feminist training policy issues, see Rees (1998); Good (1998); Mazur (2001a).

9 For more on comparable worth/equal value policies see Kahn and Meehan (1992) on Great Britain and the USA ; McCann (1994) on the USA ; O'Connor (1999) on Great Britain, the USA, Australia, and Canada; and Wilborn (1991) on Australia, Canada, Sweden, Great Britain, and the USA.

10 For more on how EU equality policy interfaces with national policy see for example Meehan (1992; 1994); Hoskyns (1996); Vallance and Davies (1986); Gardiner (1999); Egan (1998);and Meehan and Collins (1996). For nation-based analyses in a legal perspective see the encyclopaedia series published by Martinus Nijhoff; for example, Nielsen (1995) on Denmark; Bertelsmann and Rust (1995) on Germany; Asscher-Vonk (1995) on the Netherlands; McCrudden (1994) on the UK; and Callender and Meenan (1995) on Ireland.

11 Lovenduski (1994; 1995) and Outshoorn (1986b) both emphasize 'the rules of the game'—for example, organizational rules and constitutional design—in feminist policy successes.

12 Borchorst (1995) introduces the notion of 'political niche' to explain the limited arena of action for Denmark's Equal Status Council, which has not been able to go beyond employment equality issues to indirect causes of sex- based employment inequities. Denmark's political niche is much broader in scope than Ireland's.

13 It is interesting to note that, despite the feminist content of the act, the language used to describe discrimination would be considered sexist by many analysts today: 'where by reason of his sex a person is treated less favourably than another person of the same sex' (Art. 2.a in Callender and Meenan 1995: 113).

14 For more about the weaknesses of autonomous feminism in Sweden in the 1970s see Dahlerup and Gulli (1985); Elman (1996a); Bergman (1999).

15 Kahn (1992) introduces the two models from Cockburn's (1989) more general assessment of two different types of equal employment opportunity policies: radical and liberal.

16 This analysis comes out of my research on the formation of French equal-employment legislation published in Mazur (1995a, b).

6 ❖ Reconciliation Policy

❖ OVERVIEW

The fourth sub-sector of feminist policy covers policies that aim to reconcile women's and men's work and family responsibilities. The concept of reconciling employment with family life is not always used for feminist purposes. As one feminist analyst asserts:

> In the sixties and seventies it [the concept of reconciliation] was understood as reconciling women's roles in paid and unpaid work to promote equality. Today, it tends to be associated with work force strategies used by individual firms to promote part-time or flexible work rather than with any larger goal of equality between men and women. (Tobío 2001: 63 n.3).

Other feminist policy analysts use the term to describe feminist work and family policies that promote 'a more equal sharing of paid and unpaid work' (Hantrais 2000a: 1). Hantrais argues that there has been an important shift, at least in European Union member countries, from 'measures designed to bring women into line with men as workers' to 'gender policy aimed at tackling socially constructed inequalities at work and in the home': what she calls 'reconciliation policy' (2000a: 2). Given the emphasis on gender in Hantrais' conceptualization of policies in this area, this study opts for the label 'reconciliation'.

Government action that explicitly addresses the relationship between work and family to improve women's situation is arguably at the heart of feminist thinking, mobilization, and scholarship. From an activist perspective, liberal, socialist, and social feminists have focused, to varying degrees in different countries, on the need to help women alleviate the double burden of work and home to promote women's equality in paid labour. Some radical feminists associated with the new women's movements, have called for the elimination of the traditional family and the patriarchal institutions that keep women down as well.[1]

Feminist analysts construct studies that show the direct connection between dominant notions about women's alleged natural role as mother and family caretakers, the duties that come from these expectations, and women's inferior positions not just in paid labour but in all spheres of society. As one feminist scholar articulates, 'The persistent economic inequality and dependency of women can be directly attributable to gender differences in family responsibilities' (Stetson 1997b: 257). Some feminist economic theorists show that women's family caring duties can prevent them from competing in the labour market. Others maintain that women's marginal position in the labour force makes staying at home a more attractive option.

The issue of the division of labour between work and home, as a recent and growing literature on gender and the welfare state illuminates, also directly bears upon the development of the welfare state and social policy, so central to the social and economic orders of post-industrial democracies. The feminist scholarship documents how the contemporary welfare state was developed on the assumption that the family is the major caring unit for society. The assumption dictates that men earn the main wage and women bear and raise children as well as care for sick family members and the elderly. Non-feminist social policy provisions, ranging from health care to social security and family benefits, therefore, are based on the 'male breadwinner-female caretaker' model, with important cross-national differences.[2]

The model continued to drive the expanding market economies of most post-industrial economies when women became a cheap source of flexible and home-grown labour that would, according to the conventional wisdom, return to their permanent maternal duties once economic growth had run its course. Labour-force statistics do not necessarily contradict the pattern outside the Nordic countries. Women's labour-force participation continues to be in part-time work and/ or in feminized occupations with much lower salaries than male-dominated occupations. Women's overall labour-force participation has increased significantly. Drew and Emerek (1998: 90) and others assert that women's ever-increasing entrance into paid labour in EU member states indicates the 'emergence of a dual breadwinner model whereby both men and women take responsibility in supporting the family'. Feminist analyses that focus on social-welfare policy packages disagree about the prevalence of the dual bread-winner model. In any case, feminist policies that aim to improve women's status through reconciling employment and family responsibilities must take on the structural importance of established gender roles and the gendered development of the contemporary welfare state.

Given the multiplicity of feminist thought and action, there is obviously no single feminist way to tackle such pervasive and structural impediments. 'Economic independence' may be the common ground on which divergent feminist views on reconciliation policy come together: that is, the notion that women as well as men should be able to 'reach a situation in which every adult can build an independent livelihood regardless of gender, marital status or living arrangement'.[3] Of course, the notion of an 'independent livelihood' is open to feminist debate.

There are three feminist approaches to achieving women's economic independence in reconciling work and family obligations for both men and women. All three can exist side by side in a specific country or in the same set of policy reforms.[4] Reconciliation policy that takes a 'traditional sex roles' stance assumes that women should stay in the home and take care of the family. The major aim of policy is to help women to be economically independent of the husband's salary. Examples of these policies include social security benefits for stay-at-home mothers and housewives' salaries. While liberal feminists do not support traditional sex-role policies, social feminists do.

In the second approach, the traditional model is slightly shifted, but established gender roles are not completely challenged. The assumption is that women are more or less compelled, because of dominant divisions of labour between work and home, to take on the primary parenting role. The family responsibility, however, should not keep women from entering the labour market and other public spheres on the same footing as men. From this perspective, government policies are supposed to protect women from being penalized for being mothers. The third approach is the most radical in terms of 'gender role change' (Gelb and Palley 1987). Public policy aims to redefine traditional gender roles so that men and women share family caretaking. Government action promotes shared parenting through helping both parents or extending incentives to men to accept more responsibility in parenting.

The operational definition of reconciliation policy has the potential to incorporate all three of these stances: any policy that seeks to promote women's economic independence within the purview of the predominant division of labour between work and family. The policy may work within the established gender division or seek to change it. What is key here is that the actors who define the policy are conscious of the negative aspects of the dominant family model. Reconciliation policy, therefore, seeks ultimately to improve women's situation by dealing explicitly with the full complexity and political ramifications of their roles, both socially constructed and concrete, as mothers, wives, workers, and citizens.

While there are certainly grey areas of overlap between reconciliation policy and other sub-sectors of feminist policy, there are distinct parameters. Equal employment policies do not have women's economic independence in work and family as a primary goal. They focus on other impediments than the work-family relationship. Family law policies, covered in Chapter 7, explicitly target the legal rights of mothers, fathers, wives, and husbands in the family. Whereas some family law policies may take into consideration the way in which family roles relate to paid and unpaid work, mediating between the two spheres is not their major aim. Public service-delivery policies focus on the provision of services for women and are not necessarily articulated on the backdrop of dominant work and family patterns.

Reconciliation policy also potentially overlaps with policies that do not take an explicitly feminist frame. This book differentiates between reconciliation and non-feminist family policy.[5] Although some policy experts refuse to define such a vast policy area (for example, Gauthier 1996), Kammerman and Kahn (1978) define family policy as 'what the state does by action or inaction to affect people in their roles as family members or to influence the future of the family as an institution' (cited in Lewis 1983*b*: 13). Family policy, therefore, is not involved with the direct pursuit of women's economic independence. In fact, feminist critics assert that much family policy takes a pro-natalist view that women should stay in the home and have children (Hobson and Berggren 1997; Lewis 1983; Heitlinger 1993).

Reconciliation policy is also not the same as social policy. Like family policy, social policy is difficult to define as a discrete area of policy. Jones (1985: 14) asserts that it is impossible to pinpoint a single definition of social policy because of the different meanings of 'social' in different cultural contexts. 'Social policy . . . is a blanket expression . . . blanket in that it can also stand for different sorts of "social" objectives and motivations.' Family policy is often counted as a social policy. Whatever social policy is or is not, it does not have an inherently feminist intent; a case made thoroughly on both theoretical and empirical grounds by feminist gender and welfare state literature.

Insofar as the gender and welfare state literature points out that social policies are not feminist, it does not assess comprehensively social policies that actually are feminist. Heitlinger (1993) implies that protective legislation, maternity and pre-natal leaves, 'childcare politics and programmes' and 'fiscal support for parent and children' have feminist goals. Gornick, Meyers, and Ross (1997: 45) focus on 'provisions that support mothers employment parental leave; child care and scheduling of public education'. Windebank (1996:147) examines 'ways in which welfare regimes may have helped challenge the dominant ideology of mothering' through 'fostering a distribution of childcare which assists mothers in their employment and which gives child care providers social and economic status'. Other feminist analysts of the welfare state identify new areas for future government action that do not involve existing policies: for example, lone-mothers policy (Lewis 1997; Hobson 1994); women's poverty policy (Scheiwe 1994*b*); school scheduling (Gornick, Meyers, and Ross 1997); and status of child care providers (Windebank 1996).

Given the potential for overlap with other policy areas, policies must clearly aim for women's economic independence within the frame of work and family issues to be considered a part of the reconciliation sub-sector. For example, childcare policies that primarily promote children's welfare do not fall into the reconciliation sub-sector. As Franzway, Court, and Connell (1989: 5) posit from a more radical feminist perspective:

The feminist demand for childcare seeks the liberation of women. And liberation requires the transformation of women's status as wives and mothers, since it is this status that embodies women's dependence.

Women's economic independence can be included in sex-neutral concepts of equality as long as policy actors state publicly that women are the targets of policy. Some sex-neutral notions are used to exclude women; others are intended to help women. In this light, the issue of whether universal notions of equality in public policy are feminist or not becomes a question for empirical research to investigate in individual policy efforts. This chapter explores whether sex-neutral notions of equality are feminist in the case of childcare policy in Denmark.

Table 6.1 presents the range of reconciliation policies found in post-industrial democracies. They include social security—pensions, health benefits, and family allowances; childcare; parental/family leave; taxation reform; and lone-mothers policies. The Table does not intend to show either the timing of policy development or general national policy approaches.

Social security has been an important object of feminist government action. Feminist reforms of social security are quite difficult to identify because of the highly complex nature of social security reform more generally. The 1979 and 1986 Directives on Social Security set European Union standards for equal treatment of men and women in general social security schemes. The reforms listed in the Table for Great Britain and the Netherlands represent national efforts to bring policies into line with the EU directives. The Irish pension reforms for home-makers and 'survivors' sought to equalize pensions for widows and widowers as well as to establish pensions for full-time homemakers (Hoskyns 1996: 218). They

Table 6.1 Range of reconciliation policy in core countries

Country	Policy
Italy	1989 Law in the Emilia-Romagna region on lone mothers
Ireland	1994 Pensions for homemakers
Spain	1989 Parental leave introduced and maternity leave extended/tax reform
Denmark	1993 Childcare guarantee for municipalities announced by Prime Minister
Sweden	1976 Act on reform of childcare system
Norway	1970s Work Environment Act: paid maternity and unpaid paternity leave
France	1970s Reforms in natalist family allowances
Germany	1986 Federal Childcare Benefit Act
Netherlands	Reforms in social security provisions to comply with EC Directives
United States	1993 Family and Medical Leave Act
Great Britain	Reforms in social security provisions to comply with EC Directives
Canada	1987 National Strategy on Child Care
Australia	1972 Childcare Act

are an example of policy that reinforces women's economic rights in relation to men's within the male bread-winner model and with sex-neutral language. While often used for pro-natalist ends, family allowances, if paid directly to the women, can be a source of economic independence to stay-at-home mothers. France has some of the most developed family allowances. In the 1970s the centre-right government made a series of reforms that aimed to redefine these allowances as a way to support mothers, working or not (Hantrais 1993*b*: 125).

Another important instrument of reconciliation policy is the provision of government-mandated leave for working parents, often called 'family leave'. As Table 6.1 shows, parental leave may be combined with reforms in pensions, as in the case of Spain and Germany. In most post-industrial countries, outside of the USA, there is at least a minimum guarantee of job security for parental leaves, if not of full pay. Mandated leave can also cover absences for care of sick family members, including elderly parents. Some European feminists argue that when mandated leave is given only to mothers it can contribute to marginalizing women in the labour force. In the US context, where nationally mandated paid family leave is impossible, feminists counter that some form of mandated leave is better than none.

The most feminist-oriented leave has been made available to both parents, single or married, has been paid, and is available for a variety of caring situations. In some countries, policies were developed to provide incentives for men to take advantage of family leave opportunities; 'daddy leave' or 'daddy quotas' (for example, Leira 1992). A European Union Council recommendation (cited in Randall 1996: 191) that 'promote[s] and encourage[s] increased participation of men' in family responsibilities provides a EU framework for this more recent reconciliation policy.

Childcare reform is a major feminist demand. Not all childcare policies have a feminist intent. The reforms listed in Table 6.1 are clearly feminist, except the policy listed for Canada. The 1987 National Strategy on Childcare was elaborated by a Conservative government within a questionably feminist frame (Hetlinger 1993: 236). It was not adopted by Parliament due to the outcome of parliamentary elections (Hetlinger 1993: 236). Childcare reforms can begin with chief executive commitments that lead to legislation or administrative regulations. This is the case of the Childcare Guarantee for Municipalities announced by the Prime Minister in Denmark (Borchorst 1999*a*: 8). In addition to services, governments provide direct transfer payments to families for childcare—'cash for care' (Borchorst 1999*a*: 5)—or give tax deductions for childcare. Subsidies for childcare are often included in social security reform or taxation policy. Lone-mothers policy has only been recently placed on government agendas. Very few countries make policy specifically to deal with single mothers. The Italian regional law in Table 6.1 defines for the first time mothers as 'rights-bearing individuals' instead of social problems (Bimbi 1997: 194). Often, solo mothers policy can be attached to women's poverty issues, particularly in the US where the welfare state has not gone as far as others in making universal social provisions.

There are two problems in studying the formation of reconciliation policies. The first stems from the nature of reconciliation policy. Policy is often embedded in highly intricate welfare reform. Specific policy tends to be difficult to identify and seldom consists of discrete decisions through which the different stages of the policy process can be traced. Reforms occur often through executive-based decision-making behind closed doors, distinguished by a low-profile administrative policy style. The 'low agenda status' (Baumgartner 1996: 87) and transversal nature of reconciliation policy make it difficult to study policy development.

A second problem is the focus of published work on reconciliation policy.[6] While some literature does focus on the policy process—for example, Meyer (1998); Borchorst (1999a); Ungerson (1997); R. Mahon (1997); Randall (1996); Hetlinger (1993)—most feminist literature assesses the social impact of general social policies in a cross-national perspective. Whether studies use cross-national data sets, like the Luxembourg Income Study, or comparative national studies, much of the feminist literature on social policy ignores the politics of feminist policy formation. As a consequence, the extensive feminist policy literature on social policy does not provide systematic and/or detailed analyses of how individual reconciliation policies are developed and implemented.

The selection of cases for analysis for this chapter is more restricted than the previous three sub-sectors in part because of the dearth of feminist policy studies. The four cases presented here still represent a range of reconciliation policies: social security reforms, childcare, and family leave. Given the importance of the childcare issue in Nordic countries and the extent of this issue's coverage, childcare policy formation in Denmark is examined. The continuous nature of childcare policy makes studying an individual policy difficult. The evolution of Danish policy over time, therefore, is scrutinized. Germany provides a particularly interesting context in which to study childcare policies in Christian Democrat countries in the formulation and implementation of the 1985 Federal Child Care Benefit Act. Feminist analysts argue that German policy and attitudes institutionalized the male breadwinner model more than in many other post-industrial countries (for example, Ostner 1993). The traditional model presents German feminist policy with quite pronounced structural obstacles.

Ireland's treatment of social security reform in the 1990s and family-leave policy in the USA present clear cases of non-decision-making.[7] In the USA, there are few federal policy statements on family leave. When national-level policy does exist, it is quite restricted. The 1993 Family and Medical Leave Act displays well the politics of family-leave policy; years of resistance to feminist calls for federal legislation produce a policy that is highly restricted. The poor feminist showing of reconciliation policy in the US also serves as a contrast to the image of feminist movement policy successes oft portrayed in analyses of American feminist politics (for example, Gelb and Palley 1987; Gelb 1989).

❖ THE POLICY CASES

❖ 1. The Evolution of Childcare Policy in Denmark: A Woman-Friendly Society in Action (Pre/Form.: 2/2 Post-form.: 2/2 = 8)

Denmark has arguably the best day-care coverage of any European country (Borchorst 1999a). Even so, parents have to contribute roughly 30 per cent of the costs (Siim 1997: 161). Moreover, day-care provision cannot keep up with demand coming from recent increases in birth rates. The highly developed state-run system, since the early 1980s at the municipal level, was a product of a cross-party consensus defined in universal terms of children's interests and shared parenting and based on a dual bread-winner family model. In general, parental duties in Denmark are seen in non-gendered terms. A 1987 law codified the equal rights of cohabiting partners (Siim 1997: 161).

Since the 1950s, Danish policy pursued a universalist approach to childcare. The first major push for expansion was in the 1960s and 1970s (Borchorst 1999a: 7; Siim 1997: 155; Dahlerup 1987:111). The major political force behind this expansion was the progressive pedagogues who emphasized the importance of play and social interaction in child development. Pedagogical motivations were not the only logic behind the expansion of childcare. The economic boom and the need for women to enter the labour force were also important, as were egalitarian notions of providing equal educational opportunities to all children.

The Social Democratic Party translated the proposals of the progressive pedagogues into policy in the 1960s and 1970s; right-wing governments have not undone the scope of childcare provision. In 1982–3, in the context of neo-liberal government restructuring, the number of children was increased in each childcare unit; thus sacrificing quality but not coverage. The control of childcare was also decentralized. Centralized responsibility for childcare was handed over to the municipalities during this period as well (Borchorst 1999b: 8). Today, there continues to be a broad-based consensus on childcare provisions with concerted efforts to compel municipalities to respond to all childcare needs.

Women have been intimately involved with the formulation and implementation of this highly woman-friendly system. Their involvement, however, was in the context of sex-neutral groups and movements without any explicitly feminist agendas. They were active as progressive pedagogues, philanthropists who first began to provide private childcare before the government took it over in the 1960s, as members in the Social Democrat party, and as a majority of the trained professional childcare providers (Borchorst 1999b: 5). Mothers were active members of self-identified parents' organizations that have played an extremely important role in childcare management. In 1993, municipalities were required to set up parental advisory boards for childcare with budgetary and decision-making powers (Siim 1997: 163). Mothers and fathers share equally the work of the boards. Thus, overall descriptive representation of women has been quite important in childcare policy formation.

Self-identified feminist groups and/or feminists were remarkably absent. In the 1950s, a Social Democrat women's organization became involved with the campaign for childcare facilities. Otherwise, 'women's organizations did not play a major role in the establishment of child care facilities' (Borchorst 1999b: 8). One explanation for the absence of feminist mobilization may be linked to the all-party consensus among non-feminist groups on childcare as a national priority. In this light, feminist demands were met before second-wave feminist movements became active in the 1970s. Unlike women's policy machineries in many other countries, the Equal Status Commission did not make childcare one of its prominent demands for women's employment equality (Borchorst 1995). Thus, the policy subsystem that has emerged around daycare does not include women's groups. Its members consist of the Minister of Family Affairs, municipal governments, parent organizations, and childcare provider organizations Generally, these actors work together in corporatist commissions and parliament.

Ruggie (1984) argues that childcare is less overtly linked to women's employment equality in Denmark than in Sweden . However, one of the original motivations for expanding childcare was to 'increase the participation rates of women in the labour market' (Siim 1997: 155). As the political consensus around childcare developed, gender equality was an increasingly important justification (Borchorst and Siim 1987, cited in Siim 1997: 161). Danish childcare policy, therefore, emerged in a sex-neutral frame in the 1950s in which women were defined as equal partners to men (Borchorst 1999a: 1).

❖ 2. The 1986 Federal Childcare Benefit Act in Germany: The Limits of a Social Feminist Policy (Pre/Form.: 1/3 Post-form.: 1/2 = 7)

The 1986 act was a social feminist policy adopted by a Christian Democratic government.[8] West German feminism tended to focus on how to improve women's condition within the context of women having the flexibility to combine work and home and or opt out entirely from entering the work-force. In fact, feminists were 'reluctant to identify independence with employment' (Ostner 1993: 94). Not only were liberal feminists ' rarely to be seen' in West Germany (Ferree 1987: 177), but an important demand of German feminists was 'pay for housework'. It is important to differentiate social feminist positions from the conservative, arguably anti-feminist positions of certain areas of German policy. For example, social feminists agree that the restrictions on abortion imposed by the German Constitution and Constitutional Court decisions impede women's autonomy. German conservatism and social feminism both emphasize the importance of motherhood.

In pre-formulation and formulation, the 1986 act was feminist in content conferring new rights on both parents (Schiersmann 1991; Kolinsky 1989). Family policy under the law extended family leave to the mother. The law stipulated that men and women could get credit in their pensions for up to one year of family leave and extended mandated leave from work beyond pregnancy leave, a 'child-rearing vacation'. It also reinforced job security during pregnancy and allowed non-working parents to receive 'child-rearing payments' (Kolinksy 1989: 68–71). Analyses of the act do not cover details of pre-formulation or formulation. Kolinksy (1989: 67) does discuss how the social feminist ideas of the 'bourgeois women's movement' served as a foundation for the Christian Democrats' approach to feminist policy. This approach aimed to promote 'a new flexibility into the juxtaposition of home and work and a new flexibility of roles for women and men'.

In addition, the Christian Democratic Union (CDU) was rejuvenating its image in the mid-1980s to capture younger women voters who, in the words of a 1985 party document, 'no longer endorsed conservative notions of women's roles and family commitments and who increasingly felt that opportunities were unequal' (cited in Kolinksy 1993: 132). In 1985, the CDU presented 'an imaginative package of policy blueprints that matched almost identically the social feminist content of the 1986 Act' (Kolinsky 1993: 132).

If there is some evidence to support the substantive representation of women's interests, it is more difficult to discern whether women were involved with formulation. Analyses of the CDU and women's policy issues do not mention the presence of women in the party's decisions to rejuvenate the party and define its new women's programme, whether as individuals or groups (Kolinksy 1993; Lemke 1994). The Christian Democrat government appointed Rita Süssmuth Minister of Health, Family and Youth in 1986. Süssmuth, inspired by 'autonomous feminism', was an important leader in the CDU and was 'former director of an institute promoting gender equality' (Ferree 1995: 99). Ferree (1995: 99) indicates that the CDU appointed her because of its 'concern with women's policy'.

The government allowed Süssmuth to add 'and Women' to the title of the Ministry and to bring in staff members with expertise in women's policy. Although this was after the adoption of the 1986 law and there is no clear indication that Süssmuth's ministry took feminist action on the new law, her portfolio implicated her in implementation of family policy. Still, as Ferree (1995) points out, the German federal government, particularly the Christian Democrats, were not supportive of state feminist women's policy offices. Also, the autonomous women's movements of the 1970s were grass-roots-oriented and suspicious of involvement with the government, particularly at the federal level. Thus, if there was any descriptive representation of women, it was brought about through the CDU by individual feminists like Süssmuth or possibly through an older network of social feminist groups.

The post-formulation phases of this law were even less feminist. On the one hand, the act generated clear outputs. In 1987, the government was responsive to demands for extending the 'baby-year pensions' to older-age groups of women. The benefits were fully honoured and funded with some States offering similar entitlements, although with significant variation. Lower Saxony even adopted feminist policies prior to the 1986 law (Schiersmann 1991). On the other hand, there is little evidence that women were empowered. For example, women's groups did not appear to be concerned with making sure that the original social feminist intent of the laws was implemented.

Even more importantly, it is unclear whether the social feminist intent of the original act was followed. With only 1.3 per cent of men taking advantage of the benefits in 1987, the law did not appear to give women a real choice between work and home. Policies were not designed to give men incentives to take the new leave either. Indeed, the failure of the social feminist content to translate into the post-formulation phases of the 1986 act may have been the result of the way German social policy more generally reinforces the traditional male bread-winner model (Hantrais 1993a). Without any strong state-based or society-based feminist influence, social feminist reconciliation policies like the 1986 act may very well have limited feminist results unless the model changes.

❖ 3. The 1993 Family and Medical Leave Act in the USA: Breaking Non-Decision-making with Questionably Feminist Reform (Pre/Form.: 1/1 Post-form.: 1/1 = 4)

When compared with other countries, the USA has the most limited national policy on family leave. In 1995, all 15 European Union member countries had some form of paid maternity leave. Six guaranteed full pay for women taking maternity leave. Parental leave in all EU states is broadly defined. Leaves are made available to men as well as women and include mandated leave for family needs outside childbirth. Jobs are guaranteed for parental leave for periods of between three years in France and Germany to three and a half months in Greece. Paid leave is provided for men in five of the EU countries.[9] All of the arrangements are required by national-level policy; a good portion of the financial costs are covered by the government.

Family-leave policies in the USA are piecemeal at best. Trade unions in the USA pursued some benefits packages for parental leave in specific industries (Conway, Ahern, and Steuernagel 1999: 162); five States adopted maternity leave laws in the 1980s (Stetson 1997b: 269); and a handful of corporations have quite feminist family-leave policies. There was no federal national policy on family leave until the 1993 Family and Medical Leave Act (FMLA). Up until 1993, the 1978 Pregnancy Discrimination Act (PDA) required employers to give women pregnancy leave if they requested it as a physical disability (Conway, Ahern, and Steuernagel 1997; Stetson 1997*b*).

The 1993 FMLA was a clear improvement, but still did not require businesses with more than 50 employees to provide paid leave. Government offices were also given the same requirement. The act did not provide state funds to support the newly mandated leaves, up to twelve weeks, for both men and women either. The act did mandate that the leave could be taken for bearing or adopting children, for caring for a family member, or for a worker's own serious illness. Thus, leave was unpaid, restricted to firms with over 50 employees, and limited to three months, less than the minimum offered in European Union countries

Unlike the Pregnancy Discrimination Act, seen by many observers as a feminist movement success (for example, Gelb and Palley 1987), the FMLA was not a direct product of American-style feminist lobbying techniques. Feminists did work with Congress in the 1980s to develop a gender-neutral leave act. The act was supposed to redefine pregnancy from a disability to 'a medical condition', protect employees' rights to take leave, and extend leave to men. The focus of the bill presented to Congress in 1985 was general 'labour rights' rather than 'women's rights' (Stetson 1997*b*: 270–1). As a consequence, the debates around the bill centred on the government's role in assuring the extension of worker rights, as parents, family members, and sick workers. Republican and Democratic members of Congress supported the law for different reasons, none of which was feminist. For Republicans, the bill was a pro-family measure and for Democrats it was a pro-labour measure. The bipartisan consensus produced a far less feminist bill than the version originally proposed by the feminists, a bill on which both houses of Congress could agree in the context of two presidential vetoes.

It was not until Democrat Bill Clinton was elected to the presidency in 1992 that the act was finally adopted. President Bush's veto of the family-leave bill became a campaign issue. While Clinton promised to sign the bill as one of his first acts, Bush proposed an alternative: a tax credit for parents who take leave. After Clinton won the election, Congress passed quickly the FMLA and the Democratic President signed it into law in 1993. Clinton's support of the law appeared to be more a result of his election promises and his efforts to court the women's vote than of any direct pressure from feminists. To be sure, the content of the bill corresponded to liberal feminist demands; it is questionable whether supporters or opponents of the law in Congress and the White House saw the bill as a feminist policy.

The degree to which women's interests were represented descriptively was also unclear. Throughout the process, pressure from women's groups appeared to take a back seat to the partisan politics of President-Congress relations. Indeed, the 1980s marked a low point for feminist activism following the defeat of the Equal Rights Amendment (ERA) in 1982 and the open hostility of the Reagan administration to feminist issues. As Bashevkin (1998) argues, the anti-feminist backlash was more pronounced and successful in US policy during the 1980s than in Great Britain or Canada. The family-leave issue was particularly divisive for American feminists (Stetson 1997b). 'Equal treatment feminists', with their focus on individual rights, were reticent about supporting a policy that treated women differently from men and 'difference feminists' felt strongly that women should be given special consideration to combine work and home. Feminists who supported an active maternity leave also found themselves in an uncomfortable alliance with supporters of a pro-family and conservative position on family leave.

All of these complexities combined to make it quite difficult to develop a unified feminist coalition on this issue. Organized feminism, therefore, in the 1980s did not supply an important avenue for women to become involved in the policy formation process on family leave, although individual feminists had been involved with drafting the original bill in 1985. The normal avenues of access for women in other countries, like women's policy offices and political parties, are less developed in the USA. The ability of the Women's Bureau to be a major player in feminist policy formation is restricted by its low-level cabinet status and the degree to which its is connected to the President's agenda (Stetson 1995a). Women's Bureau feminists may have wanted to get involved with the FMLA, but they were constrained by President Bush's agenda. The Women's Bureau participated more in defining the terms of the 1978 PDA than in the formulation of FMLA (Stetson 1995a; 1997b). Political parties do not play as important a role in determining the content of public policy in the USA either. Outside of airing major feminist movement issues like abortion and the ERA at national presidential conventions, parties do little else on feminist policy formation (Gelb 1987: 278). Women's groups within the parties have not served as transmission belts for individual women or feminist ideas in the USA as they have in political parties in other countries. Any feminist influence from parties was structurally absent from the politics of the FMLA.

Although the act was automatically implemented when it became law, no governmental agencies were given specific implementation oversight. As with most family policy measures in the USA, implementation remains voluntary until individuals take businesses to court for violating the law. Feminist lobbying and litigation groups and State-level women's policy offices have had the potential to make the Family and Medical Leave Act more feminist around efforts to implement the new regulations. The Commission on Family and Medical Leave issued a report produced by the Women's Bureau for Congress. The report shows that only 4 per cent of those eligible actually take leave

(Commission on Family and Medical Leave 1996: xix). Efforts to implement the law in private firms, therefore, may not have received a great deal of support. What is clear is that there has been no significant institutional trail left by state or society actors in the implementation of the act.

 ❖ *4. The 1995 Reform of Social Welfare Legislation in Ireland:*
   Feminist Demands and Non-Decision-making (Pre/Form.: 2/0
   Post-form.: 2/0 = 4)

In 1995, left-wing Minister of Social Welfare Prionsias de Rossa announced that his Fianna Fáil-Labour coalition government would introduce a stipulation in social security reform to change entitlements for men and women. The reform was intended to address the social security benefits for divorced couples following the legalization of divorce in 1995. As Conroy (1997: 88) argues,

> ... this might have been an opportunity to review the legislation and abolish all the various male-defined categories under which women were or were not entitled to benefits and allowances as dependent wife, widow, deserted wife, and prisoner's wife in addition to unmarried mothers.

The policy process did not unfold in such a feminist manner.

The Irish system was also in violation of provisions of the 1979 EC Social Security directive. In the early 1990s, for example, Irish analysts showed that many social security benefits continued to be mostly paid to men even when women as wives were not financially dependent on men. Several key court decisions reinforced the payment of benefits to men (Sohrab 1994: 274). In general, Irish efforts to implement the EC directive were incremental and piecemeal: 'an ill-prepared attempt to implement the Directive at the least possible cost to the State, followed by a panic-stricken effort to alleviate the worst effects of policy' (Callender 1988: 14, cited in Sohrab 1994: 274).

Feminist calls for individualization of social security entitlements to eliminate indirect discriminations, as well as other feminist reforms in the Irish social security system, have been made by state feminist offices and women's groups since the 1980s. The Second Commission on the Status of Women Report in 1993, the Joint Oreachtas Committee on Women's Rights—a parliamentary committee on women's rights established in 1983—the Ministry of State of Woman's Affairs, and the National Women's Council of Ireland—an umbrella group of 115 organizations—all had made recommendations for feminist social security reform (E. Mahon 1995; Galligan 1998). Up until the legalization of divorce in 1995, the state feminist offices could not support reforms that were related to divorce (Mahon 1995). The divorce reform gave a green light to state feminist agencies to support measures that involved divorced women. Whereas non-feminist political interest in women's issues had been on the wane in the

1980s, the early 1990s was marked by 'a renewed political interest in women' (Galligan 1997: 62), particularly with the arrival of a reform government and a woman president.

The final version of the 1995 Social Welfare Act failed to include any feminist components. It enhanced men's rights to entitlements to the detriment of women's. The resulting situation for divorced couples was called 'social welfare polygamy' where men could declare benefits through their present and former wives. None of the weaknesses of social security for women was addressed by the law. In Parliament, a coalition of the Labour Party and Fianna Fáil supported the non-feminist bill against efforts to introduce feminist amendments by the Commission of the Status of Women, women senators, and opposition parties. The debate went beyond Parliament when a social policy researcher, most likely a feminist, criticised the bill in the *Irish Times* (Conroy 1997: 89). In what Conroy calls an 'unusual step', the Minister of Social Welfare wrote back a response in the same newspaper defending his law; ' . . . it will take time and major restructuring of the social welfare code to adequately address feminist demands for individualisation of entitlements' (cited in Conroy 1997: 89).

Thus, while descriptive representation of women's interests was quite high in both pre-formulation and formulation, the final content of the bill ignored feminist demands for reform. The outcome was a bill that was confusing and enhanced men's rights over women's. In other words, the government decided not to make feminist policy. The Minister's comments on the reform suggest that the non-decision-making may have been a result of the entrenched social security bureaucracy defending the prevailing social security system, a system still mostly based on the highly institutionalized and constitutionally reinforced male bread-winner-female caretaker family model.

❖ COMPARATIVE DISCUSSION: POLICY LOGICS AND CULTURAL ATTITUDES ABOUT GENDER MAY MATTER MORE THAN STRATEGIC PARTNERSHIPS

More than the other three sub-sectors of feminist policy, as Table 6.2 indicates, it seems that the four cases of reconciliation policy have met with mixed feminist results. In Ireland, feminist demands for reforms in entitlements met a response of non-decision-making, even when the political conditions were favourable for such reform. In the USA, a right-wing President hostile to government intervention in the economy resisted bipartisan demands for a policy that was only tangentially feminist. When the centre-left President finally signed the bill into law, it still did not explicitly advance a feminist approach to family leave. The feminist policy profile was slightly better in Germany, with a social feminist policy being elaborated with little significant involvement of either women or feminists. Even this feminist showing was diluted in post-formulation by a larger non-feminist social policy. The policy profile of Danish childcare policy shows the highest level of feminist policy formation within a sex-neutral feminist policy and a relatively high level of women's participation in both formulation and implementation. Given the absence of any explicitly feminist intellectual or organizational purview in policy formation, the highest feminist profile scores were not given to the Danish policy case.

With the exception of Ireland, there seems to be a tendency for governments to make feminist policy with little direct participation by organized feminists and, in the cases of the USA and Germany, without many women. An argument can be made for societal feminism in Denmark, or woman-friendly society as in other Nordic countries. In a woman-friendly society universal notions of social justice are underpinned by feminist assumptions that men and women should be equal partners in parenting and should be able to combine reconciliation duties to assure their well-being. As in other Nordic countries, childcare may not have become a feminist issue because of the high levels of provision and underlying feminist commitment.

In contrast to the similarities in the policy profiles, the styles of the policy communities were quite different. In Ireland, a closed social security sub-system centred on the Social Welfare Ministry elaborated policy and held tight control over the parliamentary process. Feminist and opposition party critics of the reforms were unable to make the government budge from it position, even in the context of a public debate in the national newspaper. The top-down resistance to challenges from Parliament and interest groups is a contrast to the bottom-up way the childcare policy community emerged in Denmark. The open and consensual collaboration between the social pedagogues, childcare providers, municipalities after 1983, and parents contributed to continuing expansion of childcare in the 1970s and its resilience in times of economic crisis. In Germany, it appears that the style of the policy community was more political party-based and that the social feminist agenda of the Christian Democrats created a favourable environment for limited feminist reform.

In Denmark and Germany more than in Ireland, the styles of the communities tended to be low-profile, engendering little public debate. In the USA, the

Table 6.2 Policy profile scores for cases of reconciliation policy

	Pre/Form.		Post-form.		Total
	D	S	D	S	
Denmark: Evolution of childcare policy	2	2	2	2	8
Germany: 1986 Federal Child Care Benefit Act	1	3	1	2	7
USA: 1993 Family and Medical Leave Act	1	2	1	1	5
Ireland: 1995 Reform of social welfare legislation	2	0	2	0	4

policy style was the most high-profile, with Congress the major arena for action. The dynamics of the partisan make-up of the Congress and the presidency were far more influential than other actors like women's groups, political parties, or bureaucrats. The absence of a developed welfare state in the USA excludes the possibility of an entrenched bureaucracy blocking feminist reforms as in the cases of Ireland and Germany. The US case highlights the role of the social policy bureaucracy in policy formation: as a hindrance in Ireland and Germany, and as a boost in Denmark.

An interesting common point between all four cases is that the strategic partnerships between organized women's groups, women's policy offices, and individual women in public office and in political parties were not important aspects of policy formation. Feminist policy in Denmark and Germany was made without any evidence of this feminist triangle of empowerment. In Denmark, women leaders in the childcare movement were important, but not women's policy offices or organized feminism. In Germany, individual women in the party, the legislature, and the government played important roles; organized feminism did not. In Ireland, the feminist strategic partnership was present; however, it was unable to stop the Irish government's non-decision-making. In the USA, policy formation unfolded without a strategic partnership, although feminist groups did play a role in proposal generation.

The ideology of the party in power did not appear to matter in the development of feminist policies either. Feminist policies in Denmark and Germany were pursued under right-wing governments. In Ireland, resistance to feminist demands was spearheaded by a left-wing minister with strong ties to working class ideas and constituencies (Conroy 1997). Only in the USA did the arrival of a centre-left president reverse the trend of non-decision-making. Even in this case, bipartisan consensus in Congress produced a bill that was only indirectly feminist. More than the importance of party in power, it may be the particularities of the American presidential system that drove policy development. Indeed, all four policy instances suggest that reconciliation policies are a product of all-party consensus.

For the three EU members, EU policy directives were seldom used as a political tool in getting feminist policy measures adopted. Irish non-decision-making occurred along with its poor performance on EU directives. More than domestic resistance to the Social Security Directives, however, the minor role of EU policy may be due to the limited way in which this policy has been applied in Commission action and European Court of Justice jurisprudence. As Hervey and Shaw (1998) and Luckhaus and Ward (1997) assert, EU equality law tends to emphasize more 'formal' analyses of sex equality that do not touch upon work and care issues. This has become the case in recent years when 'the earlier case law [based on the broader approach to equality] has gradually lost ground once more to a formalist approach especially in relation to the interaction of pregnancy, maternity and equal pay' (Hervey and Shaw 1998: 43). Meehan and Collins (1996: 235) also finds that 'the Court has stated categorically that the two Social Security Directives are not intended to address the general condition of sex equality but only the situations of men and women as workers'. As such, EU policy may provide disincentives for reconciliation policy in member states.

Finally, all four cases seem to suggest that the logics[10]—the particular mix of gender relations and social policy in a given country—of the larger policy in which feminist policy is injected are important in determining outcomes. In the USA, the tradition of a 'stateless state' (Wilsford 1991) with limited government involvement in social matters and the economy seems to continue to drive family-leave policy. In Germany, the importance of the male bread-winner model appeared to be a major factor in diluting the original social feminist intent of the 1986 act. In Denmark, the feminist successes of childcare policy were a result of sex-neutral social policy that promoted social justice based on shared parenting roles. The prevalence of the male-breadwinner model in the social policy system played an important role in the resistance to feminist demands in Ireland. In all four cases, the most decisive forces in policy formation were quite removed from feminist political mobilization.

❖ NOTES

1 See Nelson (1997) for recent feminist writing on the family.

2 For comparative analyses of the women's rights-welfare state nexus see, for example, Lewis (1993a; 1997) or Sainsbury (1999a); for a mixture of theoretical and empirical analysis see Sainsbury (1994); Hobson and Berggren (1997); Drew, Emerek, and Mahon (1998), or Lewis (1997).

3 Introduced by Bussemaker (1991) in her discussion of economic independence, this particular citation is from the Dutch government's 1985 Equality Plan.

4 These three stances are adapted from Heitlinger's 'matrix of egalitarian components of specific pro-natalist policies' (1993: 312–13). Much feminist scholarship takes a similar frame of a reference. For instance Gelb and Palley (1987: 10) define feminist policies in terms of sex-role change or sex-role equity; Cockburn (1989) talks about radical versus liberal approaches to equal opportunity; and Chamberlayne (1993) presents four different approaches to feminist social policy: gender neutral, gender recognition, gender reconstruction, and gender reinforcement. These classification systems are routinely cited in feminist analyses of policy, but there is no uniform vocabulary for expressing feminist policy approaches. Hetlinger's taxonomy is used for this policy area because it is developed from reconciliation policies in action in different countries, and is arguably more applicable to different cultural contexts.

5 The literature on feminist family policy also differentiates between feminist and non-feminist family policy (for example, Gauthier 1996; Drew, Emerek, and Mahon 1998; Diamond 1983).

6 The following examples examine feminist issues in different areas of social policy: on caring, Knijn and Ungerson (1997*a*); Knijn and Kremer (1997); Ungerson (1997) ; R. Mahon (1997); Hobson and Berggren (1997); on childcare, Gustafsson (1994); Joshi and Davies (1992); on daddy leave, Leira (1998*a*); on pensions, Meyer (1998); Luckhaus and Ward (1997); Döring *et al.* (1994); Sohrab (1994); and on lone mothers, Lewis (1997); Hobson (1994). In addition, the *Journal of European Social Policy* and *Social Politics* publish regularly work on issues in feminist social policy.

7 Bachrach and Baratz (1970) identified non-decision-making for the first time in the 1960s in ethnic-minority politics in Baltimore in the USA. Essentially, non-decisions occur when decision-makers in government purposefully ignore, avoid, or even block demands for policy change. As Bachrach and Baratz (1970: 43–4) state: 'A non decision is a decision that results in suppression or thwarting of a latent or manifest challenge to the values or interest of the decision maker. Non decision-making is a means by which demands for change in the existing allocation of benefits and privileges in the community can be suffocated before they are even voiced; or kept covert or killed before they gain access to the relevant decision-making arena; failing these things, maimed or destroyed in the decision-implementing process.'

8 Since the 1986 act was adopted and implemented prior to reunification, the analysis does not evaluate specifically how reunification changed the policy. In general, studies of feminist policy in the post-reunification period indicate that conservative West German policy tends to cancel out more feminist policies made in communist East Germany (for example, Ferree 1995; Ostner 1997).

9 Papadopoulos (1998: 51) provides a summary table of parental leave polices in EU member states compiled from Ruxton (1996) and Ditch *et al.* (1999). There may be some factual errors in this table in reporting and the sheer complexity of policies, but the overall picture is clear. Leave policies in EU member states are highly developed, broad in scope, and financially supported by the state.

10 The term 'policy logics' was developed to discuss lone-mothers policies (Lewis 1997) and has been applied in the cross-national studies of gender and welfare regimes (for example, Sainsbury 1999*b*).

7 ❖ Family Law Policy

❖ OVERVIEW

In some ways, family law policy is easier to identify than reconciliation policy. One feminist legal expert describes this areas of policy as 'strategies to improve the lives of women by reforming the family' (Olsen 1993: 79). Family law reform occurs through state policy and effects changes in the body of law on the family. Individual policies in other feminist sub-sectors unfold in the legal arena and often involve the courts. The family law sub-area of policy is the only one in which policy formation plays out uniquely in the legal arena, through the elaboration of legal norms in legislation and court decisions and their application, interpretation, and, often, re-interpretation in the justice system. In common and customary law systems in the Anglo-American and Nordic countries, a major share of policy formation occurs through court decisions and customary practice, with some important legislation on the family. In Romano-Germanic code law systems in France, Germany, Italy, and Spain, jurisprudence is also important for setting legal precedent; most law is specified in legislation that changes the law codes.[1] In federal systems, policy is determined through the interplay among State laws, court decisions, and national-level laws through the appeals process and in the USA through judicial review by the Supreme Court.

In contrast to work that groups family law policy with other areas of policy, like non-feminist family policy or reconciliation policy, this study separates out family law policies for several reasons. First, the policy formation dynamics of policies that focus on the law are quite distinct. Second, family law policies focus on the family as the locus for feminist change. Third, family law in general constitutes a separate branch of law. It is distinct from other areas of law such as 'public assistance, employment, social security, taxation'. Family law focuses on 'marriage, divorce, family support obligations, inheritance, the relationship of the parent and child, and the status of children born out of marriage' (Glendon 1989: 1). Feminist family law policy injects a feminist stance into family law either in its reform or in its practice. The study of family law policy, therefore, combines necessarily public policy and legal studies approaches. It examines feminist views of jurisprudence, case law, and the practice of law.

Whereas it is relatively easy to identify the parameters of family law policy in terms of substantive areas of focus, arenas, and policy instruments, it is more difficult to answer the empirical question of which family law policies have a feminist intent, arguably more than other sub-sectors of feminist policy. First, there is no clear feminist consensus over the content of a feminist family law. Second-wave feminists were initially suspicious of using family law as an avenue for change. In the USA, for example, 'feminists have not been central to the debates over family in legislatures and courts' (Stetson 1997*b*: 175). One of the major debates in the feminist legal community as it cuts across political science (for example, Kenney 1995) and legal studies (for example, Smith 1993; MacKinnon 1989; Bartlett and Kennedy 1991; Friedman 1992), is over whether feminist family law should accentuate equality or difference between men and women. Olsen (1993: 79), for example, raises the issue of the limits of an individual equality approach in family law: 'Reforms that increase the juridical equality of wives . . . also tend to undermine altruism and foster individual selfishness. Moreover, some of these reforms legitimate actual inequality by individualising and particularising it.'

Second, there is gap between the intent of legislation and its implementation in the justice system. Policy formation in the judicial system involves much more bottom-up political processes than administrative-oriented policy implementation. On one hand, a law with clear feminist intent may be interpreted in quite non-feminist ways by judges and lawyers who are not interested in promoting feminist interests. On the other hand, feminist legal practitioners as well as judges and lawyers with feminist viewpoints can take family law policies adopted with little feminist intent and make them quite feminist.

Despite the ambivalence and apathy of some parts of contemporary feminist movements towards the law, reform in family law has been an important rallying cry for many feminists. 'Bourgeois feminist movements', a part of the first wave of feminism in the nineteenth and early twentieth centuries, placed the reform of highly discriminatory laws in property and family at the centre of their struggles (Lovenduski 1986*a*: 21). Contemporary liberal feminists with their focus on women's rights are the most obvious advocates of feminist family law. Radical feminists trained in the law, like Carol Smart, who emphasize women's difference and the patriarchal nature of the legal system also look to family law as a means of social change. Feminist jurisprudence and feminist legal theory are necessary to the pursuit of feminist family law policy, particularly in countries with Anglo-American systems of law where judicial policy-making is the norm.

Family law policy is made in the following areas: men's and women's rights in the contract of marriage, divorce, property rights, parental rights and responsibilities, and families without marriage.[2] The first area involves equalizing men's and women's rights within the marriage contract. The second focuses on the legalization of divorce and the ability of both men and women to get divorces and equalized settlements. The third area focuses on the attribution of family property, including inheritance. The fourth area deals with parental authority over children. The final area addresses all of these issues within the context of families with no marriage.

Issues of domestic violence are often raised in the formation of family law policies. In Ireland, for instance, the feminist group that spearheaded feminist family law reform identified violence against married women as a serious problem. The widespread domestic violence against women became an important argument for the legalization of divorce (Galligan 1998). Policies that specifically address domestic violence, however, are not included in this fifth sub-sector.

Each of the five areas of family law policy has been the object of two different phases of reform. Women in emerging Western democracies did not benefit from the expansion of social rights in the eighteenth and nineteenth centuries in the same way as men. As Lovenduski (1986a) and others point out, as societies became industrialized, women lost power and control over their own lives within marriage. Women's rights were usually subsumed under their husbands' and, in the event of the death of the husband, under those of their brothers, sons, nephews, or any other direct male family member. By the nineteenth century, women in most Western democracies had few formal civil rights.

> Politically they [women] had no right to vote or to hold office . . . Women were barred from owning property, their inherited wealth was transferred to their husbands upon marriage, and they were prevented from engaging in trade, running a business or joining a profession. Legally women were not persons in most countries. They could not enter into contracts and were considered to be minor persons in the eyes of the law, subject to the power of their fathers or husbands. (Lovenduski 1986a: 14)

The family, therefore, became the site of the disempowerment of women; and the empowerment of men as patriarchy was formalized systematically in code, customary, and common law in the late eighteenth and early nineteenth centuries in Europe and transported to the colonies. The code law on the family in France put into place by Napoleon is one of the most extreme cases of the institutionalization of women's legal subjugation by men. In response to the pervasive codification of patriarchy in Western democracies, the first phase of family law reform sought to remove the most blatant legal provisions that subordinated women to men within the family. First-phase reform also assured that coequal rights between men and women within the couple were formalized in law.

The timing of first-phase feminist law policy varied across Western democracies. The Protestant Social Democrat and Protestant Liberal countries undertook reforms much earlier than in the Late Female Mobilizing and Advanced Christian Democrat countries (Lovenduski 1986a; Kaplan 1992; Galligan 1998). For example, divorce was legalized in Sweden in 1915 and in

Great Britain in 1920. Divorce laws were not adopted in Italy until the 1970s and in 1995 in Ireland. In Spain divorce by consent was made a reality in 1981, three years after the transition to democracy (Cousins 1995). Whereas property rights were given to married women in the late nineteenth century in Great Britain and the Nordic countries (Bergqvist *et al.* 1999: 296), wives did not gain formal property rights within the marriage until the 1960s in France. In Ireland, the first concrete first-phase reform laws were in 1957. In Germany, women's equal status in marriage was not acknowledged until 1977 (Lemke 1994: 272).

Reflecting legal system dynamics, the first phase of reform occurred incrementally, usually through case law and/or practice in the Protestant Social Democrat and Protestant Liberal countries. In the Late Female Mobilizing and Advanced Christian Democrat countries, first-phase changes occurred through top-down legislative reforms and, in Italy and Ireland, often through national referendums. First-phase family law policies can be the object of intense feminist movement action. In Great Britain and the USA, family law was mostly a first-wave women's movement struggle; in Italy and Ireland, a second-wave feminist issue. In the Nordic countries and France, first-phase reforms occurred without significant feminist mobilization.

The second phase of fine-tuning began as soon as the most blatant legal inequities in the family were addressed in formal law. Second-phase reforms tend to involve lower-profile legislation and the messier business of the practice of law and court decisions as they relate to defining coequal rights between men and women. Swedish family law reforms in the late 1960s and 1970s on custody rights of unmarried parents and simplification of divorce are examples of feminist reforms aimed at fine-tuning (Baude 1979). The issue of judges' interpretations of the law and lawyer control is an important part of the second fine-tuning phase. For example, in the USA in the 1970s feminists became aware and drew attention to the tendency of judges and lawyers to punish women more than men for 'moral misconduct' in divorce settlements. As a result, feminists pushed for legal reform of laws that would formally recognize wives contributions in 'homemaking and building the spouse's career' (Stetson 1997b: 199). Unlike the first phase of reform, the second phase of reform is difficult to identify. It often occurs at lower levels of government, through individual court cases. Work on feminist jurisprudence in family law is often useful in identifying second-phase changes.

As Table 7.1 on second-phase reform in Great Britain, the USA, and Canada shows, there is a mix of legislative and judicial measures in Protestant Liberal countries.[3]

More than other feminist policy sub-sectors, there is a major data gap in the English-language literature on the politics of family-law policy formation.[4] The Feminist Comparative Policy literature tends not to cover family-law policy issues. When feminist family-law policy issues are treated in both cross-national

Table 7.1 Second-phase family law reforms in Great Britain, the United States, and Canada

---

GREAT BRITAIN

1970 Divorce Reform Act
1970 Matrimonial Proceedings and Property Act
1971 Guardianship of Minors Act
1973 Matrimonial Causes Act
1973 Guardianship Act
1983 Matrimonial and Family Proceedings Act
1986 Family Law Act
1989 Children Act
1991 Child Support Act
1995 *Brooks v. Brooks*
1996 Family Law Act

UNITED STATES

1973 *Gomez v. Perez*
1975 Child Support Amendments to Social Security Act
1975 Case: Stanton v Stanton
1979 *Orr v. Orr*
1984 Child Support Enforcement Act
1988 *Hick v. Feiock*
1988 Family Support Act

CANADA

1986 Divorce Act
1986 Divorce Corollary Act
1986 Family Orders Enforcement Act
1992 *Moge v. Moge*

Source: Bashevkin (1998: 249–56).

studies and nation-specific studies, the analysis is piecemeal, without any significant discussion of the politics of policy formation. The most thorough analyses of cases of family law reform are found in the USA, France, Italy, and Ireland. There are virtually no English-language studies of family law reform in the Nordic countries or in the Netherlands.

The dearth of literature on feminist legal policy is a result of the dynamics of FCP as a field of study as well as of the historical, legal, and political dynamics of feminist family law reform in post-industrial democracies. While on the one hand family law policy is grounded in the legal arena of family law, on the other FCP work tends to concentrate on policy issues within the purview of political science. In the same vein, legal analysts who study family law from a feminist stance concentrate on the practice of the law and avoid a focus on formal politics. For the Protestant Democrat and Protestant Liberal countries, politically-oriented first-phase reforms took place much earlier, and hence tend to be the object of historical analysis. More recent reform tends to be second-phase policies that are removed from political policy-making channels, the usual interest of FCP scholars. American feminist studies within both political science and legal studies focus some attention on family law policy issues; they are usually on general case law, not just family law. European feminist jurisprudence has developed around European Union law, which, as Meehan and Collins (1996), Hoskyns (1996), and others have shown, eschews family issues unless they relate directly to equality in paid employment. Feminist legal studies investigating the member state-EU legal nexus, therefore, have not included family law.

Given these empirical and disciplinary parameters, the selection of policy cases for this chapter was limited. A policy case from the Protestant Social Democrat countries could not be included. Nonetheless, a certain range of family law policies is assessed here. Australian matrimonial property reform in 1987 represents second-phase reform. Irish divorce reform and the German family law of 1987 are both examples of first-phase reform adopted in the contemporary period. For all three cases, the lack of literature on the start-to-finish policy formation process meant that some important empirical holes on the different policy stages had to be filled by best estimates and extrapolations from the available evidence.

❖ THE POLICY CASES

❖ 1. Second-phase Policy in Matrimonial Property Reform (1987) in Australia: Feminist Policy with Indirect Feminist Involvement (Pre/Form.: 2/3 Post-form.: 2/3 = 10)

A 1987 bill proposed by the Australian Legal Reform Commission (ALRC) consisted of feminist fine-tuning of marriage law to promote a feminist stance on women's and men's rights in marriage. The law on property rights in marriage had been first reformed in 1957 and then more extensively in 1975. In the context of some of the highest rates of home ownership in the world and 'a very meagre public housing sector', the issue of dividing matrimonial property at divorce, as Graycar (1990: 154) explains, was 'very much a matter of public debate among feminists and social policy analysts'. The division of property from marriage became a form of social welfare for single-parent families. The final ALRC proposal called for the law to specify that the husband's and wife's property at divorce should not automatically be equally split, but should be divided on the basis of an evaluation of the economic contributions of both 'parties'. Such evaluations were to include quantifiable direct economic contributions and indirect contributions of home-work, typically carried out by the wife (Graycar

1990: 154). The final policy proposal advocated a social feminist position and took formally gender hierarchies into consideration. Once implemented, the law would provide more precise instructions to family courts than the 1975 Family Act. In both content and application the 1975 law had given the court broad discretion to determine the division of marital property.

The support for the 'result equality model' over the 'formal equality model' reflected an emerging consensus among feminist activists and scholars in the US and Australia. This consensus was based on the need for divorce settlements to be made on a careful analysis of spousal contributions to family obligations. Not all feminists supported this position. Feminist (for example, Fineman 1983; Smart 1998) and non-feminist researchers argued that automatic 50:50 splits of property discriminated against women who do not take a wage-labour job outside of the home and whose contributions in terms of their work-time to the family were greater than 50 per cent. The 50:50 'community of property' approach was also supported by some Australian feminists, particularly in the early 1980s.

Clear evidence of women's substantive representation was a significant feature of the 1987 proposal. Women's descriptive representation was less apparent. As Graycar (1990) argues, the ALRC's feminist decision was not only a result of feminist lobbying. Research conducted by non-feminist analysts showed that 50:50 splits in property contributed to women's poverty, particularly in the context of poor public housing opportunities. The members of the executive-based Legal Rights Commission and the Family Law Court Council also came to support the equality of results model. The Labor-led government in power at the time was also quite woman-friendly, with 'the most developed women's platform of any Australian government to date' (Hetlinger 1993: 305). Public submissions given to the ALRC from feminist and non-feminist groups 'overwhelmingly' backed the equality of results approach. Many of the submissions came from women legal experts who were members of women-only organizations and femocrats from the women's policy agencies in the states (Graycar 1990: 166).

Two years prior to the decision of the Labor government to open the inquiry, women's movement activists participated in an 'acrimonious' debate over which approach was preferable; the equality in results or the formal equality approach (Graycar 1990: 166). The arena for the discussions was the Women's Electoral Lobby (WEL), 'a non-partisan and non-hierarchical organization with members from all political parties' (Sawer 1994: 76). In 1981, FLAG, a group within the Women's Electoral Lobby that advocated the formal equality approach, distributed a position paper throughout Australia. At a national meeting of WEL, the debate was mediated by a staff lawyer from the Office of Women's Affairs, the federal-level women's policy office at the time. Several publications on the debate were cited in the press and, in 1983, the head of the

ALRC and a feminist lawyer debated the issue on national television. Thus, whereas the final feminist decision may not have been directly a result of feminist action, women were clearly involved with the articulation of the issue in the public and to the Commission.

The policy subsystem around the bill consisted of two distinct groups of actors with different styles: feminist and non-feminist. In the feminist part of the policy subsystem, a broad range of women's and feminist groups as well as women's policy offices developed two opposing views within the arena of the reform-oriented feminist group WEL. The publication of position papers was an extremely important part of the process. On the non-feminist side, the executive-based ALRC spent three years conducting a study of the issue. The Australian Family Institute solicited public submissions from a variety of actors as well. The discussions of the ALRC were clearly in the public eye, particularly with the participation of the ALRC's president in a televized debate. The Commission's decisions, however, were made behind closed doors.

There were no published analyses available on the events after the ALRC's recommendations. Given the dynamics of pre-formulation and that the ALRC was a Cabinet commission charged by the Labor Party Prime Minister, also head of the parliamentary majority, the recommendations were more likely to be adopted into law. Whether the law was implemented effectively in the courts also remains an empirical question. It is likely that the feminist coalition on the law continued to oversee its enforcement and implementation in the courts, particularly given the partnership between women's groups and the women's policy offices on the reform. It is not clear whether the division in the feminist community over the approach to legal reform would have diluted the mobilization of feminists around enforcement and eventual litigation. The pro-feminist positions of the Cabinet and the bureaucracy in the non-feminist policy subsystem that emerged around the reform also indicates that there would be few structural barriers to the law's application. It is possible, of course, that the judges and lawyers outside the federal level sub-system blocked the formal intent of the law in individual cases.[5]

❖ 2. First-phase Divorce Reform in Ireland, 1981–1995: Feminist Incrementalism Breaks Non-Decision-making (Pre/Form.: 2/2 Post-form.: 2/2 = 8)

Family law policy in Ireland is arguably unique given that it is articulated in the context of what many feminists see as constitutionally enshrined and socially acceptable patriarchy. In the Irish system, social practice, Church doctrine, and the 1937 Constitution made 'power and status in Irish public life . . . the preserve of the male' (Connolly 1999: 19) and produced a legal system where women in their prescribed roles as mothers and wives by Art. of the Constitution 'were afforded little legal recognition' (Galligan 1998: 91). Women's rights within marriage in Ireland continued to be subservient to men's until the late 1950s (Galligan 1998). Divorce, unlike other areas of first-phase family law policy in Ireland undertaken from the late 1950s through the 1980s, posed a particularly daunting challenge; legalization required a referendum to change the Constitution. Prior to 1995, Art. 41.3.2 stated 'that no law shall be enacted providing for the grant of dissolution of marriage' (Connolly 1999: 22).

Thus, in addition to changing the minds of the political elite, a majority of the voting public needed to be convinced: a difficult task to achieve in any country, even more so in Ireland where family, private property, and the male bread-winner model were held sacred by many Irish people. As Galligan (1998: 103) states in explaining why the 1986 divorce referendum was lost by a two-to one margin, ' In a country such as Ireland, with the continued existence of a strong Catholic ethos, such issues went well beyond the limits of tolerable policy reform'. It took nearly ten years before the Irish government braved a second referendum. It was adopted by a 1 per cent margin (Galligan 1998: 104).

In the context of the controversial nature of divorce, reform-oriented family law groups and the major feminist action group on family law, Action, Information, Motivation (AIM), did not come together specifically to demand the legalization of divorce until 1981. It took five more years for the government to respond to the demands, 14 years for the Irish people to support them, and 16 years before legal divorce was actually practised. The first legal divorce was granted in January 1997, two years after the successful referendum (Galligan 1998: 104).

The story of Irish divorce reform is about incremental feminist strategies of coalition-building aimed at persuading and cajoling elected officials on the right and the left to support what could be quite politically costly reforms. Women's policy offices were not allowed to take official positions on divorce (Mahon 1995). Nonetheless, both Cabinet-based women's policy offices and the women's rights parliamentary committee were indirect channels for the articulation of society-based demands for divorce reform and for the women who backed those demands. For example, Nuala Fennell, one of the founders of AIM, was the Minister of State of Women's Affairs in 1982–7.

The way in which the Irish government used parliamentary and executive-based committees to delay taking concrete action on the divorce issue was a textbook case of non-decision-making (Bachrach and Baratz 1970). Two years after a coalition of feminist and non-feminist groups joined together to demand for concrete reform, the Fine Gael-Labour government set up a 'parliamentary committee on marital breakdown' that, according to Galligan (1998: 102), 'was a repeat of the device to buy political time' used in previous feminist family law reforms. In the case of divorce reform, it was even more of a stalling tactic because the commission was established in the parliamentary arena rather than in the Ministry of Justice. As a parliamentary commission, hearings were more public—the committee received 700 written and 24 oral submissions—more controversial, and gave Conservative opposition party Fianna Fáil 'greater influence on the outcome of the proceedings than would have been possible in the circumstances of regular routinized policy making' (Galligan 1998: 102). Reflecting non-decision-making dynamics, the 1985 commission report suggested several reforms to deal with the growing problem of marital breakdown, but 'stopped short of recommending the removal of its [divorce's] constitutional provisions' (Galligan 1998: 102).

To what many seemed an unplanned and last-minute decision, the government announced a divorce referendum in 1986, 'with little advance public or political discussion'. The referendum produced a 'bitter and divisive campaign' framed in terms of 'the fundamental legal and moral issue of the structure of the family' (Galligan 1998: 103). Arguments for divorce reform were further weakened by a 1986 decision by the European Court of Human Rights. The court decided that the unavailability of divorce in Ireland did not infringe plaintiffs' rights (Connolly 1999: 22). Not only was the direct pressure from the EU completely absent, but a second potential for external legal pressure was precluded.

It was not until a feminist private member's bill adopted by Parliament in 1989—an unusual occurrence—that legalized separation, and hence broadened the grounds for divorce, that the Fianna Fáil-Labour government presented a second divorce referendum in 1995 (Galligan 1998: 104). Framed within the context of women's legal rights, the debate about the second referendum did not focus on the sanctity of the family, and as a consequence was adopted (Galligan 1998: 104). The new amendment included four detailed conditions under which a court could dissolve a marriage. The wording of the amendment was-sex neutral and the word 'spouses' was used rather than 'husbands' or 'wives' (cited in Connolly 1999: 79).

Women were key players in breaking the deadlock over divorce reform. The feminist reform group AIM took a leadership role in the campaign to legalize divorce, submitting a substantial document to the parliamentary commission in 1986. AIM mobilized and lobbied a large number of women at different levels of government and society and women's groups, both feminist and non-feminist, to forward a moderate agenda (Galligan 1998). The agenda sought to frame proposals for feminist reform in non-threatening ways. AIM's moderate lobbying strategy contributed to many family law policy reforms. In divorce reform, however, AIM had 'greater difficulty in finding parliamentary and government acceptance of the need to introduce divorce legislation' (Galligan 1998: 102). Nonetheless, the mostly female organization brought women fully into the pre-formulation process, with the indirect help of the women's policy machineries in the parliament and the cabinet.[6]

AIM had much less influence on government decisions to sponsor referendums and even less on the outcome of the referendums, although the Fianna

Faíl-Labour government programme for family law policy contained some of the elements of AIM's 1986 recommendations. Substantive representation of women's interests certainly occurred to the extent that AIM's moderate demands were reflected in the final wording of the amendment. However, by comparison with the content of divorce reform in other countries, the amendment was quite conservative.

The policy community on divorce reform after 1986 was high- and low-profile. Policy debates were in the public eye and pluralist lobbying politics characterized the parliamentary-based process. The decisions to hold both divorce referendums were made behind closed doors, with little apparent input from actors outside of the Cabinet. For actors in the both public and private arenas, the divorce issue was highly controversial. Another dynamic driving both the public the and private aspects of decision-making was government instability throughout the life cycle of the divorce debate, which, as Galligan (1998) argues, undoubtedly contributed to delaying government action on such a controversial issue.[7]

❖ *3. First-phase Marriage and Divorce Reform (1977) in Germany: Feminism Diluted by 'Patriarchy in Judges Robes' or Social Feminist Implementation? (Pre/Form.: 1/2 Post-form.: 1/2 = 6)*

The content of the 1977 law was clearly feminist, emphasizing a sex-neutral approach to partnership in marriage and parenting rights. The law was a radical departure from the highly gendered and patriarchal nature of past German family law where women's rights in marriage were defined as those of a housewife, subservient to men's rights as the male bread-winner. Even after a package of amendments was adopted in 1957 to introduce real equality in the context of symbolic applications of the sex-equality provisions of the Basic Law, one German critic argued that the 1957 law still 'left the core of the patriarchal model of the family untouched' (cited in Kolinsky 1989: 49). The 1977 law not only defined marriage as a partnership but it also advocated the free choice and rights of both 'partners' to either take paid employment or not. The contrast between the two laws was striking. The 1957 law reinforced the 'housewife marriage' and stipulated that the 'woman runs the household in her own responsibility'. The 1977 legislation stated that 'the partners agree on the running of the household' (cited in Kolinsky 1989: 49). As Kolinsky (1989: 49) asserts, the 1977 law was 'ahead of its time'.

The Liberal (FDP)-Social Democrat (SPD) coalition government designed and sponsored the legislation that was feminist in content. It emphasized formal or rule equality between men and women in couples, but did not take into consideration 'result equality' in terms of how dominant gender relations in the family make women's and men's situations within the family unequal. The law also reflected the left-wing coalition's programme of 'strengthening the participatory elements in social life and organisation' (cited in Kolinsky 1989: 50).

In 1972, the SPD-led government created a small women's policy group in the Ministry of Health, Family, and Youth which was expanded in 1974. The newly expanded group, according to Ferree (1995: 98), led a government inquiry into the status of women and funded the first women's shelter in Berlin in 1977. Ferree (1995; 1991–92) did not specifically mention the involvement of women's policy offices, at the federal or State and local levels. It is difficult to determine, therefore, whether women actually participated in drafting the bill.

The policy community style is not evident either. At the very least, it was grounded in the way the governing political parties informed the decision of the chief executive and the parliament, probably with some influence from the feminists within the SPD and the Cabinet. Also, given the successful adoption of such a feminist law, it is possible that opposition parties, social feminists, and more conservative political forces in society had little input into the policy formulation process. In other words, the 1977 law appeared to be the product of Cabinet-focused German parliamentary policy-making.

Even less information is available on post-formulation. It does not appear that the federal and State-level women's policy offices were formally charged with overseeing litigation; none of the more active State-level agencies took any significant legal initiatives either. Analyses of the German women's movement in the 1980s and 1990s do not indicate that family law jurisprudence was a part of feminist mobilization (Ferree 1997). Work by one German feminist jurist indicates that there was some feminist legal interest in sexual harassment and pornography in the late 1980s and early 1990s (Baer 1988; 1996).

Kolinsky's analysis of the reception of the law by the non-feminist legal community in the late 1970s shows that there was little support for the feminist intent of the law. For example, a legal guide for lawyers indicated that the legal experts who designed it expected women to continue to take full-time mothering roles and follow their husbands' advice about working outside of the home (Kolinsky 1989: 51). An analysis in *Der Spiegel* criticized the law for being out of step with common practice and attitudes about men's and women's appropriate roles (Kolinsky 1989: 53). Court decisions and settlements in divorce cases based on the law were used in this same spirit to compel women to opt for staying in the home over working in paid employment. One 1980 analysis of the application of the law stated that the 'patriarchy in the judges' robes' prevented the full realization of the law's feminist potential (cited in Kolinsky 1989: 54).

Ostner's (1993; 1997) analyses of marriage and child-custody laws provides a slightly different viewpoint. German law reaffirmed women's roles as stay-at-home-wives, while at the same time promoting the notion of 'equal contributions' based on different men's and women's roles within marriage and the family. Women's rights were protected as long as they were stay-at-home wives.

For example, social security entitlements 'paid women for unpaid caring' (1993: 101). There was no protection for lone mothers. Such an approach where women's independence is achieved within established gender roles coincides with the principles of German social feminism. In this perspective, the legal interpretations of the 1977 law fit into the social feminist approach to social policy in Germany.

❖ COMPARATIVE DISCUSSION: IN THE CONTEXT OF PARTIAL RESULTS WITH PARTIAL DATA, CULTURAL ATTITUDES ABOUT GENDER MAY MATTER

The usual tentative nature of conclusions is exacerbated by the limitations of the literature. Neither the Australian nor the Irish cases provide much insight into the politics of implementation, although implementation politics of previous reforms in Australia were a part of the pre-formulation process on the 1987 ALRC recommendations. These empirical snapshots of such an under-studied area of feminist public policy make a compelling case for more analyses of family law policy in post-industrial democracies. Future research will necessarily rely on the collaboration of legal scholars and policy experts given the legal complexities of second-phase reform. Historians also need to be enlisted in taking a policy formation approach to analysing first-phase reform in Nordic and Anglo-American countries. Bashevkin's (1998) inventory of family law reforms in Great Britain, the USA, and Canada provides an important first step for future research by identifying which family law reforms are feminist. Also, Glendon's (1989) comparative study of divorce reform should prove to be useful.

As the summary of the policy profile scores indicates, the three cases suggest that family law reforms, both first-phase and second-phase, can be feminist in content and in women's participation in the policy process. In Ireland, feminists were key players in breaking the long pattern of non-decision-making in the context of the broad-based resistance to a constitutional amendment to legalize divorce. The moderately feminist content of the amendment, coinciding with the low-key demands of the feminist reform group AIM, was also an indication

Table 7.2 Policy profile scores for cases of family law policy

	Pre/Form.		Post-form.		Total
	D	S	D	S	
Australia: 1987 Matrimonial property reform	2	3	2	3	10
Ireland: 1981–95 Divorce reform	2	2	2	2	8
Germany: 1977 Marriage and divorce reform	1	2	1	2	6

of the feminist profile of divorce reform. Women, as members of AIM and as members of the broader coalition of groups as well as Members of Parliament who backed the referendum, were clearly empowered in the long-drawn-out divorce campaign.

In Germany, the sex-neutral wording of 'equal partnership' in the 1977 law resonated with the feminist approach of formal equality; the law did not appear to take into consideration gender hierarchies institutionalized in family law and in German family patterns. The limits of the approach were made clear with the resistance of the legal establishment to following the spirit of the law in its application and in recent developments in family law. The feminist profile of the Australian law was much clearer in terms of women's substantive and descriptive representation. The degree to which the non-feminist family-reform policy community supported a quite feminist approach to the family .

In view of the radical nature of the 1977 marriage reform in Germany, there was apparently little controversy over the content of the first-phase reform, particularly when compared with the controversy of similar first-phase reform in Ireland. The style of the German policy community was more administrative and low-level. The SPD's Cabinet and party programme drove policy development and contributions from feminist activists in the party, the women's lobby or women's policy offices, or from non-feminist women were less evident.

The styles of the policy sub-systems in Ireland and Australia appeared to be bifurcated. In Ireland a very public pro-divorce community, composed of feminist reform groups, non-feminist family reformers, and opposition politicians operated alongside a closed policy community located in the Cabinet. The second policy community was composed of government commissions and government officials who stalled divorce reform, partially as a result of government instability in the 1980s. In Australia, the two sides of the policy sub-system were feminist and non-feminist. The feminist side was in the public eye and composed of reform-oriented feminist activists and legal experts. The non-feminist community was public when issues were discussed and private when decisions were made by the Cabinet-based law reform commission. In both Australia and Ireland, the actions of non-feminist actors were substantially dictated by the larger imperatives of cabinet-based parliamentary politics.

Feminist strategic partnerships were clearly a part of the feminist breaking of non-decision-making in Ireland, but not a factor in feminist policy formation in Germany. In Germany, women's policy offices and feminist groups appeared to be absent. A strategic partnership was present in Australia. It was not clear, however, to what degree feminist policy was a result of the partnership as opposed to the woman-friendly proclivities of the Labor-led government and the ALRC.

In contrast to reconciliation policy formation, the presence of a left-wing majority in government appeared to be quite decisive in all three cases. International influences were at a minimum in the context the EU's policy silences on family law. There is a possibility that the UN declaration of the Decade of the Woman in 1975 may have reinforced the woman-friendly positions of the SPD government in Germany, but this was not mentioned in the published analyses. Social saliency of and political support for the male breadwinner model and, hence, dominant patterns in gender relations appeared to play quite decisive roles in undermining feminist policy formation in the Irish and German cases. Dominant attitudes about gender relations did not appear to get into the mix of ingredients for feminist results in Australia, perhaps because the traditional model was not as salient as in Germany and Ireland.

Given the legal nature of the sub-sector, it is important to consider the impact of the type of legal system. In the Irish case, the nature of the legal system did not come into play since the policy formation process was focused on a constitutional amendment rather than the application of law in the courts. Given that the German act was first-phase reform, reacting to policy gaps rather than problems in application, and the Australian policy was developed from the application of past feminist reform, it is difficult to draw any useful comparative lessons. The different dynamics on each might be a result of the different stages of family law policy more than the differences in legal system.

Still, it is interesting to note that the dilution of feminist policy in Germany occurred in its legal application in the court room. This is not the usual expectation of code law systems where 'The findings of the courts are based upon statutory law rather than on judge-made or common laws' (Katz 1986: 83). There may have been other factors that undercut the usual patterns of the Romano-Germanic legal system, like the prominence of the male bread-winner model mentioned above. In Australia, while court decisions were used to justify more feminist divorce reform, jurisprudence did not seem to affect the content of the feminist policy, reflecting 'the tendency of Australian judges to avoid making policy-making decisions in cases' (Graycar 1990: 167 n. 2). Both of the cases suggest that the degree of judicial activism is an important factor in the feminist success and failure of family law policies.

❖ NOTES

1 For a discussion of different types of legal systems in post-industrial democracies see, for example, Katz (1986) and Zwiegert and Kötz (1992).

2 This categorization is based on Stetson's (1997*b*) taxonomy of family law in the USA.

3 Bashevkin (1998) selected reforms that could potentially be feminist in five sectors in Great Britain, the USA, and Canada. One of these sectors was family law. She identified which reforms were feminist, partially feminist, or not feminist, according to her criteria. The inventory is listed in an appendix of her book. Table 7.1 lists her feminist and partially feminist family law policies.

4 See Appendix B for the literature on family-law reform. Sixty-five studies are listed on average for the other six sub-areas; 29 are listed for family law policy.

5 Assuming that the same dynamics continued in post-formulation, the same policy profile scores are assigned for post-formulation as for pre-formulation/formulation. These scores must be seen as estimates to be verified in actual analyses of the implementation of the law.

6 AIM accepted male members, but its leadership positions were primarily held by women (Galligan 1998: 95).

7 Given that implementation was not the focus of the detailed published analyses of policy formation, the same policy scores are given to the policy profile in post-formulation as in the formulation stages.

8 ❖ Body Politics I: Reproductive Rights Policy

❖ OVERVIEW

Body politics policy is very different from other areas of feminist government action. Its focus is on the most private elements of women's and men's lives; their bodies, their sexuality, and their reproductive capabilities. The issue of body politics has been the domain of second-wave feminism which, in Kate Millet's words (1971), made the personal political. In this perspective, the very private aspects of women's and men's bodies are brought into the public sphere of power relations, citizen rights, and public policy. As Beasley and Bacchi (2000: 335) assert, 'bodies give substance to citizenship' and 'citizenship matters for bodies'. Body politics policy, therefore, transcends the traditional divide between public and private and, in doing so, has the potential to reshape how the state operates in contemporary democracies.

Unlike many other areas of feminist policy that promote women's equality, body politics seeks to improve the status and situation of women by focusing on their biological distinctiveness and the social construction of their sexuality, often in the context of women's bodies being the object of men's desire, control, and violence. As Chowdhury *et al.* (1994: 11) assert about women's experiences worldwide, 'Women routinely experience the risk of sexual assaults in ways that have no immediate parallels with men'. When men's status and rights as a group are brought into the policy mix, it tends to be as potential violators of women's rights, for example, as doctors, sexual offenders, or wife beaters and not the benchmark for the attainment of women's rights. Studies of 'sex equality policy' often do not include body politics issues. Feminist approaches to body politics can also place issues of women's control and men's domination into the context of patriarchy and gender hierarchy and propose solutions that address inequities between men and women beyond sexual politics.[1]

Debates over the type of sex equality and the appropriate model of gender relations, so much a part of policy discussions in other feminist sub-sectors, are less prominent here. Instead of equity with men, the main concern of body politics policy is how state action can ensure women's autonomy in making choices about their bodies. To be sure, states can be in the business of regulating women's bodies without promoting women's rights. Women's bodies have been the object of puritanical policies of social propriety, pro-natalist policies, and policies to professionalize the medical profession, to name a few. In many countries, the rise of the social-conservative right in the 1980s put the conservative regulation of women's bodies back on the political agenda.

Body politics policies are divided into two separate sub-areas: reproductive rights and sexuality and violence. Reproductive rights policies seek to provide optimal situations for women to choose whether and when to have children. Sexuality and violence policies, the subject of the analysis in Chapter 9, aim to help women in situations of domestic violence and in their sexual activities, unwanted or wanted. The two areas are examined separately because of the quite distinct nature of the politics of each. Unified feminist action for abortion reform and the ensuing policy responses also came earlier than any systematic attention to sexuality and violence issues. Although radical feminists began to open women's shelters in the early 1970s and some governments adopted anti-rape laws in the 1970s, the movements did not reach their apex until the 1980s, when governments began to deal with sexuality and violence issues and to provide funding for women's shelters (Weldon 2001). In many countries, sexuality and violence issues did not become priority agenda items until well after abortion was legalized.

Reproductive rights policies include government action that promotes women's freedom of choice or 'women's self-determination' (Ketting and Van Praag 1986) in contraception, abortion, and reproductive technologies. Feminist studies typically include all three areas under the rubric of reproductive rights. Stetson (1997b) and Lovenduski and Randall (1993), for instance, in their studies of feminism and feminist policy issues in the USA and Great Britain respectively include separate chapters on reproduction. The chapters discuss aspects of all three areas. Githens and Stetson's (1996) book on abortion politics includes chapters on reproductive technologies. Other work scrutinizes one area of reproductive rights without referring to the wider category: for example, Lovenduski and Outshoorn (1986a) on abortion and Field (1983) on birth control.

Contraception policies include the legalization of the birth control pill in the 1960s and, in many countries, its state subsidization and distribution on demand. Legalizing and freely distributing the birth control pill, as analysts of feminism and women's rights have demonstrated, revolutionized women's lives. It gave women a dependable and relatively safe way of preventing pregnancy. Contraception policies are inextricably linked to abortion polices given that public acceptance and government support of contraception and family planning can preclude recourse to abortion. In many countries abortion is seen as a last resort more than a form of birth control. In the Netherlands, where government policy 'prioritised safe and widely available contraception and widespread sex education' and developed 'one of the most liberal abortion regimes', the abortion rate is 'remarkably low' (Rolston and Eggert 1994*b*: xxi). As the Dutch case indicates, contraception policies also involve public support of sex education and family planning.

Abortion policy involves the legalization, regulation, and provision of abortions. In the context of the importance of legalized abortion for women's rights, the feminist consensus around women's rights to choose and the deep political controversies it has engendered, abortion policy have received much more analytical attention than the other areas of reproductive policy. The literature on abortion policy is arguably the most developed of all of the sub-sectors of feminist policy. It provides systematic empirical coverage, well-defined analytical concepts, and theory-building studies. Also, research on comparative abortion policy speaks the language of comparative policy analysis. Abortion studies examine whether, how, and why specific governments take feminist action. They also situate the inquiry within a comparative framework that uses cross-national cultural differences to sift through analytic questions. There is a clear sense in most of this literature of an ongoing dialogue about abortion policy development.

Reproductive technology policies consist of government support of research and development of new technologies that affect women in their child-bearing choices. Many feminists see these policies as a potential danger to women's rights. Feminist policies on reproductive technology policy, therefore, are often about regulating the new technologies so as not to infringe on women's rights. Government action also includes the distribution of new technologies once they are approved for public use. These policies overlap with science and technology policy issues. In addition to new abortion and contraceptive technologies, governments can promote and fund scientific research in fertility. Feminist activists closely monitor the development and application of fertility technology on women. There is a particular feminist interest in test-tube babies and their implications for women's health and women's rights. Women's health issues are linked to many body politics policies more generally.

There are studies of contraception (for example, Field 1983) and on reproductive technologies.[2] None, however, provides the coverage and comparative theoretical purview of the abortion policy literature. This chapter focuses on abortion because of the state of comparative abortion policy analysis and, just as important, because of the issue's centrality to feminism. As Outshoorn (1986*a*: 64) states, 'Without a doubt, the abortion controversy has been the most prominent issue of the feminist movement that arose in Western Europe and the USA in the course of the 1960s'.

As comparative studies show, abortion reform can promote women's 'self-determination' only if governments assure availability through financing and providing facilities. Reforms that are relatively progressive in content, essentially assuring abortion on demand with no legal restrictions or medical qualifications, do not necessarily lead to the actual provision of abortion services. As Stetson (1996a: 112) remarks, 'There is no guarantee that legalised abortion will further women's reproductive rights'. As the case analyses show below, in both Italy and the USA relatively progressive abortion policies were undermined by poor provision of services.

For analysts and observers alike the control over issue definition is at the heart of abortion politics (for example, Lovenduski and Outshoorn 1986a; Githens and Stetson 1996). As E. E. Schattshneider (1975: 66) said about politics in the USA, 'The definition of alternatives is the supreme instrument of power'. Lovenduski and Outshoorn (1986b: 2–3) argue that abortion issues have been defined in four different ways since abortion first became a public issue over 200 years ago: feminist—defined as a woman's issue; criminal—defined as a criminal act; medical—defined as an issue for doctors and medical regulation; and moral—defined in terms of the life of the unborn. Most studies of abortion policy discuss the re-definition of abortion through the lens of the four issues.

In the 1960s, the medical profession and moderate reformers placed abortion on state policy agendas to promote the practice of safe abortion in 'special cases' (Lovenduski and Outshoorn (1986b: 3). The arrival of second-wave feminist movements expanded the issue to one of mass mobilization and concern over women's rights to choose, sparking off a highly public and divided debate. Opponents to abortion on demand have developed a moral definition of the issue. They emphasize the rights of the unborn. Another issue inextricably linked to abortion is the promotion of fertility and population growth through pro-natalist policies. In many countries, abortion reform is seen as a threat to what natalists see as the need to maintain adequate birth rates. Casting abortion rights uniquely in natalist terms does not coincide with feminist approaches to reproductive rights policy. Given the different potential frames for abortion politics, the case analyses below determine the dominant definitions of abortion articulated by government policy actors in terms of women's self-determination.

Prior to the Second World War, in the late nineteenth and early twentieth centuries in many countries, earlier ambiguities in the law were addressed in 'restrictive' policy statements that tended to criminalize abortion in part to 'protect women from unscrupulous practitioners and to professionalise the medical profession' (Lovenduski and Outshoorn 1986b: 2). In France and Italy in the 1920s and 1930s, abortion was criminalized for natalist reasons. The norm was liberalization in the 1960s and 1970s, except for Germany and Ireland (Outshoorn 1996: 159). Table 8.1 (see p. 142) shows the timing and content of abortion policy after the Second World War.[3]

Abortion policy instruments include legislation, court decisions, and referendums. In Ireland, the 1983 'right to life of the unborn' amendment formally made abortion illegal. A 1992 referendum, a 1995 Supreme Court Decision, and a 1995 act liberalized abortion by allowing women to get information and to travel abroad (Scheppele 1996; Girvin 1996). In Germany, a relatively moderate law liberalizing abortion was overturned by a Constitutional Court decision in 1975. The law was also challenged by a second similar decision in 1993 that defended the constitutional rights of the unborn fetus. A 1995 law codified the conservative approach by making abortion illegal except on medical grounds. There was, however, an understanding that abortions before twelve weeks would not to be prosecuted (Outshoorn 1986b: 159; Scheppele 1986). In the Netherlands, abortion on demand was a reality by 1973 (Ketting 1994: 175). The practice was not codified into law until 1981. Public funding of abortion was not instituted until 1984. In Australia, there is no federal law on abortion; policy varies by State (Hadley 1996: Ch. 10).

Rolston and Eggert (1994a) and Outshoorn (1996) use the same two-way categorization system to classify the extent of abortion rights listed in the third column of the table. Glendon (1989) also uses the same criteria for differentiating between countries with abortion 'on demand' and 'for cause'. An indications model stipulates that women may choose to have an abortion due to a certain number of indications: 'usually medical reasons, eugenic, rape and incest, and socio-economic' (Rolston and Eggert (1994b: xx). Narrow indications usually mean that abortion is allowed only for medical reasons. In broad indications the reasons are socio-economic. The 'term model', often seen as the more progressive of the two, means that abortion is available to women on request—in some cases with further required counselling—within a certain time limit, usually twelve weeks. The right to abortion on request is explicitly written in legislation in Norway, Sweden, and Denmark (Outshoorn 1996: 149). The last column of Table 8.1 indicates women's ability to choose to have an abortion, or women's 'self-determination'. Ketting and Van Praag's (1986: 160–1) rankings on this dimension in 1986 for eight out of the 13 countries are presented. They range from '+ + +', indicating the highest level of self-determination to the lowest, '– – –'.

Stetson's (1996a) concept of 'abortion policy triad' is a useful analytical tool to determine the feminist policy profile in implementation. It is used in the case analyses below. The abortion policy triad maps out the way in which doctors, policy-makers, and women interact in the provisions of abortion. It indicates whether and how women get their interests represented in the resource distribution of abortion provision among doctors, government, and women as clients and as advocates of women's rights (Stetson's 1996a: 97). A woman-friendly triad is one in which the government assures women's right to choose over any doctors' monopoly over women's decisions, and women or women's groups are involved with the management of how abortion services are delivered. In examining triads in Russia, France, and the USA, Stetson finds that France has the most 'women-favoured triad' (1996a: 114).

Table 8.1 Abortion policy after Second World War in core countries

Country	+Year	−Year	Type in 1996	Self-determination in 1986
Italy	1978		Indications-Broad	+
Ireland	1992,1995	1983	Illegal	
Spain	1986		Indications-Narrow	
Denmark	1970,1973		Term up to 12 weeks	+ +
Sweden	1960,1967		Term up to 18 weeks	+ + +
Norway	1978,1979		Term up to 12 weeks	
France	1975, 1979,1982		Indications-Broad	+
Germany	1975	1975,1995	Indications-Narrow	− −
Netherlands	1973, 1984		Term up to 12 weeks	+
United States	1973,1992		Term up to 24-28 weeks	+ +
Great Britain	1967		Indications-Broad	+ −
Canada	1969,1988		Indications-Broad	
Australia	Varies by State			

+Year: year in which abortion was legalized and/or liberalized.   −Year: year in which restrictions on abortion were reinforced or increased.

Given the richness of the literature on abortion policy, the selection of policy cases for this chapter is far less restricted than in other chapters. Instead of choosing a range of different policies within the sub-sector, the four cases all consist of the major reform(s) that legalized abortion and their implementation in Norway, the Netherlands, the USA, and Italy. There is still variation in policy instruments used in abortion reform across the four countries. In the Dutch and US cases, policy was articulated through several different state decisions, in the Netherlands through legislation, and in the USA through the Supreme Court. In Norway and Italy, a single piece of legislation was the major instrument of legalization.

A variety of criteria were used to select the countries for each feminist family of nation. Norway was selected for the Protestant Social Democrat countries because it has the most developed anti-choice movement of the three Nordic countries. The timing of reform in the Netherlands is unusual. Abortion services were actually provided eleven years prior to the adoption of a national-level law. As such, the Dutch case can be seen as a 'deviant case' to identify whether the politics of abortion policy formation was significantly different. The combination of strong Catholic influence and a strong women's movement, both elite and mass-based, make Italy an interesting case to scrutinize for the Late Female Mobilizing countries. The Italian case also shows the limits to developing a woman-friendly abortion triad in a Catholic country. The US case is analysed from the Protestant Liberal countries because of the successes of the anti-choice movement in blocking feminist policy reform. Indeed, the

Dutch and the Norwegian abortion policies in implementation are interesting contrasts to the US and Italian cases.

❖ THE POLICY CASES

❖ *1. The 1978 Law in Norway: High Feminist Formulation and a Probable Woman-friendly Triad (Pre/Form.: 3/2 Post-form.: 3/3 = 11)*

The demand for legalization in Norway has been associated with feminist activism and women's rights (Gulli 1994: 192). As early as 1915, a feminist placed the issue of legalization on the public agenda, partially in terms of a women's right to choose (Gulli 1994: 187). A 1960 law made abortion legal for 'socio-medical' reasons upon application to a medical commission for approval. When commissions approved applications they usually went beyond the restrictions of the law. Treatment of applications for abortions varied regionally. They tended to be rejected in areas controlled by the Christian People's Party (Gulli 1994: 192). Government consideration of laws occurred in 1935 and then in the 1950s leading up to the adoption of the first abortion reform law in 1960. It was not until 1978 that a majority of parliamentarians embraced the feminist definition of abortion on demand and enacted a law.

The 1978 law allows for abortion on demand up to twelve weeks and requires the approval after examination by a two-member doctors' commission for abortions after twelve and up to 18 weeks. Women are not required to receive advice about alternative options and they can be of any age. Abortion services are delivered by state-run hospitals and covered fully under state-run health care schemes. As Van der Ros (1994: 531) states, 'The cost of abortion has never been an issue in the debates [on abortion]'. However, health-care workers were given the 'right to refuse to participate in the operation' (Gulli 1994: 193). Arguably, the feminist demand for 'women's self-determination' is fully contained in the 1978 law.

Continuing the tradition of women's activism, in the campaign for feminist abortion reform that started in the beginning of the twentieth century women were key players in pre-formulation and formulation. The principal women's actors were the new women's movements, women in the Socialist Left Party, the Women's Caucus of the Labour Party, and women in the electorate, particularly in the 1973 parliamentary elections with the increase of left-wing pro-choice MPs (Van der Ros 1994; Wiik 1986; Gulli 1994). There were few divisions in the new women's movement over feminist abortion reform. As Van der Ros (1994: 533) asserts, 'abortion became a common cause in spite of the many disagreements of different groups in the new women's movement'. Individual women successfully persuaded recalcitrant male party officials in the Labour Party to support the feminist demands for abortion in 1968 and to keep the final parliamentary vote on the law in 1978 from being a free vote not dictated by party affiliation (Wiik 1986: 149). The first feminist bill on abortion in 1975 was considered under a free vote and, as a result, the Christian members of the Socialist Left Party voted against their party's bill.

Analyses of implementation assert that abortion was made available to women who requested it (Van der Ros 1994; Wiik 1986; Gulli 1994). The clause that allowed doctors to opt out of delivering abortions for religious reasons—the conscientious objector's clause—did not seem to be a major obstacle. Wiik (1986: 151–2) describes how in 1978 medical staff 'organised civil disobedience' to refuse to participate in abortions in eight hospitals. Van der Ros (1994) mentions that these hospitals were in rural areas. The analyses do not indicate, however, that this particular movement actually obstructed women's abortion decisions. All three studies regard the virtual disappearance of back-street abortions as evidence for the effective delivery of abortion.

Anti-choice forces were unable to continue any significant opposition after 1978. In the 1990s two priests of the Norwegian Protestant Church who presented anti-choice positions during their sermons were removed from their positions by the leadership of the state-run church (Gulli 1994: 196). A bill to restrict abortion, put forward by the anti-choice lobby and the Christian People's Party, was defeated. Women helped to defeat the bill. 'This action [defeat of the bill] expressed the attitude and power of many women, including women politicians' (Gulli: 1994: 196). From these snippets about post-formulation, it appears that the feminist dynamics of formulation continued in implementation and that a woman-friendly abortion triad developed.

The policy sub-system style that produced the feminist policy outcomes was of high-agenda politics. Once women's groups and feminist advocates within the left-wing political parties persuaded party officials to support a feminist stance on abortion and to move 'the issue out of the bureaucratic, corporatist structure, and to introduce it into the parliamentary arena' (Wiik 1986: 148), abortion reform was soon adopted. Prior to the 1970s, abortion reform politics was relegated to a more closed corporatist decision-making process with some division in the policy community over abortion reform. It is difficult to establish the degree to which the style changed on implementation. What is certain is that doctors and state-run health services continued to honour women's right to choose even though the possibility for medical staff to opt out was provided. The distribution of state resources to women was not impeded by the abortion triad and hence it was not necessary for women's groups to get involved with service delivery. The various women's policy agencies created under the Equal Status Act in 1978 were not visible players in the implementation policy community. While many women were involved with policy formation, there were no significant mass-based demonstrations for the legalization of abortion.

❖ *2. Abortion Reform in the Netherlands since 1973: The 'Politics of Accommodation' Catches Up to a Woman-friendly Triad (Pre/Form.: 2/2 Post-form.: 2/3 = 9)*

A woman-friendly triad provided abortion on demand eleven years before the Parliament, limited by the 'politics of accommodation', adopted a law officially legalizing abortion. Feminist groups and movements, comprised mostly but not entirely of women, contributed both to the development of the triad prior to 1973 and to pre-formulation. They were virtually absent from the final formulation of the 1981 law and the ensuing 1984 regulation as well as from the abortion policy triad after 1984. Thus, the policy profile was highly feminist in pre-formulation but less so once the government agreed to support a draft bill on abortion.

The woman-friendly policy triad began to develop in the 1960s, despite the legal reality of criminalized abortion after 1886. After the Second World War, as the feminist triad developed, the number of criminal convictions decreased steadily. The last three convictions were in 1973 (Ketting 1994: 174). Outshoorn (1986b: 18) calls the decision not to prosecute a 'gentlemen's agreement' of 'leaving it to the doctors'. As long as abortions were conducted on therapeutic grounds, doctors were left alone. Up until the emergence of the new women's movement in the late 1960s, doctors had complete control over the practice of abortion and the definition of the issue. They were interested in responding to an increase in individual women's demands for abortion. In both the public and private sectors, doctors sought to develop a process by which the increasing demand could be responded to 'professionally and scientifically' (*sic*). Doctors in universities experimented with panels of doctors that would determine whether women's demands for abortion were medically grounded. Stimezo was a doctor-founded private organization that created a chain of abortion clinics and lobbied for the provision of therapeutic abortions.

Overcoming divisions over other areas of feminist activity, the new women's movements united behind feminist abortion reform. A new umbrella group, We Women Demand, that brought together 'women from the women's liberation movement, the trade unions, left-wing parties, and the organisation for gay rights' (Outshoorn 1986b: 20), was formed in 1974. Feminist groups made the defence of the new private clinics created by Stimezo a 'major goal' (Ketting 1994: 177). When the Minister of Justice attempted to close some clinics in 1976, women's groups occupied them. Outshoorn (1986a, b) documents how the women's movement and non-feminist reform groups forced the government to place the formulation of reform on its agenda in 1974.

It took seven years and many different versions of the bill before the law was actually adopted, and another three years before implementation measures were approved by Parliament in 1984. Thus, the women's movement contributed to the temporary suspension of the pattern of 'postponement and de-politicisation' followed by successive coalition governments of the right and the left, a part of Dutch 'politics of accommodation' (Outshoorn 1986b: 14). The movement was less successful in getting governments to sponsor a feminist bill. The 1981 law was ambiguous about giving women the right to choose, leaving several important implementation issues unresolved until 1984.

The Dutch women's movement dissipated after 1981 over questions about the usefulness of working within the 'politics of accommodation'. The feminist groups saw the 1981 law as a step backwards from previous liberal practice. One of the reasons for the delay in adopting implementing measures, according to Outshoorn (1986b: 79), was women's movement ambivalence to the law. It was not until 1985 that the government clarified the ambiguities and announced the state funding of all abortions. At that moment, the woman-friendly abortion triad could operate with government's legal and financial backing. Ketting's (1994) analysis of policy implementation in the early 1990s shows that both in the letter of the law and in practice abortion policy was feminist. Through consultation with their doctors, women could go to either public hospitals or the private clinics still run by Stimezo. If they did not want to go through a doctor they could consult family-planning facilities. Neither doctors' refusal nor the requirements of a five-day waiting period impeded women's demand for abortion.

As in the Norwegian case, two policy communities operated. The abortion policy triad operated in the arena of the private clinics and involved doctors and their organizations, private clinics management, state-run hospitals to a far lesser degree, and, from the early 1970s to 1981, women's groups. The style of the community has been consensual and semi-public. Collaboration between feminists and doctors occurred outside of the public purview. The arena was more public in the 1976 occupations of abortion clinics. The second policy community was centred in the parliamentary process of Dutch coalition governments. The arena was public when feminist-led abortion campaigns persuaded the political elite to abandon the politics of accommodation in 1973–7. Afterwards, the arena was private with the return of postponement and depoliticization. The decisions of the Minister of Health to fund abortions, for instance, appeared to attract little public attention outside of the confines of the Cabinet and the Parliament. Women's policy agencies were absent from both policy communities. As Outshoorn (1986b: 67) argues, the offices were developed after the height of the abortion campaign. Their focus was primarily on equality rather than women's specific policies like abortion and women's health.

While there was some anti-choice activity led by the Committee to Save the Unborn Child, anti-choice demands did not undermine the feminist content of the law or its feminist implementation. Anti-choice groups lobbied against the abortion laws and persuaded some policy-makers to oppose feminist reform (Outshoorn 1986b). Dutch attitudes about sexuality, abortion, and contraception explain in part the weakness of the anti-choice movement (Ketting 1986; 1994). The Dutch accept women rights to an abortion and 'couples do everything they can to prevent abortion' (Ketting 1994: 185). This includes taking advantage of free contraception established in part because of the 'general openness regarding questions of sexuality' (Ketting 1994: 183). This openness extended into the new women's movement as well (Kaplan 1992). The Netherlands has some of the lowest levels of legal abortion: half Great Britain's rate and one fourth the rates of Denmark and Sweden. In the early 1990s, there was no record of illegal abortions (Ketting 1994: 185).

❖ *3. US Abortion Reform since 1973: Limited Feminist Politics Meets an Active Anti-choice Movement in a 'Laissez-faire Triad' (Pre/Form.: 3/2 Post-form.: 3/1 = 9)*

The complexities of the federal, presidential system where interest group politics play a greater role than party discipline in determining policy development, and federal policy often leaves a great deal of latitude to individual State policy systems, make analysing a single abortion policy decision in the USA impossible. A powerful anti-choice movement that used the arsenal of tools available to groups, ranging from attaching pro-life amendments to federal legislation to killing doctors, and the equally powerful feminist responses makes pluralist American-style politics strong in abortion policy. Abortion reform is further complicated by the way it has played out in the constitutional arena of the Supreme Court. The original *Roe v. Wade* decision in 1973 placed women's right to choose solidly within the bounds of the Constitution and the right to privacy. Since then, there have been at least five major Supreme Court decisions on abortion.

US abortion policy formation is very different from abortion reform in Europe. In European unitary states a single law redefined the direction of abortion policy throughout the entire country; and usually, after a certain period of conflict, the issue was generally resolved with some conflict over implementation. In the USA abortion reform has not been resolved. It involves many actors at different levels of government. Pitched political battles turn around women's right to choose and the rights of the unborn. Policy decisions get undone and redone on a regular basis. Abortion has been a prominent political issue for years. Taking a position on abortion can make or break the fortunes of elected officials. As Studlar and Tatalovich (1996: 91) describe, 'Some observers have gone so far as to predict that abortion could be the issue that fractures the [Republican] party coalition'. They also argue that Canadian abortion policy has been decentralized in a similar manner, but the similarities between the US and Canada stop at the strength of the US anti-choice movement and the deep ongoing controversies over policy content and implementation.

148

The issue of free abortion on demand has rarely been articulated. The absence of universal health care in the USA and Americans' penchant for small government have precluded the issue from being raised in a serious manner. Instead, discussions of public funding have focused on the extent to which the government should subsidize women without economic means. Anti-choice opposition to any public funding has been more or less embraced in federal policy. Given the propensity of 'women with low income and little education' to be 'more vulnerable to abuse of reproductive services', and the absence of funding, the right to choose in practice is not available to women in lower income brackets (Stetson 1997*b*: 127). As Stetson (1997*b*: 127) points out, 'few voices in the public debate over reproductive rights deplore the inequity in access to safe reproductive service that results from social and economic circumstance'. The content of abortion policy in the USA, therefore, is limited to establishing a women's right to choose and not the financial cost of having the right to choose.

Federal government policy takes a hands-off approach to ensuring this limited right. The development of what Stetson (1996*a*) calls a 'laissez-faire triad' where the federal government allows women and doctors to work out abortion provisions with State governments and the presence of an active anti-choice movement, has meant that there is no single policy triad across the country. Instead, 'mini policy triads' developed within each State, with three different types of triads: woman-friendly, whereby States see that women get optimal access within the federal framework of limited abortion; woman-unfriendly, whereby States do their best to prevent women from getting this access; and laissez-faire, whereby States leave the anti-choice and feminist forces to 'battle it out in the courts' (Stetson 1996*a*: 114).

Women's descriptive representation has been very high throughout the bumpy development of abortion policy. Women's and feminist groups have taken a decisive role in defending women's rights to choose for women with economic means against anti-choice attack. As in other countries, 'the abortion issue has been central to the campaign for women's rights' (Stetson 1996*a*: 114). In the early stages of repeal and legalization, women's mobilization was quite similar to that in other countries. New women's groups and movements introduced feminist stances on abortion into non-feminist reform efforts, set up women's health collectives, and took cases of abortion to court. As the abortion campaign moved beyond the extension of women's rights to their defence, the US feminist movement strengthened at the same time as movements in other countries grew weak.

Since the early stages, there has been little feminist ambivalence about working within the political establishment. Feminist groups, with mostly women members, have been the major defenders of abortion rights. Activities have been broad-ranging and have included tens of thousands of women in rallies, lobbying, fund raising, and election campaigns. The majority of feminist action has been in the form of pressure from outside government. The federal-level Women's Bureau has been absent from abortion politics (Stetson 1995a). State-level women's commissions have taken some minor roles (Parry 1998).

Despite the highly complex nature of the policy-making system, a single style appears at all levels with a quite similar line-up of actors and the use of a similar array of policy instruments. Since *Roe v. Wade*, the policy style has been of high-agenda politics: controversial, polarized, and public. The same religious anti-choice and non-religious pro-choice actors compete to influence government policy-makers who try to avoid making controversial decisions. Legislation, court cases, administrative regulations, and executive orders become the battlefields for the two opposing camps.

❖ *4. The 1978 Law in Italy: A Moderately Feminist Profile in Formulation Fails to Translate into a Woman-friendly Triad (Pre/Form.: 3/2 Post-form.: 1/1 =7)*

The content of the 1978 law legalizing abortion in Italy reflected the highly complex process of pre-formulation and the controversies over abortion reform in a Catholic country with a successful mass-based feminist movement. The law was moderately feminist when compared with other countries, but within the Italian context a disappointment for feminist advocates of strong abortion reform. As Pisciotta (1986: 41) states, 'The law is a compromise between the political parties, between the stand of women's movements for women's rights to choose and the strong position of the Catholic Church'.

The law only partially provided women an unencumbered right to choose. The feminist part of the law extended free abortions in public facilities to women over 18 years of age. The limited part of the law complicated women's rights to choose by mandating a seven-day waiting period during which women were required to get counsel about not having an abortion, permitted medical staff members the right to opt-out of performing abortion services by including a 'conscientious objection' clause, required parental consent for women under 18, and allowed abortions after 90 days only in cases where the woman's life was at risk.

The limited feminist content of the law was in contrast to the unusually high level of women's descriptive representation in pre-formulation. In all, there were three major 'women's demonstrations' to back abortion reform. Pisciotta (1986: 35) reports that 10,000 women participated in 1975, 30,000 in a second demonstration the same year, and 50,000 in 1977. Women were active in the feminist abortion self-help movement prior to legalization. As political party activists in left-wing parties, women placed pressure on the mostly men leaders to support effective reform (Beckwith 1987). An all-women left-wing party organization, the Unione Donne Italiane (UDI), also lobbied political parties to support feminist reform (Beckwith 1987). Women participated in pro-abortion reform feminist groups like the Movimento della Liberazione della Donna (MLD) (Beckwith 1987; Caldwell 1986; Pisciotta 1986). Finally, women as voters brought an increased number of women deputies to Parliament in 1976 and helped to defeat an anti-abortion referendum in 1980 (Pisciotta 1986).

Prior to the extensive political activities of women, all the parties of the right as well as the powerful Communist Party avoided the issue of abortion (Beckwith 1987; Caldwell 1986). Women's action challenged a highly organized anti-choice movement backed by the Catholic Church. Women's political mobilization, according to Caldwell (1986) and Pisciotta (1986), contributed also to the historic victory of the left in 1976 and a sea-change in public attitudes about women's status and rights. Prior to the abortion campaign, the majority of Italians, including women, were hostile to feminist reforms; afterwards, a majority of the public supported sweeping changes in public policies for women. In 1983, for instance, the Italian public was ranked first out of EU member states 'in giving importance to women's situation' (cited in Pisciotta 1987: 44) in a poll conducted by the European Union.

The relatively high feminist policy profile in formulation had not translated into implementation by 1983. The 1978 law and an earlier 1975 law made provisions for the establishment of local *consultori familiara*—'health and maternity clinics'—to provide information and abortion services. Caldwell (1986: 118–19) shows that they existed only in certain regions of Italy. The provision of state services tended to be more common in Communist-dominated areas (Pisciotta 1986: 118). Immediately following the law's adoption, in the context of an active campaign by the Catholic Church, 72 per cent of doctors in Italy declared themselves to be conscientious objectors, a stand taken by 90 per cent of doctors in some regions (Caldwell 1986 and Pisciotta 1986).

Despite the pivotal role of women's movements and organizations in preformulation, there was no evidence of women's advocates in the provision of abortion services. As Ergas and Sassaroli (1977) argue, the women's movement completely lost their impetus after the abortion reforms:

> . . . it suffered the dramatic wearing down which derives from the fact that the confrontation with the institutions takes place by definition on the most anti-feminine, most compromised and most dangerous terrain. (Cited in Pisciotta 1986: 46)

Guadagnini's (1995) study of the two women's policy agencies created in the 1980s indicates that neither of the national-level offices was given the mandate nor took the initiative to close the gaps in abortion provision. The abortion policy triad unfolded, therefore, at least in the years immediately following the law, without any active representation of women's interests.

There were two different styles of the policy sub-system in formulation and post-formulation. In formulation, the style was of high agenda-status politics with a high level of polarization between the pro-choice and the anti-choice forces. The pro-abortion reform camp included anti-system and reform feminist groups, feminist activists in political parties, and parties of the left. In the anti-choice camp were the right-wing parties, the new anti-choice groups, and the Catholic Church. The arena for the policy community on pre-formulation was parliamentary and mass-based. In addition to the women's demonstrations, two referendums on abortion were put to the Italian public. Non-parliamentary actors were pivotal in agenda-setting. When decisions about policy content were made, they were made behind closed doors, and in some cases in a free vote. Members of Parliament were, therefore, not obliged to follow the party line.

In implementation until 1983, policy community activities were determined by the way in which the abortion policy triad operated at the local level. In most localities, the style was of low agenda-status politics, whereby doctors and staff decided privately to use the conscientious-objector provision and mid-level administrators and local elected councils were unable to control the extent of service provision.

❖ COMPARATIVE DISCUSSION: RELIGION AND INSTITUTIONAL DESIGN MAY MATTER

The examination of reproductive rights policy formation in the case of abortion reform provides the opportunity to examine the ways in which the same type of feminist policy is worked out in different systems. As usual the limitations of the source literature circumscribe the case analyses. Information on implementation in Norway and Italy is partial. As the Dutch case demonstrated, evaluation of policy immediately following the adoption of implementation regulations in 1984 was less optimistic than the evaluations of policy in the 1990s. The implementation of Italian policy may very well have become more feminist after the early 1980s. Nonetheless, there are some tentative comparative lessons to draw.

Table 8.2 Policy profile scores for cases of abortion policy

	Pre/Form.		Post-form.		Total
	D	S	D	S	
Norway: 1978 Abortion law	3	2	3	3	11
Netherlands: Abortion reform since 1973	2	2	2	3	9
United States: Abortion reform since 1973	3	1	3	1	9
Italy: 1978 Abortion law	3	2	1	1	7

In the Netherlands and Norway, a woman's right to choose to have a free abortion appears to be assured. As Table 8.2 indicates, in both countries woman-friendly abortion triads developed. In Italy, a moderately feminist law was diluted in implementation to produce a situation in which provision was not assured to all women. In the USA, although women's rights to choose has been reaffirmed in a recent Supreme Court decision, that right is restricted to women with economic means. While woman-friendly triads exist in the USA, they are found in only certain States.

Women's substantive representation in all four cases was quite high in the formulation stages. Feminist groups, composed mostly of women, took major roles in injecting feminist stances on abortion into debates and policy. In the Netherlands, Norway, and Italy successful feminist movements dispersed once laws were adopted, less because of their success than because of the organizational crisis posed to anti-system groups by their involvement in establishment politics. Women's groups may not have been rejuvenated in the abortion policy triads because of their woman-friendly nature in the Netherlands and in Norway. The data gap on Italian implementation leaves the issue unresolved there. Clearly, women's descriptive representation in the USA remains high because of the need to defend the limited right of women to choose. Whether this is an indicator of a feminist policy profile is questionable given that high levels of women's involvement have not led to feminist policy in content or practice. Thus, while the score for descriptive representation is high in post-formulation, substantive representation is quite low.

Policy sub-system styles were quite similar among the European countries. Two separate communities developed, one based in parliaments focused on reform and the other based in the triads focused on implementation. The styles of each community were also similar. In the parliamentary policy community, debates were public. Groups outside of the mainstream attempted to persuade recalcitrant officials of both the right and the left to take a position. In the triads, doctors, and state actors worked together in a consensual manner to deliver abortion. In Italy, however, medical staff opted out, depending on the region. In the Dutch case, a woman-friendly triad emerged prior to the adoption of policy, although doctors were not compelled by law to give women the right to choose. In a way, feminist implementation preceded feminist formulation. The triad was based in the private sector with most abortion clinics under the authority of the private group Stimezo. In the USA, there was no single policy community style in implementation given the way abortion triads varied across States. Two similarities found in all policy communities were the role of feminist groups in articulating feminist demands for abortion and the absence of women's policy machineries in all stages of policy development.

Of all the explanations for these similarities and differences, the role of religion provides some of the most compelling. In Italy and the USA, it was the prevalence of orthodox religious values about the life of the unborn and the morality of abortion, although from different denominational origins, that contributed to feminist policy failures. In Italy, the power of the Roman Catholic Church was important but not definitive. Catholic regions were more apt to have poor abortion provision than non-Catholic regions. Moreover, similar conscientious objector provisions in Norway led to very different policy outcomes from those in Italy. The leadership of the state-run Protestant church in Norway took action against renegade pro-life priests—a sharp contrast to the Catholic Church-organized campaign to compel medical staff to declare themselves conscientious objectors in Italy.

In the Netherlands, parties affiliated with organized religion participated in stalling abortion reform; they did not, however, prevent the delivery of abortion on demand. Also, the stalling was more a product of Dutch politics of accommodation than religious influence in politics. The anti-choice movement emerged only when the confessional parties were unable to block impending abortion legislation. Thus, the dynamics of Dutch multi-party politics were more important than any religious influence. Broad-based progressive attitudes about abortion, contraception, and sexuality in the Netherlands indicate that traditional religious doctrine has had little resonance in Dutch society on reproductive issues. In the USA, the salience of orthodox Christian positions on abortion underpinned the widespread and sustained support for the pro-life movement and the policies that have been a product of that movement.

To be sure, other factors are important. Traditional hostility in the US to an active welfare state explains opposition to state-funded abortion there. Also, the particular federal design of policy-making institutions in the USA is quite important in abortion policy distinctiveness. The presence of strong women's movements was crucial in getting governments to make feminist policies. In contrast to other feminist policy sub-sectors, there appears to be an important link between left-wing governing majorities and pro-feminist reforms. The coalition governments typical of the Netherlands make it difficult to assess the influence of left-wing governments there. Nonetheless, it was only in the USA that right-wing governments pursued systematically restrictive policies, under the pressure of the religious right to roll back liberal policy. Throughout Western Europe neo-liberal governments left abortion rights alone.

❖ NOTES

1 For a discussion of the recent feminist comparative and theoretical literature on body politics in the context of citizenship and policy issues, see Beasley and Bacchi (2000).

2 See for example Stetson (1996b); in Germany, Winkler (1996); in Canada, Cameron (1996); McCormack (1996); in the USA, Stetson (1997b); Diamond (1988); and in the USA compared with France, Merchant (1996).

3 Tables in Outshoorn (1996) and Rolston and Eggert (1994*b*) provide information for the first four columns for the European countries. Information on the USA is from Studlar and Tatalovich (1996); Scheppele (1996); Stetson (1996*a*); and on Canada from Studlar and Tatalovich (1996) and Scheppele (1996).

9 ❖ Body Politics II: Sexuality and Violence Policy

❖ OVERVIEW

Sexuality and violence policies promote women's rights and status in dealing with the politics of their bodies outside reproduction. There are two interrelated components of this last policy sub-sector that can also be differentiated by the specific focus of a given policy: violent behaviour and sexual behaviour. Anti-violence policies aim to identify, punish, and prevent violence against women. The targeted violence usually occurs in the domestic arena of the couple. It is 'largely perpetrated by men over women' and can involve more than sexual violence, including 'mental, physical, sexual, emotional, or economic abuse' (Abrar 1996: 193). Violence policies focus on rape and domestic violence and are often referred to as 'woman battery'. Men can be covered by these policies as cases of man battering arise. Research, however, shows that these are quite rare.

Policies on sexuality that may indirectly address violence 'police desire' (Gotell 1996) in a feminist manner through the regulation of prostitution, pornography, and sexual harassment. Whereas sexual harassment can involve physical force, policies against sexual harassment target unwanted sexual advances and/or sexually intimidating environments at work. Men may be protected by sexuality and violence policy; however, if policy is made in a feminist frame, women are the major beneficiaries.

In the context of the personal being political, violence issues preoccupy contemporary feminists who see male violence against women as an empirical reality in every society. Nelson and Chowdhury (1994), for instance, in their study of global women's issues identify 'violence, safety, and security' as one of the four issue areas that mobilize women worldwide. In Great Britain, sexuality and violence issues were at the centre of two out of four major second-wave feminist campaigns (Lovenduski 1986a: 77–8). In Italy, after the compromises on abortion reform, the feminist movement 'sought to introduce a feminist issue directly into parliament: the issue of sexual violence' (Beckwith 1987: 162).

Radical feminism places sexuality issues at the centre of its action. In addition to being 'unambiguous in its location of the sources of women's oppression which its sees first and foremost as the fault of men', radical feminists argue that sexuality is what 'makes men the "intimate" enemy' (Lovenduski 1986a: 69). Liberation, for radical feminists, can occur only through woman-centred action that frees women from the patriarchal control of men through the family, the bedroom, and the womb. Emphasizing men's and women's biological differences and highly suspicious of the patriarchal state, radical feminists focus on 'sexuality and reproduction, including pornography, rape and violence against women' (Norris 1987: 24).

Radical feminist suspicions of working within what they see as a patriarchal system has underpinned the development of grass-roots campaigns against violence. The feminist campaigns are aimed specifically at women and are organized outside the sphere of government and mainstream actors like political parties and trade unions. Women's shelter movements, in many countries, create and maintain shelters for women victims of violence and crisis centres to help women deal with their abusive situations. The movements have been instrumental in drawing public and government attention to sexual violence issues and in providing support to women at the local level, often with the help of government funding. As Sawer (1994: 85) describes in the case of Australia, 'Through such self-help services as refuges, health centres and rape crisis centres the women's movement in the 1970s revealed a level of unmet need that required government rather than volunteer actions'.

Women's movements have been involved with campaigns for legislation, but even these tend to begin at the local level. The two feminist movement campaigns on sexuality and violence policies in Great Britain that began at the local level both led to legislation: the Sexual Offences Act in 1976 and the Domestic Violence Act in 1976 (Lovenduski 1986a: 78–9). Take-back-the-night marches organized in various parts of Italy, France, and Great Britain in the 1970s, according to Kaplan (1992: 251), were also instrumental in placing sexual violence issues on government agendas.

Non-feminist interests become involved with sexuality and violence policy issues under pressure not from feminists but usually from the political right. Right-wing activists who seek to promote social morality, usually based on fundamentalist orthodox Christianity, in sexuality issues often enter into 'uneasy alliances' with radical feminists. The alliances are found typically on prostitution and pornography. For example, when a 1985 bill in the Netherlands sought to legalize pornography, 'many feminists . . . focused themselves in an uneasy alliance with the defenders of traditional morality' (Outshoorn and Swiebel 1998: 156). In France, Catholic conservative groups and feminists often work side by side on committees to use state funds to help women prostitutes, for quite different political reasons.

❖ SEXUALITY AND VIOLENCE POLICY

Widespread interest in sexuality and violence policies came later in the second wave of feminism than did interest in reproductive rights polices, partially because the abortion issue sapped the energy resources and attention of the new women's movement. Women's movements started to organize women's shelters in the early 1970s, but as Weldon (1998: 8 n. 3) asserts, it was not until the 1980s that governments systematically began to turn their attention to violence issues, and not until the early 1990s that public policy action was taken. The sequence may have begun slightly earlier in Great Britain because of the early treatment of abortion reform in 1967. In Norway, there was 'a boom in the first half of the 1980s when about six new centres [to help women victims of violence] were established each year' (Van der Ros 1994: 538). Norris identified 'increased recognition of the need to deal with violence against women and rape crisis centres, often with government financial support' (Norris 1987: 79) as one of the new trends in women's issues, beginning in the 1980s, in post-industrial nations. Active government stances on sexual harassment in the work-place are arguably one of the more recent areas of sexuality and violence policies. Most countries adopted anti-sexual harassment legislation in the early 1990s.

The frequency of anti-violence government initiatives at the national level over the past 20 years is presented in Table 9.1 on the next page. It is based on Weldon's (1998) cross-national study of the determinants of government responses to 'violence against women'. She enumerates seven different policies that contribute to an effective response. They coincide with UN recommendations for national action on violence against women in the 1990s (for example, UN 1998): legal reform on domestic violence and sexual assault; government funding for women's shelters, for emergency housing for victims, for crisis centres for victims, for training professionals who deal with victims, and for public education; and a central coordinating agency. The pattern of anti-violence initiatives shown in Table 9.1 reflects the trend toward more policies on sexuality and violence issues in the 1990s across the core countries and post-industrial democracies more generally.

As Valiente (1997a) and other analysts point out, the first stage in the development of effective sexual violence policies is to convince non-feminist actors that sexual violence is a real problem; in other words, that violence against women is no longer an acceptable social condition but a public problem that needs to be addressed by government action. Feminist actors must spend a great deal of time convincing often recalcitrant non-feminist policy actors that sexual violence is a legitimate object of government policy. The issue of problem definition is also crucial in adopting sexual harassment policy. A major part of policy formation in this last sub-sector of policy, therefore, is the documentation and study of the incidence of violent acts against women. In many countries, the study of violence against women was initiated by women's group in the late 1970s. Women's policy offices and other non-feminist government agencies

Table 9.1 Frequency of national government initiatives on violence against women in core countries, 1974–1994

Country	1974	1984	1994
Italy	0	0	0
Ireland	0	0	5
Spain	0	1	3
Denmark	0	2	2
Sweden	0	3	4
Norway	0	0	4
France	0	4	5
Germany	0	0	2
Netherlands	0	2	3
United States	2	2	6
Great Britain	0	3	4
Canada	1	2	6
Australia	0	2	7

Source: Weldon (1998: Table 2). Seven possible initiatives per country.

in criminal justice increasingly participate in collecting data on violence. In Spain and Ireland, for example, domestic violence was identified in the context of the divorce issue when women's policy agencies and women's groups found a significant number of women seeking divorce had been victims of abuse (Galligan 1998; Threlfall 1996b; Kaplan 1992: 203).

Extra-national institutions play an important role in the formation of national sexuality and violence policy. Their role is more in agenda setting and problem definition than in formulation or implementation. The international dimension of sexuality and violence policies is even more important in prostitution issues where trafficking women across national boundaries and sexual tourism have blurred the lines between the national and the international. Students of European Union sex equality policy argue that its legal 'framework is directed at men and women as workers, not sex equality in society at large' (Meehan and Collins 1996: 223). Radical feminists are often quite critical of how European Union policy deals with sexuality and violence issues. As Elman (1996b: 1) asserts, 'The politics of European integration is rarely discussed in a manner which holds the sexual subordination of women as political in nature, economic in consequence and worthy of state or Union action'. Nonetheless, EU policy has been adopted on sexual harassment in the work place.[1] Furthermore, EU policy in the early 1990s took 'sexual identities' more into account than in the past (Hoskyns 1996: 158). A key part of the shift, according to Hoskyns, was the participation of women's networks in policy discussions at the EU level.

❖ SEXUALITY AND VIOLENCE POLICY

Other international institutions and meetings have been important levers in the pre-formulation of sexual violence policies; however, none has the authority of EU policy. For instance, in 1977 the Brussels Tribunal on Violence Against Women brought together women working in crisis centres (Van der Ros 1994: 538). The Council of Europe also held several summits on prostitution, trafficking women, and violence against women. The United Nations has treated violence against women's issues since the early 1990s. It developed recommendations for countries to take action against violence in its Declaration on the Elimination of Violence Against Women in 1993 and subsequent iterations at the Beijing World Conference on Women and its aftermath (Weldon 1998, 2001; Lycklama à Nijeholt, Swiebel, and Wieringa 1998).

While the comparative literature is quite large,[2] studies of sexuality and violence policy issues are uneven and lack a common framework or theoretical purpose. Few studies focus on the politics of policy formation or conduct separate analyses of policy formation in a given national context. Often, definitions of violence are put forward, without discussing policies.[3] When sexuality and violence policy issues are treated separately—for example, in Galligan (1998), Lovenduski and Randall (1993), or Stetson (1997*b*; 1987), the same range of issues tend to be covered: rape, domestic violence, sexual harassment, prostitution, pornography, and, in some cases, lesbian rights and race issues. This similar array of policies is not defined as a unified area of policy; although Gotell (1996) uses the label 'policing desire' to describe pornography and prostitution policies. The literature on violence policy issues is much larger than on sexuality issues.[4] Few studies have examined the politics of policies that 'police desire', particularly on prostitution and trafficking women.[5]

Weldon (1998; 2001) and Stetson (1995b) suggest some specific criteria with which to evaluate whether sexuality and violence policies are actually feminist. Stetson (1995*b*) develops an index to determine whether countries meet a 'feminist standard for human rights' based on four areas of government action, all of which fall into the category of body politics: abortion, battery, rape, and prostitution. For each, she furnishes an operational definition and a three-point ordinal 'feminist policy scale' to determine whether national policies are feminist. Countries that score the highest, according to Stetson, have policies that classify rape 'as a crime of sexual assault or against freedom and dignity, defined according to force used by the perpetrator, and law allows no marital exclusion'; that 'criminalize woman battery, the government has active policy and programs for assisting victims'; and that make 'pimping and procuring criminal' and no 'arrest of prostitutes' (Stetson 1995*b*: 77, 76, 78).

Weldon's operational definition of effective violence policy, cited below, resonates with Stetson's emphasis on criminalization and support programmes. It also emphasizes the importance of a gendered approach to policies where domestic violence is situated in the context of gender-based hierarchies.

Weldon grounds her definition solidly in the international literature on violence against women as well (Connors 1989; 1994; Bunch 1991; Davies 1994;
Dobash and Dobash 1992; Heise with Pitanguy and Germain 1994; Heise *et al.*
1994; UN 1998).[6]

> Effective government responses recognize the links between these different forms
> of violence as well as the underlying problem of male dominance. Government
> responses to violence must attend to the immediate needs of victims, such as
> shelters, medical care and protection from further abuse, as well as to long term
> preventative efforts such as public education programs (Weldon 1998: 6–7).

Given the absence of comparative studies that treat systematically sexuality
and violence policy issues, the selection of policy cases in this chapter is quite
restricted. A broad range of policies is still represented across the four policy
cases: anti-sexual harassment legislation; the subsidization of women's shelters;
and a public information campaign on domestic violence. The two cases of sexual harassment legislation capture the high politics of parliamentary policy formation and the other two cases present the feminist policy dynamics at the
grass-roots level, so prevalent in sexuality and violence policy formation. The
two cases of municipal-level policy formation show the complex coalitions that
emerge around violence issues between non-feminist state actors, women's policy offices, and radical feminist women's shelter movements.

The case of the Zero Tolerance campaign in Edinburgh was chosen for the
Protestant Liberal countries to highlight the differences between politics in the
different parts of Great Britain. There are also few studies of Scottish feminist
policy formation politics. Women's shelter movements at the municipal level in
the Protestant Social Democrat countries are quite widespread; the Swedish
case has been particularly well-documented in the English-language literature.
Sexual harassment policy is traced in Spain and France given the interesting
similarities between the two cases in timing, cultural context, and influence
from EU policy. The published analyses on both cases use a similar policy-stage
framework shared also by this book. As a result, the results of the cases of sexual
harassment policy in Spain and France may provide more uniformly comparable results.

❖ THE POLICY CASES

❖ 1. The 1992 Zero Tolerance Campaign in Edinburgh: An Effective Strategic Partnership and a Woman-friendly Political Environment Produces Radical Feminist Policy (Pre/Form.: 3/3 Post-form.: 3/3 = 12)

> The Zero Tolerance Campaign . . . seeks to challenge existing power relations and
> effect far-reaching social change; it is feminist in the way it links sexual violence,

domestic violence and child sexual abuse as a part of the 'continuum of violence'; it names emotional psychological abuse as forms of violence. The campaign uses a feminist analysis of violence as a male abuse of power and it challenges men to take responsibility for their violence. In addition it specifically uses empowering images of women rather than victim images. (Mackay 1996: 211–12)

Mackay's description of the aims of the six month-long public awareness campaign on violence against women in Edinburgh in 1992 reads as a textbook case of feminist policy. In addition to its radical feminist content, the campaign contributed to empowering women both within the process as members of the feminist strategic partnership that emerged around the policy initiative and as otherwise powerless victims of violence. Mackay's assessment of the post-formulation stages reveals the continuation of this highly feminist policy profile, with high policy feedback in state and society that included a government-sponsored impact assessment of the campaign and a level of international policy diffusion—authorities in Britain and Australia emulated the campaign—often associated with England and the USA (Mackay 1996: 208). Unlike similarly radical public awareness campaigns, the Edinburgh campaign met with little backlash: what Mackay (1996: 215) characterizes as 'wobbles rather than storms'.

The policy community on the campaign was dominated by feminist actors. The major state player and decision-maker was the Edinburgh District Council's Women's Committee. The committee worked closely with the autonomous women's movement and women members of city government in a strategic feminist partnership. Together they launched a study to identify the problem of violence against women, designed a programme in response to the identified problems, and sold the campaign to non-feminist actors in the community, including churches and all political parties as well as the municipal government. The style of the community was highly consensual with a mixture of public and private venues. Whereas the programme and the problem definition were quite public, the design of the campaign occurred behind closed doors.

Given that policy development was at the municipal level in the Scottish context, the lessons to be drawn for national-level feminist policy-making are limited. Spin-off programmes sponsored by the Scottish Home Office throughout Scotland, as well as in numerous local authorities in Britain, including in Conservative municipalities, and in South Australia may provide further evidence as to whether or not the Edinburgh case was a feminist aberration. Kelly (1999) shows that the programmes in England were not as successful as Edinburgh's, thus suggesting that the success of the Zero Tolerance Campaign success may have been an aberration.

It does not appear that the feminist successes went beyond public relations, including the Scottish Home Office's £300,000 advertizing campaign. Analyses cited by Mackay (1996: 200) indicate that there are limits to the feminist profile of national-level violence policies in Great Britain, including the treatment of violence issues as social welfare rather than gender and power problems, the absence of a national framework for violence policy, and a shortfall in funding to women's aid and rape centres.

Even if this is a deviant case limited to municipal politics, it still can provide some useful insights into the ingredients of feminist policy formation. Two major factors played a role in the feminist policy profile. First, the feminist strategic partnership included a women's policy agency, women in public office, and autonomous women's groups. Mackay emphasizes the important role of women officials as elected members of the city council and as administrative officers as well as the presence of strong state feminist offices and autonomous women's groups. The strategic partnership not only agreed on a common agenda but the leaders presented enough of the campaign to non-feminist actors to gain support without frightening them with what might have been seen as an overly feminist campaign. Second, the Edinburgh political environment provided a highly woman-friendly environment with a left-wing municipal government 'led by a youngish, progressive Labour Left administration since 1984' (Mackay 1996: 211) in a Scottish context of opposition to the Conservative-controlled national government. There was little evidence of any significant international influence, although Mackay (1996: 208) does mention that the idea of the original campaign was based on Canadian initiatives.

❖ *2. Public Funding of Women's Shelters in Sweden, 1978–1995:*
The Feminist Movement-'Democratic Order' Stand-off Produces
Incremental Feminist Policy (Pre/Form.: 3/1 Post-form.: 3/1 = 8)

This second case examines an example of the public funding of women's shelters. Shelters are usually first established by volunteers. The long-term success of shelters in helping women is dependent on external funding for staff and locale. As Elman (1996a: 35) points out, 'The battered women's movement, unlike many other movements, cannot subsist on the financial support of its constituents'. As a consequence, 'activists turned to the state for fiscal assistance'. In the Swedish context, where private sector philanthropy is rendered obsolete by high levels of state support for social services, the bulk of funding comes from the state either at the national or at the local levels.

Eduards' (1997) and Elman's (1996a) studies on the women's shelter movement are used to sketch a general picture of public funding of women's shelter since it first began in the late 1970s. Both the style of the policy community and the profile of funding policies for women's shelters can be characterised by Eduards'(1997) argument about the interface between feminist demands and the non-feminist 'democratic order'. In the 'face-off', feminist demands for gendered policies and women's culture clash with the gender-neutral dominant political culture. The woman-specific feminist demands often lose to the dominant democratic order that rejects woman-centred policies and action.

Women's shelters in Sweden have been established for the most part at the municipal level, although there are several at the county level. In 1995, there were 133 shelters. The government considered women's shelters to include safe homes for victims of violence, crisis centres, and phone-in crisis lines (Elman 1996a: 39). The National Organisation of Emergency Shelters for Battered Women (ROKS) was founded in 1984. According to Eduards, the group has followed a consistently woman-centred feminist strategy. Since its creation, ROKS has acted as a sectoral representative at the national level for the shelters and woman-battery issues. In 1995, 121 out of the 133 shelters in Sweden were members. A new regional association was founded in 1994 in western Sweden and organized 16 shelters (Elman 1996a: 142). Funding for shelters was given directly to the local shelters. ROKS began to receive limited state funds in 1988 for its staff and national office.

A survey by ROKS in 1994 showed that 96 shelters received 25m Swedish kronor ($US2.63m), 21m ($2.2m) of which came from the municipalities and 3m ($320,000) from the national government (Elman 1996a: 145).[7] The amount of state funds for shelters has increased since funding began in the late 1970s and women's shelters have remained a permanent institutional fixture in municipal social service. Their institutionalization is uneven, with most shelters being staffed by a combination of part-time professionals and volunteers. Restricted budgets have also prevented complete professionalization (Eduards 1997; Elman 1996a: 42).[8] The dependence on volunteerism should be placed within the context of its uniqueness in Swedish society where, according to Elman (1996a: 42), 'Volunteerism is viewed contemptuously'. Also, the rate of increase in state funding decreased by a net amount of 1.5m kronor ($158,000) in 1995.

Elman is more sceptical than Eduards as to the degree to which funding policy was actually feminist. Eduards (1997: 175, 148) asserts that there has been 'a greater acceptance of the feminist definition of assault as an expression of women's control' and 'a greater degree of institutional and professional responses for the situation of battered women'. Elman's assessment, particularly when compared with Sweden's record on sex equality in other areas, is that 'battering and rape programs and reforms are best characterised as weak and reserved' (1996a: 118). Combined with the decline in funding and partial professionalization of the staff, substantive representation of women's interest in both formulation and post-formulation stages was low, a score of 1 for both stages.

The politics of funding women's shelters reflects the local dynamics of Sweden's unitary system. Funding decisions are taken at the municipal levels by elected members of city councils, appointed members of corporatist commissions, and bureaucrats. It is at this level that the stand-off between the women's shelters and the non-feminist public officials takes place. Eduards calls the dynamic a 'catch-22' for the feminist women's shelters. Government officials grant money only if certain levels of institutional practice are met. Underfunded shelters are often unable or unwilling to meet those standards. The stand-off is intensified by different organizational norms and political goals. 'Taken together, one can speak of the centre's operations being based on trust, women's solidarity and anonymity, principles which are opposed to the prevailing democratic code of distance gender-neutrality and openness' (Eduards 1997: 152).

The woman-centred feminist shelters at the local and national levels are for the most part staffed by women. Their activities also have the potential to empower women victims of battering. Women in public offices at the local level have apparently played important roles in funding the feminist shelters. As a 1991 study shows, 'there is a connection between a high level of political representation of women in Swedish municipalities and the existence of women's shelters' (cited in Eduards 1997: 166). Thus, there may be a direct link between the woman-centred nature of the policy, the activities of feminist women in the shelters, and the support of women on municipal councils, committees, and boards. The only feminist actor missing in the local strategic partnership is women's policy offices. The national-level equal employment agencies do not participate in the policy at the local level.

The style of the locally-based policy community was divided between the non-feminist 'democratic order' in government and the feminist society-based women's shelters. The feminist versus non-feminist stand-off tends to take place within the arena of the councils, committees, and boards that make municipal decisions. Feminist protest activities have been covered in the press as well. There is little evidence of one party favouring feminist funding more than others.

International influence has been indirect, tending toward policy diffusion and solidarity building. Both Elman (1996a) and Eduards (1997) point out that feminist ideas about woman's battery in Sweden were inspired by smaller earlier movements in England and the USA. Also, international efforts on violence against women have been used as a touchstone for the Swedish women's shelter movement. International networking intensified in the 1990s with the creation of a Nordic association for shelters. The absence of EU policy in this area, however, means that there is little real policy authority from outside Sweden to pressure the 'democratic order' to respond to feminist demands.

❖ *3. Spanish Sexual Harassment Reform in 1989: Divided Feminist Demands; Symbolic Content; Minimal Results (Pre/Form.: 2/2 Post-form.: 1/1 = 6)*

A coalition of feminist trade unionists and femocrats in the Instituto de la Mujer (IM) persuaded the Socialist (PSOE) majority to introduce a clause prohibiting sexual harassment in a 1989 bill on family leave. The final act included a clause that defined sexual harassment at work as a punishable offence; 'employers acts against the intimacy and dignity of workers (sexual harassment included) are considered very grave, punishable by fines of between 500,000 to 15,000,000 pesetas' (cited in Valiente 1997a: 182–3). No other specifics about implementation, administrative oversight, or prevention were given in the law. As Valiente asserts, in both content and implementation, the law was highly symbolic. Legislation specifically on sexual harassment was adopted in 1995. The following discussion examines policy formation from the mid-1980s up to the adoption of the 1995 reform.

Beginning in the 1980s, feminists in the women's departments of two of the major trade unions and femocrats in the IM at the national level pursued a 'campaign to define sexual harassment as a problem that deserved state intervention' (Valiente 1997a: 177). Independently from each other, the trade unionists and femocrats collected information about the incidence of and attitudes about sexual harassment and lobbied PSOE government officials to take action. The IM included three measures on sexual harassment in its 1988–90 Equality Plan (Valiente 1997a: 179.). Party feminists had also persuaded PSOE- led town councils in the 1980s to open crisis centres (Threlfall 1996b: 133).There did not appear to be any other advocates of sexual harassment policy than femocrats and feminist trade unionists. The majority of non-feminist actors were sceptical. As Valiente (1997a: 187) states, 'It is important to stress that sexual harassment had been invisible in Spanish policy discourse until feminists in the state and trade unions raised the issue and called for government interventions'.

A majority of feminists involved with the sexual harassment campaign put forward a narrow definition of sexual harassment—'sexual blackmail by superiors'—rejecting what has been identified with an Anglo-American approach developed by US feminist jurist Catharine MacKinnon and codified in US law (Elman 1996a). This broader approach includes 'hostile environment harassment' and 'quid pro quo' harassment by colleagues as well as superiors. Valiente (1997a: 180) indicates that the majority of Spanish feminists who supported the narrower definition did so because the broader stance was 'too radical a position, alien to Latin culture'. The final clause did not specify the actual approach; however, it was clear that non-feminist actors would not go beyond the narrow approach backed by a majority of the feminist advocates. With only a few conservative opponents in parliament—the conservative position was articulated by a female MP during the debates—the article became a part of the 1989 act.

Outside of the relatively powerless IM, which published a new guide to women's rights that included sexual harassment, no other government agency took action in implementing the new policy. The law did not assign oversight responsibility to any agency. Four ministries included sexual harassment clauses in their collective agreements; a very poor showing, according to Valiente. Studies of the implementation of the law up to 1995 show few complaints have been filed, much less addressed. Non-feminist trade union leaders and representatives appeared to take little interest in the new rights; references to sexual harassment were absent 'in most collective agreements and in negotiations between 'employers and union delegates'. Even more than trade unions, employers were 'the weakest links in the implementation chain' (Valiente 1997a: 186), given that they still did not officially recognize that sexual harassment was a problem in the mid-1990s.

Both trade union and women's policy-agency feminists attempted to strengthen their positions by linking up with various international efforts on sexual harassment by attending meetings like the International Confederation of Free Trade Unions (Valiente 1997a: 177). As Valiente shows, feminists were able to gain support for the narrow approach to sexual harassment by capitalizing on the political consensus on Spain's full participation in the New Europe and by arguing that other countries in the EU that did not have puritan cultures had national policies on sexual harassment.

The policy community style is reminiscent of styles found in other instances of feminist symbolic reform. Feminist advocates, both together and independently, attempt to convince recalcitrant non-feminist policy-makers. The policy-makers respond with stalling tactics followed by watered-down policies that do not challenge the status quo. Despite feminist efforts to make the issue public, non-feminists make the non-decisions and decisions about symbolic reform behind closed doors, where it is difficult for feminists to enter: trade union commissions, cabinet councils, parliamentary committees, and so forth. These same dynamics occur in implementation; feminists attempt to apply the new law and non-feminist actors are apathetic or openly hostile to concrete implementation. Although most of the feminists involved with policy formation were women, they had a marginal position in pre-formulation and formulation. The absence of administrative outputs and of feminist mobilization on the 1989 reform also contributed to making women's descriptive representation even lower in post-formulation.

❖ 4. French Sexual Harassment Reform in 1992: Feminist Consensus; Symbolic Responses (Pre/Form.: 2/1 Post-form.: 2/1 = 6)

French sexual harassment policy displayed similar symbolic politics in its style and profile in all stages of the policy process as the Spanish case.[9] In 1992, two pieces of legislation defined sexual harassment as a punishable offence. An eleventh-hour article, introduced by former Minister of Woman's Rights and a Socialist deputy, Yvette Roudy, into ongoing penal-code reform inserted a simple legal definition of sexual harassment. A second specific law established a complaints procedure and recommended that preventive measures be developed by firm-level safety commissions. It did not require employers or trade union representatives to participate.

The High Council of Equal Employment, the advisory body established by the 1983 equal employment law, was charged with oversight. As with French equal employment policy more generally, the work inspectorate was to enforce the new provisions. The government made no effort to help the already overloaded inspectorate to deal with the new obligations. The small coalition of feminist groups, femocrats, and activists that led the campaign for authoritative policy on both direct and indirect harassment saw the law as a defeat for their cause. Reflecting the open hostility of non-feminist actors in trade unions, parliament, and the Socialist cabinet to what they saw as an inherently 'Anglo-Saxon' concept, the final bill excluded hostile environment harassment and did not use the term 'harcèlement sexuel'.

From 1985 to 1994, a Paris-based coalition of feminists from the women's policy agency, one of the five major trade union confederations, and feminist jurists led by the group Association Européenne contre les Violences Faites aux Femmes au Travail (AVFT), with early support from a more established feminist reform group, the Ligue du Droit des femmes (LDF), drew attention to the problem and lobbied the government from within and outside the state to adopt reform. Governments of the left and the right resisted the feminist demands, including, in 1989–91, the Socialist Deputy Minister of Women's Rights. Government stalling was reversed by a combination of factors that had little to do with the feminist campaign. These included a Cabinet reshuffle that brought in a pro-EU Prime Minister and a Deputy Minister of Women's Rights who wanted to present her own bill, the formulation of EU policy recommendations on indirect and direct sexual harassment, and the successful adoption of Yvette Roudy's private member's bill.

Femocrats in charge of the women's ministry's working group on sexual harassment had formulated a feminist draft bill as early as 1990. The bill included both types of harassment and authoritative provisions for implementation. Not only did they consult officially French feminist advocates but they invited a male EU femocrat who had been a key player in EU sexual harassment policy to speak at one of their meetings. Descriptive and substantive representation was very high, up to the time the femocrat bill was presented to the Council of Ministers. Even though the minister backed her femocrat's bill, the non-feminist members of the Cabinet refused to sponsor the more authoritative feminist version. The bill proposal was stripped of its more authoritative provisions before it was presented to National Assembly. Even so, parliamentarians from both sides of the aisle joined together to oppose any policy that would threaten 'individual liberty' (sic) by importing what many saw as foreign values from the USA. The fear of what one deputy called 'American repression' was quite strong in the context of widespread shock in France about the repercussions of sexual harassment for Supreme Court nominee, Clarence Thomas.

This mismatch between descriptive 'substantive' representation mismatch continued in post-formulation, particularly given the highly limited nature of the 1992 law. On the one hand, femocrats in the national ministry and, at the regional level, women in one trade union, and the feminist anti-sexual harassment group, the AVFT, tried to use the law to help victims of sexual harassment and to promote prevention programmes in firms. At one national meeting hosted by the femocrats in the ministry, a single male work inspector voluntarily attended and actively participated. On the other hand, the same line-up of non-feminist forces that had opposed authoritative policy in formulation—Ministry of Labour officials, employers, Socialist Party officials, and most trade unions—took action only when prodded by a combined feminist effort. Employers recognized that sexual harassment was a problem in the firm, but they were clearly sceptical about the degree to which sexual harassment was a costly problem. In France, as in Spain, the dynamics of the Romano-Germanic code law system prevent large settlements on any employment discrimination cases. The incentive of costly settlements, which has spurred management in other countries to take action, therefore was not present in France.

❖ Comparative Discussion: Cultural Attitudes About Sex, Local Politics, and the Type of Legal System May Matter

As the scores in Table 9.2 show, in an area of policy that many argue is the most blatant feminist challenge to the non-feminist state, often responded to with resistance or backlash, the four policy cases were quite feminist. Whereas stalling and non-decision-making were a part of pre-formulation in Spain and France, non-feminist policy actors capitulated to feminist demands with symbolic responses in a more pronounced way in Spain than in France. In Spain, non-feminist actors in the mid-1990s were still not convinced that sexual harassment was a problem. In both countries there was no consensus outside small elite feminist networks that government should pursue preventive action. The Swedish and Scottish cases displayed much more developed feminist policy profiles. In Sweden, feminist policy developed incrementally in the context of the tug-of-war between the non-feminist state and the feminist society-based women's shelter movement. Contradicting analyses of feminist policy that suggest the impossibility of bringing a radical feminist stance into public policy, the Edinburgh public awareness campaign displayed a radical feminist policy profile. In all four countries, policy profiles were marked by significant levels of women's descriptive representation throughout the whole process; but to varying degrees.

❖ Sexuality and Violence Policy

Table 9.2 Policy profile scores for cases of sexuality and violence policy

	Pre/Form.		Post-form.		Total
	D	S	D	S	
Edinburgh: 1992 Zero Tolerance campaign	3	3	3	3	12
Sweden: 1978–95 Women's shelters funding	3	1	3	1	8
Spain: 1989 Sexual harassment reform	2	2	1	1	6
France: 1992 Sexual harassment reform	2	1	2	1	6

Policy community styles in Sweden, Spain, and France displayed quite similar characteristics, with clear divisions between non-feminist and feminist camps. Feminist coalitions convinced reluctant non-feminist policy-makers that violence problems existed and needed to be addressed in government policy. In Edinburgh, the policy community was less divided; feminists successfully persuaded non-feminist actors to support feminist programmes. Unlike the other policy communities, femocrats were the major state decision-makers and collaborated in their decisions with feminist actors outside the state. Except for the French parliamentary discussion, where MPs became vocal about encroaching 'American puritanism', public controversy was relatively subdued. Non-feminist actors tended to voice their opposition and resistance in private; feminist actors tended to use the public arena to draw attention to and gain public support for their demands. Only in Spain was there any significant disagreement between feminists.

Weldon (1998; 2001) in her study of violence policies finds that feminist partnerships between women's movements and women's policy agencies go the furthest in explaining effective policy responses. This is not confirmed in the four cases. Only the Edinburgh case appears to emphasize the role of a strategic partnership between elected and appointed women officials, femocrats, and women's movements. Also, Swedish incrementalism occurred without any femocrat involvement. In France, femocrats, society-based feminist activists in the AVFT, and women deputies worked together mostly in Paris. They had little success in changing the symbolic dynamic of sexual harassment reform. Indeed, during 1989–91 the state feminist minister actually aided the non-feminist actors in stalling reform. In Spain, one could even advance the argument that the weak sexual harassment policy was due to the absence of a strategic partnership. Trade union feminist and femocrats worked independently without any significant involvement of women's groups. Each of the four cases, however, points to other salient factors.

The two cases of symbolic reform indicate that the treatment of sexual violence issues is difficult in Latin cultures where sexual relations are considered to be a private issue and in some quarters macho notions of male superiority may still be acceptable. For example, the campaign organizer for the Socialist Party in France made the following public statement about sexual harassment in 1985:

> Of course, I have had occasion to hump cute chicks on my office carpet. Sexual harassment is the demeanour of all Latin men towards women. In my country, we call that courtship. It is French men's need to seduce at work as well as in the subway. But be careful, in the final analysis, it is the woman who decides (cited in Zelensky and Gaussot 1986: 10).

Whether this statement is indicative of the attitudes of the left-wing elite in France or just an anecdotal case of public bravado is impossible to determine. Whereas violence against women may be easier to identify as a nasty social problem, the regulation of sexual harassment at work gets into the grey area of what is considered acceptable and unacceptable sexual behaviour at work. Opposition to broad-based notions of sexual harassment identified with an American approach to sexual harassment were rejected in France and Spain in the name of national cultural traditions and individual liberty.

Whether the cultural attitudes are sexist or indicative of hostility to public prying into private sexual relations is not at all clear. Radical feminists would argue that the sanctity of private sexual relations is a way to preserve male power in sexual matters. Apparent public willingness in Edinburgh and Sweden to accept policy on violence against women may have been due to the more clear-cut nature of the violent behaviour than any different line-up of social attitudes about sexual relations. Whatever the motivations for strong opposition to broad definitions of sexual harassment in Spain and France, the dynamics of the legal system precluded economic incentives for employers to address sexual harassment. The legal systems in both countries do not produce high-priced collective action suits.

More than cultural attitudes about sexual relations, the success of policy in Edinburgh appeared to be the result of the progressive political environment and the way in which gender issues were tied to larger definitions of the democratic deficit in Scotland (Mackay 1996). The other three cases do not suggest at all that a left-wing party in power matters. Left-wing governments were just as apathetic as right-wing governments to feminist demands for sexuality and violence policies. Another factor not as prevalent in these four instances as in other feminist policy areas was the international dimension. Policy ideas from other countries were used, but there was no authoritative international policy framework. In France and Spain, the introduction of foreign approaches created resistance and backlash. In the case of Edinburgh, policy diffusion went the other way as the Zero Tolerance campaign was emulated in other countries.

Finally, municipal-level politics may be more open to feminist infiltration than national-level politics, given that the two most feminist policy responses occurred in the municipal arena against the backdrop of more restrained national policies. Abrar, Lovenduski, and Margetts (1998: 198) find in their study of municipal feminism in Great Britain a pattern that resonates with Swedish incrementalism in women's shelter funding: 'Feminist success in highlighting the gender dimensions of a policy resulted from activity sustained over a long period of time and change has been localised, patchy, and gradual.'

❖ NOTES

1 In the early 1990s, the European Union passed a recommendation on 'dignity at work'. Along with guidelines for practice, EU polices suggested, but did not mandate, measures to prevent sexual harassment in the work place (Collins 1996).

2 There are 57 entries for sexuality and violence policy literature in Appendix B. Given that the average for all sub-sectors is 63 pieces, the amount of literature in this final sub-sector is comparable, at least in magnitude, to other policy sub-sectors.

3 For example, Eduards (1997: 121 n. 3) presents a definition for violence against women: 'the different types of abuse women are subjected to including assault rape, sexual harassment, prostitution and pornography.'

4 The growing feminist literature in the field of criminal justice on violence against women is not consulted here. As an academic discipline in the USA, criminal justice tends to be predominantly interested in the American criminal justice system with little interest in comparative theory-building.

5 A workshop on prostitution policies at the European Consortium for Political Research joint sessions in Copenhagen in April 2000 began to close the gap.

6 Only two of the international studies Weldon cites place violence policy in a systematic comparative perspective (Busch 1992; Heise et al. 1994); both include Western and non-Western countries. Much of the international violence literature focuses on developing countries.

7 Exchange rates from May 2001 at 9.5 kronor to the US dollar.

8 Professionalization of women's shelters staff, according to Elman (1996a), is a controversial issue among Swedish feminists. Radical feminists in Sweden argue that a trained staff would not act in women's interests. Reform-oriented feminists have pointed to trained staff as a key in effectively helping battered women.

9 This case analysis is based on my research of sexual harassment policy formation published in Mazur (1993; 1996a, b). All three pieces were based on archival research and interviews with pertinent policy actors.

10 ❖ Conclusion: The Feminist Policy Formation Puzzle

The 27 cases of feminist policy formation examined here shed new light on the highly complex puzzle of feminist policy formation in Western democracies. At the core of the puzzle is the question of whether, how, and why nominally feminist policies are feminist in action. Another piece of the puzzle is the issue of how to use the wealth of published empirical literature on feminist policy development. The first part of the puzzle's solution was to map out the parameters and aims of each sub-sector of feminist policy through the lens of the published studies. In delineating the seven sub-sectors, feminist policy was identified as a new sector of government intervention. As a policy sector in its own right, feminist policies can be identified, traced, and analysed. Next, the body of work on feminist policy was surveyed and systematized in order to map out each sub-sector, to select specific policy cases for analysis, and to assess the dynamics and determinants of each policy case. The conclusion of each sub-area chapter identified the most important forces at work across the four policy cases and advanced tentative propositions about feminist policy formation in each policy sub-sector.

This chapter now turns to the next essential piece of the theoretical puzzle: identifying the dynamics and determinants of feminist policy formation in action across all seven sub-sectors of feminist policy and all four feminist families of nations. Although the four policy cases in each sub-sector help to pinpoint some of the important influences in successful feminist policy formation at the sub-sectoral level, the propositions about specific sub-sector patterns cannot be extrapolated to policy formation across the entire sector of feminist policy. At the same time, the 27 cases were selected for analysis in order to eventually examine policy dynamics and determinants of policy cases across the four feminist families of nations and the seven sub-sectors of the feminist policy sector.

This chapter places the sub-sectoral findings in the larger comparative perspective. In presenting the findings of all 27 policy cases together, the analysis can begin to answer the following questions, initially posed in Chapter 2, on the puzzle of feminist policy formation.

1. Are nominally feminist policies actually feminist in the way they represent women descriptively and substantively in the long-term process of policy development?
2. If nominally feminist policies actually have feminist results in the policy process, what are the determinants of that feminist success? Does success correspond with a specific sub-sector of feminist policy, with a specific country, or with a specific regional cluster of countries? Are there other important factors that can be identified at the level of the policy sub-system, the nation-state, or outside the nation-state that produce feminist policy success?
3. Is there a single policy style or pattern of sectorization across the entire sector of policies with formal feminist intentions?

The chapter first presents the propositions that come out of the comparative analysis of the 27 policy cases as they respond to the original hypotheses about the dynamics and determinants of feminist policy formation. A more detailed discussion of the propositions as they play out across the 27 cases follows. These comparative findings are then placed within the context of the methodological parameters of this study. The next section touches upon several future avenues of research and analysis and the chapter concludes by highlighting the book's broader implications.

❖ GENERAL PROPOSITIONS

Given that this study was the first step in mapping out feminist policy as a new sector of public policy, it was important that the cases be analysed qualitatively through 'thick description' (Geertz 1973) and 'process-tracing' (George and McKeown 1985). As many political scientists who advocate combining qualitative and quantitative analysis assert—for example, Collier (1993); Tarrow (1995); Caporaso (1995)—first-step qualitative studies of uncharted areas necessarily must identify the complex forces at work in a thorough examination of a small number of cases. Studies with larger sample sizes can then re-examine or test the hypotheses from the detailed cases through correlational analysis and statistical models.

The propositions that come out of the comparative analysis of the 27 policy cases in this chapter, therefore, must be understood in the perspective of the larger research cycle on feminist policy formation. This study begins the cycle by mapping feminist policy as a new sector of government action, by developing a framework to identify patterns and trends, and by generating a series of propositions about the dynamics and determinants of feminist policy formation. It will be up to future studies to address and shore up the various methodological gaps that, in some ways, are an inherent part of such an initial foray.

The model for this study, developed in Chapter 2 and presented once again in Fig. 10.1, serves as a road map to guide the comparative discussion of the policy cases and the examination of the original hypotheses for this study.[1] Feminist *policy profiles* consist of the *substantive* and *descriptive representation of women* throughout all stages of the policy process, divided into *pre-formulation/ formulation* and *post-formulation.* Feminist policy profiles may be a function of the *style of the policy sub-system* and/or a series of *exogenous determinants* at the sectoral, sub-sectoral, national, regional, or extra-national levels. The model allows for the possibility that the style of the sub-system—its interactions, actors, belief systems, arenas, and instruments—may be an important *intervening influence* on the degree to which a policy profile is feminist. Whether there is a common style in policy sub-systems in each sub-sector or sector of policy is also treated by the model.

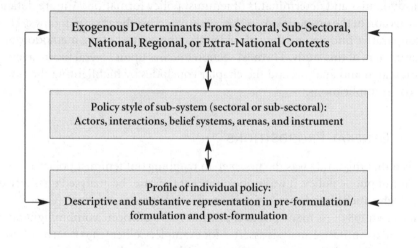

Figure 10.1 Model for hypothesized relationships
in feminist policy formation

The following list of propositions summarizes the comparative analysis of the 27 cases in terms of the various hypothesized analytical relationships of the model. The next section shows how the general propositions listed below are supported by the comparative analysis of the findings of the 27 case analyses. The propositions are presented under each original hypothesis as they were presented at the end of Chapter 2. As the general list of propositions shows, some of the original hypotheses are confirmed by the comparison of the 27 cases, while others are modified or refuted. Propositions about the influences of additional determinants are also included in this general list.

❖ CONCLUSION

❖ On the Dynamics of Feminist Policy Formation

Hypothesis 1. Nominally feminist policies are feminist in action. Feminist policies are quite feminist in women's substantive and descriptive representation throughout the entire policy process with some variation.

Hypothesis 2. Feminist policy dynamics in formulation coincide with feminist implementation and evaluation. There is a strong link between feminist policy success in pre-formulation/formulation and higher levels in post-formulation. While feminist policy dynamics in pre-formulation do not always lead to feminist implementation, feminist policy success is not generally reversed in post-formulation.

Hypothesis 3. When women are represented descriptively in policy formation they are substantively represented as well. The presence of women in the policy formation does not always coincide with high levels of feminist success in policy content and/or in administrative outputs and institutional feedback.

Hypothesis 4. Feminist policies are not guided by a uniform feminist approach; feminist success in policy formation does not correspond with a specific type of feminism. The content of feminist policies does not coincide with a single type of feminism. There is no obvious link between the type of feminist approach of a given policy and its level of feminist success.

❖ On Feminist Policy as a Sector

Hypothesis 5. Feminist policy as a sector does not have a single policy profile or style. Feminist policy is a new sector of government action in democracies; policy profiles and styles do not follow a common pattern.

❖ On the Determinants of Feminist Policy Formation

Hypothesis 6. The determinants of feminist policy formation are highly complex. The determinants of successful feminist policy formation are complex, shifting, and often case-specific. The multifaceted line-up of determinants for a given policy tends to be more related to the dynamics of the policy sub-system than political dynamics at the national, sectoral, or sub-sectoral levels.

Hypothesis 7. Variations in policy profiles and styles correspond with variations in sub-sector. There are few sub-sectoral patterns for either policy profiles or policy styles. Political representation policy displays some common dynamics in the profile of feminist policies and to a lesser degree the reconciliation sub-sector.

Hypothesis 8. Variations in policy profiles and styles correspond with variations in feminist families of nation; a specific pattern of policy profile and style is found in each country and/ or feminist family of nation. Feminist policy profiles follow to a limited degree similar policy patterns by feminist family of nation;

176

there is no single pattern of policy styles within sub-sectors. Although inconclusive, the evidence suggests that policy styles and profiles do not follow any set patterns at the national level either.

Hypothesis 9. Woman-friendly polities produce more feminist policy. Polities with more woman-friendly aspects tend to produce more feminist policy to a limited degree.

Hypothesis 10. National/regional patterns in religion correspond with patterns in the profiles of feminist policies. National religion has some impact on feminist policy formation; Protestant countries have moderately higher levels of feminist policy, and religion is an important factor in reproductive rights policies.

Hypothesis 11. Success in feminist policy formation tends to occur under left-wing governments. There is a link between highly successful feminist policies and left-wing governments; left-wing governments are not a pre-cursor to feminist policy.

Hypothesis 12. Variations in policy profiles occur in function of variations in policy styles. There are some connections between policy styles and policy profiles, but not in a systematic manner to make the style of public policies a significant intervening factor.

Hypothesis 13. Feminist policy success is a result of the emergence of feminist advocacy coalitions. The coalitions are characterized by 'a triangle of empowerment' (Vargas and Weiringa 1998) or 'strategic partnership' (Halsaa 1998) among women's policy offices, feminist-oriented women in elected office, and women's movements/organizations that share a feminist approach to the policy problem in question. There is some connection between feminist advocacy coalitions and feminist policy success. The presence of a feminist advocacy coalition is not a precursor to successful feminist policy. Feminist advocacy coalitions do not always consist of coequal strategic partnerships.

The different actors of a feminist advocacy coalition do not necessarily share the same approach to feminist politics.

Higher levels of women in public office, active women's policy offices, or strong women's movement mobilization do not separately lead to high levels of feminist policy success.

❖ On Other Determinants

Feminist policy success coincides with the presence of non-feminist allies in key decision-making positions; they tend to be men.

Successful feminist policy are sometimes a by-product of cultural attitudes about gender and/or the role of government.

Extra-national government bodies have a limited influence on the development of successful feminist policy.

❖ CONCLUSION

The specific design of state institutions and the pattern of state-society relations has some impact on feminist policy formation, but not in any consistent manner.

❖ Summary

The comparative analysis of the 27 policy cases suggests that feminist policies appear to be quite feminist in action. Successful feminist policies do not always achieve the same level of women's substantive and descriptive representation throughout the policy process. Bringing more women into the political arena may not automatically lead to concrete feminist government action that goes beyond symbolic reform to generate significant administrative outputs and societal feedback in implementation and evaluation. The style of feminist policy formation may be even less uniform than the profile of policies. There does not seem to be a single type of feminism associated with feminist policy successes either.

The multiple causes of successful feminist policies may very well be highly case-specific. Success does not seem to neatly correspond with a given subsector, country, or feminist family of nations. Political representation and reconciliation polices may have some of the most predictable policy process outcomes. Given the pronounced variation in policy styles, feminist policy successes does not seem to be a direct product of the particular line-up of state and society actors within a given policy sub-system. Whereas feminist strategic partnerships and feminist advocacy coalitions emerge around more feminist policies, they do not appear to be a prerequisite for highly successful policies. The presence of left-wing governments and more woman-friendly states and societies also may be one part of the feminist policy recipe for success; they are by no means the only ingredient. One of the most important determinants of feminist policy success may very well be the presence of sympathetic non-feminist allies in key decision-making positions. Thus, although feminist policy as a sector of government action is an undeniable feature of Western post-industrial democracy at the beginning of the twenty-first century, it appears to be quite different from more established areas of government action with more uniform and predictable dynamics and policy styles.

❖ COMPARATIVE ANALYSIS OF 27 POLICY CASES

Policy profile scores for all 27 cases are presented in Tables 10.2–10.7 to assess to what degree the original hypotheses about the dynamics and determinants of feminist policy formation played out across the 27 cases.[2] A three-point scale was used to score women's substantive and descriptive representation in the two phases of the policy process. The possible total number of points is twelve.[3] The scoring system was developed for comparative and qualitative purposes. It was designed neither to evaluate which country or feminist family of nation was the most feminist along a single universal standard of feminist success nor to be used in any eventual large 'n' correlational analysis. The numerical scores are intended to be indicators of what occurred in each policy case, within each national and policy context. They are used to sort through the determinants of a relatively large number of qualitative cases. Individual policy case scores were, therefore, assigned with an eye to cross-case comparison to ensure some level of uniformity in the final comparative analysis while still accounting for the dynamics of each case.

The missing case for family law policy in the Protestant Social Democrat countries was given an estimated score of 9 points in order to allow for more uniform comparison across all the cases.[4] The estimated score, therefore, is not meant to substitute for an actual a policy case. Feminist policy scores were also estimated in certain policy stages for the cases with insufficient literature. As the case analyses showed, the estimations were based on the dynamics of the phases that were actually covered in the consulted literature.

❖ The Dynamics of Feminist Policy Formation

Feminist policies are feminist in action. Comparing the 27 cases by their composite policy scores provides a comparison of the degree to which feminist policies are actually feminist in action, 'feminist success' in the tables. Table 10.1 places the policy cases in four different groups of feminist success: high success—cases with scores from 9 to 12 points; moderate success—cases with scores from 5 to 8 points; low success—cases with scores from 1 to 4 points; and feminist failure—cases with scores of zero. As the Table indicates, 26 of the 28 cases—including the estimated case—are ranked in the top two groups of feminist success, with an equal division of cases between the two categories. Only two policy cases are ranked in the low success group. None of the cases was a pure feminist failure. The averages of all three categories of success are at the high end of the scoring range for each category. Thus, feminist policies appear to be quite feminist in action. Whether the feminist success occurs in women's substantive or descriptive representation or in the two different stages of policy development varies across policy cases.

Connections between policy stages. As Table 10.1 suggests, there is no single pattern of feminist success across the two policy processes. The next comparative table scrutinizes more closely the feminist policy success in the two major stages. Table 10.2 classifies the policy cases by the change in the combined policy scores for substantive and descriptive representation from the first stage to the second. There is no apparent link between feminist dynamics in pre-formulation/ formulation and post-formulation. In 13 cases there was no change in the policy profile scores between the two stages. There was an increase in scores from the

Table 10.1 Feminist success in policy cases

	Pre/Form.		Post-form.		Total
	D	S	D	S	
HIGH SUCCESS (9–12 total points)					
ˣEdinburgh (SVP)1992 Zero Tolerance campaign	3	3	3	3	12
*ˣOntario (PRP)1982 Affirmative action in ONDP	3	3	3	3	12
^ˣNorway (PRP) Election campaigns in the 1980s–90s	3	3	2	3	11
#Norway (RRP) 1978 Abortion law	3	2	3	3	11
France (PRP) 1999 Constitutional Parity Amendment	3	2	2	3	10
Canada (BP)1982 Charter of Rights and Freedoms	3	2	3	2	10
Norway (BP) 1978 Equal Status Act	2	2	3	3	10
#Italy (PRP)1993 and 1995 Quota legislation	3	2	3	2	10
#Australia (FLP) 1987 Matrimonial property reform	2	3	2	3	10
#Netherlands (RRP)Abortion reform since 1973	2	2	2	3	9
Ireland (EEP) 1977 Equal Employment Act	3	2	3	1	9
^United States (RRP) Abortion reform since 1973	3	2	3	1	9
Estimated value for FLP in Protestant Social Democrat countries					9
MODERATE SUCCESS (5–8 total points)					
Sweden (EEP) 1979 Equality Act	1	2	3	2	8
#Ireland (FLP) 1981–95 Divorce reform	2	2	2	2	8
^ˣDenmark (RP) Evolution of childcare policy	2	2	2	2	8
ˣ^Sweden (SVP) 1978–95 Women's shelters funding	3	1	3	1	8
Great Britain (EEP) 1983 Equal Value Amendment	2	1	3	2	8
#Germany (RP)1986 Federal Childcare Benefit Act	1	3	1	2	7
Netherlands (BP) 1985–90 Emancipation Policy Program	2	3	1	1	7
#Spain (BP) 1988–90 Equality Plan	1	3	1	2	7
#Italy (RRP) 1978 Abortion law	3	2	1	1	7
#Spain (SVP) 1989–95 Sexual harassment reform	2	2	1	1	6
#Germany (FLP) 1977 Marriage and divorce reform	1	2	1	2	6
France (EEP) 1983 *Égalité Professionnelle* Act	2	2	1	1	6
France (SVP) 1992 Sexual harassment reform	2	1	2	1	6
LOW SUCCESS (1–4 total points)					
United States (RP) 1993 Family and Medical Leave Act	1	1	1	1	4
#Ireland (RP) 1995 Reform of social welfare legislation	2	0	2	0	4
FEMINIST FAILURES (0 total points)					
No cases					

ˣsub-national cases; *non-state case studies; #missing information on cases; ^more than one individual policy.

Table 10.2 Feminist success in policy cases presented by the two stages of policy formation

	Pre/Form.		Post-form.		Total
	D	S	D	S	
GROUP 1: NO CHANGE (13)					
×Edinburgh (SVP) 1992 Zero Tolerance campaign	3	3	3	3	12
*×Ontario (PRP) 1982 Affirmative action in ONDP	3	3	3	3	12
Canada (BP) 1982 Charter of Rights and Freedoms	3	2	3	2	10
#Italy (PRP) 1993 and 1995 Quota legislation	3	2	3	2	10
#Australia (FLP) 1987 Matrimonial property reform	2	3	2	3	10
#Ireland (FLP) 1981–95 Divorce reform	2	2	2	2	8
^×Denmark (RP) Evolution of childcare policy	2	2	2	2	8
×^Sweden (SVP) 1978–95 Women's shelters funding	3	1	3	1	8
#Germany (FLP) 1977 Marriage and divorce reform	1	2	1	2	6
France (SVP) 1992 Sexual harassment reform	2	1	2	1	6
United States (RP) 1993 Family and Medical Leave Act	1	1	1	1	4
#Ireland (RP) 1995 Reform of social welfare legislation	2	0	2	0	4
France (PRP) 1999 Constitutional Parity Amendment	3	2	2	3	10
GROUP 2: SCORES INCREASE (5)					
Norway (BP) 1978 Equal Status Act	2	2	3	3	10
Great Britain (EEP) 1983 Equal Value Amendment	2	1	3	2	8
#Norway (RRP) 1978 Abortion law	3	2	3	3	11
#Netherlands (RRP) Abortion reform since 1973	2	2	2	3	9
Sweden 1979 (RRP) Equality Act	1	2	3	2	8
GROUP 3: SCORES DECREASE (9)					
Netherlands (BP) 1985–90 Emancipation Policy Program	2	3	1	1	7
^×Norway (PRP) 1980s–90s Election campaigns	3	3	2	3	11
Ireland (EEP) 1977 Equal Employment Act	3	2	3	1	9
^United States (RRP) Abortion reform since 1973	3	2	3	1	9
#Germany (RP) 1986 Federal Childcare Benefit Act	1	3	1	2	7
#Spain (BP) 1988–90 Equality Plan	1	3	1	2	7
France (EEP) 1983 *Égalité Professionnelle* Act	2	2	1	1	6
#Spain (SVP) 1989–95 Sexual harassment reform	2	2	1	1	6
#Italy (RRP) 1978 Abortion law	3	2	1	1	7

×sub-national cases;   *non-state case studies;   #missing information on cases;
^more than one individual policy.

first to the second stage in five cases, and policy feminist scores decreased from the first stage to the second stage in one third of the cases.

Symbolic reform and non-decisions. Symbolic policies and non-decisions, policies without outputs, are a common type of feminist policy, identified in

❖ CONCLUSION

nine policy cases, in four different policy sub-sectors, across all three feminist families, and in six different countries. They include French and Spanish sexual harassment reform, the Family and Medical Leave Act in the USA, social welfare reform in Ireland, an equality plan in Spain, an equal value amendment in Great Britain, an emancipation programme in the Netherlands, and French equal employment policy. In particular, the substantive representation of women's interests in the content of the policies was quite restrained. In the French, Spanish, and Irish cases, the dynamics of symbolic politics and/or non-decisions carried over into the post-formulation phases. In Great Britain, a limited policy on equal value was transformed into a much more feminist one in post-formulation. In the Netherlands, a feminist policy in formulation became symbolic in implementation.

Links between descriptive and substantive representation. Table 10.3 classifies the policy cases in terms of the difference between descriptive and substantive representation in both stages of policy development. Cross-case comparison does not suggest that women's participation in the policy process necessarily leads to policies that have a more feminist policy content and/or feminist policy feedback. Furthermore, women's descriptive representation was at the same or higher levels as women's substantive representation in all three different groups of feminist policy success: low, medium, and high.

In many cases, women mobilized around policy formation precisely because policies were not pursuing feminist action. In Irish social welfare reform, for example, women did come forward, but were unable to reverse the non-decision-making dynamic established by the social security administration. Also, women did not participate in the formation of a significant number of policies that were quite feminist in content and/or in policy feedback and out-puts. Thus, there does not appear to be a single pattern in the way women's sub-stantive and descriptive representation interrelates.

Types of feminism(s) in feminist policy. The content of feminist policies did not coincide with any particular current of feminist ideas in Western political thought. In many cases, it was difficult to identify a single feminist approach to a given policy. In other cases policy statements formally acknowledged different feminist approaches to or assumptions about specific policy problems. A wide variety of feminist currents was represented in particular policy cases across all sub-sectors and all feminist families of nations. Radical feminist positions were incorporated into sexuality and violence policies in Sweden and Scotland; liberal feminist ideas informed political representation policies in countries from all four feminist families; social feminism was quite pronounced in reconciliation policies in Germany and the USA; and socialist feminist ideas were transformed into equal employment policies in France.

Policies that had the highest levels of feminist success represented the full range of Western feminist ideas as well. In the two cases of pure feminist success, the

Table 10.3 Feminist success in policy cases presented by the two forms of women's representation

	Pre/Form.		Post-form.		Total
	D	S	D	S	
1. No Differences in Either Stage (8)					
ˣEdinburgh (SVP) 1992 Zero Tolerance Campaign	3	3	3	3	12
*ˣOntario (PRP) 1982 Affirmative action in ONDP	3	3	3	3	12
#Ireland (FLP) 1981–95 Divorce reform	2	2	2	2	8
^ˣDenmark (RP) Evolution of childcare policy	2	2	2	2	8
United States (RP) 1993 Family and Medical Leave Act	1	1	1	1	4
Norway (BP) 1978 Equal Status Act	2	2	3	3	10
France (EEP) 1983 *Égalité Professionnelle* Act	2	2	1	1	6
#Spain (SVP) 1989–95 Sexual harassment reform	2	2	1	1	6
In pre/formulation (1)					
^ˣNorway (PRP) Election campaigns in the 1980s–90s	3	3	2	3	11
In post-formulation (3)					
#Norway (RRP) 1978 Abortion law	3	2	3	3	11
#Italy (RRP) 1978 Abortion law	3	2	1	1	7
Netherlands (BP)1985–90 Emancipation Policy Program	2	3	1	1	7
2. Descriptive Lower Than Substantive					
In both stages (4)					
#Australia (FLP) 1987 Matrimonial property reform	2	3	2	3	10
#Germany (FLP) 1977 Marriage and divorce reform	1	2	1	2	6
#Spain (BP) 1988–90 Equality Plan	1	3	1	2	7
#Germany (RP) 1986 Federal Childcare Benefit Act	1	3	1	2	7
In pre/formulation (2)					
Sweden (EEP) 1979 Equality Act	1	2	3	2	8
Netherlands (BP) 1985–90 Emancipation Policy Program	2	3	1	1	7
In post-formulation (2)					
France (BP) 1999 Constitutional Parity Amendment	3	2	2	3	10
^ˣNorway (PRP) 1980s–90s Election campaigns	3	3	2	3	11
3. Descriptive Higher than Substantive					
in both stages (8)					
Canada (BP) 1982 Charter of Rights and Freedoms	3	2	3	2	10
#Italy (PRP) 1993 and 1995 Quota legislation	3	2	3	2	10
France (SVP) 1992 Sexual harassment reform	2	1	2	1	6
Ireland (EEP) 1977 Equal Employment Act	3	2	3	1	9
^United States (RRP) Abortion reform since 1973	3	2	3	1	9
Great Britain (EEP) 1983 Equal Value Amendment	2	1	3	2	8
ˣ^Sweden (SVP) 1978–95 Women's shelters funding	3	1	3	1	8
#Ireland (RP) 1995 Reform of social welfare legislation	2	0	2	0	4

❖ Conclusion

	Pre/Form.		Post-form.		Total
	D	S	D	S	
In pre/formulation (3)					
France (PRP)1999 Constitutional Parity Amendment	3	2	2	3	10
#Norway (RRP) 1978 Abortion law	3	2	3	3	11
#Italy (RRP) 1978 Abortion law	3	2	1	1	7
In post-formulation (1)					
Sweden (EEP) 1979 Equality Act	1	2	3	2	8

ˣsub-national cases; *non-state case studies; #missing information on cases; ^more than one individual policy.

Edinburgh Zero Tolerance Campaign and the Ontario National Democratic Party resolution, the policies were formally based on radical feminist assumptions, articulated by individual feminists who identified with this current of thought. Liberal feminist ideas were quite clearly incorporated in the abortion and political representation reforms that reached some of the highest levels of policy success. The content of the final Australian family law reform arguably blended both liberal and radical feminist approaches to matrimonial property issues. The imprint of social, Marxist, and socialist feminist ideas was not apparent in the twelve cases of high feminist policy success.

❖ *Feminist Policy as a Sector*

The case for feminist policy as a separate sector has been made throughout the book in terms of the overall goals of feminist government action. There is no single pattern in either the policy profiles or the policy styles. High feminist policy successes were found in all feminist families of nations, in all feminist sub-sectors, and in nine out of the 13 countries; moderately successful policies occurred in all sub-sectors, in all feminist families of nations, and in nine countries; and low feminist policies took place in two feminist families of nations in one sub-sector. The style of the sub-systems of state and society actors that emerged around specific policy issues in the policy cases was quite varied as well.

❖ *The Determinants of Successful Feminist Policy Formation*

Multiple and case-specific determinants. Reflecting the highly transversal nature of the feminist policy sector, there was no single line-up of determinants that surfaced in the policy analyses. Furthermore, as the rest of the comparative analysis of the policy case findings indicate, a particular combination of determinants did not tend to come together within a certain sub-sector of policy, within a certain country, or within a particular feminist family of nation.

Ultimately, the determinants of feminist policy formation are highly case-specific, located at the level of the sub-system rather than at the more aggregate national, sectoral, or sub-sectoral levels.

Patterns by sub-sector. Certain policy sub-sectors display some common patterns. As Table 10.4 illustrates, the democratic representation and reconciliation sub-sectors have the highest degree of distinctiveness in composite policy-profile scores. The four cases of democratic representation policies all display quite similar levels of policy success. The policy success ranking for the entire sub-sector is only slightly higher, however, than the next highest sub-sector of policies.

Table 10.4 Feminist success in policy cases presented by sub-sector

	Pre/Form.		Post-form.		Total
	D	S	D	S	
DEMOCRATIC REPRESENTATION POLICIES (DRP): 0.90@					
*ˣOntario 1982 Affirmative action in ONDP	3	3	3	3	12
^Norway 1980s–90s election campaigns	3	3	2	3	11
France 1999 Constitutional Parity Amendment	3	2	2	3	10
#Italy 1993 and 1995 Quota legislation	3	2	3	2	10
REPRODUCTIVE RIGHTS POLICIES (RRP): 0.75					
#Norway 1978 Abortion law	3	2	3	3	11
#Netherlands Abortion reform since 1973	2	2	2	3	9
^United States Abortion reform since 1973	3	2	3	1	9
#Italy 1978 Abortion law	3	2	1	1	7
FAMILY LAW POLICIES (FLP): 0.69					
#Australia 1987 Matrimonial property reform	2	3	2	3	10
Estimated Value for FLP in Protestant Social Democrat Countries					9
#Ireland 1981–95 Divorce reform	2	2	2	2	8
#Germany 1977 Marriage and divorce reform	1	2	1	2	6
BLUEPRINT POLICIES (BP): 0.69					
Canada 1982 Charter of Rights and Freedoms	3	2	3	2	10
Norway 1978 Equal Status Act	2	2	3	3	10
Netherlands 1985–90 Emancipation Policy Program	2	3	1	1	7
#Spain 1988–90 Equality Plan	1	3	1	2	7
SEXUALITY AND VIOLENCE POLICIES (SVP): 0.66					
ˣEdinburgh 1992 Zero Tolerance campaign	3	3	3	3	12
ˣ^Sweden 1978–95 Women's shelters funding	3	1	3	1	8
#Spain 1989–95 Sexual harassment reform	2	2	1	1	6
France 1992 Sexual harassment reform	2	1	2	1	6

	Pre/Form.		Post-form.		Total
	D	S	D	S	
EQUAL EMPLOYMENT POLICIES (EEP): 0.65					
Ireland 1977 Equal Employment Act	3	2	3	1	9
Sweden 1979 Equality Act	1	2	3	2	8
Great Britain 1983 Equal Value Amendment	2	1	3	2	8
France 1983 *Égalité Professionnelle* Act	2	2	1	1	6
RECONCILIATION POLICIES (RP): 0.48					
^×Denmark Evolution of childcare policy	2	2	2	2	8
#Germany 1986 Federal Childcare Benefit Act	1	3	1	2	7
USA 1993 Family and Medical Leave Act	1	1	1	1	4
#Ireland 1995 Reform of social welfare legislation	2	0	2	0	4

×sub-national cases;   *non-state case studies;   #missing information on cases;
^more than one individual policy;   @calculated from number of total points/48 for each category; out of 1.00.

The next five sub-sectors group around the same ten-point range of policy success rates. The family law and blueprint sub-areas received identical feminist success ratings and the rates of sexuality and violence and equal employment are very close. The reconciliation sub-sector has the lowest feminist policy-success rating. The four policy cases in this lowest-ranked sub-sector still show a relatively high degree of variation, significantly more than the democratic representation cases. Reconciliation policy cases also fall into both the moderate and low feminist success categories. There is even more variation in the feminist successes of individual policy cases within each of the mid-ranking sub-sectors.

The absence of distinct patterns in feminist policy profiles is echoed in the policy styles of the policy cases within each policy sub-sector. Policy sub-system dynamics displayed some similar traits in the sub-areas of equal employment, reproductive rights, and sexuality and violence; the rest of the sub-sectors were characterized by quite divergent policy styles. Often two separate policy sub-systems—non-feminist and feminist—converged over policies; in many cases feminist advocacy coalitions came forward. Some of the feminist advocacy coalitions consisted of strategic partnerships between femocrats, women's movement activists, and female public officials.

Equal employment policies were characterized by the highest degree of uniformity in policy styles. Labour-oriented strategic partnerships composed of women's movement advocates, equality agency actors, and labour union feminists emerged around the formulation and implementation of laws. Even within the context of the similar line-up of actors, there was variation between the influence of feminists within trade unions and the strength of equal employment agencies. In all four countries, non-feminist organized labour had the potential to limit the feminist content and implementation of policy even when organized labour was fragmented and weak.

Policy sub-system styles were also somewhat similar in sexuality and violence policies. In three out of the four cases the policy sub-system was divided between feminist and non-feminist camps. In Sweden, Spain, and France, feminist advocacy coalitions faced reluctant non-feminist actors who had to be convinced of the need to address sexual violence issues. Strategic partnerships between femocrats, women's movement activists, and female public officials emerged only in Edinburgh. The femocrats in the city government were the major decision-makers; and non-feminists and feminists worked together in relatively close collaboration. Whereas femocrats played active roles in Spain, Scotland, and France, they were absent from the Swedish policy scene.

Even with four similar cases of abortion reform, there were important differences among the policy sub-systems in the reproductive rights sub-sector. Policy styles were somewhat similar between the three European cases. Two separate policy communities emerged in each case; one based in parliament around formulation and a second located in the abortion policy triad in post-formulation. While parliamentary sub-systems were public, the abortion triads were more closed and consensual. In the USA, the policy style of the sub-system was anything but consensual. Both formulation and implementation divided the constellation of actors around the issue into two hostile camps of pro- and anti-choice advocates that articulated their positions in highly vocal and public ways. The arenas for abortion policy-making in the USA were quite different from those in the other three countries. Policies were made in the streets and the courts rather than in parliament or in abortion triads. The feminist advocacy coalitions that emerged in all four cases of abortion reform did not include femocrats as active participants.

In two cases of blueprint policy, the policy style was decidedly feminist. An equal partnership between femocrats, women's movement activists, and women in elected office emerged in both Norway and Canada. The other two cases in Spain and the Netherlands did not generate this type of feminist advocacy coalition. In democratic representation, feminist advocacy coalitions developed in the Italian and the Norwegian cases. The French sub-system on the parity law was divided between a more publicly feminist-oriented sub-system and a closed sub-system composed of non-feminist actors. Unlike in Italy and Norway where women's policy offices were present, the French feminist advocacy coalition did not include femocrats. The sub-system for the Canadian case that emerged in the confines of the political party was closed and characterized by partisan dynamics quite different from the dynamics of the other three cases.

In contrast to the relative similarities among the policy profiles of the four cases of reconciliation policies (Table 10.4), their policy styles were quite divergent. In

❖ CONCLUSION

both Ireland and Germany, policy formation took place within the public bureaucracy in closed administrative arenas. Social policy bureaucrats had important roles in both cases. In Germany, Social Democratic Party leaders were also involved in policy formation. The Danish and US cases were more public and open. Family leave policy in the USA was made in Congress and childcare was delivered at the municipal level in Denmark, which also involved a different set of actors. One common point in all four cases of reconciliation policy was the absence of any prominent feminist advocacy coalitions.

Similar levels of variations in policy sub-system styles were found across the four cases of family law policies. In Australia and in Ireland two policy communities emerged around family law policy—non-feminist and feminist—but not in the case of Germany. Also, whereas strategic partnerships were a part of feminist policy development in Australia and Ireland, there was no triangle of empowerment evident in German divorce and marriage reform.

Patterns by feminist family of nations. There is no systematic pattern in either policy profiles or styles across the four feminist families of nations. Cross-group variations are more pronounced for the policy styles than for the success of feminist policies. As Table 10.5 shows, the Protestant Social Democrat countries and the Advanced Christian Democrat countries share to a certain degree common patterns in feminist policy success. Policy cases fall into the top two groups of policy success in the Protestant Social Democrat countries with only a three-point difference between the highest and the lowest scores. In the Advanced Christian Democrat countries policy cases are situated in the two middle groups of feminist policy success, with four points separating the lowest and the highest cases. In contrast, the Protestant Liberal countries had the most variation across feminist profiles. The seven policy cases were distributed across three groups of policy success; and the widest difference between policy profiles was eight points. The cases covered for the Late Female Mobilizing countries also fell into the three different groups of feminist policy success, with a six-point difference between the most and least successful cases.

Patterns by country. Policy profiles do not follow a common pattern within the countries either. Policy cases reached identical levels of success only in Sweden. In France and Norway, two out of the three cases received identical feminist policy profile scores. The third case in Norway diverged by only one point, but the third case in France was much more successful than the other two, by four points. In Germany and Spain, the two policy cases differed by one point as well. In the remaining countries—Great Britain, Canada, the USA, the Netherlands, Ireland, and Italy—policy profiles score differences went from two to four points. It is important to note that the small number of feminist policy cases precludes any conclusive observation about policy profile patterns at the national level, particularly given that several cases took place at lower levels of government.

CONCLUSION ❖

Table 10.5 Feminist success in policy cases by feminist family of nation and by country

	Pre/Form.		Post-form.		Total
	D	S	D	S	
PROTESTANT LIBERAL: 0.77@					
ˣEdinburgh (SVP)1992 Zero Tolerance Campaign	3	3	3	3	12
Great Britain (EEP) 1983 Equal Value Amendment	2	1	3	2	8
*ˣOntario (PRP) 1982 Affirmative action in ONDP	3	3	3	3	12
Canada (BP) 1982 Charter of Rights and Freedoms	3	2	3	2	10
^United States (RRP) Abortion reform since 1973	3	2	3	1	9
United States (RP) 1993 Family and Medical Leave Act	1	1	1	1	4
#Australia (FLP) 1987 Matrimonial property reform	2	3	2	3	10
PROTESTANT SOCIAL DEMOCRAT: 0.77					
^Norway (PRP) 1980s–90s Election campaigns	3	3	2	3	11
#Norway (RRP) 1978 Abortion law	3	2	3	3	11
Norway (BP) 1978 Equal Status Act	2	2	3	3	10
Estimated value for FLP in Protestant Social Democrat countries					9
Sweden (EEP) 1979 Equality Act	1	2	3	2	8
^ˣSweden (SVP) 1978–95 Women's shelters funding	3	1	3	1	8
^ˣDenmark (RP) Evolution of childcare policy	2	2	2	2	8
ADVANCED CHRISTIAN DEMOCRAT: 0.61					
#Netherlands (RRP) Abortion reform since 1973	2	2	2	3	9
Netherlands (BP) 1985–90 Emancipation Policy Program	2	3	1	1	7
#Germany (RP) 1986 Federal Childcare Benefit Act	1	3	1	2	7
#Germany (FLP) 1977 Marriage and divorce reform	1	2	1	2	6
France (PRP)1999 Constitutional Parity Amendment	3	2	2	3	10
France (EEP)1983 *Égalité Professionnelle* Act	2	2	1	1	6
France (SVP) 1992 Sexual harassment reform	2	1	2	1	6
LATE FEMALE MOBILIZING: 0.61					
Ireland (EEP) 1977 Equal Employment Act	3	2	3	1	9
#Ireland (FLP) 1981–95 Divorce reform	2	2	2	2	8
#Ireland (RP) 1995 Reform of social welfare legislation	2	0	2	0	4
#Italy (PRP)1993 and 1995 Quota legislation	3	2	3	2	10
#Italy (RRP) 1978 Abortion law	3	2	1	1	7
#Spain (SVP) 1989–95 Sexual harassment reform	2	2	1	1	6
#Spain (BP) 1988–90 Equality Plan	1	3	1	2	7

ˣsub-national cases; *non-state case studies; #missing information on cases; ^more than one individual policy; @calculated from number of total points/84 for each category; out of 1.00.

❖ CONCLUSION

Woman-friendly polities. Comparing the 27 policy cases by feminist family of nation in Table 10.5 does suggest a certain link between feminist policy success-es and woman-friendly polities. The most woman-friendly feminist families of nations, Protestant Democrat and Protestant Liberal, share the same high pol-icy ranking. The lower overall ranking of the Advanced Christian Democrat and Late Female Mobilizing also coincides to a certain degree with the typology of woman-friendly states. At the same time, the Late Female Mobilizing and Protestant Liberal countries are not shown to be significantly lower in feminist policy success than the other two feminist families of nations as they are in the original woman-friendly typology used for this study. The presence of woman-friendly policy logics, the interplay play between gender and welfare regimes, was an important factor in determining feminist successes in reconciliation policies, but not in any other feminist policy sector. Thus, the policy cases do not provide strong evidence either for or against the assertion that woman-friendly states produce more feminist policies.

Religion. Table 10.5 also suggests that religion may be an important factor in determining feminist policy success given that the two highest feminist families of nations had strong Protestant influences. Religion was also salient to the dynamics of abortion reform. Higher levels of feminist policy were achieved in countries where fundamentalist Christianity was less socially salient and polit-ically influential.

The influence of the left. The conventional wisdom that left-wing govern-ments are more favourable to feminist-oriented policies is partially confirmed by the 27 cases. Of the 13 cases of strong feminist policy successes, over half clear-ly unfolded under the influence of left-wing labour governments. In the cases of continuous policy, it is more difficult to link a particular party in power to policy outcomes at a give stage of the policy process. High levels of feminist policy success were also clearly associated with more right-wing governments in two cases. Similarly, moderate feminist policy formation occurred under left-wing governments in six out of the 13 cases. In Spain and France, four cases of symbolic reform with low levels of feminist policy success were pursued under governments with Socialist Party majorities. Finally, the two cases of low feminist policy success both unfolded in the context of left-wing governments. Left-wing governments, therefore, do not always coincide with feminist policy successes and right-wing governments are not necessarily hostile to proactive feminist policy.

Policy styles as an intervening influence. Given the variation in policy styles across the 27 policy cases, there is no systematic link between policy styles and lev-els of feminist policy success in policy profiles. For example, the four policy cases with the highest feminist policy scores all displayed different types of policy sub-system styles. As was already pointed out for each policy sub-sector, there were some similarities in policy styles for only some of the policy sub-sectors; even the commonalties in the interactions within those sectors were limited. Thus, the particular style of a policy sub-system does not appear to be an important intervening factor in feminist policy formation. Instead, policy styles should be seen as one determinant out of many that dictate the dynamics of feminist policy formation.

Strategic partnerships and feminist advocacy coalitions. Feminist strategic partnerships were clearly important players in the development of feminist policy. Partnerships between women's movement activists, femocrats in women's policy offices, and women in public office developed in over half of the policy cases. In many other cases, feminist partnerships that did not involve all three sets of actors participated actively in feminist policy formation. For example, femocrats did not participate in the feminist advocacy coalitions in abortion reform. These coalitions included women parliamentarians and women's movement activists. In the equal employment sub-sector, strategic partnerships linked feminists in trade unions with femocrats in equal employment agencies and other women's movement activists without the participation of women MPs.

Feminist policy successes occurred without the emergence of triangles of empowerment on specific issues as well. Full strategic partnerships played key roles in making and implementing seven out of the 13 high-success feminist policy cases. There were also strategic partnerships that contributed to seven out of the 13 cases of moderate feminist successes. Non-decision in an Irish policy case was made in the face of an active strategic partnership. The formation of reconciliation policies, the sub-sector with the lowest feminist policy scores, was marked by the absence of any significant feminist advocacy coalitions.

The different feminist actors in the feminist advocacy coalitions did not necessarily share fixed visions of feminist values linked to Western feminism(s), particularly given that the three sets of actors often came from significantly different social, economic, and political worlds. In some policy cases, like the Italian quota legislation, feminists were quite divided on particular issues. When feminist values were shared by actors in the feminist policy coalitions, they were pragmatic, goal-oriented, and focused on the specific policy in question. In many cases, the feminist advocacy coalition collapsed even before the policy was implemented, particularly in abortion reforms in Europe. Moreover, policy success for strategic partnerships was not always good for women's movement mobilization and organization. Women's movements in several cases lost organizational impetus as the result of relatively successful feminist reform.

Feminist advocacy coalitions must be actively forged by feminist actors around specific policy issues. High levels of women in elected office, active women's policy agencies, and strong women's movement mobilization do not by themselves produce successful feminist policies. For example, high numbers of women in elected office are found consistently in the Protestant Social Democrat countries,

❖ CONCLUSION

but not in the Protestant Liberal countries. Both feminist families of nations achieved the same aggregate levels of policy success. Women's policy offices, furthermore, do not have an active presence in all of the Protestant Social Democrat countries either. With some of the most extensively developed women's policy machineries at all levels of the state (Mazur *et al.* 2000), French feminist policy reached relatively moderate levels of success. Likewise, periods of significant women's movement mobilization and institutionalization did not correspond with feminist policy success. As Table 10.6 (on the next page) shows, policy cases did not follow any patterns of success over time that might correspond with the appearance of the new women's movements on the political scene in Western countries in the 1970s and their institutionalization in the 1980s and 1990s.

Many additional exogenous determinants were important in explaining the development of feminist policy. The following four factors were salient in a critical mass of cases. As with the other determinants, their effects on feminist policy formation were not systematic across policy sub-sectors, feminist families of nations, or countries. The specific impact of each factor on the relative success of feminist policy formation, therefore, must be seen in light of the particular combination of determinants on a given policy case.

Non-feminist allies. In the most successful feminist policy cases, non-feminist allies in the government played important roles in supporting feminist demands for policy. In order for feminist policy to be formulated, non-feminist decision-makers—for example, chief executives, ministers, and party and trade union leaders—had to provide some level of support to feminist ideas and feminist policy proposals. Non-feminist allies included women and men who were outside feminist advocacy coalitions. Some were allies with an independent interest in feminist ideas; others were converted to a feminist cause by activists in the feminist advocacy coalition on a given policy. Reluctant non-feminist policy actors were a part of policy formation in many of the cases of lower policy success across a range of countries and policy sub-sectors. Upper civil servants, in particular, entrenched in the established employment and social security bureaucracies were often resistant to demands for feminist reform in the equal employment and reconciliation sub-sectors.

National cultural attitudes and norms. National cultural attitudes were important in three policy sub-areas: attitudes about sexual relations and government's role in policing them in sexuality and violence policies; predominant views on gender relations in reconciliation and family law policies; and attitudes about the role of government in society in reconciliation policy. Countries with more woman-friendly policy logics in reconciliation policy produced higher levels of feminist policy success. The effect of norms and attitudes about government's role on feminist policy formation was quite important when the USA is compared with other democracies, but not as important when examining the degree of feminist success among the other countries.

CONCLUSION ❖

Table 10.6 Feminist success in policy cases of discrete decisions over time

	Pre/Form.		Post-form.		Total
	D	S	D	S	
THE 1970S					
#Germany (FLP) 1977 Marriage and divorce reform	1	2	1	2	6
Ireland (EEP)1977 Equal Employment Act	3	2	3	1	9
#Italy (RRP) 1978 Abortion law	3	2	1	1	7
#Norway (RRP) 1978 Abortion law	3	2	3	3	11
Norway (BP) 1978 Equal Status Act	2	2	3	3	10
Sweden (EEP) 1979 Equality Act	1	2	3	2	8
THE 1980S					
*×Ontario (PRP) 1982 Affirmative action in ONDP	3	3	3	3	12
Canada (BP) 1982 Charter of Rights and Freedoms	3	2	3	2	10
Great Britain (EEP) 1983 Equal Value Amendment	2	1	3	2	8
France (EEP) 1983 *Égalité Professionnelle* Act	2	2	1	1	6
^×Norway (PRP) 1980s–90s Election campaigns	3	3	2	3	11
#Netherlands (RRP) Abortion reform since 1973	2	2	2	3	9
Netherlands (BP) 1985–90 Emancipation Policy Program	2	3	1	1	7
#Australia (FLP) 1987 Matrimonial property reform	2	3	2	3	10
#Germany (RP)1986 Federal Childcare Benefit Act	1	3	1	2	7
#Ireland (FLP) 1981–95 Divorce reform	2	2	1	2	8
#Spain (BP) 1988–90 Equality Plan	1	3	1	2	7
#Spain (SVP) 1989–95 Sexual harassment reform	2	2	1	1	6
THE 1990S					
×Edinburgh (SVP) 1992 Zero Tolerance campaign	3	3	3	3	12
United States (RP) 1993 Family and Medical Leave Act	1	1	1	1	4
France (SVP) 1992 Sexual harassment reform	2	1	2	1	6
#Italy (PRP) 1993 and 1995 Quota legislation	3	2	3	2	10
#Ireland (RP)1995 Reform of social welfare legislation	2	0	2	0	4
France (PRP) 1999 Constitutional Parity Amendment	3	2	2	3	10

×sub-national cases;   *non-state case studies;   #missing information on cases;
^more than one individual policy;

Institutional design. The design of state institutions appeared to have an important effect on successful feminist outcomes in some cases. The type of legal system was important in equal employment and sexual harassment polices. Ironically, the type of legal system was not an important factor in family law policies. The particular national territorial distribution of power appeared to influence the dynamics of feminist policy in the federal systems of Canada, USA, and Germany. Federalism seemed to do little to produce feminist

❖ CONCLUSION

policy outcomes in Spain. The type of executive-legislative relations—pure parliamentary, semi-presidential as in France, or presidential as in the USA— had some impact on where policies were debated and the degree to which women gained access to decision-making. The way in which interest groups organized and obtained access to the state was also important to a certain degree, particularly in equal employment policies. In this sub-sector, the hold of the non-feminist trade unions over policy-making often shut out demands for more feminist approaches to public policy. The institutional design of state-society relations was also an important factor in abortion reform in the USA.

Extra-national influences. International and supra-national government bodies had a mitigated impact in feminist policy successes. European Union policy statements and European Court of Justice (ECJ) decisions sent conflicting messages to EU member states about their feminist policy. On the one hand, EU policy directives placed a certain degree of pressure on governments to pursue feminist policy in equal employment and political representation policies; and ECJ jurisprudence was an important rallying point for feminist advocacy coalitions in equal employment policy in Great Britain. On the other hand, the restricted scope of EU sex equality policy, for the most part limited to equality issues in paid labour, made it easier for governments of EU member countries to avoid taking action in sub-sectors of feminist policy outside the purview of EU sex equality policy. Thus, feminist policy success is not guaranteed for EU countries. Only five out of the 13 cases of high feminist policy success occurred in EU member states and only one member of the EU was among the top four cases (Table 10.1).

In EU and non-EU countries alike, the United Nations policies on women and women's conferences served as important touchstones for feminist policy-advocacy coalitions, particularly in drawing government attention to feminist policy issues in the pre-formulation stages. The limited power of the UN meant that the policy influence was necessarily indirect and symbolic. Other international organizations like the Council of Europe and the International Labour Organisation served similar symbolic functions in certain policy cases.

❖ METHODOLOGICAL PARAMETERS

The answer to Feick's (1992: 257) question about non-feminist policy studies— 'do the studies selected for secondary analyses lend themselves to integrative comparisons?'—with regard to the feminist policy formation literature is mixed. Many policy studies that were used in the case analyses did allow for uniform comparisons Complete studies of the start-to-finish process of feminist policy formation were not available for all sub-sectors or all feminist families of nations. There were no English-language analyses of family and law policies in any of the Protestant Social Democratic countries. Furthermore, as Table 10.7 shows, only ten out of the 27 cases were uncompromised by data problems.

CONCLUSION ❖

Table 10.7 Validity of observed cases

Compromised cases:	
Insufficient literature	11
Unit/level of analysis problems	6
Total	17
Uncompromised cases	10
Total observed cases	27

Compromised cases are marked in Tables 10.1–10.6; a key for the different validity problems is given at the bottom of each table.

The eleven cases which did not have sufficient literature coverage included cases for which there was only one published source available or the available sources did not cover the entire policy process. The literature gap occurred most frequently on recent post-formulation, in eight out of the eleven cases of insufficient information. There was inadequate information on the details of formulation on cabinet-level and parliamentary decisions in five cases as well. Five out of the eleven policy cases with insufficient literature were analysed with only a single major source. Out of the eleven cases, one was on Italy in the political representation sub-sector; three in reproductive rights on Norway, the Netherlands, and Italy; three in family law on Australia, Ireland, and Germany; one in blueprint on Spain; one in sexuality and violence on Spain; and two in the reconciliation sub-sector on Germany and Ireland. Equal employment policy was the only sub-sector with full literature coverage for all four cases.

The absence of complete studies of policy formation at the national level and the need to conduct case studies in all sub-sectors across all feminist families of nations underpinned the decision to shift the level and/or unit of analysis from the national arena of state-centred processes in six policy cases. Four policy cases took place below the national level: the affirmative action resolution in Ontario, the Zero Tolerance Campaign in Edinburgh, women's shelter funding at the municipal-level in Sweden, and the implementation of childcare policy at the municipal level in Denmark. The Ontario case took place in a political party rather than in any formal government arena. Four out of the six cases covered the evolution of a series of policy decisions over time rather than a discrete policy decision. Several election campaigns were observed in Norway; a series of Supreme Court decisions and national legislation on abortion were studied in the USA; funding decisions were analysed in Sweden; and childcare service delivery in Denmark was assessed.

It is difficult to determine to what extent the 17 compromised cases fail to provide an accurate portrayal of policy formation, or to what degree the limitations in the source literature undermine the lessons that can be drawn from the policy

✦ CONCLUSION

cases. In terms of the five cases for which only one source was analysed, it is obviously impossible to ascertain whether looking at a second source would have changed the outcome of the case. The high feminist successes of the three policy cases that took place outside national-level state arenas, shown in Table 10.7, may have been less a product of specific contextual factors than of policy decisions that were removed from the high stakes of national-level politics. Non-feminist actors may have more of a vested interest in blocking material reforms at the national level than at the sub-national level of the state. Similarly, for the cases observed in a series of policies, it is difficult to differentiate between the effects of specific determinants in policy formation and the dynamics of several different policy decisions as opposed to the dynamics of a single discrete decision.

Selecting cases for even distribution across sub-sectors and feminist families of nations within the limits of the available policy literature also meant that the policies analysed were not necessarily exemplars of a given policy sub-area, within a given country or feminist family of nations. The policy dynamics of a given case, therefore, have the potential to be an aberration for that policy sub-area and/or country. This case selection bias certainly applies to the cases covered in the sexuality and violence sub-sector. The politics of sexual harassment reform in Spain and in France are by no means the same as the politics of policies that seek to regulate rape or other extreme forms of violence like wife battery. Similarly, the four cases covered for reproductive rights policy were all on abortion reform, because of the extensive comparative literature on abortion policy. The selection of different types of reproductive rights policy may have produced quite different outcomes. Although the case selection bias problems obviously cannot be resolved at this point, it is important to raise them and to situate the comparative analysis of the 27 cases in the context of these limitations.

❖ NEXT STEPS

First and foremost, the propositions generated by this study need to be systematically tested in both qualitative and quantitative studies. The finding that feminist policy success is case-specific, a product of a shifting and complex line-up of influences, is significant. The particular way in which the long list of determinants actually combines in feminist policy formation remains an open-ended question. Although feminist policy coalitions appear to be key, additional work needs to be done on the connection between feminist policy success and the specific structure and shared belief systems of the coalitions. Understanding when strategic partnerships are important players should also be a part of future inquiry. The influence of cultural factors was also under-explored, particularly in how cultural attitudes play out differently within a single country across different policy sub-sectors. More work needs to be done on determining the relative impact of the institutional determinants on feminist policy outcomes as well.

The design of this study was to examine policy cases across all four feminist families of nations and all seven sub-sectors. Future studies that aim to test the propositions about feminist policy do not need to follow this sample-selection criterion. In this light, a variety of research avenues may be taken. The following are just a few examples. Small 'n' studies could take a sample of policy cases across sub-sectors within a certain country to control for national-level factors, or within a specific sub-sector to control for sub-sectoral effects. Cases could also be re-examined within a single feminist family of nations. A within-country design could be used to assess feminist policy formation at different levels of government or in different time periods to control for national-level factors. The case analyses from this study could be re-used in any one of these focused comparisons.

The small 'n' studies would help to sort through the relative influence of the various causal factors; they could not, however, provide any definitive statement, due to the 'small "n" too many variables' problem that typifies comparative qualitative analysis (Lijphart 1971). Thus, a second avenue to theory development is needed through the quantitative analysis of a statistically significant number of cases. In order to conduct a correlational analysis of feminist policy formation, the qualitative case analyses would need to be converted into a data set. The number of cases also would need to be increased significantly and numerical indicators would need to be developed for the different analytical elements of the model. Once a data set is created, different analyses of the data could be conducted that would control for the influences of feminist family of nation, nation, sub-sector, and other relevant exogenous factors.

Whether the next steps are qualitative or quantitative, new cases analyses need to be conducted. The cases with insufficient information could be fleshed out by more thorough searches of national-research collections. This study's inventory shows that there is sufficient literature for at least 50 additional cases of feminist policy formation. There is also an ever-growing literature on the politics of reconciliation policy (for example, Hantrais 2000a), particularly with the turn toward politics as an important factor in explaining welfare development in gender and welfare state scholarship (for example, Sainsbury 1999a) and a plethora of new studies on the politics of caring (for example, Lewis 1998). Legal studies of family law could be more consistently consulted to conduct case analyses of family law policies as well. New case analysis could be conducted by FCP scholars with expertise in feminist policy.

Given the rising interest in feminist politics at the sub-national and local levels, additional policy cases at levels of government below the national level could augment current case analyses. With more cases at the municipal level, the differences between local and national feminist politics could be more closely examined. Urban studies of public service delivery could fill the gaps left by this study for this eighth sub-sector of feminist policy. As the field becomes more developed, existing work may be translated into English. Whatever the route to the development of a more systematic theory, future work would be greatly facilitated by the creation of an international network of scholars in the tradition of previous FCP-networked groups.

❖ BROADER IMPLICATIONS

❖ *For Feminist Comparative Policy*

From the beginning, the major goal of this book has been to strengthen and to contribute to the new field and to follow the larger feminist empirical project of FCP in carrying out this study. The book will, one hopes, help other FCP scholars in a variety of ways: by defining feminist policy as a distinct field of policy, by taking stock of the literature on feminist policy, by developing a framework to analyse feminist policy, and by generating propositions about the dynamics and determinants of feminist policy formation.

The findings of this project shed new light on the major question of FCP: whether, how, and why the contemporary state in Western democracies is feminist. This book has argued throughout that states do take feminist ideas and demands and put them into action. Beyond the clear assertion that Western democracies pursue purposefully feminist action, the findings of this study are more nuanced. The dynamics of feminist policy formation is variegated, multiform, and most of all transversal in the way it cross-cuts many different sectors of state action. Thus, whereas assertions about the monolithic and patriarchal state are refuted, this study does not supply as satisfactory an explanation of the how and why of feminist policy formation.

Likewise, the role of women and women's movements is not clear-cut. Feminist policy definitely brings women into the state both substantively and descriptively. Women do not have to be present, however, in the formulation or implementation of feminist policy. Women can be quite involved with the development of policies that are seen as feminist successes. Women's descriptive representation does not necessarily lead to their substantive representation. Women's movements, women-centred feminist policy coalitions, and strategic partnerships are clearly a part of feminist policy formation; they do not appear to be the decisive ingredient. The findings also suggest that the agency of individual women is not the only road to optimal feminist policy and that policy under left-wing governments is not always a feminist success.

❖ For Non-feminist Political Science

Intersecting feminist with non-feminist scholarship has been an important part of this project . This book has sought to make feminist-informed contributions to comparative politics, comparative public policy, and public policy analysis. It has also applied non-feminist theory and methods to the feminist analysis of a feminist issue. The major finding of this study—that feminist policy is a new sector of government action—speaks directly to comparative policy scholarship that has missed or purposefully ignored the sector. It contributes to work that focuses on the policy sub-system as an object of analysis and an explanatory factor in policy development. The study follows the lead of other FCP work that uses the advocacy-coalition framework as a heuristic and theoretical device. This book also contributes to the application and development of the qualitative research techniques of 'process tracing' and 'thick description' in comparative analysis. The template used to record the case analyses provides a useful tracking tool for this type of analysis.

❖ For Practical Politics

Feminist policy practitioners, femocrats, activists in feminist and women's organizations and movements, as well as non-feminist policy actors interested in pursuing and monitoring feminist policy have the potential to benefit from the findings in this book. In recognizing that their efforts are part of a larger trend in government policy in Western democracies, feminist policy actors often dispersed across many different sectors may be able to begin to or to further develop a common awareness and political identity about their individual work. With the broader purview of feminist policy as a sector and the backdrop of feminist policy success, policy actors frequently marginalized in feminist bureaucracies, women's organizations, political parties, and trade unions and worn down by non-feminist resistance might be able to develop a more optimistic view about their work. In examining cases of feminist policy success, the constellation of state and society actors involved with feminist policy can learn more about the specific ingredients for success within their policy niche. Many may take comfort in learning that there is no single route to feminist policy success; some may even consider experimenting with different approaches and strategies.

In conclusion, this book has sought to constructively participate and contribute to the lively, vital, and essential ongoing dialogue among activists, practitioners, and scholars in feminist and non-feminist worlds on government performance, democracy, feminism, and feminist policy in action. Hopefully, the lessons drawn from this study will prove to be useful to the range of individuals engaged in making the state more feminist.

❖ CONCLUSION

❖ Notes

1 See Chapter 2 for the way the different components of the model were operational-
ized and the analytical logic behind the original hypotheses

2 The sub-sector of each policy is marked in all of the tables by an abbreviation: BP
for blueprint policies; PRP for political representation policies; EEP for equal employment policies; RP for reconciliation policies; FLP for family law policies; RRP for reproductive rights policies; and SVP for sexual violence policies. Uncompromised cases
are flagged in all of the tables. These problems are discussed at further length in the next
section. A key for the different validity problems is at the bottom of each table.

3 See Chapter 2 for the criteria used for assigning policy profile scores (pp. 37–39).
The case analyses in the sub-sector chapters provide the rationale for the score of each
specific case. Summary tables in the conclusion of each sub-sector channel present the
scores of the policy cases.

4 The average of the six observed policy cases in the Protestant Democrat family was
taken to provide an estimated policy profile score of 9.

❖ Appendix A

Labelling Feminist Political Action in Western Post-industrial Democracies

The operational definitions of feminist policy and feminism presented in Chapters 1 and 2 follow the Feminist Comparative Policy approach. As a result, these general definitions are not identified with any specific current of ideas in Western political thought. At the same time, labels typically used to distinguish between different currents of Western feminism are used in the 27 case analyses of feminist policy formation conducted for this study to identify actors and action. It is important to clarify the meanings of the various labels for feminist ideas and action used throughout this comparative study of feminist policy formation. The aim of the following discussion, however, is not to replicate the many extensive treatments of the different strands of Western feminism (for example, Beasley 1999; Tong 1989; Offen 2000). This appendix seeks to provide working definitions of the pertinent labels used to refer to feminist positions taken by individuals, groups, actors, and policies in the full range of countries found in the four feminist families of nations covered by this study.

It is also important to recognize the limits of labelling specific feminist positions. Given the complex and all-encompassing nature of feminist action, it is difficult to place individuals and specific actions into a single feminist category. Several distinct currents of feminism are often intertwined in the outlook of individuals and in the content of policy in the real political world. Nonetheless, it is useful to identify the origins of feminist ideas in the process of tracing the development of policy over time. This discussion should be seen as a key to the feminist terminology used in the study to orient the reader; it is not intended to delineate a limited range of possible types of feminism along which all feminists must align themselves. Given that this study is about public policy, the different labels incorporate feminist ideas that are associated with demands for social change through the state. Feminist currents of thought directed at intellectual and cultural production like standpoint, postmodern, or psychoanalytic feminism, therefore, are not treated in this Appendix.

Feminist action is classified on two dimensions: *positions towards political change* and *ideological approach*. There are two types of feminist positions on political change. Moderate or *reform-oriented* feminist approaches are based on the assumption that feminist goals should be pursued within the established political system, usually through the reform of public policy. Political action is oriented toward creating coalitions and convincing decision-makers to support a specific policy line through informal and formal channels. *Anti-system* feminist stances are associated with action that seeks to break with the status quo and to create a new feminist order. Feminists who follow more anti-system positions typically shun working with established groups, like political parties and trade unions, as well as with government actors. Feminist action on the reform/anti-system dimension consists of a range of actions located on a continuum from anti-system to reform rather than in dichotomous categories whereby actors and actions take either a reform or an anti-system approach.

Four labels for feminist action used in this study are based on political ideology: liberal, radical, socialist/Marxist, and social. Often, analysts identify liberal feminism with reform feminism. This study does not, because feminists favourable to reform can include socialist, social, radical and, in some cases, Marxist feminism. For example, radical feminists in many different countries work—reluctantly—with government agencies to develop shelters for battered women.

When the label *liberal feminist* is used to describe feminist action, the action tends to focus on social change in the public spheres of formal politics and paid employment and to emphasize individual rights and equality between the sexes. Liberal feminism has been associated in some countries with classical liberal ideas that define government as a limited legal cage. Contemporary liberal feminist positions, however, tend to embrace notions of redistributive liberalism whereby government is seen as a corrective for social inequities between men and women.

The *radical feminist* label covers ideas that emphasize the private sphere and what feminist analysts refer to as 'body politics' (see Chapter 8). The source of women's oppression is traced to the patriarchal nature of society and the sexual power men have over women. This feminist set of ideas is based on the premise that women and men are profoundly different. Gender differences are seen in a positive light as long as they are not translated into gender-based discrimination again women. In this light, social change should take into consideration women's interests as a group and strike down patriarchy.

Feminist labels associated with socialism fall into two groups: Marxist feminism and socialist feminism. In *Marxist feminist* action, women's emancipation is intertwined with the revolution of the working class. Systems of gender domination are based on class-based inequities and the bourgeois control of capital. *Socialist feminist* ideas and action are based on the assertion that gender domination exists alongside class inequities. Social change, therefore, must take into consideration patriarchy within the context of socialist emancipation. Marxist feminists tend to be associated with communist parties and movements and socialist feminists with more moderate socialist and social democratic political parties. Socialist feminists are arguably more oriented toward reform than Marxist feminists. However, in countries where the communist parties have Euro-communized—that is, they have abandoned the pursuit of complete working-class revolution—communist feminists can also operate within the democratic system and pursue social change through public policy.

Social feminist ideas embrace the notion that women are different from men. They do not focus on patriarchy as the cause of women's oppression. Action that is pursued in a social feminist optic seeks to maintain the status quo in gender relations, where men are the bread-winners and women are the homemakers. Women's rights tend to be defined in terms more of women's maternal roles than their roles outside the home. Social feminism has been identified as a major current of feminism in Germany (Black 1989; Ferree 1997). It was also an important influence in the United States prior to the Second World War (Stetson 1997b).

❖ Appendix B

Guide to Feminist Policy Formation Literature

The following guide classifies the published work on feminist policy formation used for this study into three categories: (1) general work that covers feminist policy and contextual factors in several different sub-sectors of feminist policy and/or several different feminist families of nations; (2) studies that focus on a single country or feminist family of nations in more than one sub-sector of feminist policy; and (3) literature that looks at specific sub-sectors of feminist policy in a given feminist family of nation or country. Works listed under the rubric 'general' in the feminist family nations and sub-sector categories cover two or more countries within a feminist family of nations or treat the issues relevant to that sub-sector in a comparative perspective.

All entries are listed in the larger bibliography for the book. A variety of sources was consulted to compile the general bibliography. They include 86 social science journals,[1] US-based library indexes, and state-of-the-field articles on gender and politics (Lovenduski 1981; Boals 1975; Carroll 1980; Ferguson 1984; Nelson 1989; Sapiro 1991; Carroll and Zerilli 1993; Randall 1991; Silverberg 1992; Githens 1983; Meehan 1986; Staudt and Weaver 1997; Kelly and Fisher 1993; Hawkesworth 1994; Ackelsberg 1992; Lief Palley 1976; Cichowski 2000; Orloff 1993, 1993; Kornbluh 1996; O'Connor 1996; Outshoorn 1992; Valiente 1998a; Lovenduski 1998; Acker 1992; Nelson 1992).

Four graduate students worked a total of over 300 hours compiling the bibliography. The US-based searches were cross-checked with extensive country-specific bibliographies on all of European Union member countries in the study. These country-specific bibliographies were collected for a report on research on women and decision-making conducted for the European Union in 1997–8 (Lovenduski and Stephenson 1999). Policy experts from each EU member country submitted an inventory of published work on women in political, economic, and social decision-making and on evaluations of equality policy in their country for the report. Over 50 FCP scholars were also contacted directly for their suggestions on current literature in their areas.

Given that the case analysis selection for the cross-national analysis of feminist policy formation was partially based on literature coverage, it is useful to present the number of published pieces cited for each policy sub-sector. The substantive coverage of this literature is discussed in the overview section of each sub-sector chapter. While the search conducted for English-language work was quite thorough, it was by no means

[1] List available on request

exhaustive. None the less, given the scope and intensity of the search, the following numerical summary provides a relatively accurate picture of the extent of literature published through 2001 on feminist policy formation for each sub-sector. Only work that went into some level of detail on the politics of policy formation was included.

There are 462 separate entries classified by sub-sector under the third category of literature. Taking into consideration pieces that covered more than one country or sub-sector, the actual number of individual pieces that examine the specific details of the politics of feminist policy is probably closer to 400. This total does not include additional work in the first and second categories that is not listed with the third group of literature. There were 60 pieces on blueprint policies, 56 on political representation policies, 116 on equal employment policies, 81 on reconciliation policies, 29 on family law policies, 62 on reproductive rights policies, and 56 on sexuality and violence policies. The average number of pieces for all seven sub-sectors was 65 pieces for each sub-sector and the largest difference in literature coverage between individual sub-sectors was for equal employment and family law sub-sectors; there were 87 more pieces on equal employment policies than on family law policies.

1. GENERAL COMPARATIVE WORK ON FEMINIST POLICY FORMATION ISSUES = 53

Adams and Padamsee (2001); Andreasen *et al.* (1991); Bacchi (1999); Baldock and Cass (1983); Bashevkin (1998); Basu (1995); Bayes (1991); Black (1989); Black and Cottrell (1981); Buckley and Anderson (1988a); Burrell (1997); Bystydzienski (1992a); Bystydzienski and Sekhon (1999); Chamberlayne (1993); Chow and Berheide (1996); Dahlerup (1986a); Davis (1997); Dominelli (1991); Drew, Emerek, and Mahon (1998); Ferre and Martin (1995); García-Ramoan and Monk (1996); Gardiner (1997a); Gardiner and Leijenaar (1997); Gelb (1989); Hallett (1996); Hayes, MacAllister, and Studlar (2000); Heatlinger (1993); Hernes (1987); Hobson and Berggren (1997); Inglehart and Norris (2000); Kaplan (1992); Katzenstein and Mueller (1986); Lipman-Bluman and Bernard (1979); Lovenduski and Hills (1981); Lovenduski and Norris (1993; 1996); Lovenduski (1986a; 1997c); Lycklama à Nijeholt, Vargas, and Wieringa (1998); Mahon (2001); Mutari and Figart (2001); Nelson and Chowdhury (1994); Norris (1987); O'Regan (2000); Randall (1982; 1987); Randall and Weylen (1998); Safilios-Rotschild (1974); Singh (1998); Stetson and Mazur (1995); Threlfall (1996a); Tremblay (2000); Walby (1997); Young (2000).

2. GUIDE BY FEMINIST FAMILY OF NATION AND/OR COUNTRY = 110

Late Female Mobilizing = 17

Ireland: Connelly (1993); Connolly (1999); Galligan (1998); Galligan, Ward, and Wilford (1999); Mahon (1995; 1996); Mahon and Morgan (1999).
Italy: Becalli (1994;1996); Beckwith (1987); Guadagini (1995).
Spain: Cousins (1995); Duran and Gellego (1986); Mendez (1994); Threlfall (1996a); Valiente (1995; 1997a, b).

Protestant Social Democrat = 21

General: Bergqvist *et al.* (1999); Haavio-Mannila *et al.* (1985); Karvonen and Selle (1995); Skjeie and Siim (2000).

Denmark: Borchorst (1995).

Sweden: Elman (1995); Gustafsson, Eduards, and Rönnblom (1997); Hirdman (1998); Rönnblom (1997); Sainsbury (2001).

Norway: Bystydzienski (1992*a*, *b*; 1995*a*, *b*); Halsaa (1991; 1995; 1998); Skjeie (1991*a*, *b*; 1993); Van der Ros (1994; 1997).

Advanced Christian Democrat = 30

France: Baudino and Mazur (2001); Duchen (1986); Jenson (1980; 1985); Jenson and Sineau (1994); Mazur (1995*a*, *b*); Mazur *et al.* (2000); Raissiguier (2001); Stetson (1987); Allwood and Wadia (2000).

Germany: Baer (1988); Ferree (1987; 1991–92; 1995; 1997); Kolinsky (1989); Lemke (1994).

The Netherlands: Asscher-Vonk (1995); Bussemaker and Voet (1998); Dutch (forthcoming); Leijenaar and Niemöller (1994); Oldersma (1999); Outshoorn (1992; 1994*a*, *b*; 1995; 1997; 1998*a*, *b*); Outshoorn and Swiebel (1998).

Protestant Liberal English Speaking = 42

USA: Costain (1992); Conway, Ahern, and Steuernagel (1999); Ferree (1987); Ferree and Hess (1985); Gelb and Palley (1982,1987); Mathews and DeHart (1990); Nelson and Carver (1994); Stetson (1995*a*; 1997*b*);

Great Britain: Abrar, Lovenduski, and Margetts (1998); Lovenduski (1994); Lovenduski and Randall (1993); Norris and Lovenduski (1995); Walby (1999); Bashevkin (1998; 2000).

Scotland: Brown (1996).

Canada: Andrew and Rodgers (1997); Arscott (1995; 1998); Bakker (1996); Bashevkin (1985*a*, *b*; 1994; 1998); Bégin (1997); Brodie (1996); Burt (1995); Evans and Wekerle (1997); Geller-Schwartz (1995); Gingras (1995); Haussman (1992); Paltiel (1997); Tremblay and Andrew (1998); Tremblay and Pelletier (2000).

Australia: Eisenstein (1996); Franzway, Court, and Connell (1989); Sawer (1990; 1994; 1995); Sullivan (1990); Watson (1990).

3. GUIDE BY SUB-SECTOR OF FEMINIST POLICY = 462
A. Blueprint = 60

General: Vogel-Polsky (1995).

Late Female Mobilizing

Ireland: Connolly (1999); Gardiner (1999); Mahon (1995); Mahon and Morgan (1999).

Italy: Guadagini (1995).

Spain: Mendez (1994); Threlfall (1996*b*); Valiente (1995; 1997*a*).

Protestant Social Democrat

General: Borchorst (1999*b*).

Denmark: Borchorst (1995).

Sweden: Elman (1995).
Norway: Bystydzienski (1992*a*; 1995*b*); Halsaa (1991; 1995; 1998); Skjeie (1991*a*); Van der Ros (1994; 1997).

Advanced Christian Democrat

France: Jenson and Sineau (1994*a*, *b*); Mazur (1995*a*, *b*); Stetson (1987).
Germany: Ferree (1991–92; 1995); Kolinsky (1989); Lemke (1994).
The Netherlands: Leijenaar and Niemöller (1994); Oldersma (1999); Outshoorn (1994*a*; 1995; 1998*a*); Outshoorn and Swiebel (1998).

Protestant Liberal English Speaking

USA: Ferree and Hess (1995); Haussman (1992); Mathews and DeHart (1990); Nelson and Carver (1994); Parry (1998); Stetson (1995*a*; 1997*b*).
Great Britain: Lovenduski (1994); Lovenduski and Randall (1993).
Canada: Arscott (1995; 1998); Bashevkin (1994; 1998); Bégin (1997); Brodsky and Day (1989); Burt (1995); Geller-Schwartz (1995); Haussman (1992); Paltiel (1997).
Australia: Eisenstein (1996); Gingras (1995; Sawer (1990; 1994; 1995); Sullivan (1990).

B. Political Representation = 56

General: Bacchi (1996); Outshoorn (1994*b*); Haavio-Mannila *et al.* (1985).

Late Female Mobilizing

Ireland: Galligan (1993; 1998).
Italy: Guadagnini (1993; 1998*a*, *b*); Becalli (1996).
Spain: Mendez (1994).

Protestant Social Democrat

General: Bergqvist *et al.* (1999); Karvonen and Selle (1995).
Denmark:
Sweden: Bergqvist (1995*a*, *b*); Sainsbury (1993).
Norway: Bystydzienski (1995*a*, *b*); Halsaa (1991); Skjeie (1993); Van der Ros (1994).

Advanced Christian Democrat

France: Appleton and Mazur (1993); Gaspard (1997); Gaspard, Servan-Schreiber, and LeGall (1992); Hause and Kenney (1984); Jenson and Sineau (1994); Mazur (2001*b*); Mossuz-Lavau (1998); Praud (2001); Sihean (2001).
Germany: Ferree (1987;1995); Kolinksy (1989; 1991; 1993); Lemke (1994).
The Netherlands: Leijenaar and Niemöller (1994); Oldusma (2002).

Protestant Liberal English-Speaking

USA: Burrell (1997); Saloma and Sontag (1972); Kelber (1994); Kirkpatrick (1975); Stetson (1997*b*).
Great Britain: Bashevkin (1985*b*); Lovenduski (1994); Norris and Lovenduski (1995); Squires (1999*b*).

Canada: Arscott (1995); Erickson (1993); Geller-Schwartz (1995); Praud (1997); Young (1998).
Australia: Simms (1993); Sawer (1994).

C. Equal Employment = 116

General: Bacchi (1996); Bellace (1991); Cockburn (1989); Cook (1989); Corcoran and Donnelly (1988); Good (1998); Hoskyns (2001); Kahn and Meehan (1992); Laatikainen (2001); Mazur (2001*a*); Meehan and Sevenhuijsen (1991*a*); Pillinger (1992); Steinberg-Ratner (1980*a*); Steinberg-Ratner and Cook (1988); Rees (1995; 1998).

Late Female Mobilizing

Ireland: Callender and Meenan (1995); Galligan (1998); Gardiner (1999); Good (2001); E. Mahon (1995; 1996); Mahon and Morgan (1999).
Italy: Bimbi (1993); Del Boca (1998); Del Re (2000); Guadagnini (2001).
Spain: Cousins (1995); Mendez (1994); Threlfall (1996*a*); Valiente (1995; 2001*a*).

Protestant Social Democrat

General: Eduards, Halsaa, and Skjeie (1985); Borchorst (1999*b*).
Denmark: Borchorst (1995); Siim (1991).
Sweden: Bergqvist and Jungar (2000); Elman (1995); Gelb (1989); Leira (1992; 1993); Nielsen (1995); Ruggie (1984; 1987; 1988); Victorin (1991).
Norway: Halsaa (1991; 1998); Leira (1992; 1993); Skjeie (1993); Van der Ros (1994).

Advanced Christian Democrat

France: Hantrais (1993*a*, *b*); Jenson (1987); Jenson and Sineau (1994); Kilpatrick (1997); Lanquetin, Laufer, Letablier (2000); Mazur (1995*a*; 2001*c*); Stetson and Mazur (2000).
Germany: Bertelsmann and Rust (1995); Daubler-Gmelin (1980); Erler (1988); Lemke (1994); Kolinsky (1989); Ostner (1993); Scheiwe (2000).
The Netherlands: Leijenaar and Niemöller (1994); Outshoorn (1991); Outshoorn and Swiebel (1998).

Protestant Liberal English-Speaking

USA: Bashevkin (1998); Gregory (1992); Hart (1994); Kelly and Bayes (1988); Kahn and Meehan (1992); McCann (1994); E. Meehan (1983*a*, *b*; 1985); Nelson and Carver (1994); O'Connor (1999); Remick (1980); Ruggie (1984; 1987); Stetson (1997*b*; 2001*b*); Stetson and Mazur (2000).
Great Britain: Bagilhole and Byrne (2000); Bashevkin (1998); Byrne and Lovenduski (1978); Forbes (1989; 1997); Gelb (1989); Gregory (1992; 1999); Hart (1994); Kahn (1992); Kahn and Meehan (1992); Kilpatrick (1997); Lovenduski (1995); Lovenduski and Randall (1993); McCrudden (1994); E. Meehan (1983*a*, *b*; 1985); Nandy (1980); O'Connor (1999); Seear (1980).
Canada: Bashevkin (1994; 1998); Fudge (1996); Gunderson and Robb (1991); McDermott (1996); O'Connor (1999); Teghtsoonian and Grace (2001).
Australia: O'Connor (1999); Sawer (1994); Ronalds (1990).

D. Reconciliation = 81

General: Bradshaw (1996); Bradshaw *et al.* (1993); Diamond (1983); Ditch *et al.* (1999); Döring *et al.* (1994); Gauthier (1996); Hantrais (2000*a*); Hervey and Shaw (1998); Hirschmann and Liebert (2001); Jenson and Sineau (2001); Joshi and Davies (1992); Kammerman and Kahn (1978; 1991); Lewis (1993*a*, *b*; 1997*a*, *b*; 1998); Lohnka-Himmighofen and Dienel (2000); Luckhaus and Ward (1997); Meyers, Gornick, and Ross (1999); Michel and Mahon (forthcoming); E. Mahon 1998*a*, *b*); Morgan (2001); Sainsbury (1994; 1996; 1999*a*, *b*); Sohrab (1994); Yohalem (1980).

Late Female Mobilizing

Ireland: Conroy (1997); Jackson (1993).
Italy: Becalli (1996); Bimbi (1993; 1997); Bimbi and Della Sal (1998); Del Boca (1998); Del Re (2000).
Spain: Cousins (1995); Valiente (2000).

Protestant Social Democrat

General: Leira (1992; 1993; 1998*a*); Bergqvist *et al.* (1999); Sainsbury (2001).
Denmark: Borchorst (1999*a*).
Sweden: Bergqvist and Jungar (2000); Daune-Richard and Mahon (1998); R. Mahon (1997).
Norway: Bergqvist *et al.* (1999); Leira (1992).

Advanced Christian Democrat

France: Hantrais (1993*a*); Jenson and Sineau (1998*b*); Lanquetin, Laufer, Letablier (2000); Morgan (forthcoming); Stetson (1987).
Germany: Kolinsky (1989); Lankau and Langkau-Hermann (1980); Meyer (1998); Scheiwe (1994*a*; 2000); Schiersmann (1991).
The Netherlands: Bussemaker and Voet (1998).

Protestant Liberal English Speaking

USA: Conway, Ahern, and Steuernagel (1999); Gelb and Palley (1987); Joffe (1983); Stetson (1997*b*); Teghtsoonian (1993; 1995; 1996).
Great Britain: Bagilhole and Byrne (2000); Bashevkin (1998); Brannen (1999); Ginn and Arber (1999); Lovenduski and Randall (1993); Millar and Whiteford (1993); Randall (1996).
Canada: Bashevkin (1998); Evans (1996); Teghtsoonian (1993; 1996).
Australia: Millar and Whiteford (1993); Sawer (1994).

E. Family Law = 29

General: Glendon (1989); Nelson (1997); Smart (1998).

Late Female Mobilizing

Ireland: Galligan (1998); Connolly (1999).
Italy: Beckwith (1987); Becalli (1996); Pisciotta (1986).
Spain: Cousins (1995); Threlfall (1996*a*).

Protestant Social Democrat
Denmark:
Sweden: Baude (1979).
Norway:

Advanced Christian Democrat
France: Stetson (1987).
Germany: Ferree (1991–92;1995; 1997); Kolinsky (1989); Lemke (1994); Ostner (1993; 1997).
The Netherlands:

Protestant Liberal English Speaking
General: Bashevkin (1998).
USA: Conway, Ahern, and Steuernagel (1999); Fineman (1983); Stetson (1997*b*); Stoper and Boneparth (1988).
Great Britain: Stetson (1982).
Canada: Cossman (1996).
Australia: Graycar (1990).

F. Reproductive Rights = 62

General: Crighton and Ebert (2001); Dahlerup (1986*a*); Field (1983); Githens and Stetson (1996); Ketting (1986); Lovenduski and Outshoorn (1986*a*); Outshoorn (1988; 1996); Rolston and Eggert (1994*a);* Stetson (1996*a*; 2001*a*).

Late Female Mobilizing
Ireland: Eggert and Rolston (1994); Galligan (1998); Girvin (1996); Jackson (1986); E. Mahon (2001); Randall (1986); Smyth (1996); Taylor (1999).
Italy: Beckwith (1987); Caldwell (1986); Pisciotta (1986).
Spain: Mendez (1994); Valiente (2001*b*).

Protestant Social Democrat
Denmark: Rasmussen (1994).
Sweden: Lindahl (1994).
Norway: Gulli (1994); Van der Ros (1994); Wiik (1986).

Advanced Christian Democrat
France: Batiot (1986); Jenson (1987); Mossuz-Lavau (1986); Robinson (2001); Stetson (1987).
Germany: Kolinsky (1989); Kamenitsa (2001); Kelin-Schonnefeld (1994); Lemke(1994); Winkler (1996).
The Netherlands: Ketting (1994); Outshoorn (1986*a, b*; 2001).

Protestant Liberal English Speaking
USA: Cohan (1986); Craig and O'Brien (1993); Diamond (1988); Graber (1996); McDonagh (1996); Scheppele (1996); Stetson (1996*a*; 1997*b*; 2001*d*); Studlar and Tatalovich (1996); Woliver (1996).

Great Britain: Cohan (1986); Lovenduski (1986a; 1994); Lovenduski and Randall (1993); Randall (1992); Stetson (2001c).
Canada: Brodie, Gavigan, and Jenson (1992); Cameron (1996); Haussman (2001); McCormack (1996); Studlar and Tatalovich (1996).
Australia: Sawer (1994); Simms (1994).

G. Sexuality And Violence = 56

General: Baer (1996); Barry (1988); Bunch (1991); Cameron (1996); Carver and Mottier (1998); Collins (1996); Connors (1994); Corrin (1996); Davies (1994); Dobash and Dobash (1992); Elman (1996); Leidholt (1996); Stetson (1995b); Weldon (1998; 2001).

Late Female Mobilizing

Ireland: Galligan (1998).
Italy: Becalli (1996); Beckwith (1987).
Spain: Valiente (1997a; 1998a); Threlfall (1996b).

Protestant Social Democrat

General: Morken and Selle (1995)
Denmark:
Sweden: Elman (1996a); Eduards (1997).
Norway: Van der Ros (1994).

Advanced Christian Democrat

France: Mazur (1993; 1996a, b); Merchant (1996); Stetson (1987).
Germany: Baer (1996); Kolinsky (1989); Winkler (1996).
The Netherlands: Outshoorn (1998b).

Protestant Liberal English Speaking

USA: Daniels (1997); Diamond (1988); Elman (1996a); Mathews (1995); Stetson (1997b).
Great Britain: Abrar (1996); Itsin (1996); Kelly (1999); Lovenduski and Randall (1993); Merchant (1996).
Scotland: Mackay (1996)
Canada: Cossman (1996); Cossman *et al.* (1997); Gotell (1996); Gwinnett (1998); Johnson (1995); Levan (1996); McCormack (1996); Ursel (1997).
Australia: Franzway, Court, and Connell (1989); McFerren (1990); Sawer (1994); Gorjanicyn (1998).

❖ Appendix C

Research Network on Gender, Politics, and the State (RNGS) Template for Analysis of Policy Cases

Policy Sub-Sector/ Country:
Specific Policy:
Policy Profile Score   *Pre/Form.:*   *Post-form.:*   =
Literature:

I. PROGRESS IN PROCESS

II. POLICY PROFILE

Pre-Formulation/Formulation:
  Descriptive:

  Substantive:

Post-Formulation:
  Descriptive:

  Substantive:

Outputs/Feedback:

III. POLICY COMMUNITY STYLE

Actors:

Interactions:

Arenas:

Instruments:

Shared Belief System:

IV. How Feminist?

V. Significant Determinants

❖ Bibliography

See Appendix B for a guide to the feminist policy formation literature and the different sources used to compile this bibliography.

Abbot, P. and Wallace, C. (1992). *The Family and the New Right*. London and Boulder, CO: Pluto Press.

Abels, G., and Sifft, S. (eds) (1999). *Halbierte Demokratie Weltweit? Feministische Perspektiven auf Transitions—und Demokratisierungsprozesse.* (Unfinished Democracy World-wide? Feminist Perspectives of Transition and Democratization). Frankfurt: Campus Verlag.

Abrar, S. (1996). 'Feminist Intervention and Local Domestic Violence Policy', in J. Lovenduski and P. Norris (eds), *Women in Politics*. Oxford: Oxford University Press.

——Lovenduski, J., and Margetts, H. (1998). 'Sexing London: The Gender Mix of Urban Policy Actors'. *International Review of Political Science*, 19: 147–71.

—————(2000). 'Feminist Ideas and Domestic Violence Policy Change'. *Political Studies*, 48: 239–62.

Ackelsberg, M. A. (1992). 'Feminist Analyses of Public Policy'. *Comparative Politics*, 24/3: 477–93.

Acker, J. (1992). 'From Sex Roles to Gendered Institutions'. *Contemporary Sociology*, 21/5: 565–9.

Adams, J. and Padamsee (2001). 'Signs and Regimes: Rereading Feminist Work on Welfare States'. *Social Politics*, 8/1: 1–28.

Adolino, J. R. and Blake, C. H. (2001). *Comparing Public Policies: Issues and Choices in Six Industrialized Countries*. Washington, DC: CQ Press.

Allwood, G. and Kinsheed, W. (2000). *Women and Politics in France, 1958–2000*. London and New York: Routledge.

Andersen, S. and Kjell, A.E. (eds) (1993). *Making Policy in Europe: The Europeification of National Policy-making*. London: Sage.

Anderson, J. E. (1994). *Public Policymaking: An Introduction*. Boston, MA: Houghton Mifflin.

Anderson, J. L. (1997a). 'Governmental Suasion: Refocusing the Lowi Policy Typology'. *Policy Studies Journal*, 25/2: 266–82.

——(1997b). 'Response to Theodore J. Lowi's "Comments on Anderson", Governmental Suasion Adding to the Lowi Policy Typology'. *Policy Studies Journal*, 25/4: 283–85.

Andreasen, T., Borchorst, A., Dahlerup, D., Louis, E., and Nielsen Rimmen, H. (eds) (1991). *Moving On: New Perspectives on the Women's Movements*. Aarhus: Aarhus University Press.

Andrew, C. and Rodgers, S. (eds) (1997). *Women and the Canadian State.* Montréal: McGill-Queen's University Press.

ANEF (Association Nationale des Étude Féministes) (1994). 'Pouvoir, Parité et Représentation Politiques'. *Bulletin de l'ANEF.* Supplement to no. 16.

Appleton, A. and Mazur, A. G. (1993). 'Transformation or Modernization: The Rhetoric and Reality of Gender and Party Politics in France', in J. Lovenduski and P. Norris (eds), *Gender and Party Politics.* London: Sage.

Armstrong, P. (1996). 'Unraveling the Safety Net: Transformations in Health Care and Their Impact on Women', in J. Brodie (ed.), *Women and Canadian Public Policy.* Toronto: Harcourt Brace and Company.

Arscott, J. (1995). 'A Job Well Begun . . . Representation, Electoral Reform, and Women', in F.-P. Gingras (ed.), *Gender and Politics in Contemporary Canada.* Toronto: Oxford University Press.

——(1998). 'More Women: The RCSW and Political Representation', in M. Tremblay and C. Andrew (eds), *Women and Political Representation in Canada.* Ottawa: University of Ottawa Press.

Ashford, D. E. (ed.) (1978). *Comparing Public Policies: New Concepts and Methods.* Beverly Hills: Sage Publications.

——(ed.) (1992). *History and Context in Comparative Public Policy.* Pittsburgh: University of Pittsburgh Press.

Asscher-Vonk, I. (1995). *Equality in Law Between Men and Women in the European Community: The Netherlands.* Dordrecht: Martinus Nijhoff.

Atkinson, M. M. and Coleman, W. D. (1989). 'Strong States and Weak States: Sectoral Policy Networks in Advanced Capitalist Economies'. *British Journal of Political Science,* 19: 47–67.

AVFT (Association Européene contre les Violences Faites aux Femmes au Travail) (1996). 'Actualité de la Parité'. *Projets Féministes,* February, 4–5.

Bacchi, C. L. (1990). *Same Difference: Feminism and Sexual Difference.* Sydney: Allen and Unwin.

——(1996). *The Politics of Affirmative Action: Women, Equality and Category Politics.* London, Thousand Oaks, and New Delhi: Sage.

——(1999). *Women, Policy and Politics: The Construction of Policy Problems.* London, Thousand Oaks, and New Delhi: Sage.

Bachrach, P. and Baratz, M. S. (1970). *Power and Poverty: Theory and Practice.* New York: Oxford University Press.

Baer, S. (1988). 'State, Law and Women In Germany', in *Test the West: Gender Democracy and Violence.* Vienna: Austrian Federal Ministry of Women's Affairs and the Federal Chancellery.

——(1996). 'Pornography and Sexual Harassment in the EU', in A. R. Elman (ed.), *Sexual Politics and the European Union: The New Feminist Challenge.* Oxford: Berghahn Books.

Bagilhole, B. and Byrne, P. (2000). 'From Hard to Soft Law and From Equality to Reconciliation in the United Kingdom', in L. Hantrais (ed.), *Gendered Policies in Europe.* London: Macmillan Press.

Bakker, I. (ed.) (1996). *Rethinking Restructuring: Gender and Change in Canada.* Toronto: University of Toronto Press.

Baldcock, C. V. and Cass, B. (eds) (1983). *Women, Social Welfare, and the State.* Sydney: George Allen and Unwin.

Banaszak, L. A. (1996). *Why Movements Succeed or Fail: Opportunity, Culture, and the Struggle for Woman Suffrage.* Princeton: Princeton University Press.

——Beckwith, K., and Rucht, D. (1996). 'Research Planning Group: The State and Women's Movements: Expanding Theories Through Comparative Analysis'. *Council for European Studies Newsletter,* 25/6: 1–3.

Barry, K. (1988). 'Female Sexual Slavery: The Problem, Policies and Cause for Feminist Action', in E. Boneparth and E. Stoper (eds), *Women, Power, and Policy: Toward the Year 2000.* New York: Pergamon.

Bartlett, T. K. and Kennedy, R. (eds) (1991). *Feminist Legal Theory: Readings in Law and Gender.* Boulder, CO: Westview Press.

Bashevkin, S. (1985*a*). *Toeing the Lines Women in Party Politics in Canada.* Toronto: University of Toronto Press.

——(1985*b*). *Women and Politics in Western Europe.* Frank Cass: London.

——(1994). 'Building a Political Voice: Women's Participation and Policy Influence in Canada', in P. Nelson and N. Chowdhury (eds), *Women and Politics Worldwide.* New Haven and London: Yale University Press.

——(1998). *Women on the Defensive: Living Through Conservative Times.* Toronto: Toronto University Press.

——(2000). 'From Tough Times to Better Times: Feminism, Public Policy, and New Labour Politics', *International Political Science Review,* 21: 407–24.

Basu, A. (ed.) (1995). *The Challenge of Local Feminisms.* Boulder, CO: Westview Press.

Batiot, A. (1986). 'Radical Democracy and Feminist Discourse: The Case of France', in D. Dahlerup (ed.), *The New Women's Movement: Feminism and Political Power in Europe and the USA.* London: Sage.

Baude, A. (1979). 'Public Policy and Changing Family Patterns In Sweden, 1930–1977', in J. Lipmen-Bluman and J. Bernard (eds), *Sex Roles and Social Policy: A Complex Social Science Equation.* London and Beverly Hills: Sage.

Baudino, C. and Mazur, A. G. (2001). 'Le Genre Gâché: La Féminisation de l'Action Publique.' *Espace-Temps,* November/12: 12–25.

Baumgartner, F. R. (1996). 'The Many Styles of Policymaking in France', in J. Keller and M. Schain (eds), *Chirac's Challenge: Liberalization, Europeanization, and Malaise in France.* New York: St. Martin's Press.

Bayes, J. (ed.) (1991). *Women in Public Administration: International Perspectives.* London: The Haworth Press.

Beasley, C. (1999). *What is Feminism: An Introduction to Feminist Theory.* London, Thousand Oaks, and New Delhi: Sage.

——and Bacchi, C. (2000). 'Citizen Bodies: Embodying Citizens—A Feminist Analysis', *International Feminist Journal of Politics,* 2–3: 335–58.

Becalli, B.(1984). 'Italy', in A. Cook *et al.* (eds), *Women in Trade Unions in Eleven Industrialized Countries.* Philadelphia: Temple University Press.

——(1994). 'The Modern Women's Movement in Italy'. *New Left Review,* 204: 135–51.

——(1996). 'The Modern Women's Movement in Italy', in M. Threlfall (ed.), *Mapping the Women's Movement.* London: Verso.

Beckman, P. R. and D'Amico, F. (eds) (1994). *Women, Gender, and World Politics: Perspectives, Policies, and Prospects.* Westport, CT: Bergin and Garvey.

Beckwith, K. (1980). 'The Cross-Cultural Study of Women and Politics: Methodological Problems'. *Women and Politics,* 29/2: 295–328.

——(1987). 'Response to Feminism in the Italian Parliament: Divorce, Abortion, and Sexual Violence Legislation', in M. Katzenstein and G. Mueller (eds), *The Women's Movements of the United States and Western Europe.* Philadelphia: Temple University Press.

——(2000). 'Beyond Compare? Women's Movements in Comparative Perspective'. *European Journal of Political Research,* 37: 431–68.

——(2001). 'Gender Frames and Collective Action: Configurations of Masculinity in the Pittston Coal Strike'. *Politics and Society,* 29/2: 295–328.

Bégin, M. (1997). 'The Canadian Government and the Commissions Report', in C. Andrew and S. Rodgers (eds), *Women and the Canadian State.* Montreal and Kingston: McGill-Queens University Press.

Bellace, J. (1991). 'The Role of the Law in Effecting Gender Pay Equity: A Comparison of Six Countries Experience', in S. L. Wilborn (ed.), *Women's Wages: Stability and Change in Six Industrialized Countries.* Greenwich, CT: JAI Press.

Bergman, S. (1999). 'Women in New Social Movements', in C. Bergvist *et al.* (eds), *Equal Democracies: Gender Politics in the Nordic Countries.* Oslo: Scandinavian University Press.

Bergqvist, C. (1995a). 'Changing the Institutions—State Feminism in Sweden'. Paper presented at the ECPR Joint Session Workshops. Bordeaux.

——(1995b). 'The Declining Corporatist State and the Political Gender Dimension in Sweden', in L. Karvonen and P. Selle (eds), *Closing the Gaps: Women in Nordic Politics.* Aldershot: Dartmouth.

——(1999). 'Family Policy in the Nordic Welfare States', in C. Bergvist *et al.* (eds), *Equal Democracies: Gender and Politics in the Nordic Countries.* Oslo: Scandinavian University Press.

——and Jungar, A.-C. (2000). 'Adaptation or Diffusion of the Swedish Gender Model?', in L. Hantrais (ed.), *Gendered Policies in Europe.* London: Macmillan.

——Kuuispalo, J., and Strykarsdóttir, A. (1999). 'The Debate on Childcare Policies', in C. Bergvist *et al.* (eds), *Equal Democracies: Gender Politics in the Nordic Countries.* Oslo: Scandinavian University Press.

——Borchorst, A., Christensen, A.-D., Ramstedt-Silén, V., Raaum, N. C., and Styrkasdottir, A. (eds) (1999). *Equal Democracies? Gender Politics in the Nordic Countries.* Oslo: Scandinavian University Press.

Bertelsmann, K. and Rust, U. (1995). *Equality in Law Between Men and Women in the European Community: Germany.* Dordrecht: Martinus Mijhoff.

Bimbi, F. (1993). 'Gender, "Gift Relationship", and the Welfare State Cultures in Italy', in J. Lewis (ed.), *Women and Social Policies in Europe: Work, Family and the State.* Aldershot: Edward Elgar.

——(1997). 'Lone Mothers in Italy: A Hidden and Embarrassing Issue in a Familist Welfare Regime', in J. Lewis (ed.), *Lone Mothers in European Welfare Regimes: Shifting Policy Logics.* London: Jessica Kingsley.

——and Della Sala, V. (1998). 'L'Italie. Concertation sans Représentation', in J. Jenson and M. Sineau (eds), *Qui Doit Garder le Jeune Enfant?Modes d'Acceuil et Travail des Mères dans l'Europe en Crise*. Paris: Librairie Générale de Droit et Jurisprudence.

Black, N. (1989). *Social Feminism*. Ithaca: Cornell University Press.

——and Cottrell, A. B. (eds) (1981). *Women and World Change: Equity Issues in Development*. Beverly Hills and London: Sage Publications.

Blank, R. and Merrick, J. (1995). *Human Reproduction, Emerging Technologies, and Conflicting Rights*. Washington, DC: CQ Press.

Blum, L. M. (1992). 'Gender and Class in Comparable Worth', in P. Kahn and E. Meehan (eds), *Equal Value/Comparable Worth in the UK and the USA*. New York: Martin's Press.

Boals, K. (1975). 'Political Science'. *Signs*, 1/1: 161–74.

Bock, G. and James, S. (eds) (1992). *Beyond Equality and Difference*. London: Routledge.

——and Thane, P. (eds) (1991). *Maternity and Gender Policies: Women and the Rise of the European Welfare States, 1880s–1950s*. London and New York: Routledge

Boje, T. P. and Leira, A. (eds) (2000), *Gender, Welfare State and the Market: Towards a New Division of Labour*. London: Falmer Press.

Boneparth, E. and Stoper, E. (eds) (1982a, 1988). *Women, Power and Policy*. New York: Pergamon Press.

————(1982b). 'A Framework for Policy Analysis', in E. Boneparth and E. Stoper (eds), *Women, Power and Policy*. New York: Pergamon Press, 1–16.

Borchorst, A. (1994a). 'The Scandinavian Welfare States—Patriarchal, Gender-Neutral or Woman-Friendly?'. *International Journal of Contemporary Sociology*, 1/8: 3–21.

——(1994b). 'Welfare State Regimes, Women's Interests, and the EC', in D. Sainsbury (ed.), *Gendering Welfare States*. London: Sage.

——(1995). 'A Political Niche: Denmark's Equal Status Council', in D. M. Stetson and A. Mazur (eds), *Comparative State Feminism*. Thousand Oaks: Sage.

——(1999a). 'The State and the "Social Pedagogic" Universal Child Care Services—Danish Child Care Policy and Gender Equality'. Paper presented at the Labour Market and Social Policy-Gender Relations in Transition Workshop. Brussels.

——(ed.) (1999b). 'Institutionalised Gender Equality', in C. Bergvist *et al.* (eds), *Equal Democracies: Gender and Politics in the Nordic Countries*. Oslo: Scandinavian University Press.

——and Siim, B. (1987). 'Women and the Advanced Welfare State—A New Kind of Patriarchal Power?', in A. S. Sassoon (ed.), *Women and the State: The Shifting Boundaries of Public and Private*. London: Unwin Hyman.

——Christensen, A. D., and Rauum, N. (1999). 'Equal Democracies? Conclusions and Perspectives', in C. Bergqvist *et al.* (eds), *Equal Democracies?* Oslo: Universitetsforlaget.

Borrelli, M. A. and Martin, J. M. (eds) (1997). *Women, Politics, and Power in the Executive Branch*. Boulder, CO and London: Lynne Rienner.

Bradshaw, J., Ditch, J., Holmes, H., and Whiteford, P. (1993). 'A Comparative Study of Child Support in Fifteen Countries'. *Journal of European Social Policy*, 3/4: 255–71.

Bradshaw, J. (1996). *The Employment of Lone Parents: Comparison of Policy in 20 Countries*. London: Family Policy Studies Centre.

Braithwaite, M. and Byrne, C. (1995). *Women in Decision-making in Trade Unions* (Report for the European Trade Union Congress and the European Expert Network on 'Women in Decision-making', part of the third Equal Opportunities Programme of the Commission of the European Community). Brussels.

Brannen, J. (1999). 'Caring for Children', in S. Walby (ed.), *New Agendas for Women*, London: Macmillan.

Brodie, J. (1995). *Politics on the Margin: Restructuring and the Canadian Women's Movement*. Halifax: Fernwood.

——(ed.) (1996). *Women and Canadian Public Policy*.Toronto: Harcourt Brace.

——Gavigan, S. A. M., and Jenson, J. (1992). *The Politics of Abortion*. Toronto: Oxford University Press.

Brodsky, G. and Day, S. (1989). *Canadian Charter Equality Rights for Women: One Step Forward or Two Steps Back?* (Report for the Canadian Advisory Council on the Status of Women). Ottawa.

Brown, A. (1996). 'Women and Politics in Scotland'. *Parliamentary Affairs*, 49/1: 26–40.

Brown, B. E. and Macridis, R. (1996). *Comparative Politics: Notes and Readings* (8th edn). Belmont, CA: Wadsworth.

Buchinger, B. and Sieglinde, K. R. (2001). 'A Women-Friendly Employment Administration Pursues Symbolic Policies in Austria', in A. G. Mazur (ed.), *State Feminism, Women's Movements, and Job Training: Making Democracies Work in the Global Economy*. New York and London: Routledge.

Buckley, M. and Anderson, M. (1988*a*). 'Introduction: Problems, Policies and Politics', in M. Buckley and M. Anderson (eds), *Women. Equality and Europe*. London: Macmillan.

————(1988*b*). *Women, Equality and Europe*. London: Macmillan.

Bunce, V. (1981). *Do Leaders Make a Difference? Exclusive Succession and Public Policy Under Capitalism and Socialism*. Princeton: Princeton University Press.

Bunch, C. (ed.) (1991). *Violence Against Women*. New York: Ford Foundation.

Burrell, B. (ed.) (1997). 'Women and Public Policy: A Special Symposium Issue'. *Journal of Policy Studies*, 25/4: 565–647.

Burt, S. (1988). 'The Charter of Rights and the Ad Hoc Lobby: The Limits of Success'. *Atlantis*, 14/1: 74–81.

——(1995). 'Gender and Public Policy: Makings Some Difference in Ottawa', in F.-P. Gingras (ed.), *Gender and Politics in Contemporary Canada*. Toronto: Oxford University Press.

Busch, D. M. (1992). 'Women's Movement and State Policy Reform Aimed at Domestic Violence Against Women: A Comparison of the Consequences of Movement Mobilization in the United States and India'. *Gender and Society*, 6/4: 587–608.

Bussemaker, J. (1991). 'Equality, Autonomy and Feminist Politics', in E. Meehan and S. Sevenhuijsen (eds), *Equality Politics and Gender*. London: Sage.

——(1997). 'Citizenship, Welfare State Regimes and Breadwinner Arrangements', in F. Gardiner (ed.), *Sex Equality Policy in Western Europe*. London: Routledge.

——and Voet, R. (eds) (1998). *Gender, Participation and Citizenship in the Netherlands*. Aldershot: Ashgate.

Byrne, P., and Lovenduski, J. (1978). 'The Equal Opportunities Commission'. *Women's Studies International Quarterly*, 1.

Bystydzienski, J. M. (ed.) (1992a). *Women Transforming Politics: Worldwide Strategies for Empowerment.* Bloomington: Indiana University Press.

—— (1992b). 'Influence of Women's Culture on Public Policies', in J. M. Bystydzienski (ed.), *Women Transforming Politics.* Bloomington: Indiana University Press.

—— (1995a). 'Women's Equality Structures in Norway: The Equal Status Council', in D. M. Stetson and A. Mazur (eds), *Comparative State Feminism.* Thousand Oaks: Sage.

—— (1995b). *Women in Electoral Politics: Lessons From Norway.* Westport, CT: Praeger.

—— and Sekhon, J. (eds) (1999). *Democratization and Women's Grassroots Movements.* Bloomington and Indianapolis, IN: Indiana University Press.

Caldwell, L. (1986). 'Feminism and Abortion in Italy', in J. Lovenduski and J. Outshoorn (eds), *The New Politics of Abortion.* London: Sage.

Callender, R. (1988). 'Ireland and the Implementation of Directive 79/7/EEC: The Social, Political, and Legal Issues', in G. Whyte (ed.), *Sex Equality, Community Rights and Irish Social Welfare Law.* Dublin: Irish Centre for European Law.

—— and Meenan, F. (1995). *Equality in Law Between Men and Women in the European Community: Ireland.* Dordrecht: Martinus Mijhoff.

Calloni, M. (2001). 'Debates and Controversies on Abortion in Italy', in D. M. Stetson (ed.), *Abortion Politics, Women's Movements and the Democratic State: A Comparative Study of State Feminism.* Oxford: Oxford University Press.

Cameron, B. (1996). 'Brave New Roles for Women: NAFTA and New Reproductive Technologies', in J. Brodie (ed.), *Women and Canadian Public Policy.* Toronto: Harcourt Brace.

Caporaso, J. A. (1995). 'Research Design, Falsification, and the Qualitative-quantitative Divide', in Review Symposium, 'The Qualitative-quantitative Disputation: Gary King, Robert Keohane, and Sidney Verba's *Designing Social Inquiry: Scientific Inference in Qualitative Research'. American Political Science Review*, 89: 457–60.

—— and Jupille, J. (2000). 'The Europeanization of Gender Equality Policy and Domestic Structural Change', in M. G. Cowles, J. A. Caporaso, and T. Risse (eds), *Europeanization and Domestic Structural Change.* Ithaca, NY: Cornell University Press.

Carlsen, S. and Larsen, J. E. (eds) (1993). *The Equality Dilemma: Reconciling Working Life and Family Life.* Copenhagen: Murksgaard International Publisher.

Caroll, S. J. and Zerilli, L. M. G. (1993). 'Feminist Challenges to Political Science', in A. W. Finifter (ed.), *The State of the Discipline II.* Washington, DC: American Political Science Association.

Carroll, B. A. (1980). 'Political Science, Part II: International Politics, Comparative Politics, and Feminist Radicals'. *Signs*, 5/3: 449–58.

Carver, T. (1995). *Gender is Not a Synonym for Women.* Boulder, CO: Lynne Rienner.

—— and Mottier, V. (eds) (1998). *Politics of Sexuality: Identity, Gender, Citizenship.* London and New York: Routledge.

Castles, F.G. (ed.) (1989a). *The Comparative History of Public Policy.* New York: Oxford University Press.

Castles, F.G. (1989*b*). 'Introduction: Puzzles of Political Economy', in F. G. Castles (ed.), *The Comparative History of Public Policy*. New York: Oxford University Press.

—— (ed.) (1993). *Families of Nations: Patterns of Public Policy in Western Democracies*. Aldershot: Dartmouth.

—— (1999). *Comparative Public Policy*. Northampton, MA: Edward Elgar.

—— and Flood, M. (1993). 'Why Divorce Rates Differ: Law, Religious Belief and Modernity', in F. G. Castles (ed.), *Families of Nations: Patterns of Public Policy in Western Democracies*. Aldershot: Dartmouth.

Catt, H. and McLeay, E. (eds) (1993). *Women and Politics in New Zealand*. Wellington: Victoria University Press.

Cerny, P. (1990). *The Changing Architecture of Politics: Structure, Agency, and the Future of the State*. London: Sage.

Chamberlayne, P. (1993). 'Women and the State: Changes in Roles and Rights in France, West Germany, Italy and Britain, 1970–1990', in J. Lewis (ed.), *Women and Social Policies in Europe: Work, Family and the State*. Aldershot: Edgar Elgar.

Chow, E. N. and Berheide, C.W. (eds) (1996). *Women, the Family and Policy: A Global Perspective*. Albany: SUNY Press

Chowdhury, N. and Nelson, B. with Carver, K. A., Johnsons, N. J., and O'Loughlin, P. L. (1994). 'Redefining Politics: Patterns of Women's Political Engagement from a Global Perspective', in B. Nelson and N. Chowdhury (eds), *Women and Politics Worldwide*. New Haven: Yale University Press.

Cichowski, R. A. (2000). 'Gender and Policy in Comparative Perspective'. *Women and Politics*, 21/1: 107–15.

Cobb, R.W. and Elder, C. D. (1983). *Participation in American Politics: The Dynamics of Agenda-setting*. Baltimore: Johns Hopkins University Press.

Cockburn, C. (1989). 'Equal Opportunities: The Short and Long Agenda'. *Industrial Relations Journal*, 20: 213–25.

—— (1991). *In the Way of Women: Men's Resistance to Sex Equality in Organizations*. Ithaca, NY: ILR Press.

—— (1995). 'Strategies for Gender Democracy: Women and the European Social Dialogue', in *Social Europe*. Supplement 4.

—— *et al.* (1994). *Women in the Europeanising of Industrial Relations—A Study in Five Member States* (Report for the European Commission. No. 664). Brussels.

Cohan, A. (1986). 'Abortion as a Marginal Issue: The Use of Peripheral Mechanisms in Britain and the United States', in J. Lovenduski and J. Outshoorn (eds), *The New Politics of Abortion*. London: Sage.

Collier, D. (1993). 'The Comparative Method', in A. W. Finifter (ed.), *Political Science: The State of the Discipline II*. Washington, DC: American Political Science Association.

—— (1995). 'Translating Quantitative Methods for Qualitative Researchers: The Case of Selection Bias', in Review Symposium 'The Qualitative-quantitative Disputation: Gary King, Robert Keohane, and Sidney Verba's *Designing Social Inquiry: Scientific Inference in Qualitative Research'*. *American Political Science Review*, 89: 461–66.

—— and Mahon, J. E. (1993). 'Conceptual "Stretching" Revisited: Adapting Categories in Comparative Analysis'. *American Political Science Review*, 87: 845–55.

Collins, E. (1996). 'The European Union Sexual Harassment Policy', in A. R. Elman (ed.), *Sexual Politics and the European Union: The New Feminist Challenge.* Providence and Oxford: Berghahn.

Commission on Family and Medical Leave (1996). *A Workable Balance: Report to Congress on Family and Medical Leave Policies.* Washington, DC: Women's Bureau, US Department of Labor.

Connelly, A. (1993). 'The Constitution', in A. Connelly (ed.), *Women and the Law in Ireland.* Dublin: Gill and Macmillan.

Connolly, E. (1999). 'The Republic of Ireland's Equality Contract: Women and Public Policy', in Y. Galligan, E. Ward, and R. Wilford (eds), *Contesting Politics: Women in Ireland, North and South.* London: Westview.

Connors, J. F. (1989). *Violence Against Women in the Family.* Vienna: United Nations.

——(1994). 'Government Measures to Confront Violence Against Women', in M. Davies (ed.), *Women and Violence: Realities and Responses Worldwide.* London and New Jersey: Zed Books.

Conroy, P. (1997). 'Lone Mothers: The Case of Ireland', in J. Lewis (ed.), *Lone Mothers In European Welfare Regimes: Shifting Policy Logics.* London: Jessica Kingsley.

Conway, J., Bourque, S. C., and Scott, J.W. (1987). 'The Concept of Gender'. *Daedalus,* 116/4: xxi–xxix.

Conway, M. M, Ahern, D.W, and Steuernagel, G. A. (1999). *Women and Public Policy: A Revolution in Progress.* Washington, DC: CQ Press.

Cook, A. H., Lorwin, W., and Daniels, J. (eds) (1984). *Women and Trade Unions in Eleven Industrialized Countries.* Philadelphia: Temple University Press.

——(1989). 'Collective Bargaining as a Strategy for Achieving Equal Opportunities and Equal Pay: Sweden and West Germany', in R. Steinberg-Ratner (ed.), *Equal Employment Policy For Women: Strategies for Implementation in the United States, Canada, and Western Europe.* Philadelphia: Temple University Press.

Corcoran, J. and Donnelly, E. (1988). *Report of a Comparative Analysis of the Provision for Legal Redress in Member States of the European Community in Respect to Article 119 of the Treaty of Rome and the Equal Pay, Equal Treatment and Social Security Directives* (V/564/84-EN). Brussels.

Corrin, C. (ed.) (1996). *Women in a Violent World: Feminist Analyses of Resistance Across Europe.* Edinburgh: Edinburgh University Press.

Crighton, E. and Ebert, M. (2001). 'RU 486 and Abortion Practices in Europe: From Legalization to Utilization'. Paper presented at the Western Political Science Association Meetings.

Cossman, B. (1996). 'Same-sex Couples and the Politics of Family Status', in J. Brodie (ed.), *Women and Canadian Public Policy.* Toronto: Harcourt Brace.

——and Bell, S. (1997). 'Introduction', in B. Cossman *et al.* (eds), *Bad Attitudes on Trial: Pornography, Feminism, and the Butler Decision.* Toronto: University of Toronto Press.

————Gotell, L., and Ross, B. L. (1997). *Bad Attitudes on Trial: Pornography, Feminism, and the Butler Decision.* Toronto: University of Toronto Press.

Costain, A. N. (1992). *Inviting Women's Rebellion: A Political Process Interpretation of the Women's Movement.* Baltimore and London: The Johns Hopkins University Press.

Cousins, C. (1995). 'Women and Social Policy in Spain: The Development of a Gendered Welfare Regime'. *Journal of European Social Policy*, 5/3: 175–97.

Craig, H. B. and O'Brien, D. M. (1993). *Abortion and American Politics*. New Jersey: Chatham House.

Dahlerup, D. (ed.) (1986*a*). *The New Women's Movement: Feminism and Political Power in Europe and the USA*. London: Sage.

——(1986*b*). 'Is the New Women's Movement Dead? Decline and Change of the Danish Movement', in D. Dahlerup (ed.), *The New Women's Movement: Feminism and Political Power in Europe and the USA*. London: Sage.

——(1987). 'Confusing Concepts—Confusing Reality: A Theoretical Discussion of the Patriarchal State', in A. S. Sassoon (ed.), *Women and the State: the Shifting Boundaries of Public and Private*. London: Hutchinson.

——(1988). 'From a Small to Large Minority: Women in Scandinavian Politics'. *Scandinavian Political Studies*, 11/4: 275–98.

——and Gulli, B. (1985). 'Women's Organization in the Nordic Countries: Lack of Force or Counterforce', in E. Haavio-Mannila (ed.), *Unfinished Democracy*. Oxford: Pergamon Press.

Daley, M. (2000). *The Gender Division of Welfare: The Impact of the British and German Welfare States*. Cambridge: Cambridge University Press.

Daniels, C. R. (ed.) (1997). *Feminists Negotiate the State: The Politics of Domestic Violence*. Lanham, New York, and Oxford: University Press of America.

Daubler-Gmelin, S. (1980). 'Equal Employment Opportunity for Women on West Germany Today', in R. Steinberg-Ratner (ed.), *Equal Employment Policy For Women: Strategies for Implementation in the United States, Canada, and Western*. Philadelphia: Temple University Press.

Daune-Richard, A.-M. and Mahon, R. (1998). 'La Suède. Le Modèle Égalitaire en Danger?', in J. Jenson and M. Sineau (eds), *Qui Doit Garder le Jeune Enfant? Modes d'Acceuil et Travail des Mères dans l'Europe en Crise*. Paris: Librairie Générale de Droit et Jurisprudence.

Davies, M. (ed.) (1994). *Women and Violence: Realities and Responses Worldwide*. London and New Jersey: Zed Books.

Davis, R. H. (1997). *Women and Power in Parliamentary Democracies: Cabinet Appointments in Western Europe, 1968–1992*. Lincoln: University of Nebraska Press.

de Leon, P. (1998). 'Introduction: The Evidentiary Basis of Policy Analysis: Empiricist vs. Postpositivist Positions'. *Policy Studies Journal*, 26/1: 109–13.

Del Boca, D. (1998). 'Labour Policies, Economic Flexibility and Women's Work', in E. Drew, R. Emerek, and E. Mahon (eds), *Women, Work and the Family in Europe*. London and New York: Routledge.

Delmar, R. (1986). 'What is Feminism?', in J. Mitchell and A. Oakley (eds), *What is Feminism?* Oxford: Blackwell.

Del Re, A. (2000). 'The Paradoxes of Italian Law and Practice', in L. Hantrais (ed.), *Gendered Policies in Europe*. London: Macmillan.

DeSario, J. P. (ed.) (1989). *International Public Policy Sourcebook. Volume 1: Health and Social Welfare*. New York: Greenwood Press.

Di Stefano, C. (1991). *Configurations of Masculinity: A Feminist Perspective on Modern Political Theory.* Ithaca, NY: Cornell University Press.

——(1997). 'Integrating Gender in the Political Science Curriculum: Challenges, Pitfalls, and Opportunities'. *PS: Political Science and Politics*, 3/2: 204–6.

Diamond, I. (ed.) (1983). *Families, Politics, and Policy: A Feminist Dialogue on Women and the State.* New York: Longman.

——(1988). 'Medical Science and the Transformation of Motherhood: The Promise of Reproductive Technologies', in E. Boneparth and E. Stoper (eds), *Women, Power and Policy: Toward the Year 2000.* New York: Pergamon.

Ditch, J., Barnes, H., Bradshaw, J., Commaille, J., and Eardley, T. (1999). *A Synthesis of National Family Policies.* York: European Observatory on Family Policies, University of York.

Dobash, R., and Dobash, E. (1992). *Women, Violence and Social Change.* New York: Routledge.

Dominelli, L. (1991). *Women Across Continents: Feminist Comparative Social Policy.* London: Harvester/Wheatsheaf.

Doremus, P. N., Kelly, W. W., Pauly, L. W., and Reich, S. (1998). *The Myth of Global Corporations.* Princeton, NJ: Princeton University Press.

Döring, D., Hauser, R., Rolf, G., and Tbitanzl, F. (1994). 'Old-age Security for Women in Twelve EC Countries'. *Journal of European Social Policy*, 4/1: 1–18.

Dowding, K. (2001). 'There Must Be End to Confusion: Policy Networks, Intellectual Fatigue, and the Need For Political Science Methods Courses in British Universities'. *Political Studies*, 49: 89–105.

Drew, E. and Emerek, R. (1998). 'Employment, Flexibility and Gender', in E. Drew, R. Emerek, and E. Mahon (eds), *Women, Work and the Family in Europe.* New York: Routledge.

————and Mahon, E. (eds) (1998). *Women, Work and the Family in Europe.* London: Routledge.

Duchen, C. (1986). *Feminism in France from May 1968 to Mitterrand.* London: Routledge and Kegan Paul.

Duerst-Lahti, G. and Kelly, R. M. (eds) (1995). *Gender Power, Leadership, and Governance.* Ann Arbor: The University of Michigan Press.

Duncan, S. (1995). 'Theorizing European Gender Systems'. *Journal of European Social Policy*, 5/4: 263–84.

Duran, M. A., and Gallego, M. T. (1986). 'The Women's Movement and the New Spanish Democracy', in D. Dahlerup (ed.), *The New Women's Movement: Feminism and Political Power in Europe and the USA.* London: Sage.

Durham, M. (1991). *Sex and Politics: The Family and Morality in the Thatcher Years.* London: Macmillan.

Edelman, M. (1985). *The Symbolic Uses of Politics.* Urbana: University of Illinois Press.

Eduards, M. (1997). 'The Women's Shelter Movement', in G. Gustafsson *et al.* (eds), *Towards a New Democratic Order: Women's Organizing in Sweden in the 1990s.* Stockholm: Publica.

——Halsaa, B., and Skjeie, H. (1985). 'Equality: How Equal?', in E. Haavio-Mannila *et al.* (eds), *Unfinished Democracy.* Oxford: Pergamon.

Egan, M. (1998). 'Gendered Integration: Social Policies and the European Market'. *Women and Politics*, 19/4: 23–52.

Eggert, A. and Rolston, B. (1994). 'Ireland', in B. Rolston and A. Eggert (eds), *Abortion in the New Europe: A Comparative Handbook.* Westport, CT and London: Greenwood Press.

Ehrmann, H. (1975). *Comparative Legal Cultures.* Inglewood Cliffs, NJ: Prentice-Hall.

Eisenstein, H. (1996). *Inside Agitators: Australian Femocrats and the State.* Philadelphia: Temple University Press.

Eliason, L. C. (1997). 'Women and Gender in European Political Course: Exploring the Scandinavian Welfare States'. *PS: Political Science and Politics*, 3/2: 198–9.

Elison, S. (1997). 'Integrating Women into the Study of Politics'. *PS: Political Science and Politics*, 3/2: 202–4.

Elman, A. R. (1995). 'The State's Equality for Women: Sweden's Equality Ombudsman', in D. M. Stetson and A. G. Mazur (eds), *Comparative State Feminism.* Thousand Oaks: Sage.

—— (1996*a*). *Sexual Subordination and State Intervention: Comparing Sweden and the United States.* Providence/Oxford: Berghahn Books.

—— (ed.) (1996*b*). *Sexual Politics and the European Union: The New Feminist Challenge.* London: Berghahn Books.

—— (1996*c*). 'Introduction: The EU From Feminist Perspectives', in A. R. Elman (ed.), *Sexual Politics and the European Union: The New Feminist Challenge.* Providence and Oxford: Berghahn Books.

Epstein, C. F. and Laub, R. (eds) (1981). *Access to Power: Cross-National Studies of Women and Elites.* Boston: Allen and Unwin.

Ergas, Y. and Sassaroli, S. (1977). Instituzioni scantro o confronto'. *Effe*, 5: 49–50.

Erickson, L. (1993). 'Making Her Way In: Women, Parties, and Candidacies', in J. Lovenduski and P. Norris (eds), *Gender and Party Politics.* London: Sage.

Erikson, R., Jansen, E J., Ringen, S., and Uusitalo, H. (1987). *The Scandinavian Model: Welfare States and Welfare State Research.* London: M. E. Sharpe.

Erler, G. (1988). 'The German Paradox: Non-feminization of the Labor Force and Post-industrial Social Policies', in J. Jenson *et al.* (eds), *Feminization of the Labor Force: Paradoxes and Promises.* New York: Oxford University Press.

Esping-Andersen, G. (1990). *The Three Worlds of Welfare Capitalism.* Cambridge: Polity Press.

—— (1999). *Social Foundations of Post Industrial Economies.* Oxford: Oxford University Press.

European Commission (1995). *Strategies for a Gender Balance in Decision-making* (Report of the European Seminar for the European Network 'Women in Decision-making'). 23–4 March: Dublin.

Evans, P. (1996). 'Single Mothers and Ontario's Welfare Policy: Restructuring the Debate', in J. Brodie (ed.) *Women and Canadian Public Policy.* Toronto: Harcourt Brace.

Evans, P. M and Wekerle, G. R. (eds) (1997). *Women and the Canadian Welfare State: Challenges and Change.* Toronto: University of Toronto Press.

Feick, J. (1992). 'Comparing Comparative Policy studies—A Path Toward Integration?'. *Journal of Public Policy*, 12: 257–85.

Ferguson, K. E. (1984). *The Feminist Case Against Bureaucracy*. Philadelphia: Temple University Press.

Ferree, M. M. (1987). 'Equality and Autonomy: Feminist Politics in the United States and West Germany', in M. Katzenstein and G. Mueller (eds), *The Women's Movements of the United States and Western Europe*. Philadelphia: Temple University Press.

——(1991–92). 'Institutionalizing Gender Equality: Feminist Politics and Equality Offices'. *German Politics and Society*, 24–25: 53–66.

——(1995). 'The Women's Affairs Offices in the Federal Republic of Germany', in D. M. Stetson and A. G. Mazur (eds), *Comparative State Feminism*. Thousand Oaks: Sage.

——(1997). 'Patriarchies and Feminisms: The Two Women's Movements of Postunification Germany', in B. Hobson and A.M. Berggren (eds), *Crossing Borders: Gender and Citizenship in Transition*. Stockholm: Swedish Council for Planning and Coordination of Research.

——and Hess, B. B. (1985). *Controversy and Coalition: The New Feminist Movement*. Boston: Twayne.

——and Martin, P. Y. (eds) (1995). *Feminist Organizations*. Philadelphia: Temple University Press.

Field, M. J. (1983). *The Comparative Politics of Birth Control: Determinants of Policy Variation and Change in the Developed Nations*. New York: Praeger.

Fineman, M. (1983). 'Implementing Equality: Ideology, Contradictions and Social Change: A Study of Rhetoric and Results in Regulation of the Consequences of Divorce'. *Wisconsin Law Review*, 1983/4: 789–866.

Forbes, I. (1989). 'Unequal Partners: The Implementation of Equal Opportunities Policies in Western Europe'. *Public Administration*, 67/1: 19–38.

——(1991). 'Equal Opportunity: Radical, Liberal and Conservative Critiques', in E. Meehan and S. Sevenhuijsen (ed.), *Equality Politics and Gender*. London: Sage.

——(1996). 'The Privatisation of Sex Equality Policy', in J. Lovenduski and P. Norris (ed.), *Women and Politics*. Oxford: Oxford University Press.

——(1997). 'The Privatisation of Equality Policy in the British Employment Market For Women', in F. Gardiner (ed.), *Sex Equality Policy in Western Europe*. London: Routledge.

Fouque, A. (1995). 'International Action: United Nations Conferences, from Nairobi to Beijing', in Report of the European Seminar for the European Network. Brussels.

Franzway, S., Court, D., and Connell, R.W. (1989). *Staking a Claim: Feminism, Bureaucracy and the State*. Cambridge: Polity Press.

Freeman, G. P. (1985). 'National Styles and Policy Sectors: Explaining Structured Variation'. *Journal of Public Policy*, 15: 467–96.

Friedman, L.G. (ed.) (1992). *Feminist Jurisprudence: The Difference Debate*. Lanham, MD: Rowman and Littlefield.

Fudge, J. (1996). 'Fragmentation and Feminization: The Challenge of Equity for Labour-Relations Policy', in J. Brodie (ed.), *Women and Canadian Public Policy*. Toronto: Harcourt Brace.

Gallard, C. (1994). 'France', in B. Rolston and A. Eggert (eds), *Abortion in the New Europe: A Comparative Handbook*. Westport, CT and London: Greenwood Press.

Galligan, Y. (1993). 'Party Politics and Gender in the Republic of Ireland', in J. Lovenduski and P. Norris (eds), *Gender and Party Politics*. London: Sage.

—— (1998). *Women and Politics in Contemporary Ireland: From the Margins to the Mainstream*. London and Washington: Pinter

——Ward, E., and Wilford, R. (eds) (1999). *Contesting Politics: Women in Ireland, North and South*. London: Westview Press.

Gamson, W. A. (1988). 'Political Discourse and Collective Action', in B. Klandermans, H. Kriesi, and S. Tarrow (eds), *International Social Movement Research*, i. Greenwich, CT: JAI Press.

Garcia, A. (1995). 'The Enlargement of the Recruitment Pool', in Report of the European Seminar for the European Network 'Women in Decision-making', 23–4 March. Dublin.

García-Ramon, M. D., and Monk, J. (eds) (1996). *Women of the European Union: The Politics of Work and Daily Life*. London: Routledge.

Gardiner, F. (1995). 'The Use of Quotas' and 'The Enlargement of the Recruitment Pool', in Report of the European Seminar for the European Network 'Women in Decision-making', 23–4 March. Dublin.

—— (ed.) (1997*a*). *Equality Policy and the European Union*. London: Routledge.

—— (1997*b*). 'Introduction: Welfare and Sex Equality Policy Regimes', in F. Gardiner (ed.), *Sex Equality Policy in Western Europe*. London: Routledge.

—— (1999). 'The Impact of EU Equality Legislation on Irish Women', in Y. Y. Galligan, E. Ward, and R. Wilford (eds), *Contesting Politics: Women in Ireland, North and South*. Boulder, CO: Westview Press.

——and Leijenaar, M. (1997). 'The Timid and the Bold: Analysis of the "woman-friendly state" in Ireland and the Netherlands', in F. Gardiner (ed.), *Sex Equality Policy in Western Europe*. London: Routledge.

Gaspard, F. (1997). 'Les Françaises en Politiques au Lendemain des Élections Legislatives de 1997'. *French Politics and Society*, 15: 1–13.

——Servan-Schreiber, C., and LeGall, A. (1992). *Au Pouvoir les Citoyennes! Liberté, Egalité, Parité*. Paris: Le Seuil.

Gatens, M. (1991). *Feminism and Philosophy: Perspectives on Difference and Equality*. Cambridge: Polity Press.

Gauthier, H. A. (1996). *The State and the Family Policies in Industrialized Countries*. Oxford: Clarendon Press.

Geertz, C. (1973). 'Thick Description: Toward an Interpretive Theory of Culture', in C. Geertz (ed.), *The Interpretation of Cultures*. New York: Basic Books.

Gelb, J. (1987). 'Social Movement "Success": A Comparative Analysis of Feminism in the United States and the United Kingdom', in M. Katzenstein and G. Mueller (eds), *The Women's Movements of the United States and Western Europe*. Philadelphia: Temple University Press.

—— (1989). *Feminism and Politics*. Berkeley: University of California Press.

——and Palley, L. M. (1982, 1987). *Women and Public Policies*. Princeton: Princeton University Press.

Geller-Schwartz, L. (1995). 'An Array of Agencies: Feminism and State Institutions in Canada', in D. M. Stetson and A. G. Mazur (eds), *Comparative State Feminism*. Thousand Oaks: Sage.

George, A. and McKeown, T. J. (1985). 'Case Studies and Theories of Organization Decision-making'. *Advances in Information Processes and Organization*, 2: 21–58.

Ginn, J. and Arber, S. (1999). 'Women's Pension Poverty: Prospects and Opinions for Change', in S. Walby (ed.), *New Agendas for Women*. London: Macmillan.

Girvin, B. (1996). 'Ireland and the European Union: The Impact of Integration and Social Change on Abortion Policy', in M. Githens and D. M. Stetson (eds), *Abortion Politics: Public Policy in Cross-Cultural Perspective*. New York and London: Routledge.

Githens, M. (1983). 'The Elusive Paradigm: Gender, Politics and Political Behavior', in A. W. Finifter (ed.), *Political Science: The State of the Discipline*. Washington, DC: American Political Science Association.

——(1987). *Abortion and Divorce in Western Law*. Cambridge: Harvard University Press.

——and Stetson, D. (eds) (1996). *Abortion Politics: Public Policy in Cross-national Perspective*. New York and London: Routledge.

Glendon, M. A. (1989). *The Transformation of Family Law*. Chicago: The University of Chicago Press.

Gonzáles, E. B. (1994). 'Spain', in B. Rolston and A. Eggert (eds), *Abortion in the New Europe: A Comparative Handbook*. Westport, CT and London: Greenwood Press.

Good, A. (1998). 'Gender Equality and European Training Policy 1971–97'. *Administration*, 46/3: 29–36.

——(2001). 'Femocrats Work with Feminists and the EU Against Gender-Bias in Ireland', in A. G. Mazur (ed.), *State Feminism, Women's Movements, and Job Training: Making Democracies Work in the Global Economy*. New York and London: Routledge.

Gordon, L. (ed.) (1990). *Women, the State, and Welfare*. Madison: The University of Wisconsin Press.

Gorjanicyn, K. (1998). 'Sexuality and Work: Contrasting Prostitution Policies in Victoria and Queensland', in T. Carver and V. Mottier (eds), *Politics of Sexuality: Identity, Gender, Citizenship*. London and New York: Routledge.

Gornick, J. (1995). 'Bringing Gender into Comparative Welfare State Research: An Assessment of the Typological Approach'. Paper presented at the annual meeting of the American Political Science Association. Chicago.

——Meyers, M. K., and Ross, K. E. (1997). 'Supporting the Employment of Mothers: Policy Variation Across Fourteen Welfare States'. *Journal of European Social Policy*, 7/1: 45–70.

Gotell, L. (1996). 'Policing Desire: Obscenity Law, Pornography Politics, and Feminism in Canada', in J. Brodie (ed.), *Women and Canadian Public Policy*. Toronto: Harcourt Brace.

Graber, M. (1996) *Rethinking Abortion: Equal Choice, the Constitution, and Reproductive Politics*. Princeton, NJ: Princeton University Press.

Graycar, A. (1990). 'Feminism and Law Reform: Matrimonial Property Law and Models of Equality', in S. Watson (ed.), *Playing the State: Australian Feminist Interventions*. London and New York: Verso.

Gregory, J. (1987). *Sex, Race, and the Law*. London: Sage.

Gregory, J. (1992). 'Equal Value/ Comparable Worth: National Statute and Case Law in Britain and the USA', in F. Kahn and E. Meehan (eds), *Equal Value/Comparable Worth in the UK and the USA*. New York: St. Martin's Press.

—— (1999). 'Revisiting the Sex Equality Laws', in S. Walby (ed.), *New Agendas for Women*. London: Macmillan.

Guadagnini, M. (1993). 'A "Partitocrazia" Without Women: the Case of the Italian Party System', in J. Lovenduski and P. Norris (eds), *Gender and Party Politics*. London: Sage.

—— (1995). 'The Latecomers: Italy's Equal Status and Equal Opportunities Agencies', in D. M. Stetson and A. G. Mazur (eds), *Comparative State Feminism*. Thousand Oaks: Sage.

—— (1998a). 'The Debate on Women's Quotas in Italian Elections'. *Swiss Political Science Review*, 4/3: 97–102.

—— (1998b). 'Gender and Political Citizenship in Italy in the 1990s'. Paper presented at the Colloquium 'Fifty Year of Women's Suffrage: Now What?'. Brussels, 27 November.

—— (2001). 'Limited Women's Policy Agencies Produce Limited Results in Italy', in A. G. Mazur (ed.), *State Feminism, Women's Movements, and Job Training: Making Democracies Work in the Global Economy*. New York and London: Routledge.

Gulli, B. (1994). 'Norway', in B. Rolston and A. Eggert (eds), *Abortion in the New Europe: A Comparative Handbook*. Westport, CT and London: Greenwood Press.

Gunderson, M. and Robb, R. E. (1991). 'Legal and Institutional Issues Pertaining to Women's Wages in Canada', in S. L. Wilborn (ed.), *Women's Wages: Stability and Change in Six Industrialized Countries*. Greenwich, CT: JAI Press.

Gustafsson, G., Eduards, M., and Rönnblom, M. (1997). *Towards a New Democratic Order? Women's Organizing in Sweden in the 1990s*. Stockholm: Publica.

—— (1994). 'Childcare and Types of Welfare States', in D. Sainsbury (ed.), *Gendering Welfare States*. London: Sage.

Gutman, A. (ed.) (1998). *Democracy and the Welfare State*. Princeton, N.J.: Princeton University Press.

Gwinnett, B. (1998). 'Policing Prostitution: Gender, the State and Community Politics', in V. Randall and G. Weylen (eds), *Gender, Politics and the State*. London and New York: Routledge.

Haavio-Mannila, E., Dahlerup, D., Eduards, M., Gudmundsdóttir, E., Halsaa, B., Hernes, H. M., Hänninene-Salmelin, E., Sigmundsdóttir, B., Sinkkonene, S., and Skard, T. (1985). *Unfinished Democracy: Women in Nordic Politics*. New York: Pergamon.

Hadley, J. (1996). *Abortion: Between Freedom and Necessity*. Philadelphia: Temple University Press.

Hallett, C. (ed.) (1996). *Women and Social Policy: An Introduction*. London: Prentice Hall.

Halsaa, B. (1991). 'Policies and Strategies on Women in Norway'. Revised version of Norwegian paper presented at the workshop on 'Policies and Strategies related to Women's Issues'. Lima, Peru, September.

—— (1995). 'Equal Status: National Standards and Local Implementation'. Paper presented at the ECPR Joint Sessions of Workshops. Bordeaux, April.

——(1998). 'A Strategic Partnership for Women's Policies in Norway', in G. Lycklama à Nijeholt, V. Vargas, and S. Wieringa (eds), *Women's Movements and Public Policy in Europe, Latin America, and the Caribbean*. New York: Garland.

Hancock, D. M. (1983). 'Comparative Public Policy: An Assessment', in A. W. Finifter (ed.), *Political Science: The State of the Discipline*. Washington, DC: American Political Science Association.

Hanmer, J. (1996). 'The Common Market of Violence', in A. R. Elman (ed.), *Sexual Politics and the European Union: The New Feminist Challenge*. Providence and Oxford: Berghahn Books.

Hantrais, L. (1993a). 'Comparing Family Policy in Britain, France and Germany'. *Journal of Social Policy*, 28/2: 135–60.

——(1993b). 'Women, Work and Welfare in France', in J. Lewis (ed.), *Women and Social Policies in Europe: Work, Family and the State*. Aldershot: Edgar Elgar.

——(ed.) (2000a). *Gendered Policies in Europe*. London: Macmillan.

——(2000b). 'From Equal Pay to Reconciliation of Employment and Family Life', in L. Hantrais (ed.), *Gendered Policies in Europe*. London: Macmillan.

Harding, S. (ed.) (1987a). *Feminism and Methodology*. Bloomington and Indianapolis: Indiana University Press.

——(1987b). 'Conclusion: Epistemological Questions', in S. Harding (ed.), *Feminism and Methodology*. Bloomington and Indianapolis: Indiana University Press.

Harrington, M. (ed.) (2000). *Gender, Labor and the Welfare State*. London and New York: Routledge.

Harrop, M. (ed.) (1992). *Power and Policy in Liberal Democracies*. Cambridge: Cambridge University Press.

Hart, V. (1994). *Bound by Our Constitution: Women, Workers, and the Minimum Wage*. Princeton: Princeton University Press.

Hartsock, N. C. M. (1983). *Money, Sex, and Power: Toward a Feminist Historical Materialism*. New York: Longman.

Hause, S. C. and Kenney, A. R. (1984). *Women's Suffrage and Social Politics in the French Third Republic*. Princeton: Princeton University Press.

Haussman, M. A. (1992). 'The Personal is Constitutional: Feminist Struggles for Equality Rights in the United State and Canada', in J. M. Bystydzienski (ed.), *Women Transforming Politics*. Bloomington: Indiana University Press.

——(2001). 'Of Rights and Power: Canada's Federal Abortion Policy 1969–1991', in D. M. Stetson (ed.), *Abortion Politics, Women's Movements and the Democratic State: A Comparative Study of State Feminism*. Oxford: Oxford University Press.

Hawkesworth, M. (1994). 'Policy Studies Within a Feminist Frame'. *Policy Sciences*, 27: 97–114.

Hayes, B. C., McAllister, I., and Studlar, D. T. (2000). 'Gender, Postmaterialism, and Feminism in Contemporary Perspective', *International Political Science Review*, 21: 425–40.

Hayward, J. (1992). 'The Policy Community Approach to Industrial Policy', in D. A. Rustow and K. P. Erickson (eds), *Comparative Political Dynamics: Global Research Perspectives*. New York: Harper Collins.

Heclo, H. (1974). *Modern Social Politics in Britain and Sweden: From Relief to Income Maintenance*. New Haven: Yale University.

Heidenheimer, A. J., Heclo, H., and Adams, C. T. (1990). *Comparative Public Policy: The Politics of Social Choice in European and America*. New York: St Martin's Press.

Heise, L. with Pitanguy, J. and Germain, A. (1994). *Violence Against Women: The Hidden Health Burden* (World Bank Discussion Papers). Washington, DC: World Bank.

——Raikes, A., Watts, C. H., and Zwi, A. B. (1994). 'Violence Against Women: A Neglected Public Health Issue in Less Developed Countries'. *Social Science and Medicine*, 39: 1165–79.

Heitlinger, A. (1993). *Women's Equality Demography and Public Policies*. London: Macmillan.

Hendrick, R. M. and Nachmias, D. (1992). 'The Policy Sciences: The Challenge of Complexity'. *Policy Studies Review*, 11: 303–9.

Hernes, H. M. (1987). *Welfare State and Woman Power: Essays in State Feminism*. London: Norwegian University Press.

Hervey, T. and Shaw, J. (1998). 'Women, Work and Care: Women's Dual Role and Double Burden in EC Sex Equality Law'. *Journal of European Social Policy*, 8/1: 43–63.

Hirdman, Y. (1998). 'State Policy and Gender Contracts: the Swedish Experience', in E. Drew, R. Emerek, and E. Mahon (eds), *Women, Work and the Family in Europe*. London and New York: Routledge.

Hirschmann, N. J. (1992). *Rethinking Obligations: A Feminist Method for Political Theory*. Ithaca, NY: Cornell University Press.

——and Liebert, U. (eds) (2001). *Women and Welfare: Theory and Practice in the United States and Europe*. Rutgers, NJ: Rutgers University Press.

Hobson, B. (1994). 'Solo Mothers, Social Policy Regimes, and the Logics of Gender', in D. Sainsbury (ed.), *Gendering Welfare States*. London: Sage.

——(ed.) (2000a). 'Faces of Inequality'. Special Issue of *Social Politics*, 7/2.

——(ed.) (2000b). *Gender and Citizenship in Transition*. New York and London: Routledge.

——and Berggren, A. M. (eds) (1997). *Crossing Borders: Gender and Citizenship in Transition*. Stockholm: Swedish Council for Planning and Coordination.

Holli, A. M. (1992). 'Why the State? Reflection on the Politics of the Finnish Equality Association 9', in M. Keränen (ed.), *Gender and Politics in Finland*. Aldershot: Avebury.

——(2001). 'A Shifting Policy Environment Divides the Impact of State Feminism in Finland', in A.G. Mazur (ed.), *State Feminism, Women's Movements, and Job Training: Making Democracies Work in the Global Economy*. New York and London: Routledge.

Hoskyns, C. (1996). *Integrating Gender: Women, Law and Politics in the European Union*. London: Verso.

——(2001). 'Gender Politics in the European Union: The Context for Job Training.' in A.G. Mazur (ed.) *State Feminism, Women's Movements, and Job Training: Making Democracies Work in the Global Economy*. New York and London: Routledge.

Inglehart, R. (1990). *Culture Shift in Advanced Industrial Society*. Princeton: Princeton University Press.

——and Norris, P. (2000). 'The Developmental Theory of the Gender Gap: Women's and Men's Voting Behavior in Global Perspective'. *International Political Science Review*, 21: 441–63.

Ingram, H. and Smith, S. R. (1998). 'Institutions and Policies for Democracy: A Discussion Paper and Comments'. *Policy Currents*, 8/1: 1–8.

Itsin, C. (1996). 'Pornography, Harm, and Human Rights: The UK in European Context', in A. Elman (ed.), *Sexual Politics and the European Union: The New Feminist Challenge*. Providence and Oxford: Berghahn Books.

IU (Inter-Parliamentary Union) (1995). *Women in Parliaments 1945–1995. A World Statistical Survey* (Reports and Documents No. 23).Geneva: IU.

Jackson, P. C. (1986). 'Women's Movement and Abortion: The Criminalization of Irish Women', in D. Dahlerup (ed.), *The New Women's Movement: Feminism and Political Power in Europe and the USA*. London: Sage.

——(1993). 'Managing Mothers: The Case of Ireland', in J. Lewis (ed.), *Women and Social Policies in Europe: Work, Family and the State*. Aldershot: Edgar Elgar.

Jaggar, A. (1977). 'Political Philosophies of Women's Liberation', in M. Vetterling-Braggin *et al.* (eds), *Feminism and Philosophy*. Totwa, NJ: Rowman and Littlefield.

Jarman, J. (1991). 'Equality or Marginalization: The Repeal of Protective Legislation', in E. Meehan and S. Sevenhuijsen (eds), *Equality Politics and Gender*. London: Sage.

Jenkins-Smith, H. C. and Sabatier, P. (1993). ' The Study of Public Policy Processes', in H. C. Jenkins-Smith and P. A. Sabatier (eds), *Policy Change and Learning: An Advocacy Coalition Approach*. Boulder, CO: Westview.

Jenson, J. (1980). 'The French Communist Party and Feminism'. *The Socialist Register*, 121–48.

——(1985). 'Struggling for Identity: The Women's Movement and the State in Western Europe'. *West European Politics*, 8/4: 5–18.

——(1987). 'Changing Discourse, Changing Agendas: Political Rights and Reproductive Policies in France', in M. Katzenstein and G. Mueller (eds), *The Women's Movement of the United States and Western Europe*. Philadelphia: Temple University Press.

——(1988). 'The Limits of "and the" Discourse', in J. Jenson *et al.* (ed.), *Feminization of the Labor Force: Paradoxes and Promises*. New York: Oxford University Press.

——Hagen, E., and Reddy, C. (eds) (1988). *Feminization of the Labor Force: Paradoxes and Promises*. London: Oxford.

——and Sineau, M. (1994). 'The Same or Different? An Unending Dilemma for French Women', in B. Nelson and N. Chowdhury (eds), *Women and Politics Worldwide*. New Haven and London: Yale University Press.

——————(1995). *Mitterrand et les Françaises*. Paris: Presse Science Po.

——————(eds) (1998*a*). *Qui Doit Garder le Jeune Enfant? Modes d'Acceuil et Travail des Mères dans l'Europe en Crise*. Paris: Librairie Générale de Droit et Jurisprudence.

——————(1998*b*). 'La France, Quand la "liberté de choix" ne rime pas avec égalité républicaine', in J. Jenson, and M. Sineau (eds), *Qui Doit Garder le Jeune Enfant? Modes d'acceuil et travail des Mères dans l'Europe en Crise*. Paris: Librairie Générale de Droit et Jurisprudence.

———— ——(eds.) (2001). *Who Cares? Womens' Work, Childcare and Welfare State Design*. Toronto, Buffalo and London: University of Toronto Press.

Joffe, C. (1983). 'Why the United State Has no Child-Care Policy', in. I. Diamond (ed.), *Families, Politics and Public Policy: A Feminist Dialogue on Women and the State.* New York and London: Longman.

Johnson, K. (1995). *Undressing the Canadian State: The Politics of Pornography from Hickman to Butler.* Halifax, Nova Scotia: Fernwood Publishing.

Jones, C. (1985). *Patterns of Social Policy: An Introduction to Comparative Analysis.* London and New York: Tavistock Publications.

Jones, K. (1990). 'Citizenship in a Woman-Friendly Polity'. *Signs*, 15: 781–812.

——and Jonasdottir, A. G. (eds) (1988). *The Political Interests of Gender: Developing Theory and Research with a Feminist Face.* London: Sage.

Jordan, G. and Shubert, K. (eds) (1992). 'Policy Networks'. Special Issue of *European Journal of Political Research,* 21/1–2.

Joshi, H. and Davies, H. (1992). 'Day Care in Europe and Mother's Forgone Earnings'. *International Labour Review,* 131: 561–78.

Kahn, P. (1992). 'Introduction: Equal Pay for Work of Equal Value in Britain and the USA', in P. Kahn and E. Meehan (eds), *Equal Value/Comparative Worth in the UK and the USA.* New York: St Martin's Press.

——and Meehan, E. (eds) (1992). *Equal Value/Comparative Worth in the UK and the USA.* New York: St. Martin's Press.

Kamenitsa, L. (2001). 'Abortion Debates in Germany', in D. M. Stetson (ed.), *Abortion Politics, Women's Movements and the Democratic State: A Comparative Study of State Feminism.* Oxford: Oxford University Press.

Kamienicki, S. (1991). 'Pursuing Alternative Directions in Policy Research'. *Policy Currents,* 13/1: 4–5.

Kammerman, S. B. and Kahn, A. J. (eds) (1978). *Family Policy: Government and Families in Fourteen Countries.* New York: Columbia University Press.

————(eds) (1991). *Child Care, Parental Leave, and the Under Three's: Policy Innovation in Europe.* New York: Auburn House.

Kaplan, G. (1992). *Contemporary Western Feminism.* London: UCL Press and Allen and Unwin.

Karvonen, L. and Selle, P. (eds) (1995) *Closing the Gaps: Women in Nordic Politics.* Aldershot: Dartmouth.

Katz, A. K. (1986). *Legal Traditions and Systems: An International Handbook.* New York: Greenwood Press.

Katzenstein, M. and Mueller, C. (eds) (1987). *The Women's Movements of the United States and Western Europe.* Philadelphia: Temple University Press.

Kelber, M. (1994). *Women in Government: New Ways to Political Power.* Westport: Praeger.

Kelin-Schonnefeld, S. (1994). 'Germany', in B. Rolston and A. Eggert (eds), *Abortion in the New Europe: A Comparative Handbook.* Westport, CT and London: Greenwood Press.

Kellow, A. (1988). 'Promoting Elegance in Policy Theory: Simplifying Lowi's Arenas of Power'. *Policy Studies Journal,* 16: 713–24.

Kelly, L. (1999). 'Violence Against Women: A Policy of Neglect or a Neglect of Policy?', in S. Walby (ed), *New Agendas for Women.* London: Macmillan.

Kelly, R. M. (1992). 'Policy Inquiry and a Policy Science of Democracy', in S. Dunn and R. M. Kelly (eds), *Advances in Policy Studies Since 1950* (*Policy Studies* Review Annual No. 10). New Brunswick: Transaction Books.

——and Bayes, J. (eds) (1988). *Comparable Worth, Pay Equity and Public Policy.* New York: Greenwood Press.

——and Fisher, K. (1993). 'An Assessment of Articles About Women in the "Top 15" Political Science Journals'. *PS: Political Science and Politics*, 26: 544–58.

——and Newman, M. (2001). 'The Gendered Bureaucracy: Agency Mission, Equality of Opportunity and Representative Bureaucracies'. *Women and Politics*, 22/3: 1–33.

Kenney, S. J. (1995). 'Women, Feminism, Gender and Law in Political Science: Ruminations of a Feminist Academic'. *Women and Politics*, 15/3: 43–69.

Keränen, M. (1992). *Gender and Politics in Finland.* Aldershot: Avebury.

Ketting, E. (1986). 'The Marginal Relevance of Legislation Relating to Induced Abortion', in J. Lovenduski and J. Outshoorn (eds), *The New Politics of Abortion.* London: Sage.

——(1994). 'Netherlands', in B. Rolston and A. Eggert (eds), *Abortion in the New Europe: A Comparative Handbook.* Westport, CT and London: Greenwood Press.

——and van Praag, P. (1986) 'The Marginalization of Legislation Relating to Individual Abortion', in J. Lovenduski and J. Outshoorn (eds), *The New Politics of Abortion.* London: Sage.

Keuzenkamp, S. (1985). 'You Cannot Make an Omelette without Breaking Eggs: Emancipation Policy in the Netherlands'. Paper presented at the Fourth International Interdisciplinary Congress on Women. New York.

Kilpatrick, C. (1997). 'Effective Utilisation of Equality Rights: Equal Pay for Work of Equal Value in France and the UK', in F. Gardiner (ed.), *Sex Equality Policy in Western Europe.* London: Routledge.

King, G., Keohane, R. O., and Verba, S. (1994). *Designing Social Inquiry: Scientific Inference in Qualitative Research.* Princeton: Princeton University Press.

Kingdon, J. (1995). *Agendas, Alternatives and Public Policies.* New York: Harper Collins.

Kirkpatrick, J. (1975). 'Representation in the American National Conventions: The Case of 1972'. *British Journal of Political Science*, 5: 265–322.

Knijn, T. and Kremer, M. (1997). 'Gender and the Caring Dimension of Welfare States: Toward Inclusive Citizenship'. *Social Politics*, 4/3.

——and Ungerson, C. (eds) (1997*a*). 'Special Issue: Gender and Care Work in Welfare States'. *Social Politics*, 4/3.

————(1997*b*). 'Introduction: Gender and Care Work in Welfare Regimes'. *Social Politics*, 4/3.

Kolinsky, E. (1989). *Women in West Germany.* Oxford, New York, Munich: Berg.

——(1991). 'Political Participation and Parliamentary Careers: Women's Quotas in West Germany'. *West European Politics*, 14/1: 56–71.

——(1993). 'Party Change and Women's Representation in Unified Germany', in J. Lovenduski and P. Norris (eds), *Gender and Party Politics.* London: Sage.

Kornbluh, F. A. (1996). 'The New Literature on Gender and the Welfare State: The U.S. Case'. *Feminist Studies*, 22/1: 171–97.

Kriesi, H. (ed.) (1994). *Yearbook of Swiss Political Science*. Bern, Stuttgart, and Vienna: Paul Haupt Verlag.

Laatikainen, K. V. (2001). 'Caught Between Access and Activism in the Multi-level European Union Labyrinth', in A.G. Mazur (ed.), *State Feminism, Women's Movements, and Job Training: Making Democracies Work in the Global Economy*. New York and London: Routledge.

Laitin, D. (1995). 'Disciplining Political Science', in Review Symposium 'The Qualitative-quantitative Disputation: Gary King, Robert Keohane, and Sidney Verba's *Designing Social Inquiry: Scientific Inference in Qualitative Research*', *American Political Science Review*, 89: 454–6.

Lane, R. (1990). 'Concrete Theory: An Emerging Political Method'. *American Political Science Review*, 84: 927–40.

Langan, M. and Ostner, L. (1991). 'Gender and Welfare: Towards a Comparative Framework', in G. Roon (ed.), *Towards a European Welfare State*. London: Routledge.

Langkau, J. and Langkau-Herrmann, M. (1980). 'Federal Republic of Germany', in A. M. Yohalem (ed.), *Women Returning to Work: Policies and Progress in Five Countries*. Allnheld: Landmark Studies.

Lanquetin, M.-T., Laufer, J., and Letablier, M.-T. (2000). 'From Equality to Reconciliation in France', in L. Hantrais (ed.), *Gendered Policies in Europe*. London: Macmillan.

LaPalombara, J. (1968). 'Macrotheories and Microapplications in Comparative Politics: A Widening Chasm'. *Comparative Politics*, 1: 52–78.

Laroche-Reef, M. (1995). 'The Enlargement of the Recruitment Pool', in *Women in Decision-making* (Report of the European Seminar for the European Network). Brussels: European Community.

Lawlor, E. F. (1996). 'Review Essay'. *Journal of Policy Analysis and Management*, 15/1: 110–21.

Leidholt, D. (1996). 'Sexual Trafficking of Women in Europe: A Human Rights Crisis for the European Union', in A. R. Elman (ed.), *Sexual Politics and the European Union: The New Feminist Challenge*. Providence and Oxford: Berghahn Books.

Leijenaar, M. and Niemöller, K. (1994). 'Political Participation of Women: The Netherlands', in B. Nelson and N. Chowdhury (eds), *Women and Politics Worldwide*. New Haven and London: Yale University Press.

Leira, A. (1992). *Welfare States and Working Mothers: The Scandinavian Experience*. New York: Cambridge University Press.

——(1993). 'The "woman-friendly" Welfare State: The Case of Norway and Sweden', in J. Lewis (ed.), *Women and Social Policies in Europe: Work, Family and the State*. Aldershot: Edgar Elgar.

——(1998*a*). 'Caring as Social Right: Cash for Child Care and Daddy Leave'. *Social Politics*, 4: 362–78.

——(1998*b*). 'The Modernisation of Motherhood', in E. Drew *et al.* (eds), *Women, Work and the Family in Europe*. London and New York: Routledge.

Lemke, C. (1994). 'Women and Politics: The New Federal Republic of Germany', in B. Nelson and N. Chowdhury (eds), *Women and Politics Worldwide*. New Haven and London: Yale University Press.

Levan, A. (1996). 'Violence Against Women', in J. Brodie (ed.), *Women and Canadian Public Policy*. Toronto: Harcourt Brace.

Lewis, J. (ed.) (1983*a*). *Women's Welfare: Women's Rights*. London and Canberra: Croom Helm.

——(1983*b*). 'Introduction', in J. Lewis (ed.), *Women's Welfare, Women's Rights*. London and Canberra: Croom Helm.

——(1992). 'Gender and the Development of Welfare Regimes'. *Journal of European Social Policy*, 2/3: 159–73.

——(1993*a*). *Women and Social Policies in Europe: Work, Family and the State*. Aldershot: Edward Elgar.

——(1993*b*). 'Introduction: Women, Work, Family and Social Policies in Europe', in J. Lewis (ed.) *Women and Social Policies in Europe: Work, Family and the State*. Aldershot: Edgar Elgar.

——(ed.) (1997). *Lone Mothers in European Welfare Regimes: Shifting Policy Logics*. London: Jessica Kingsley Publishers.

——(ed.) (1998). *Gender and Social Care: Welfare State Restructuring in Europe*. Aldershot: Ashgate.

——and Hobson, B. (1997). 'Introduction', in J. Lewis (ed.), *Lone Mothers in European Welfare Regimes: Shifting Policy Logics*. London: Jessica Kingsley.

Liebert, U. (1999). 'Gender Politics in the European Union: The Return of the Public'. *European Society*, 1/2: 191–232.

Liebfried, S. and Pierson, P. (eds) (1995). *European Social Policy: Between Fragmentation and Integration*. Washington, DC: Brookings Institution.

Lief Palley, M. (1976). 'Women and the Study of Public Policy'. *Policy Studies Journal*, 4/3: 288–96.

Lijphart, A. (1971). ' Comparative Politics and Comparative Method'. *American Political Science Review*, 65: 682–93.

——(1975). 'The Comparable Cases Strategy in Comparative Research'. *Comparative Political Studies*, 8: 481–96.

Liljestrom, R. (1980). 'Integration of Family Policy and Labor Market Policy in Sweden', in R. Steinberg-Ratner (ed.), *Equal Employment Policy For Women: Strategies for Implementation in the United States, Canada, and Western Europe*. Philadelphia: Temple University Press.

Lindahl, K. (1994). 'Sweden', in B. Rolston and A. Eggert (eds), *Abortion in the New Europe: A Comparative Handbook*. Westport, CT and London: Greenwood Press.

Lipman-Bluman, J. and Bernard, J. (eds) (1979). *Sex Roles and Social Policy: A Complex Social Science Equation*. Beverly Hills: Sage.

Lohnka,-Himmighofen, M. and Dienel, C. (2000). 'Reconciliation Policies from a Comparative Perspective', in L. Hantrais (ed.), *Gendered Policies in Europe*. London: Macmillan.

Lovenduski, J. (1981). 'Toward the Emasculation of Political Science: The Impact of Feminism', in D. Spender (ed.), *Men's Studies Modified*. New York: Pergamon.

——(1986*a*). *Women and European Politics: Contemporary Feminism and Public Policy*. London: Wheatsheaf.

——(1986*b*). 'Parliament, Pressure Groups, Networks and the Women's Movements: The Politics of Abortion Law Reform in Britain (1967–1983)', in J. Lovenduski and J. Outshoorn (eds), *The New Politics of Abortion*. London: Sage.

Lovenduski, J. (1993). 'Introduction: The Dynamics of Gender and Party', in J. Lovenduski and P. Norris (eds), *Gender and Party Politics*. London: Sage.

—— (1994). 'The Rules of the Political Game: Feminism and Politics in Great Britain', in B. Nelson and N. Chowdhury (eds), *Women and Politics Worldwide*. New Haven and London: Yale University Press.

—— (1995). 'An Emerging Advocate: The Equal Opportunities Commission in Great Britain', in D. M. Stetson and A. G. Mazur (eds), *Comparative State Feminism*. Thousand Oaks: Sage.

—— (1997*a*). 'Women and Party Politics in Western Europe'. *PS: Political Science and Politics*, 3: 200–2.

—— (1997*b*). 'Sex Equality and the Rules of the Game', in F. Gardiner (ed.), *Sex Equality Policy in Western Europe*. London: Routledge.

—— (1997*c*). 'The Integration of Feminism into West European Politics', in M. Rhodes, P. Heywood, and V. Wright (eds), *Developments in West European Politics*. New York: St Martin's Press.

—— (1998). 'Gendering Research in Political Science'. *Annual Review of Political Science*, 1: 333–56.

—— (1999). 'Sexing Political Behaviour in Britain', in S. Walby (ed.), *New Agendas for Women*. London: Macmillan.

—— (ed.) (in progress). 'Feminism and the Political Representation of Women in Europe and North America.' Manuscript.

—— and Hills, J. (eds) (1981). *The Politics of the Second Electorate*. London: Routledge and Kegan Paul.

—— and Norris, P. (eds) (1993). *Gender and Party Politics*. London: Sage.

———— (eds) (1996). *Women in Politics* (special issue of *Parliamentary Affairs*). Oxford: Oxford University Press.

—— and Outshoorn, J. (eds) (1986*a*). *The New Politics of Abortion*. London: Sage.

———— (1986*b*). 'Introduction: The New Politics of Abortion', in J. Lovenduski and J. Outshoorn (ed.), *The New Politics of Abortion*. London: Sage.

—— and Randall, V. (1993). *Contemporary Feminist Politics: Women and Power in Great Britain*. Oxford: Oxford University Press.

—— and Stephenson, S. (1998). *Women in Decision-making: Report on Existing Research in the European Union*. Brussels: Employment and Social Affairs, European Commission.

Lowi, T. J. (1964). 'American Business, Public Policy, Case-Studies, and Political Theory'. *World Politics*, 16: 677–715.

—— (1972). 'Four Systems of Policy, Politics, and Choice'. *Public Administration Review*, 11: 298–310.

—— (1988). 'An Assessment of Kellow's "Promoting Elegance Theory"'. *Policy Studies Journal*, 16: 725–8.

—— (1997). '"Comments on Anderson," Governmental Suasion Adding to the Lowi Policy Typology'. *Policy Studies Journal*, 25: 283–5.

Luckhaus, L. and Ward, S. (1997). 'Equal Pension Rights for Men and Women: A Realistic Perspective'. *Journal of European Social Policy*, 7: 237–53.

Lycklama à Nijeholt, G., Vargas, V., and Wieringa, S. (eds) (1998). *Women's Movements and Public Policy in Europe, Latin America, and the Caribbean*. New York: Garland.

——G., Swiebel, J., and Wieringa, S. (1998). 'The Global Institutional Framework', in G. Lycklama à Nijeholt, V. Vargas, and S. Wieringa (eds), *Women's Movements and Public Policy in Europe, Latin American and the Caribbean*. New York: Garland.

Mackay, F. (1996). 'The Zero Tolerance Campaign: Setting the Agenda', in J. Lovenduski and P. Norris (eds), *Women in Politics*. Oxford: Oxford University Press.

MacKinnon, C. (1989). *Toward A Feminist Theory of the State*. Cambridge: Harvard University Press.

Mahon, E. (1995). 'Ireland's Policy Machinery: The Ministry of State for Women's Affairs and the Joint Oireachtas Committees for Women's Rights', in D. M. Stetson and A. G. Mazur (eds), *Comparative State Feminism*. Thousand Oaks: Sage.

——(1996). 'Women's Rights and Catholicism in Ireland', in M. Threlfall (ed.), *Mapping the Women's Movement*. London: Verso.

——(1998a). 'Changing Gender Roles, State, Work and Family', in E. Drew. R. Emerek, and E. Mahon (eds), *Women, Work and the Family in Europe*. London and New York: Routledge.

——(1998b). 'Class, Mothers and Equal Opportunities to Work', in E. Drew, R. Emerek, and E. Mahon (eds), *Women, Work and the Family in Europe*. London and New York: Routledge.

——(2001). 'Abortion Debates in Ireland: An On-going Issue'. in D. M. Stetson (ed.), *Abortion Politics, Women's Movements and the Democratic State: A Comparative Study of State Feminism*. Oxford: Oxford University Press.

——and Morgan, V. (1999). 'State Feminism in Ireland', in Y. Galligan, E. Ward, and R. Wilford (eds), *Contesting Politics: Women in Ireland, North and South*. London: Westview Press.

Mahon, R. (1997). 'Child Care in Canada and Sweden: Policy and Politics'. *Social Politics*, 4/.

——(2001). 'Theorizing Welfare Regimes: Toward a Dialogue'. *Social Politics*. 8/1: 24–35.

March, J. G. and Olsen, J. P. (1984). 'The New Institutionalism: Organizational Factors in Political Life'. *American Political Science Review*, 78: 734–49.

Mathews, D. G. and DeHart, J. S. (1990). *Sex, Gender, and the Politics of the ERA*. New York: Oxford University Press.

Matthews, N. (1995). 'Feminist Clashes with the State: Tactical Choices by State-Funded Rape Crisis Centers', in M. M. Ferree and P. Y. Martin (eds), *Feminist Organizatons: Harvest of the New Women's Movement*. Philadelphia: Temple University Press.

Mazey, S. (1988). 'European Community Action on Women'. *Journal of Common Market Studies*, 1.

Mazur, A.G. (1993). 'Sexual Harassment Policy in France: Another Case of French Exceptionalism?'. *French Politics and Society*, 11/2: 12–31.

——(1995a). *Gender Bias and the State: Symbolic Reform at Work in Fifth Republic France*. Pittsburgh: Pittsburgh University Press.

——(1995b). 'Strong State and Symbolic Reform: The Ministère des Droits de la Femme in France', in D. M. Stetson and A. G. Mazur (eds), *Comparative State Feminism*. Thousand Oaks: Sage.

Mazur, A.G. (1996*a*). 'The Interplay: The Formation of Sexual Harassment Legislation in France and EU Policy Initiatives', in A. R. Elman (ed.), *Sexual Politics and the European Union: The New Feminist Challenge*. Providence and Oxford: Berghahn Books.

——(1996*b*). 'Sexual Harassment, Gender Politics, and Symbolic Reform', in J. Keeler and M. Schain (eds), *Chirac's Challenge Liberalization, Europeanizaton and Malaise in France*. New York: St Martin's Press.

—— (1999). 'Feminist Comparative Policy: A New Field of Study'. *European Journal of Political Research*, 35: 483–506.

——(ed.) (2001*a*). *State Feminism, Women's Movements, and Job Training: Making Democracies Work in the Global Economy*. New York and London: Routledge.

——(2001*b*). 'Drawing Lessons From The French Parity Movement'. *Contemporary French Civilization*, 25/3.

——(2001*c*). 'Republican Universalism Resists State Feminist Approaches to Gendered Equality in France', in A. G. Mazur (ed.), *State Feminism, Women's Movements, and Job Training: Making Democracies Work in the Global Economy*. New York and London: Routledge.

—— and Appleton, A. (1997). 'Mainstreaming Gender and Research into the Classroom: Cases from Contemporary Western Europe—Introductory Essay'. *PS: Political Science and Politic*, 3: 194–5.

—— and Parry, J. (1998). 'Choosing Not to Choose in Comparative Policy Research Design: The Case of the Research Network on Gender, Politics, and the State'. *Policy Studies Journal*, 26: 384–97.

—— and Reiter, S. (forthcoming). 'EU Sex Equality Policy in France: Feminist Leader or Lagger?', in U. Liebert (ed.), *The Implementation of EU Sex Equality Policy*.

—— Baudino, C., Appleton, A., and Robinson, J. (2000). *Appareils Gouvernementaux Chargés de la Politique en Direction des Femmes* (Report for the Ministère de l'Emploi et de la Solidarité—Service des Droits des Femmes). Paris, May.

McCann, M. (1994). *Rights at Work and the Politics of Legal Mobilization*. Chicago: University of Chicago Press.

McCool, D. C. (1995). 'The Theoretical Foundations of Policy Studies', in D. C. McCool (ed.), *Public Policy Theories, Models, and Concepts: An Anthology*. Englewood Cliffs, NJ: Prentice Hall.

McCormack, T. (1996). 'Reproductive Technologies: Rights, Choice, and Coercion', in J. Brodie (ed.), *Women and Canadian Public Policy*. Toronto: Harcourt Brace.

McCrudden, C. (1994). *Equality in Law Between Men and Women in the European Community: The United Kingdom*. Dordrecht: Martinus Mijhoff.

McDermott, P. (1996). 'Pay and Employment Equity: Why Separate Policies?', in J. Brodie (ed.), *Women and Canadian Public Policy*. Toronto: Harcourt Brace.

McDonagh, E. L. (1996). *Breaking the Abortion Deadlock: From Choice to Consent*. New York: Oxford University Press.

McFerren, L. (1990). 'Interpretation of a Frontline State: Australian Women's Refuges and the State', in S. Watson (ed.), *Playing the State*. New York: Verso.

Mead, L. (1995). 'Public Policy: Vision, Potential, Limits'. *Policy Currents*, 3/February: 1–4.

Meehan, E. (1983*a*). 'Equal Opportunity Policies: Some Implications for Women of Contrasts Between Enforcement Bodies in Britain and the USA', in J. Lewis (ed.), *Women's Welfare, Women's Rights*. London and Canberra: Croom Helm.

——(1983*b*). 'Implementing Equal Opportunity Policies: Some British American Comparisons'. *Politics*, 2/1.

——(1985). *Women's Rights at Work: Campaigns and Policy in Britain and the United States*. New York: St Martin's Press.

——(1986). 'Women's Studies and Political Studies', in P. Evans *et al.* (eds), *Feminism and Political Theory*. London: Sage.

——(1989). 'Equal Value/ Comparable Worth'. Paper for ECPR Joint Sessions Workshop on Equality Principles and Gender Politics. Paris, April.

——(1992). 'Researching Women in Europe: European Community Policies on Sex Equality: A Bibliographic Essay'. *Women's Studies International Forum*, 15/1: 57–64.

——(1994). *Citizenship and the European Community*. London: Sage.

——and Collins, E. (1996). 'Women, the European Union and Britain', in J. Lovenduski and P. Norris (eds), *Women in Politics*. Oxford: Oxford University Press.

——and Sevenhuijsen, S. (eds) (1991*a*). *Equality Politics and Gender*. London: Sage.

————(1991*b*). 'Problems in Principles and Policies', in E. Meehan and S. Sevenhuijsen (eds), *Equality Politics and Gender*. London: Sage.

Mendez, M. T. G. (1994). 'Women's Political Engagement in Spain', in B. Nelson and N. Chowdhury (eds), *Women and Politics Worldwide*. New Haven and London: Yale University Press.

Merchant, J. (1996). 'Confronting the Consequences of Medical Technology: Policy Frontiers in France and the USA', in M. Githens and D. M. Stetson (eds), *Abortion Politics: Public Policy in Cross-Cultural Perspective*. New York and London: Routledge.

Merton, R. K. [1949] (1968). *Social Theory and Social Structure*. New York: Free Press.

Meyer, T. (1998). 'Retrenchment, Reproduction, Modernization: Pension Politics and the Decline of the German Breadwinner Model'. *Journal of European Social Policy*, 8/3: 195–211.

Meyers, M. K, Gornick, J., and Ross, K. E. (1999). 'Public Childcare, Parental Leave, and Employment', in D. Sainsbury (ed.), *Gender and Welfare State Regimes*. Oxford: Oxford University Press.

Michel, S. and Mahon, R. (forthcoming, 2002) (eds), *Gender and Welfare State Restructuring: Through the Lens of Childcare*. London and New York: Routledge.

Millar, J. and Whiteford, P. (1993). 'Support in Lone-parent Families: Policies in Australia and UK', in P. Rist (ed.), *Policy Evaluation* (International Library of Comparative Public Policy Series). Brookfield, VT: Edward Elgar.

Millett, K. (1971). *Sexual Politics*. New York: Avon Books.

Molyneux, M. (1985). 'Mobilization with Emancipation? Women's Interests, the State and Revolution in Nicaragua'. *Feminist Studies*, 11: 227–55.

Morgan, K. (2001). *Whose Hand Rocks the Cradle: The Politics of Child Care Policy in Advanced Industrialized States*. Princeton: Princeton University Press.

——(forthcoming, 2002). 'Child Care Policy and the Crisis of the Welfare State in France', in S. Michel and R. Mahon (eds), *Gender and Welfare State Restructuring: Through the Lens of Childcare*. London and New York: Routledge.

Morken, K. and Selle, P. (1995). 'An Alternative Movement in a 'state-friendly' society: the Women's Shelter Movement', in L. Karvonen and P. Selle (eds), *Women in Nordic Politics*. Aldershot: Dartmouth.

Mossuz-Lavau, J. (1986). 'Abortion Policy in France Under Governments of the Right and Left (1973–1984)', in J. Lovenduski and J. Outshoorn (eds), *The New Politics of Abortion*. London: Sage.

Mossuz-Lavau, J. (1998). *Femmes/Hommes Pour la Parité*. Paris: Presses de Science Po.

Mutari, E. and Figart, D. M. (2001). 'Europe at a Crossroads: Harmonization, Liberalization, and Gender of Work Time'. *Social Politics*, 8/1: 36–64.

Nandy, D. (1980). 'Administering Anti-Discrimination Legislation in Great Britain', in R. Ratner (ed.), *Equal Employment Policy for Women*. Philadelphia: Temple University Press.

Nelson, B. J. (1992). 'The Role of Sex and Gender in Comparative Political Analysis: Individuals, Institutions and Regimes'. *American Political Science Review*, 86: 491–5.

——(1989). 'Women and Knowledge in Political Science: Texts, Histories, and Epistemologies'. *Women and Politics*, 9: 1–25.

——and Carver, K. A. (1994). 'Many Voices But Few Vehicles: The Consequences for Women of Weak Political Infrastructure in the United States', in B. J. Nelson and N. Chowdhury (eds), *Women and Politics Worldwide*. New Haven and London: Yale University Press.

——and Chowdhury, N. (eds) (1994). *Women and Politics Worldwide*. New Haven: Yale University Press.

Nelson, H. L. (1997). *Feminism and Families*. New York and London: Routledge.

Nettl, J. P. (1968). 'The State as a Conceptual Variable'. *World Politics*, 20: 559–92.

Newman, M. (1995). 'The Gendered Nature of Lowi's Typology; or, Who would Guess You Could Find Gender Here?', in G. Duerst-Lahti and R. M. Kelly (eds), *Gender Power, Leadership, and Governance*. Ann Arbor: The University of Michigan Press.

Nielsen, R. (1995). *Equality in Law Between Men and Women in the European Community: Denmark*. Dordrecht: Martinus Mijhoff.

Norris, P. (1987). *Politics and Sexual Equality: The Comparative Position of Women in Western Democracies*. Boulder, CO: Lynne Reiner.

——(1997a). 'Towards a More Cosmopolitan Political Science?'. *European Journal of Political Research*, 31/1–2: 17–34.

——(1997b). 'Equality Strategies and Political Representation', in F. Gardiner (ed.), *Sex Equality Policy in Western Europe*. London: Routledge.

——and Lovenduski, L. (1995). *Political Recruitment: Gender, Race and Class in the British Parliament*. Cambridge: Cambridge University Press.

O'Connor, J. (1996). 'From Women in the Welfare State to Gendering Welfare State Regimes'. Special Issue of *Current Sociology*, 44/2.

——(1999). 'Employment Strategies in Liberal Welfare State: Similar Principles Different Strategies', in D. Sainsbury (ed.), *Gender Regimes and Welfare States*. Oxford: Oxford University Press.

——Shaver, S., and Orloff, A. S. (1999). *States, Markets, Families: Gender, Liberalism and Social Policy in Australia, Canada, Great Britain, and the Untied States*. Cambridge: Cambridge University Press.

O'Regan, V. (2000). *Gender Matters: Female Policymakers' Influences in Industrialized Nations*. Westport, CT and London: Praeger.

Offen, K. (1988). 'Defining Feminism: A Comparative Historical Approach'. *Signs*, 14/11: 119–57.

—— (2000). *European Feminisms, 1700–1950: A Political History*. Stanford, CA: Stanford University Press.

Oldersma, J. (1999). 'Gendering Constitutional Reforms'. Paper presented at the Joint Session of Workshops of the ECPR. Mannheim.

—— (2002). 'More Women or More Feminists in Politics? Advocacy Coalitions and the Representation of Women in the Netherlands, 1967–1992'. *Acta Politica*, 3.

Olsen, F. (1993). 'The Family and the Market: A Study of Ideology and Legal Reform', in P. Smith (ed.), *Feminist Jurisprudence*. New York: Oxford University Press.

Orloff, A. S. (1993). 'Gender and the Social Rights of Citizenship: The Comparative Analysis of Gender Relations and Welfare States'. *American Sociological Review*, 58: 303–28.

—— (1996), 'Gender in the Welfare State'. *Annual Review of Sociology*, 22: 51–78.

Ostner, I. (1993). 'Slow Motion: Women, Work, and the Family', in J. Lewis (ed.), *Women and Social Policies in Europe: Work, Family and the State*. Aldershot: Edward Elgar.

—— (1997). 'Lone Mothers in Germany Before and after Unification', in J. Lewis (ed.), *Lone Mothers in European Welfare Regimes: Shifting Policy Logics*. London: Jessica Kingsley.

—— and Lewis, J. (1995). 'Gender and the Evolution of European Welfare States', in S. Liebfried and P. Pierson (eds), *European Social Policy: Between Fragmentation and Integration*. Washington, DC: Brookings Institution.

Outshoorn, J. (1986a). 'The Feminist Movement and Abortion Policy in the Netherlands', in D. Dahlerup (ed.), *The New Women's Movement: Feminism and Political Power in Europe and the USA*. London: Sage.

—— (1986b). 'The Rules of the Game: Abortion Politics in the Netherlands', in J. Lovenduski and J. Outshoorn (eds), *The New Politics of Abortion*. London: Sage.

—— (1988). 'Abortion Law Reform: A Woman's Right to Choose', in M. Buckley and M. Anderson (eds), *Women, Equality, and Europe*. London: Macmillan.

—— (1991). 'Is This What We Wanted? Positive Action as Issue Perversion', in E. Meehan and S. Sevenhuijsen (eds), *Equality Politics and Gender*. London: Sage.

—— (1992). 'Women and Politics in the Netherlands'. *European Journal of Political Research*, 21: 453–67.

—— (1994a). 'Between Movement and Government: Femocrats in the Netherlands'. *Annuaire Suisse de Science Politique*, 34: 141–64.

—— (1994b). 'Being Present to Make Difference Visible? "Parity Democracy" and the Question of the Political Representation of Women'. Paper prepared for the 1994 APSA meeting, 1–4 September.

—— (1995). 'Administrative Accommodation in the Netherlands: The Department for the Coordination of Equality Policy', in D. M. Stetson and A.G. Mazur (eds), *Comparative State Feminism*. Thousand Oaks: Sage.

Outshoorn, J. (1996). 'The Stability of Compromise: Abortion Politics in Western Europe', in M. Githens and D. M. Stetson (eds), *Abortion Politics: Public Policy in Cross-Cultural Perspective.* New York and London: Routledge.

——(1997). 'Incorporating Feminism: The Women's Policy Network in the Netherlands,' in F. Gardiner, (ed.) *Sex Equality Policy in Western Europe.* London and New York: Routledge.

——(1998*a*). 'Furthering the "Cause"; Femocrat Strategies in National Government', in J. Bussemaker and R. Voet (eds), *Gender, Participation and Citizenship in the Netherlands.* Aldershot: Ashgate.

——(1998*b*). 'Sexuality and International Commerce: The Traffic in Women and Prostitution Policy in the Netherlands', in T. Carver and V. Mottier (eds), *Politics of Sexuality: Identity, Gender, Citizenship.* London and New York: Routledge.

—— (2001). 'Policymaking on Abortion: Arenas, Actors, and Arguments in the Netherlands', in D. M. Stetson (ed.), *Abortion Politics, Women's Movements and the Democratic State: A Comparative Study of State Feminism.* Oxford: Oxford University Press.

——and Swiebel, J. (1998). 'Feminism and the State in the Netherlands', in G. Lycklama à Nijeholt, V. Vargas, and S. Weiringa (eds), *Women's Movements and Public Policy in Europe, Latin America, and the Caribbean.* New York: Garland.

Paltiel, F. A. (1997). 'State Initiatives: Impetus and Effects', in C. Andrew and S. Rodgers (eds), *Women and the Canadian State.* Montreal and Kingston: McGill-Queens University Press.

Papadopoulos, T. N. (1998). 'Greek Family Policy From a Comparative Perspective', in E. Drew *et al.* (eds), *Women, Work and the Family in Europe.* New York: Routledge.

Parry, J. (1998). 'Institutionalizing Interests: Women's Commissions in the United States'. Ph.D. thesis, Washington State University.

Parvikko, T. (1991). 'Conceptions of Gender Equality: Similarities and Differences', in E. Meehan and S. Sevenhuijsen (eds), *Equality Politics and Gender.* London: Sage.

Pateman, C. (1988). *The Sexual Contract.* Stanford: Stanford University Press.

Phillips, A. (1991). *Engendering Democracy.* University Park, Pennsylvania: The University of Pennsylvania Press.

——(1995). *The Politics of Presence.* Oxford: Clarendon Press.

Pierson, P. (2000). 'Three Worlds of Welfare State Research'. *Comparative Political Studies,* 33: 791–821.

Pietila, H. and Vickers, J. (1996). *Making Women Matter: The Role of the United Nations* (3rd edn). London: Zed Books.

Pillinger, J. (1992). *Feminising the Market: Women's Pay and Employment in the European Community.* London: Macmillan.

Pisciotta, E. E. (1986). 'The Strength and the Powerlessness of the New Italian Women's Movement: The Case of Abortion', in D. Dahlerup (ed.), *The New Women's Movement.* London Sage.

Pitkin, H. F. (1967). *The Concept of Representation.* Berkeley: University of California Press.

Pouvoirs (1997). 'Femmes en Politiques'. Special Issue. 82.

Praud, J. (1997). 'Affirmative Action and Women's Representation in the Onitario Democratic Party', in M. Tremblay and C. Andrew (eds), *Women and Political Representation in Canada*. Ottawa: University of Ottawa Press.

——(ed.) (2001). 'Towards Parity Democracy? Women's Political Representation in Fifth Republic France'. *Contemporary French Civilization*, 24/5.

Pringle, R. and Watson, S. (1992). 'Women's Interests and the Post-structuralist State', in M. Barrett and A. Phillips (eds), *Destabilizing Theory: Contemporary Feminist Debates*. Cambridge: Polity Press.

Putnam, C. C. (1993). *Making Democracy Work: Civic Traditions in Modern Italy*. Princeton: Princeton University Press.

Ragin, C. (1987). *The Comparative Method: Moving Beyond Qualitative and Quantitative Strategies*. Berkeley: University of California Press.

Raissiguier, C. (2001). 'Gender, Race and Exclusion: A New Look at the French Republican Tradition'. *International Feminist Journal of Politics*, 1: 433–57.

Randall, V. (1982, 1987). *Women and Politics*. Chicago: University of Chicago Press.

——(1986). 'The Politics of Abortion in Ireland', in J. Lovenduski and J. Outshoorn (eds), *The New Politics of Abortion*. London: Sage.

——(1991). 'Feminism and Political Analysis'. *Political Studies*, 39: 513–32.

——(1992). 'Great Britain and Dilemmas for Feminist Strategy in the 1980s: The Case of Abortion and Reproductive Rights', in J.M. Bystydzienski (ed.), *Women Transforming Politics: Worldwide Strategies for Empowerment*. Bloomington: Indiana University Press.

——(1996). 'The Politics of Childcare Policy', in J. Lovenduski and P. Norris (eds), *Women in Politics*. Oxford: Oxford University Press.

——and Weylen, G. (eds) (1998). *Gender, Politics, and the State*. London: Routledge.

Rasmussen, N. (1994). 'Denmark', in B. Rolston and A. Eggert (eds), *Abortion in the New Europe: A Comparative Handbook*. Westport, CT and London: Greenwood Press.

Rees, T. (1995). *Women and the EC Training Programmes: Tinkering, Tailoring, and Transforming*. Bristol: SAUS Publishing.

——(1998). *Mainstreaming Equality in the European Union: Education, Training and Labour Market Policies*. London and New York: Routledge.

Reinharz, S. (1992). *Feminist Methods and Social Research*. New York and Oxford: Oxford University Press.

Remick, H. (1980). 'Beyond Equal Pay for Equal Work: Comparable Worth in the State of Washington', in R. Ratner (ed.), *Equal Employment Policy for Women*. Philadelphia: Temple University Press.

Richardson, J. (ed.) (1982). *Policy Styles in Western Europe*. London: George Allen and Unwin.

Robinson, J. (2001). 'Gendering the Abortion Debate: the French Case', in D. M. Stetson (ed.), *Abortion Politics, Women's Movements and the Democratic State: A Comparative Study of State Feminism*. Oxford: Oxford University Press.

Rochon, T. R. and Mazmanian, D. A. (1993). 'Social Movements and the Policy Process'. *Annals of the American Academy of Political and Social Science*, 528: 75–87.

Rolston, B. and Eggert A. (eds) (1994a). *Abortion in the New Europe: A Comparative Handbook*. Westport, CT and London: Greenwood Press.

Rolston, B. and Eggert A. (1994*b*). 'Introduction: Abortion in the Europe, Present and Future', in B. Rolston and A. Eggert (eds), *Abortion in the New Europe: A Comparative Handbook*. Westport, CT and London: Greenwood Press.

Romao, I. (1995). 'The Use of Quotas: The Enlargement of the Recruitment Pool', in *Women in Decision-making* (Report of the European Seminar for the European Network), 23–4 March. Dublin.

Ronalds, C. (1990). 'Government Action Against Employment Discrimination', in S. Watson (ed.), *Playing the State: Australian Feminist Interventions*. London: Verso.

Rönnblom, M. (1997). 'Local Women's Projects', in G. Gustafsson (ed.), *Towards a New Democratic Order: Women's Organizing in Sweden in the 1990s*. Stockholm: Publica.

Rosenbloom, D. H. (1984). 'What Have Policy Studies Told Us About Affirmative Action'. *Policy Studies Review*, 4/1: 43–8.

Rossi, A. S. (1973). *The Feminist Papers: From Adams to Beauvoir*. New York: Columbia University Press.

Roth, P. (1987). *Meaning and Method in Social Sciences*. Ithaca, NY: Cornell University Press.

Ruggerini, M. G. (1995). 'The Use of Public Awareness Campaigns', in *Women in Decision-making* (Report of the European Seminar for the European Network), 23–4 March. Dublin.

Ruggie, M. (1984). *The State and Working Women: A Comparative Study of Britain and Sweden*. Princeton: Princeton University Press.

——(1987). 'Workers' Movements and Women's Interests: The Impact of Labor State Relations in Britain and Sweden', in M. Katsenstein and G. Mueller (eds), *The Women's Movements of the United States and Western Europe: Consciousness, Political Opportunity, and Public Policy*. Philadelphia: Temple University Press.

——(1988). 'Gender, Work and Social Progress: Some Consequence of Interest Aggregation in Sweden', in J. Jenson *et al.* (ed.), *Feminization of the Labor Force: Paradoxes and Promises*. New York: Oxford University Press.

Ruxton, S. (1996). *Children in Europe*. London: NCH Action for Children.

Sabatier, P. A. (1993). 'Policy Change over a Decade or More', in H. C. Jenkins-Smith and P. A. Sabatier (eds), *Policy Change and Learning: An Advocacy Coalition Approach*, Boulder, CO: Westview.

——and Jenkins-Smith, H. C. (eds) (1993). *Policy Learning: An Advocacy Coalition Approach*. Boulder, CO: Westview Press.

Safilios-Rothschild, C. (1974). *Women and Social Policy*. Englewood Cliffs: Prentice-Hall.

Sainsbury, D. (1993). 'The Politics of Increased Women's Representation: The Swedish Case', in J. Lovenduski and P. Norris (eds), *Gender and Party Politics*. London: Sage.

——(ed.) (1994). *Gendering Welfare States*. London: Sage.

——(1996). *Gender, Equality, and Welfare States*. Cambridge: Cambridge University Press.

——(ed.) (1999*a*). *Gender Regimes and Welfare States*. Oxford: Oxford University Press.

——(1999*b*). 'Taxation, Family Responsibilities, and Employment', in D. Sainsbury (ed.), *Gender and Welfare State Regimes*. Oxford: Oxford University Press.

——(2001). 'Gender and the Making of Welfare States: Norway and Sweden.' *Social Politics*, 8/1:113–43.

Salimen, K. (1993). *Pensions Schemes in the Making: A Comparative Study of the Scandinavian Countries*. Helsinki: The Central Pension Security Institute.

Saloma, J. S. and Sontag, F. S. (1972). *Parties*. New York: Knopf.

Sapiro, V. (1981). 'Research Frontier Essay: When are Interests Interesting? The Problem of the Political Representation of Women'. *American Political Science Review*, 75: 701–16.

——(1991). 'Gender Politics, Gendered Politics: The State of the Field', in W. Crotty (ed.), *The Theory and Practice of Political Science*, i. Evanston IL: Northwestern University Press.

Sartori, G. (1970). 'Concept Misformation in Comparative Politics'. *American Political Science Review*, 64: 1033–53.

Sassoon, A. S. (ed.) (1992). *Women and the State* (third reprint). Routledge: New York.

Savage, M. and Witz, A. (1992). *Gender and Bureaucracy*. Oxford and Cambridge: Blackwell/*Sociological Review*.

Sawer, M. (1990). *Sisters in Suits: Women and Public Policy in Australia*. Sydney: Allen and Unwin.

——(1994). 'Locked Out or Locked In? Women and Politics in Australia', in B. Nelson and N. Chowdhury (eds), *Women and Politics Worldwide*. New Haven, CT: Yale University Press.

——(1995). 'Femocrats in Glass Towers?: The Office of the Status of Women in Australia', in D. M. Stetson and A. G. Mazur (eds), *Comparative State Feminism*. Thousand Oaks: Sage.

Schattschneider, E. E. (1975). *The Semi Sovereign People: A Realist's View of Democracy in America*. Hinsdale, IL: Dryden Press.

Scheiwe, K. (1994*a*). 'German Pension Insurance, Gendered Times and Stratification', in D. Sainsbury (ed.), *Gendering Welfare States*. London: Sage.

——(1994*b*). 'Labour Market, Welfare State and Family Institutions: The Links to Mothers' Poverty Risks'. *Journal of European Social Policy*, 4: 201–24.

——(2000). 'Equal Opportunities Policies and the Management of Care in Germany', in L. Hantrais (ed.), *Gendered Policies in Europe*. London: Macmillan.

Scheppele, K. L. (1996). 'Consitutionalizing Abortion', in M. Githens and D. M. Stetson (eds), *Abortion Politics: Public Policy in Cross-Cultural Perspective*. New York and London: Routledge.

Schiersmann, C. (1991). 'Germany: Recognizing the Value of Child Rearing', in B. Kamerman and A. J. Kahn (eds), *Child Care, Parental Leave and the Under 3s*. New York: Auburn House.

Schmidt, M. G. (1993). 'Gendered Labour Force Participation', in F. G. Castles (ed.), *Families of Nations*. Aldershot: Dartmouth.

Schneider, A. and Ingram, H. (1993). 'Social Construction of Target Populations: Implications for Politics and Policy'. *American Political Science Review*, 87: 334–47.

Scott, J. (1986). 'Gender: A Useful Category of Historical Analysis'. *American Historical Review*, 91: 1053–75.

——Kaplan, C., and Keates, D. (eds) (1997). *Transitions, Environments, Translations: Feminisms in International Politics*. New York and London: Routledge.

Seear, N. (1980). 'Implementing Equal Pay and Equal Opportunity Legislation in Great Britain', in R. Ratner (ed.), *Equal Employment Policy for Women*. Philadelphia: Temple University Press.

Seeland, S. (1995). 'The Enlargement of the Recruitment Pool', in *Women in Decision-making* (Report of the European Seminar for the European Network), 23–4 March, Dublin.

Siaroff, A. (1994). 'Work, Welfare, and Gender Equality: A New Typology', in D. Sainsbury (ed.), *Gendering Welfare States*. London. Sage.

Siim, B. (1991). 'Welfare State, Gender Politics and Equality Policies: Women's Citizenship in the Scandinavian Welfare States', in E. Meehan and S. Sevenhuijsen (eds), *Equality Politics and Gender*. London: Sage.

—— (1993). 'The Gendered Scandinavian Welfare States: The Interplay Between Women's Roles as Mothers, Workers and Citizens in Denmark', in J. Lewis (ed.), *Women and Social Policies in Europe: Work, Family and the State*. Aldershot: Edward Elgar.

—— (1997). 'Dilemmas of Citizenship in Denmark: Lone Mothers Between Work and Care', in J. Lewis (ed.), *Lone Mothers in European Welfare Regimes: Shifting Policy Logics*. London: Jessica Kingsley.

Simms, M. (1993). 'Two Steps Forward, One Step Back: Women and the Australian Party Systems' in L. Lovenduski and P. Norris (eds), *Gender and Party Politics*. London: Sage.

—— (1994). 'Britain', in B. Rolston and A. Eggert (eds), *Abortion in the New Europe: A Comparative Handbook*. Westport, CT and London: Greenwood Press.

Siltanen, J. and Stanworth, M. (eds) (1984). *Women and the Public Sphere*. London: Hutchinson.

Silverberg, H. (1990). 'What Happened to the Feminist Revolution in Political Science: A Review Essay'. *Western Political Quarterly*, 43: 887–903.

—— (1992). 'Gender Studies and Political Science: The History of the "Behavioralist Compromise"', in J. Farr and R. Seidelman (eds), *Discipline and History: Political Science in the United States*. Ann Arbor: University of Michigan Press.

Sineau, M. (2001). *Profession Femme Politique: Sexe et Pouvoir sous la Cinquième République*. Paris: Presses de Sciences Po.

Singh, R. (1998). *Gender Autonomy in Western Europe*. London: Macmillan.

Skjeie, H. (1991a). 'The Rhetoric of Difference: On Women's Inclusion into Political Elites'. *Politics and Society*, 19: 233–63.

—— (1991b). 'The Uneven Advance of Norwegian Women'. *New Left Review*, 187: 79–102.

—— (1993). 'Ending the Male Political Hegemony: the Norwegian Experience', in J. Lovenduski and P. Norris (eds), *Gender and Party Politics*. London: Sage.

—— and Siim, B. (2000). 'Scandinavian Feminist Debates on Citizenship', *International Political Science Review*, 21: 345–60.

Skocpol, T. (1985). 'Bringing the State Back In: Strategies of Analysis in Current Research', in P. B. Evans *et al.* (eds), *Bringing the State Back*. New York: Cambridge University Press.

—— (1993). *Protecting Soldiers and Mothers: The Political Origins of Social Policy in the United States*. Cambridge: Harvard University Press.

——and Somers, M. (1980). 'The Uses of Comparative History in Macrosocial Inquiry'. *Comparative Studies in Society and History*, 22: 174–97.

Smart, C. (1998). *The Ties that Bind: Law, Marriage and the Reproduction of Patriarchal Relations*. London: Routledge and Kegan Paul.

Smith P. (1993). *Feminist Jurisprudence*. New York: Oxford University Press.

Smith, T. A. (1975). *The Comparative Policy Process*. Santa Barbara, CA: Clio Books.

Smyth, A. (1996). 'And Nobody Was Any the Wiser: Irish Abortion Rights and the European Union', in A. R. Elman (ed.), *Sexual Politics and the European Union: The New Feminist Challenge*. Providence and Oxford: Berghahn Books.

Snow, D. A. and Benford, R. D. (1992). 'Master Frames and Cycles of Protest', in A. Morris and C. M. Mueller (eds), *Frontiers in Social Movement Theory*. New Haven: Yale University Press.

Sohrab, J. A. (1994). 'An Overview of the Equality Directive on Social Security and Its Implementation in Four Social Security Systems'. *Journal of European Social Policy*, 4: 263–76.

Squires, J. (1999*a*). *Gender in Political Theory*. Cambridge: Polity Press.

——(1999*b*). 'Rethinking the Boundaries of Political Representation', in S. Walby (ed.), *New Agendas for Women*. London: Macmillan.

Sratigaki, M. (2000). 'The European Union and the Equal Opportunities Process', in L. Hantrais (ed.), *Gendered Policies in Europe*. London: Macmillan.

Staudt, K. (1998). *Policy, Politics, and Gender*. West Hartford, CT: Kumarian Press.

——and Weaver, W.G. (1997). *Political Science and Feminisms: Integration or Transformation*. New York: Twayne Publishers.

Steinberg-Ratner, R. (ed.) (1980*a*). *Equal Employment Policy for Women: Strategies for Implementation in the United States, Canada, and Western Europe*. Philadelphia: Temple University Press.

——(1980*b*). 'The Policy and Problem: Overview of Seven Countries', in R. Steinberg-Ratner (ed.), *Equal Employment Policy For Women: Strategies for Implementation in t he United States, Canada, and Western Europe*. Philadelphia: Temple University Press.

——(1988). 'The Unsubtle Revolution: Women, the State and Equal Employment', in J. Jenson *et al.* (eds), *Feminization of the Labor Force: Paradoxes and Promises*. New York: Oxford University Press.

——and Cook, A. (1988). 'Policies Affecting Women's Employment in Industrial Countries', in A. Stromberg and S. Harkness (eds), *Women Working: Theories and Facts in Perspective*. Mountain View, CA: Mayfield Publishing Company.

Stetson, D. M. (1982). *A Woman's Issue: The Politics of Family Law Reform in England*. Westport, CT: Greenwood Press.

——(1987). *Women's Rights in France*. New York: Garland.

——(1995*a*). 'The Oldest Women's Policy Agency: The Women's Bureau in the United States', in D. M. Stetson and A.G. Mazur (eds), *Comparative State Feminism*. Thousand Oaks: Sage.

——(1995*b*). 'Human Rights for Women: International Compliance with a Feminist Standard'. *Women and Politics*, 15/3: 71–95.

Stetson, D. M. (1996a). 'Abortion Triads and Women's Rights in Russia, the United States, and France', in M. Githens and D. M. Stetson (eds), *Abortion Politics: Public Policy in Cross-Cultural Perspective*. New York and London: Routledge.

——(1996b). 'Feminist Perspectives on Abortion and Reproductive Technologies', in M. Githens and D. M. Stetson (eds), *Abortion Politics: Public Policy in Cross-Cultural Perspective*. New York and London: Routledge.

——(1997a). 'Gender and European Politics: The Limits of Integration'. *PS: Political Science and Politics*, 3: 195–7.

——(1997b). *Women's Rights in the USA* (2nd edn). New York: Garland.

——(ed.) (2001a). *Abortion Politics, Women's Movements and the Democratic State: A Comparative Study of State Feminism*. Oxford: Oxford University Press.

——(2001b) 'Federal and State Women's Policy Agencies Help to Represent Women in the USA', in A.G. Mazur (ed.), *State Feminism, Women's Movements, and Job Training: Making Democracies Work in the Global Economy*. New York and London: Routledge.

——(2001c). 'Women's Movements' Defense of Legal Abortion in Great Britain', in D. M. Stetson (ed.), *Abortion Politics, Women's Movements and the Democratic State: A Comparative Study of State Feminism*. Oxford: Oxford University Press.

——(2001d) 'U.S. Abortion Debates 1959–1998: The Women's Movement Holds On', in D. M. Stetson (ed.), *Abortion Politics, Women's Movements and the Democratic State: A Comparative Study of State Feminism*. Oxford: Oxford University Press.

——and Mazur, A. G. (eds) (1995). *Comparative State Feminism*. Newbury Park, CA: Sage.

————(2000). 'Women's Movements and the State: Job Training Policy in France and the US'. *Political Research Quarterly*, 53: 597–623.

————(2001). 'RNGS Project Description'. Working Draft.

Stone, Alec (1992). *The Birth of Judicial Politics in France: The Constitutional Council in Comparative Perspective*. Oxford: Oxford University Press.

Stoper, E. and Boneparth, E. (1988).'Divorce and Transition to the Single-parent Family', in E. Boneparth and E. Stoper (eds), *Women, Power and Policy*. New York: Pergamon.

Studlar, D.T. and Tatalovich, R. (1996). 'Abortion Policy in the United States and Canada', in M. Githens and D. M. Stetson (eds), *Abortion Politics: Public Policy in Cross-Cultural Perspective*. New York and London: Routledge.

Sullivan, B. (1990). 'Sex Equality and the Australian Body Politic', in S. Watson (ed.), *Playing the State*. London: Verso.

Tarrow, S. (1995). 'Bridging the Quantitative-qualitative Divide in Political Science', in Review Symposium, 'The Qualitative-Quantitative Disputation: Gary King, Robert Keohane, and Sidney Verba's *Designing Social Inquiry: Scientific Inference in Qualitative Research*'. *American Political Science Review*, 89: 471–4.

Tatalovich, R. and Daynes, B. (1984). 'Moral Controversies and the Policymaking Process: Lowi's Framework Applied to the Abortion Issue'. *Policy Studies Review*, 3: 206–22.

Taylor, J. (1999). 'Case X: Irish Reproductive Policy and European Influence'. *Social Politics*, 6: 203–29.

Teghtsoonian, K. (1993). 'Neo-Conservative Ideology and Opposition to Federal Regulation of Child Care Services in the United States and Canada'. *Canadian Journal of Political Science*, 26/1: 97–121.

——(1995). 'Work and Motherhood: The Ideological Construction of Women's Options in Canadian Child Care Policy Debates'. *Canadian Journal of Women and the Law*, 8: 411–39.

——(1996). 'Promises, Promises: Choices of Women in Canadian and American Child Care Policy Debates'. *Feminist Studies*, 22/1: 119–46.

——and Grace, J. (2001). '"Something More is Necessary": The Mixed Achievements of Women's Policy Agencies in Canada.' in A.G. Mazur (ed.), *State Feminism, Women's Movements, and Job Training: Making Democracies Work in the Global Economy*. New York and London: Routledge.

Thomas, S. (1994). *How Women Legislate*. New York: Oxford University Press.

Threlfall, M. (ed.) (1996*a*). *Mapping the Women's Movement: Feminist Politics and Social Transformation*. London and New York: Verso.

——(1996*b*). 'Feminist Politics and Social Change in Spain', in M. Threlfall (ed.), *Mapping the Women's Movement: Feminist Politics and Social Transformation*. London: Verso.

Tobío, C. (2001). 'Women's Strategies and the Family-Employment Relationship in Spain', in A.G. Mazur (ed.), *State Feminism, Women's Movements, and Job Training: Making Democracies Work in the Global Economy*. New York and London: Routledge.

Tolleson, R. S. (1992). *Gender Consciousness and Politics*. Routledge: New York.

Tong, R. (1989). *Feminist Thought: A Comprehensive Introduction*. Boulder, CO and San Francisco: Westview Press.

Tremblay, M. (ed.) (2000). 'Women, Citizenship, and Representation'. Special Issue of *International Political Science Review*, 21/4.

——and Andrews, C. (eds) (1998). *Women and Political Representation in Canada*. Ottawa: University of Ottawa Press.

——and Pelletier, R. (2000). 'More Women or More Feminist? Descriptive and Substantive Representations of Women in the 1997 Canadian Federal Elections'. *International Political Science Review*, 21: 381–406.

True, J. and Mintrom, M. (2001). 'Transnational Networks and Policy Diffusion: The Case of Gender Mainstreaming'. *International Studies Quarterly*, 45: 27–57.

Tuohy, C. (1992). *Canada: Institutionalized Ambivalence*. Philadelphia: Temple University Press.

UN (United Nations) (2000). *The World's Women: Trends and Statistics*. New York and Geneva: United Nations.

——(2000). *Women and Men in Europe and North America*. New York and Geneva: United Nations.

——Commission on the Elimination of all Forms of Discrimination Against Women (CEDAW) (1998). *Report of the Special Rapporteur on Violence Against Women, Its Causes and Consequences*. New York: United Nations.

Ungerson, C. (1997). 'Social Politics and the Commodification of Care'. *Social Politics*, 4/3. 362–81.

Ursel, J. (1997). 'Considering the Impact of Battered Women's Movement on the State: The Example of Manitoba', in C. Andrew and S. Rodgers (eds), *Women and the Canadian State*. Montreal and Kingston: McGill-Queens University Press.

Vaillancourt, P. R. (1993). 'Anticipating a Post-Modern Policy Current?'. *Policy Currents*, 3/2: 1–4.

Valiente, C. (1995). 'The Power of Persuasion: The Instituto de la Mujer in Spain', in D. M. Stetson and A. G. Mazur (eds), *Comparative State Feminism*. Thousand Oaks: Sage.

——(1997*a*). 'The Regulation of Sexual Harassment in the Workplace in Spain', in B. Hobson and A. M. Berggren (eds), *Crossing Borders: Gender and Citizenship in Transition*. Stockholm: Swedish Council for Planning and Coordination.

——(1997*b*). 'State Feminism and Gender Equality Policies: The Case of Spain, 1983–1995', in F. Gardiner (ed.), *Sex Equality Policy in Europe*. London: Routledge.

——(1998*a*). 'Sexual Harassment in the Workplace: Equality Policies in Post-Authoritarian Spain', in T. Carver and V. Mottier (eds), *Politics of Sexuality: Identity, Gender, Citizenship*. London and New York: Routledge.

——(1998*b*). 'An Overview of the State of Research on Women and Politics in Spain'. *European Journal of Political Research*, 33: 459–474.

—— (2000). 'Reconciliation Policies in Spain', in L. Hantrais (ed.), *Gendered Policies in Europe*. London: Macmillan.

——(2001*a*). 'A Closed Subsystem and Distant Feminist Demands Block Women-Friendly Outcomes in Spain', in A.G. Mazur (ed.), *State Feminism, Women's Movements, and Job Training: Making Democracies Work in the Global Economy*. New York and London: Routledge.

——(2001*b*). 'Gendering Abortion Debates: State Feminism in Spain', in D. M. Stetson (ed.), *Abortion Politics, Women's Movements and the Democratic State: A Comparative Study of State Feminism*. Oxford: Oxford University Press.

Vallance, E. and Davies, E. (1986). *Women of Europe: Women MEPs and Equality Policy*. Cambridge: Cambridge University Press.

Van der Ros, J. (1994). 'The State and Women: A Troubled Relationship in Norway', in B. Nelson and N. Chowdhury (eds), *Women and Politics Worldwide*. New Haven, CT: Yale University Press.

——(1995). '"Femocrat" you said? What kind of bird is that?'. Paper presented at the ECPR Joint Sessions of Workshops. Bordeaux, April.

——(1997). 'The Organisation of Equality Policies at the Local Level', in F. Gardiner (ed.), *Sex Equality Policy in Western Europe*. London: Routledge.

Van Doorne-Huiskes, J. and Roelofs, E. (eds) (1995). *Women and the European Labour Markets*. London: Paul Chapman.

Van Waarden, F. (1992). 'Dimensions and Types of Policy Networks'. *European Journal of Political Research*. 21/1–2: 29–52.

Vargas, V. and Wieringa, S. (1998). 'The Triangles of Empowerment: Processes and Actors in the Making of Public Policy', in G. Lycklama à Nijeholt *et al.* (eds), *Women's Movements and Public Policy in Europe, Latin America, and the Caribbean*. New York: Garland.

Victorin, A. (1991). 'Equal Pay in Sweden', in S. L. Wilborn (ed.), *Women's Wages: Stability and Change in Six Industrialized Countries*. Greenwich, CT: JAI Press.

Vogel-Polsky, E. (1994). 'Les femmes et la citoyenneté européene', in *Women in Decision-making* (Report for the European Network, European Commission). Brussels

——(1995). 'The Use of Legislation', in *Strategies for a Gender Balance in Political Decision-making* (Report on European Seminar). Dublin, 23–4 March.

Walby, S. (1997). *Gender Transformations*. London and New York: Routledge.

——(1999). *New Agendas for Women*. New York: St Martin's Press.

Watson, S. (ed.) (1990). *Playing the State: Australian Feminist Interventions*. London: Verso.

Weaver, K. R. and Rockman, B. A. (eds) (1993). *Do Institutions Matter? Government Capabilities in the United States and Abroad*. Washington, DC: Brookings Institution.

Weldon, L. (1998). 'Feminists, Femocrats and Institutions: Explaining Cross-National Variations in Government Responses to Violence Against Women'. Paper presented at the Conference for Women's Progress at the Institute for Women's Policy Research. Washington DC, 12–13 June.

——(2001). *Protest, Policy and the Problem of Violence Against Women*. Pittsburgh: University of Pittsburgh Press.

Wiarda, H. J. (2001). *Introduction to Comparative Politics: Concepts and Processes*. Belmont, CA: Wadsworth.

Wieringa, S. (ed.) (1995). *Subversive Women: Women's Movements in Africa, Asia, Latin America, and the Caribbean*. London: Zed Books.

Wiik, J. (1986). 'The Abortion Issue, Political Cleavage and the Political Agenda in Norway', in J. Lovenduski and J. Outshoorn (ed.), *The New Politics of Abortion*. London: Sage.

Wilborn, S. L. (ed.) (1991). *Women's Wages: Stability and Change in Six Industrialized Countries*. Greenwich, CT: JAI Press.

Wilensky, H. L., Luebbert, G. M., Hahn, S. R., and Jamieson, A. M. (1985). *Comparative Social Policy: Theories, Methods, Findings*. Berkeley: Institute of International Studies, University of California.

Williams, F. (1989). *Social Policy: A Critical Introduction: Issues of Race, Gender, and Class*. London: Polity Press.

——(1993). 'Gender, "Race", and Class in British Welfare Policy', in A. Cochrane and J. Clarke (eds), *Comparing Welfare States: Britain in International Context*. Milton Keynes: The Open University.

Wilsford, D. (1991). *Doctors and the State: The Politics of Healthcare in France and the United States*. Durham, N. C.: Duke University Press.

Windebank, J. (1996). 'To What Extent Can Social Policy Challenge the Dominant Ideology of Mothering: A Cross-National Comparison of Sweden, France and Britain'. *Journal of European Social Policy*, 6: 147–61.

Winkler, U. (1996). 'Reproductive Technologies in Germany: An Issue for the European Union', in A. R. Elman (ed.), *Sexual Politics and the European Union: The New Feminist Challenge*. Providence and Oxford: Berghahn Books.

Winslow A. (ed.) (1995). *Women, Politics, and the United Nations*. Westport, CT: Greenwood Press.

Woliver, L. R. (1996). 'Rhetoric and Symbols in American Abortion Politics', in M. Githens and D. M. Stetson (eds), *Abortion Politics: Public Policy in Cross-Cultural Perspective.* New York and London: Routledge.

Yohalem, A. M. (ed.) (1980). *Women Returning to Work: Policies and Progress in Five Countries.* Montclair, NJ: Allenheld, Osmun.

Young, L. (2000). *Feminist and Party Politics.* Vancouver: UBC Press.

——(1998). 'The Canadian Women's Movement and Political Parties, 1970–1993', in M. Tremblay and C. Andrew (eds), *Women and Political Representation in Canada.* Ottawa: University of Ottawa Press.

Zelensky, A. and Gaussot, M. (1986). *Le harcèlement sexuel: Scandales et Réalités'* Paris: Garancière.

Zirakzadeh, C. E. (1997). *Social Movements in Politics: A Comparative Study.* London and New York: Longman.

Zwiegert, K. and Kötz, H. (1992). *Introduction to Comparative Law.* Oxford: Oxford University Press.

❖ Index